Student Solutions Manual

COST ACCOUNTING

Twelfth Edition

Charles T. Horngren
Srikant M. Datar
George Foster
Ratna Sarkar

PEARSON

Prentice
Hall

Upper Saddle River, New Jersey 07458

VP/Editorial Director: Jeff Shelstad
Senior Acquisitions Editor: Wendy Craven
Project Manager: Kerri Tomasso
Associate Director Manufacturing: Vincent Scelta
Manager, Print Production: Christy Mahon
Production Editor & Buyer: Carol O'Rourke
Printer/Binder: Banta Book Group, Harrisonburg

10 9 8 7 6 5 4 3 2 1
ISBN 0-13-149601-8

CONTENTS

***This Student Solutions Manual by Charles T. Horgren, Srikant M. Datar, George Foster, and Ratna Sarkar, assists with even-numbered end-of-chapter problems.

CHAPTER 1
THE ACCOUNTANT'S ROLE IN THE ORGANIZATION

See the front matter of this Solutions Manual for suggestions regarding your choices of assignment material for each chapter.

1-2 Financial accounting is constrained by generally accepted accounting principles. Management accounting is not restricted to these principles. The result is that
- management accounting allows managers to charge interest on owners' capital to help judge a division's performance, even though such a charge is not allowed under GAAP,
- management accounting can include assets or liabilities (such as "brand names" developed internally) not recognized under GAAP, and
- management accounting can use asset or liability measurement rules (such as present values or resale prices) not permitted under GAAP.

1-4 The business functions in the value chain are
- **Research and development**—generating and experimenting with ideas related to new products, services, or processes.
- **Design of products, services, and processes**—the detailed planning and engineering of products, services, or processes.
- **Production**—acquiring, coordinating, and assembling resources to produce a product or deliver a service.
- **Marketing**—promoting and selling products or services to customers or prospective customers.
- **Distribution**—delivering products or services to customers.
- **Customer service**—providing after-sale support to customers.
-

1-6 "Management accounting deals only with costs." This statement is misleading at best, and wrong at worst. Management accounting measures, analyzes, and reports financial *and nonfinancial* information that helps managers define the organization's goals, and make decisions to fulfill them. Management accounting also analyzes revenues from products and customers in order to assess product and customer profitability. Therefore, while management accounting does use cost information, it is only a part of the organization's information recorded and analyzed by management accountants.

1-8 *Planning decisions* focus on (a) selecting organization goals, predicting results under various alternative ways of achieving those goals, deciding how to attain the desired goals, and (b) communicating the goals and how to attain them to the entire organization.

Control decisions focus on (a) taking actions that implement the planning decisions, and (b) deciding how to evaluate performance and what related feedback to provide that will help future decision making.

1-10 The three guidelines for management accountants are
1. Employ a cost-benefit approach.
2. Recognize behavioral and technical considerations.
3. Apply the "different costs for different purposes" notion.

1-12 The new controller could reply in one or more of the following ways:

(a) Demonstrate to the plant manager how he or she could make better decisions if the plant controller was viewed as a resource rather than a deadweight. In a related way, the plant controller could show how the plant manager's time and resources could be saved by viewing the new plant controller as a team member.

(b) Demonstrate to the plant manager a good knowledge of the technical aspects of the plant. This approach may involve doing background reading. It certainly will involve spending much time on the plant floor speaking to plant personnel.

(c) Show the plant manager examples of the new plant controller's past successes in working with line managers in other plants. Examples could include
  - assistance in preparing the budget,
  - assistance in analyzing problem situations and evaluating financial and nonfinancial aspects of different alternatives, and
  - assistance in submitting capital budget requests.

(d) Seek assistance from the corporate controller to highlight to the plant manager the importance of many tasks undertaken by the new plant controller. This approach is a last resort but may be necessary in some cases.

1-14 The Institute of Management Accountants (IMA) sets standards of ethical conduct for management accountants in the following areas:
  - Competence
  - Confidentiality
  - Integrity
  - Objectivity

1-16 (15 min.) **Value chain and classification of costs, computer company.**

Cost Item	Value Chain Business Function
a.	Production
b.	Distribution
c.	Design
d.	Research and Development
e.	Customer Service or Marketing
f.	Design (or Research and Development)
g.	Marketing
h.	Production

1-18   (25 min.)   **Management accounting system and its customers.**

1. Management accounting's customers are managers of departments such as marketing, production and R&D. Management accounting focuses on providing financial and nonfinancial information to the managers to help them make better decisions to achieve the organization's goals.

2. The value of a management accounting system can be enhanced and, simultaneously, expectations of managers can be exceeded by providing relevant and timely information to the managers so that they achieve their strategic goals and make good planning and control decisions. This means that management accounting must have customer focus. The information needs of the managers for decision making must be met and exceeded in order to retain them as users of management accounting information. Management accounting systems should address the information needs of the managers by helping with problem solving, scorekeeping, and directing their attention to the following key success factors:

- Cost control
- High quality
- Timely response to customer demand
- Innovation

Management accountants have several tools that can help managers concentrate on continuous improvement of various aspects of their operations.

Value chain and supply chain analysis performed by the management accounting function can contribute to the achievement of key success factors. When each business function adds value and all business functions are coordinated and well integrated, it contributes to cost control, high quality, timely response, and innovation.

1-20 (15 min.) **Planning and control decisions.**

1. a. Planning—Barnes & Noble (B&N)'s cash needs for the future.
    b. Control—B&N's annual financial performance evaluation.

2. a. Planning—whether to increase or decrease local marketing support.
    b. Control—whether recent sales promotion led to an increase in revenues.

3. a. Planning—whether or not to expand B&N's internet-based lines of business.
    b. Control—evaluation by VP of New Business Development of the performance of managers of individual lines of business.

4. a. Planning—which books to advertise more or which books to include in a special chat-room site.
    b. Control—decision by publisher to pay additional bonuses to each author whose book reaches the bestseller list and stays on the list for a certain period of time.

5. a. Planning—decision by B&N on the amount and type of insurance to purchase next year.
    b. Control—follow up by B&N with the insurance company regarding a cash payment to B&N.

1-22 (15 min.) **Problem solving, scorekeeping, and attention directing.**

The accountant's duties are often not sharply defined, so some of these answers might be challenged:

1. Attention directing
2. Problem solving
3. Scorekeeping
4. Scorekeeping
5. Scorekeeping
6. Attention directing
7. Problem solving
8. Scorekeeping
9. Problem solving
10. Attention directing

1-24 (15 min.) **Planning and control decisions, Internet company.**

1. **Planning decisions**
    a. Decision to raise monthly subscription fee
    c. Decision to upgrade content of online services (later decision to inform subscribers and upgrade online services is an implementation part of control)
    e. Decision to decrease monthly subscription fee

    Control decisions
    b. Decision to inform existing subscribers about the rate of increase—an implementation part of control decisions
    d. Dismissal of VP of Marketing—performance evaluation and feedback aspect of control decisions

2. Other planning decisions that may be made at WebNews.com: decision to raise or lower advertising fees; decision to charge a fee from on-line retailers when customers click-through from WebNews.com to the retailers' websites.
    Other control decisions that may be made at WebNews.com: evaluating how customers like the new format for the weather information, working with an outside vendor to redesign the website, and evaluating whether the waiting time for customers to access the website has been reduced.

1-26 (15 min.) **Management accounting guidelines.**

1. Cost-benefit approach
2. Behavioral and technical considerations
3. Different costs for different purposes
4. Cost-benefit approach
5. Behavioral and technical considerations
6. Cost-benefit approach
7. Behavioral and technical considerations
8. Different costs for different purposes
9. Behavioral and technical considerations

1-28 (30 min.)   **Software procurement decisions, ethics.**

1.   Michael faces an ethical problem. The trip appears to be a gift which could influence his purchase decision. The ethical standard of integrity requires Michaels to refuse the gift. Companies with "codes of conduct" frequently have a "supplier clause" that prohibits their employees from accepting "material" (in some cases, any) gifts from suppliers. The motivations include

      (a) Integrity/conflict of interest. Suppose Michaels recommends that a Horizon 1-2-3 product should subsequently be purchased by Fiesta. This recommendation could be because he felt obligated to them as his trip to the Cancún conference was fully paid by Horizon.

      (b) The appearance of a conflict of interest. Even if the Horizon 1-2-3 product is the superior one at that time, other suppliers likely will have a different opinion. They may believe that the way to sell products to Fiesta is via "fully-paid junkets to resorts." Those not wanting to do business this way may downplay future business activities with Fiesta even though Fiesta could gain much from such activities.

Some executives view the meeting as "suspect" from the start given the Caribbean location and its "rest and recreation" tone.

2.   Fiesta should not allow executives to attend user meetings while negotiating with other vendors about a purchase decision. The payment of expenses for the trip constitutes a gift that could appear to influence their purchase decision.

Pros of attending user meeting
      (a) Opportunity to learn more about Horizon's software products.
      (b) Opportunity to interact with other possible purchasers and get their opinions.
      (c) Opportunity to influence the future product development plans of Horizon in a way that will benefit Fiesta. An example is Horizon subsequently developing software modules tailored to food product companies.
      (d) Saves Fiesta money. Visiting suppliers and their customers typically cost money, whereas Horizon is paying for the Cancún conference.

Cons of Attending
      (a) The ethical issues raised in requirement 1.
      (b) Negative morale effects on other Fiesta employees who do not get to attend the Cancún conference. These employees may reduce their trust and respect for Michaels's judgment, arguing he has been on a "supplier-paid vacation."

Conditions on Attending that Fiesta Might Impose
      (a) Sizable part of that time in Cancún has to be devoted to business rather than recreation.
      (b) Decision on which Fiesta executive attends is <u>not</u> made by the person who attends (this reduces the appearance of a conflict of interest).
      (c) Person attending (Michaels) does not have final say on purchase decision (this reduces the appearance of a conflict of interest).
      (d) Fiesta executives go only when a new major purchase is being contemplated (to avoid the conference becoming a regular "vacation").

A Conference Board publication on *Corporate Ethics* asked executives about a comparable situation. Following are the results:

- 76% said Fiesta and Michaels face an ethical consideration in deciding whether to attend.
- 71% said Michaels should not attend, as the payment of expenses is a "gift" within the meaning of a credible corporate ethics policy.

3.   The company does not need its own code of ethics. They can use the code of ethics developed by the IMA.

Pros of having a written code

The Conference Board outlines the following reasons why companies adopt codes of ethics:

(a) Signals commitment of senior management to ethics.
(b) Promotes public trust in the credibility of the company and its employees.
(c) Signals the managerial professionalism of its employees.
(d) Provides guidance to employees as to how difficult problems are to be handled. If adhered to, employees will avoid many actions that are unethical or appear to be unethical.
(e) Drafting of the policy (and its redrafting in the light of ambiguities) can assist management in anticipating and preparing for ethical issues not yet encountered.

Cons of having a written code

(a) Can give appearance that all issues have been covered. Issues not covered may appear to be "acceptable" even when they are not.
(b) Can constrain the entrepreneurial activities of employees. Forces people to always "behave by the book."
(c) Cost of developing code can be "high" if it consumes a lot of employee time.

1-30   (40 min.)   Global company, ethical challenges with bribery.

1.   It is clear that bribes are illegal according to U.S. laws. It is not clear from the case whether bribes are illegal in Vartan. However, knowledgeable people in global business would attest to the fact that it is virtually impossible to find any country in the world that specifically sanctions bribery. The major point, however, that deserves discussion is: Should ZenTel engage in any unethical activities even if they are not illegal?

It is difficult to make a generalization about all shareholders of the company. It is, however, safe to assume that not all shareholders would want to keep their investment in a company that is engaged in unethical and/or illegal activities. There is historical evidence to substantiate this point: When apartheid laws were in effect in South Africa, many investors divested shares of companies doing business in South Africa.

Apart from the ethical issues, it should also be noted that bribery can be very costly in some parts of the world. Bribes may not generate revenues sufficient enough to offset their cost.

2.   Apparently Hank thinks that local culture and common practice are one and the same. This, in fact, is not the case. There are many common practices in developing countries, which are against the native culture.

Specifically, bribery often leads to decisions that are not made on the basis of the merits of the alternative selected. This results in misallocation of meager resources of the developing country. Misallocation of resources has adverse effects on the economy of a country and the living standard of its population. The negative impact is intensified in developing countries because they can least afford the misallocation of resources.

As it applies to local common practice, multinational companies make some small allowances but draw a hard line against paying the $1 million "commission."

3.   ZenTel might have an articulated corporate policy against such payments to get the message across that regardless of laws, the top management would not tolerate any bribery payments made by its employees. A strong and consistent message from the top often has a noticeable effect on the corporate culture and employee behavior.

U.S. laws specifically prohibit bribery payments. Such payments can result in heavy penalties to the corporation making the payments.

4.   If this contract is of great importance to ZenTel's global strategy, it is likely that this kind of issue will come up again as ZenTel expands into very diverse cultures and the company should tackle it head on and make a policy decision against offering bribes. Steve Cheng should discuss the situation with the top management at ZenTel and re-affirm his goal to get the Vartan contract with legal means. He could seek the help of the U.S. commercial attaché in Vartan to continue a dialogue with Vartan's deputy minister of communications. He could propose other creative, legal changes to the ZenTel's bid, even at the cost of reducing the profitability of the current project. Concessions such as training programs, schools and other public works projects may be legal, get the attention of the Vartan government and raise ZenTel's profile both at home and abroad. In the worst case, if the Vartan government does not agree to any of the creative, legal "extras" that ZenTel can provide in order to win the contract, Cheng should report this to ZenTel's management and be willing to walk away from the Vartan project.

CHAPTER 2
AN INTRODUCTION TO COST TERMS AND PURPOSES

2-2 Direct costs of a cost object are related to the particular cost object and can be traced to that cost object in an economically feasible (cost-effective) way.

Indirect costs of a cost object are related to the particular cost object but cannot be traced to that cost object in an economically feasible (cost-effective) way.

Cost assignment is a general term that encompasses the assignment of both direct costs and indirect costs to a cost object. Direct costs are *traced* to a cost object while indirect costs are *allocated* to a cost object.

2-4 Factors affecting the classification of a cost as direct or indirect include
- the materiality of the cost in question,
- available information-gathering technology,
- design of operations, and
- contractual arrangements.

2-6 A *cost driver* is a variable, such as the level of activity or volume, which causally affects total costs over a given time span. A change in the cost driver results in a change in the level of total costs. For example, the number of vehicles assembled is a driver of the costs of steering wheels on a motor-vehicle assembly line.

2-8 A unit cost is computed by dividing some amount of total costs (the numerator) by the related number of units (the denominator). In many cases, the numerator will include a fixed cost that will not change despite changes in the denominator. It is erroneous in those cases to multiply the unit cost by activity or volume change to predict changes in total costs at different activity or volume levels.

2-10 Manufacturing companies typically have one or more of the following three types of inventory:
1. *Direct materials inventory.* Direct materials in stock and awaiting use in the manufacturing process.
2. *Work-in-process inventory.* Goods partially worked on but not yet completed. Also called *work in progress*.
3. *Finished goods inventory*. Goods completed but not yet sold.

2-12 No. Service sector companies have no inventories and, hence, no inventoriable costs.

2-14 *Overtime premium* is the wage rate paid to workers (for both direct labor and indirect labor) in excess of their straight-time wage rates.

Idle time is a subclassification of indirect labor that represents wages paid for unproductive time caused by lack of orders, machine breakdowns, material shortages, poor scheduling, and the like.

2-16 (15 min.) **Computing and interpreting manufacturing unit costs.**

1.

	Supreme	Deluxe	Regular	Total
	(in millions)			
	Supreme	**Deluxe**	**Regular**	**Total**
Direct material cost	$ 84.00	$ 54.00	$ 62.00	$200.00
Direct manuf. labor costs	14.00	28.00	8.00	50.00
Indirect manuf. costs	42.00	84.00	24.00	150.00
Total manuf. costs	$140.00	$166.00	$ 94.00	$400.00
Fixed costs allocated at a rate of $20M ÷ $50M (direct mfg. labor) equal to $0.40 per dir. manuf. labor dollar (0.40 × $14; 28; 8)	5.60	11.20	3.20	20.00
Variable costs	$134.40	$154.80	$ 90.80	$380.00
Units produced (millions)	80	120	100	
Cost per unit (Total manuf. costs ÷ units produced)	$1.7500	$1.3833	$0.9400	
Variable manuf. cost per unit (Variable manuf. costs ÷ Units produced)	$1.6800	$1.2900	$0.9080	

	Supreme	Deluxe	Regular	Total
	(in millions)			
	Supreme	**Deluxe**	**Regular**	**Total**
2. Based on total manuf. cost per unit ($1.75 × 120; $1.3833 × 160; $0.94 × 180)	$210.00	$221.33	$169.20	$600.53
Correct total manuf. costs based on variable manuf. costs plus fixed costs equal Variable costs ($1.68 × 120; $1.29 × 160; $0.908 × 180)	$201.60	$206.40	$163.44	$571.44
Fixed costs				20.00
Total costs				$591.44

The total manufacturing cost per unit in requirement 1 includes $20 million of indirect manufacturing costs that are fixed irrespective of changes in the volume of output per month, while the remaining variable indirect manufacturing costs change with the production volume. Given the unit volume changes for August 2007, the use of total manufacturing cost per unit from the past month at a different unit volume level (both in aggregate and at the individual product level) will yield incorrect estimates of total costs of $600.53 million in August 2007 relative to the correct total manufacturing costs of $591.44 million calculated using variable manufacturing cost per unit times units produced plus the fixed costs of $20 million.

2-18 (15–20 min.) **Classification of costs, service sector.**

Cost object: Each individual focus group
Cost variability: With respect to the number of focus groups

There may be some debate over classifications of individual items, especially with regard to cost variability.

Cost Item	D or I	V or F
A	D	V
B	I	F
C	I	V[a]
D	I	F
E	D	V
F	I	F
G	D	V
H	I	V[b]

[a]Some students will note that phone call costs are variable when each call has a separate charge. It may be a fixed cost if Consumer Focus has a flat monthly charge for a line, irrespective of the amount of usage.
[b]Gasoline costs are likely to vary with the number of focus groups. However, vehicles likely serve multiple purposes, and detailed records may be required to examine how costs vary with changes in one of the many purposes served.

2-20 (15–20 min.) **Classification of costs, manufacturing sector.**

Cost object: Type of car assembled (Corolla or Geo Prism)
Cost variability: With respect to changes in the number of cars assembled

There may be some debate over classifications of individual items, especially with regard to cost variability.

Cost Item	D or I	V or F
A	D	V
B	I	F
C	D	F
D	D	F
E	D	V
F	I	V
G	D	V
H	I	F

2-22 (15–20 min.) **Variable costs and fixed costs.**

1.   Variable cost per ton of beach sand mined

Subcontractor	$ 80 per ton
Government tax	50 per ton
Total	$130 per ton

   Fixed costs per month

0 to 100 tons of capacity per day	=	$150,000
101 to 200 tons of capacity per day	=	$300,000
201 to 300 tons of capacity per day	=	$450,000

2.

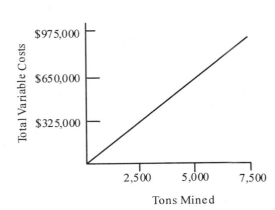 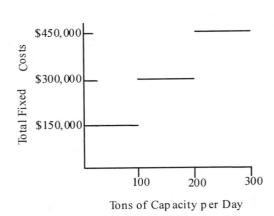

The concept of relevant range is potentially relevant for both graphs. However, the question does not place restrictions on the unit variable costs. The relevant range for the total fixed costs is from 0 to 100 tons; 101 to 200 tons; 201 to 300 tons, and so on. Within these ranges, the total fixed costs do not change in total.

3.

Tons Mined per Day (1)	Tons Mined per Month (2) = (1) × 25	Fixed Unit Cost per Ton (3) = FC ÷ (2)	Variable Unit Cost per Ton (4)	Total Unit Cost per Ton (5) = (3) + (4)
(a) 180	4,500	$300,000 ÷ 4,500 = $66.67	$130	$196.67
(b) 220	5,500	$450,000 ÷ 5,500 = $81.82	$130	$211.82

The unit cost for 220 tons mined per day is $211.82, while for 180 tons it is only $196.67. This difference is caused by the fixed cost increment from 101 to 200 tons being spread over an increment of 80 tons, while the fixed cost increment from 201 to 300 tons is spread over an increment of only 20 tons.

2-24 (10–15 min.) **Cost drivers and functions.**

1.

Function	Representative Cost Driver
1. Accounting	Number of transactions processed
2. Personnel	Number of new hires
3. Data Processing	Hours of computer processing unit (CPU)
4. Research and Development	Number of research scientists
5. Purchasing	Number of purchase orders
6. Billing	Number of invoices sent

2.

Function	Representative Cost Driver
1. Accounting	Hours of technical work
2. Personnel	Number of employees
3. Data Processing	Number of computer transactions
4. Research and Development	Number of new products being developed
5. Purchasing	Number of different types of materials purchased
6. Billing	Number of credit sales transactions

2-26 (15 min.) **Total costs and unit costs.**

1. (a) $100,000 ÷ 2,000 = $50.00 per package
   (b) $100,000 ÷ 6,000 = $16.67 per package
   (c) $100,000 ÷ 10,000 = $10.00 per package
   (d) [$100,000 + (10,000 × $8)] ÷ 20,000 = $180,000 ÷ 20,000 = $9.00 per package

The unit cost to ECG decreases on a per-unit base due to the first $100,000 payment being a fixed cost. The $8 amount per package beyond 10,000 units is a variable cost.

The cost function is

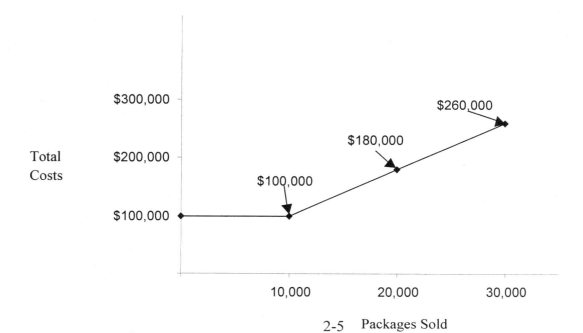

ECG should not use any of the unit costs in requirement 1 when predicting total costs. Up to 10,000 units, the total cost is a fixed amount. Beyond 10,000 units, the total cost is a combination of a fixed amount plus a per-unit (beyond 10,000 unit) variable amount. The total costs at different volume levels cannot be predicted by using the unit cost at a specific volume level. The total cost should be predicted by combining the total fixed costs and total variable costs rather than multiplying a unit cost amount by the predicted number of packages sold.

2-28 (20 min.) **Flow of Inventoriable Costs.**

(All numbers below are in millions).

1.

Direct materials inventory 8/1/2007	$	90
Direct materials purchased		360
Direct materials available for production		450
Direct materials used		375
Direct materials inventory 8/31/2007	$	75

2.

Total manufacturing overhead costs	$	480
Subtract: Variable manufacturing overhead costs		(250)
Fixed manufacturing overhead costs	$	230

3.

Total manufacturing costs	$	1,600
Subtract: Direct materials used (from requirement 1)		(375)
Total manufacturing overhead costs		(480)
Direct manufacturing labor costs	$	745

4.

Work-in-process inventory 8/1/2007	$	200
Total manufacturing costs		1,600
Work-in-process available for production		1,800
Subtract: Cost of goods manufactured (moved into FG)		(1,650)
Work-in-process inventory 8/31/2007	$	150

5.

Finished goods inventory 8/1/2007	$	125
Cost of goods manufactured (moved from WIP)		1,650
Finished goods available for sale in August	$	1,775

6.

Finished goods available for sale in August (from requirement 5)	$	1,775
Subtract: Cost of goods sold		(1,700)
Finished goods inventory 8/31/2007	$	75

2-30 (30–40 min.) **Cost of goods manufactured.**

Canseco Company
Schedule of Cost of Goods Manufactured
Year Ended December 31, 2007
(in thousands)

Direct materials:		
Beginning inventory, January 1, 2007	$ 22,000	
Purchases of direct materials	75,000	
Cost of direct materials available for use	97,000	
Ending inventory, December 31, 2007	26,000	
Direct materials used		$ 71,000
Direct manufacturing labor		25,000
Indirect manufacturing costs:		
Indirect manufacturing labor	15,000	
Plant insurance	9,000	
Depreciation—plant building & equipment	11,000	
Repairs and maintenance—plant	4,000	
Total indirect manufacturing costs		39,000
Manufacturing costs incurred during 2007		135,000
Add beginning work-in-process inventory, January 1, 2007		21,000
Total manufacturing costs to account for		156,000
Deduct ending work-in-process inventory, December 31, 2007		20,000
Cost of goods manufactured (to Income Statement)		$136,000

Canseco Company
Income Statement
Year Ended December 31, 2007
(in thousands)

Revenues		$300,000
Cost of goods sold:		
Beginning finished goods, January 1, 2007	$ 18,000	
Cost of goods manufactured	136,000	
Cost of goods available for sale	154,000	
Ending finished goods, December 31, 2007	23,000	
Cost of goods sold		131,000
Gross margin		169,000
Operating costs:		
Marketing, distribution, and customer-service costs	93,000	
General and administrative costs	29,000	
Total operating costs		122,000
Operating income		$ 47,000

2-32 (15–20 min.)   **Interpretation of statements (continuation of 2-31).**

1.   The schedule in 2-31 can become a Schedule of Cost of Goods Manufactured and Sold simply by including the beginning and ending finished goods inventory figures in the supporting schedule, rather than directly in the body of the income statement. Note that the term *cost of goods manufactured* refers to the cost of goods brought to completion (finished) during the accounting period, whether they were started before or during the current accounting period. Some of the manufacturing costs incurred are held back as costs of the ending work in process; similarly, the costs of the beginning work in process inventory become a part of the cost of goods manufactured for 2007.

2.   The sales manager's salary would be charged as a marketing cost as incurred by both manufacturing and merchandising companies. It is basically an operating cost that appears below the gross margin line on an income statement. In contrast, an assembler's wages would be assigned to the products worked on. Thus, the wages cost would be charged to Work in process and would not be expensed until the product is transferred through Finished Goods Inventory to Cost of Goods Sold as the product is sold.

3.   The direct-indirect distinction can be resolved only with respect to a particular cost object. For example, in defense contracting, the cost object may be defined as a contract. Then, a plant supervisor working only on that contract will have his or her salary charged directly and wholly to that single contract.

4.   Direct materials used = \$320,000,000 ÷ 1,000,000 units = \$320 per unit
        Depreciation   = \$ 80,000,000 ÷ 1,000,000 units = \$ 80 per unit

5.   Direct materials unit cost would be unchanged at \$320 per unit. Depreciation cost per unit would be \$80,000,000 ÷ 1,200,000 = \$66.67 per unit. Total direct materials costs would rise by 20% to \$384,000,000 (\$320 per unit × 1,200,000 units), whereas total depreciation would be unaffected at \$80,000,000.

6.   Unit costs are averages, and they must be interpreted with caution. The \$320 direct materials unit cost is valid for predicting total costs because direct materials is a variable cost; total direct materials costs indeed change as output levels change. However, fixed costs like depreciation must be interpreted quite differently from variable costs. A common error in cost analysis is to regard all unit costs as one—as if all the total costs to which they are related are variable costs. Changes in output levels (the denominator) will affect *total variable costs*, but not *total fixed costs*. Graphs of the two costs may clarify this point; it is safer to think in terms of total costs rather than in terms of unit costs.

2-34 (15–20 min.) **Terminology, interpretation of statements (continuation of 2-33).**

1.

Direct materials used	$105 million
Direct manufacturing labor costs	40 million
Prime costs	$145 million

Direct manufacturing labor costs	$ 40 million
Indirect manufacturing costs	51 million
Conversion costs	$ 91 million

2. Inventoriable costs (in millions) for Year 2007

Plant utilities	$ 5
Indirect manufacturing labor	20
Depreciation—plant, building, and equipment	9
Miscellaneous manufacturing overhead	10
Direct materials used	105
Direct manufacturing labor	40
Plant supplies used	6
Property tax on plant	1
Total inventoriable costs	$196

Period costs (in millions) for Year 2007

Marketing, distribution, and customer-service costs	$ 90

3.   Design costs and R&D costs may be regarded as product costs in case of contracting with a governmental agency. For example, if the Air Force negotiated to contract with Lockheed to build a new type of supersonic fighter plane, design costs and R&D costs may be included in the contract as product costs.

4.   Direct materials used = $105,000,000 ÷ 1,000,000 units = $105 per unit
        Depreciation   = $ 9,000,000 ÷ 1,000,000 units = $ 9 per unit

5.   Direct materials unit cost would be unchanged at $105. Depreciation unit cost would be $9,000,000 ÷ 1,500,000 = $6 per unit. Total direct materials costs would rise by 50% to $157,500,000 ($105 per unit × 1,500,000 units). Total depreciation cost of $9,000,000 would remain unchanged.

6.   In this case, equipment depreciation is a variable cost in relation to the unit output. The amount of equipment depreciation will change in direct proportion to the number of units produced.
        (a) Depreciation will be $4 million (1 million × $4) when 1 million units are produced.
        (b) Depreciation will be $6 million (1.5 million × $4) when 1.5 million units are produced.

2-36 (30–40 min.)   **Fire loss, computing inventory costs.**

1. Finished goods inventory, 2/26/2007 = $50,000
2. Work-in-process inventory, 2/26/2007 = $28,000
3. Direct materials inventory, 2/26/2007 = $62,000

This problem is not as easy as it first appears. These answers are obtained by working from the known figures to the unknowns in the schedule below. The basic relationships between categories of costs are:

Prime costs (given)   = $294,000
Direct materials used = $294,000 – Direct manufacturing labor costs
                      = $294,000 – $180,000 = $114,000
Conversion costs   = Direct manufacturing labor costs ÷ 0.6
                        $180,000 ÷ 0.6 = $300,000
Indirect manuf. costs = $300,000 – $180,000 = $120,000 (or 0.40 × $300,000)

Schedule of Computations

Direct materials, 1/1/2007		$ 16,000
Direct materials purchased		160,000
Direct materials available for use		176,000
Direct materials, 2/26/2007	3 =	62,000
Direct materials used ($294,000 – $180,000)		114,000
Direct manufacturing labor costs		180,000
Prime costs		294,000
Indirect manufacturing costs		120,000
Manufacturing costs incurred during the current period		414,000
Add work in process, 1/1/2007		34,000
Manufacturing costs to account for		448,000
Deduct work in process, 2/26/2007	2 =	28,000
Cost of goods manufactured		420,000
Add finished goods, 1/1/2007		30,000
Cost of goods available for sale (given)		450,000
Deduct finished goods, 2/26/2007	1 =	50,000
Cost of goods sold (80% of $500,000)		$400,000

Some instructors may wish to place the key amounts in a Work in Process T-account. This problem can be used to introduce students to the flow of costs through the general ledger (amounts in thousands):

Work in Process				Finished Goods			Cost of Goods Sold	
BI	34			BI	30			
DM used	114	COGM 420	------->		420	COGS 400	---->400	
DL	180							
OH	120			Available				
To account for	448			for sale	450			
EI	28			EI	50			

2-38 (30 min.)   **Cost analysis, litigation risk, ethics.**

1.   Reasons for Keely not wanting Nash to include the potential litigation costs include the following:

      (a) Genuine belief that the product has no risk of future litigation. Note that she asserts "she has total confidence in her medical research team."

      (b) Concern that the uncertainties about litigation are sufficiently high to make any numerical estimate "meaningless."

      (c) Concern that inclusion of future litigation costs would cause the board of directors to vote against the project. Keely may be "overly committed" to the project and wants to avoid showing information that prompts questions she prefers not to be raised.

      (d) Avoid "smoking gun" memos being included in the project evaluation file. Keely may believe that if subsequent litigation occurs, the plaintiffs will "inappropriately" use a litigation cost line item as "proof" that FY knew the product had health problems that were known to management at the outset.

2.

Unit costs excluding litigation costs	$100
Add unit litigation costs	110
Total unit costs	210
Add 20% markup	42
Selling price per unit	$252

Since each treatment is planned to cost patients $300, the new selling price of $252 will drop the doctors' margin to only $48 (16%) from the planned margin of $180 (60%) based on FY's originally intended selling price of $120. This would probably result in the doctors not having much incentive to promote the product. In fact, it may be quite possible that the doctors may not attempt to prescribe the treatment at such low margin because of their own exposure to liability.

3.

Doctor's fee	$300
Doctor's minimum gross margin per treatment (40% × 300)	(120)
Doctor's maximum cost per treatment	180
FY's maximum selling price per unit =	180
FY's maximum total cost = 180/1.2 =	150
FY's per unit purchase cost =	(100)
FY's maximum per treatment insurance cost =	$ 50

4.   Nash has expressed his concerns to Keely. He should try to negotiate for an insurance fee of no more than $50 per treatment and point out to Keely that at the $180 price, they can still make Enhance attractive to doctors and also profitable for FY. If she still will not let Nash document and present his concerns and possible solutions, then he is in a difficult position.

      (a) He may be implicated in future litigation, and in particular, he may be accused of withholding damaging evidence.

      (b) Keely may find ways to portray him as not a "team player" and this may damage his career trajectory and future in the company.

      (c) He may have serious on-going issues with Keely's ethical standards. He should talk to her, to her manager/supervisor, and in the worst case, be prepared to resign if his concerns are not heard and documented. This type of problem is likely to occur again and again in the "cosmeceuticals" business.

CHAPTER 3
COST-VOLUME-PROFIT ANALYSIS

NOTATION USED IN CHAPTER 3 SOLUTIONS

   SP: Selling price
VCU: Variable cost per unit
CMU: Contribution margin per unit
  FC: Fixed costs
 TOI: Target operating income

3-2   The assumptions underlying the CVP analysis outlined in Chapter 3 are

1.   Changes in the level of revenues and costs arise only because of changes in the number of product (or service) units produced and sold.
2.   Total costs can be separated into a fixed component that does not vary with the output level and a component that is variable with respect to the output level.
3.   When represented graphically, the behavior of total revenues and total costs are linear (represented as a straight line) in relation to output level within a relevant range and time period.
4.   The selling price, variable cost per unit, and fixed costs are known and constant.
5.   The analysis either covers a single product or assumes that the sales mix, when multiple products are sold, will remain constant as the level of total units sold changes.
6.   All revenues and costs can be added and compared without taking into account the time value of money.

3-4   Contribution margin is the difference between total revenues and total variable costs. Contribution margin per unit is the difference between selling price and variable cost per unit. Contribution-margin percentage is the contribution margin per unit divided by selling price.

3-6   Breakeven analysis denotes the study of the breakeven point, which is often only an incidental part of the relationship between cost, volume, and profit. Cost-volume-profit relationship is a more comprehensive term than breakeven analysis.

3-8   An increase in the income tax rate does not affect the breakeven point. Operating income at the breakeven point is zero, and no income taxes are paid at this point.

3-10   Examples include:
        Manufacturing—substituting a robotic machine for hourly wage workers.
        Marketing—changing a sales force compensation plan from a percent of sales dollars to a fixed salary.
        Customer service—hiring a subcontractor to do customer repair visits on an annual retainer basis rather than a per-visit basis.

3-12   Operating leverage describes the effects that fixed costs have on changes in operating income as changes occur in units sold, and hence, in contribution margin. Knowing the degree of operating leverage at a given level of sales helps managers calculate the effect of fluctuations in sales on operating incomes.

3-14 A company with multiple products can compute a breakeven point by assuming there is a constant sales mix of products at different levels of total revenue.

3-16 (10 min.) **CVP computations.**

	Revenues	Variable Costs	Fixed Costs	Total Costs	Operating Income	Contribution Margin	Contribution Margin %
a.	**$2,000**	$ 500	**$300**	$ 800	$1,200	$1,500	**75.0%**
b.	2,000	**1,500**	300	**1,800**	200	500	**25.0%**
c.	1,000	700	**300**	1,000	**0**	**300**	**30.0%**
d.	1,500	**900**	300	**1,200**	**300**	**600**	40.0%

3-18 (35–40 min.) **CVP analysis, changing revenues and costs.**

1a.
SP $= 8\% \times \$1,000 = \$80$ per ticket
VCU $= \$35$ per ticket
CMU $= \$80 - \$35 = \$45$ per ticket
FC $= \$22,000$ a month

$$Q = \frac{FC}{CMU} = \frac{\$22,000}{\$45 \text{ per ticket}}$$

$= 489$ tickets (rounded up)

1b.
$$Q = \frac{FC + TOI}{CMU} = \frac{\$22,000 + \$10,000}{\$45 \text{ per ticket}}$$

$$= \frac{\$32,000}{\$45 \text{ per ticket}}$$

$= 712$ tickets (rounded up)

2a.
SP $= \$80$ per ticket
VCU $= \$29$ per ticket
CMU $= \$80 - \$29 = \$51$ per ticket
FC $= \$22,000$ a month

$$Q = \frac{FC}{CMU} = \frac{\$22,000}{\$51 \text{ per ticket}}$$

$= 432$ tickets (rounded up)

2b. $Q = \dfrac{FC + TOI}{CMU} = \dfrac{\$22,000 + \$10,000}{\$51 \text{ per ticket}}$

$= \dfrac{\$32,000}{\$51 \text{ per ticket}}$

= 628 tickets (rounded up)

3a.   SP   = \$48 per ticket
      VCU = \$29 per ticket
      CMU = \$48 – \$29 = \$19 per ticket
      FC   = \$22,000 a month

$Q = \dfrac{FC}{CMU} = \dfrac{\$22,000}{\$19 \text{ per ticket}}$

= 1,158 tickets (rounded up)

3b. $Q = \dfrac{FC + TOI}{CMU} = \dfrac{\$22,000 + \$10,000}{\$19 \text{ per ticket}}$

$= \dfrac{\$32,000}{\$19 \text{ per ticket}}$

= 1,685 tickets (rounded up)

The reduced commission sizably increases the breakeven point and the number of tickets required to yield a target operating income of \$10,000:

	8% Commission (Requirement 2)	Fixed Commission of \$48
Breakeven point	432	1,158
Attain OI of \$10,000	628	1,685

4a.   The \$5 delivery fee can be treated as either an extra source of revenue (as done below) or as a cost offset. Either approach increases CMU \$5:

SP   = \$53 (\$48 + \$5) per ticket
VCU   = \$29 per ticket
CMU   = \$53 – \$29 = \$24 per ticket
FC   = \$22,000 a month

$Q = \dfrac{FC}{CMU} = \dfrac{\$22,000}{\$24 \text{ per ticket}}$

= 917 tickets (rounded up)

4b. $$Q = \frac{FC + TOI}{CMU} = \frac{\$22{,}000 + \$10{,}000}{\$24 \text{ per ticket}}$$

$$= \frac{\$32{,}000}{\$24 \text{ per ticket}}$$

$$= 1{,}334 \text{ tickets (rounded up)}$$

The $5 delivery fee results in a higher contribution margin which reduces both the breakeven point and the tickets sold to attain operating income of $10,000.

3-20   (20 min.)   **CVP exercises.**

1a.   [Units sold (Selling price − Variable costs)] − Fixed costs   = Operating income
                [5,000,000 ($0.50 − $0.30)] − $900,000   = $100,000

1b.   Fixed costs ÷ Contribution margin per unit   = Breakeven units
                $900,000 ÷ [($0.50 − $0.30)] = 4,500,000 units
                Breakeven units × Selling price = Breakeven revenues
            4,500,000 units × $0.50 per unit   = $2,250,000
        or,

$$\text{Contribution margin ratio} = \frac{\text{Selling price - Variable costs}}{\text{Selling price}}$$

$$= \frac{\$0.50 \text{-} \$0.30}{\$0.50} = 0.40$$

Fixed costs ÷ Contribution margin ratio   = Breakeven revenues
                $900,000 ÷ 0.40   = $2,250,000

2.   5,000,000 ($0.50 − $0.34) − $900,000   = $ (100,000)

3.   [5,000,000 (1.1) ($0.50 − $0.30)] − [$900,000 (1.1)]   = $ 110,000

4.   [5,000,000 (1.4) ($0.40 − $0.27)] − [$900,000 (0.8)]   = $ 190,000

5. $900,000 (1.1) ÷ ($0.50 − $0.30)   =   4,950,000 units

6.   ($900,000 + $20,000) ÷ ($0.55 − $0.30)   =   3,680,000 units

3-22 (20–25 min.) **CVP analysis, income taxes.**

1. Variable cost percentage is $3.20 \div \$8.00 = 40\%$

$$\text{Let } R = \text{Revenues needed to obtain target net income}$$

$$R - 0.40R - \$450,000 = \frac{\$105,000}{1 - 0.30}$$
$$0.60R = \$450,000 + \$150,000$$
$$R = \$600,000 \div 0.60$$
$$R = \$1,000,000$$

or,

$$\text{Breakeven revenues} = \frac{\dfrac{\text{Target net income}}{1 - \text{Tax rate}}}{\text{Contribution margin percentage}} = \frac{\$450,000 + \dfrac{\$105,000}{1 - 0.30}}{0.60} = \$1,000,000$$

Proof:

Revenues	$1,000,000
Variable costs (at 40%)	400,000
Contribution margin	600,000
Fixed costs	450,000
Operating income	150,000
Income taxes (at 30%)	45,000
Net income	$ 105,000

2.a. Customers needed to earn net income of $105,000:
   Total revenues ÷ Sales check per customer
   $1,000,000 ÷ \$8 = 125,000$ customers

b. Customers needed to break even:

Contribution margin per customer = $8.00 - \$3.20 = \$4.80$
Breakeven number of customers = Fixed costs ÷ Contribution margin per customer
   = $450,000 \div \$4.80$ per customer
   = 93,750 customers

3. Using the shortcut approach:

$$\text{Change in net income} = \left(\begin{array}{c}\text{Change in}\\ \text{number of customers}\end{array}\right) \times \left(\begin{array}{c}\text{Unit}\\ \text{contribution}\\ \text{margin}\end{array}\right) \times (1 - \text{Tax rate})$$

$$= (150,000 - 125,000) \times \$4.80 \times (1 - 0.30)$$
$$= \$120,000 \times 0.7 = \$84,000$$
$$\text{New net income} = \$84,000 + \$105,000 = \$189,000$$

The alternative approach is:

Revenues, 150,000 × $8.00	$1,200,000
Variable costs at 40%	480,000
Contribution margin	720,000
Fixed costs	450,000
Operating income	270,000
Income tax at 30%	81,000
Net income	$ 189,000

3-24 (10 min.) CVP analysis, margin of safety.

1.
$$\text{Breakeven point revenues} = \frac{\text{Fixed costs}}{\text{Contribution margin percentage}}$$

$$\text{Contribution margin percentage} = \frac{\$400,000}{\$1,000,000} = 0.40 \text{ or } 40\%$$

2.
$$\text{Contribution margin percentage} = \frac{\text{Selling price} - \text{Variable cost per unit}}{\text{Selling price}}$$

$$0.40 = \frac{SP - \$12}{SP}$$

$$0.40\ SP = SP - \$12$$

$$0.60\ SP = \$12$$

$$SP = \$20$$

3.

Revenues, 80,000 units × $20	$1,600,000
Breakeven revenues	1,000,000
Margin of safety	$ 600,000

3-26 (15 min.) CVP analysis, international cost structure differences.

Country	Sales price to retail outlets (1)	Annual Fixed Costs (2)	Variable Manufacturing Cost per Sweater (3)	Variable Marketing & Distribution Cost per Sweater (4)	Contribution Margin Per Unit (5)=(1)-(3)-(4)	Breakeven Units (6)=(2)÷(5)	Breakeven Revenues (6) × (1)	Operating Income for Budgeted Sales of 800,000 Sweaters (7)=[800,000 ×(5)] – (2)
Singapore	$32.00	$ 6,500,000	$ 8.00	$11.00	$13.00	500,000	$16,000,000	$3,900,000
Thailand	32.00	4,500,000	5.50	11.50	15.00	300,000	9,600,000	7,500,000
United States	32.00	12,000,000	13.00	9.00	10.00	1,200,000	38,400,000	(4,000,000)

Requirement 1

Requirement 2

Thailand has the lowest breakeven point since it has both the lowest fixed costs ($4,500,000) and the lowest variable cost per unit ($17.00). Hence, for a given selling price, Thailand will always have a higher operating income (or a lower operating loss) than Singapore or the U.S.

The U.S. breakeven point is 1,200,000 units. Hence, with sales of only 800,000 units, it has an operating loss of $4,000,000.

3-28 (20 min.) **CVP analysis, multiple cost drivers.**

1a. $\text{Operating income} = \text{Revenues} - \left(\begin{matrix}\text{Cost of picture}\\ \text{frames}\end{matrix} \times \begin{matrix}\text{Quantity of}\\ \text{picture frames}\end{matrix}\right) - \left(\begin{matrix}\text{Cost of}\\ \text{shipment}\end{matrix} \times \begin{matrix}\text{Number of}\\ \text{shipments}\end{matrix}\right) - \begin{matrix}\text{Fixed}\\ \text{costs}\end{matrix}$

$= (\$45 \times 40,000) - (\$30 \times 40,000) - (\$60 \times 1,000) - \$240,000$

$= \$1,800,000 - \$1,200,000 - \$60,000 - \$240,000 = \$300,000$

1b. $\text{Operating income} = (\$45 \times 40,000) - (\$30 \times 40,000) - (\$60 \times 800) - \$240,000 = \$312,000$

2. Denote the number of picture frames sold by Q, then

$\$45Q - \$30Q - (500 \times \$60) - \$240,000 = 0$

$\$15Q = \$30,000 + \$240,000 = \$270,000$

$Q = \$270,000 \div \$15 = 18,000 \text{ picture frames}$

3. Suppose Susan had 1,000 shipments.

$\$45Q - \$30Q - (1,000 \times \$60) - \$240,000 = 0$

$15Q = \$300,000$

$Q = 20,000 \text{ picture frames}$

The breakeven point is not unique because there are two cost drivers—quantity of picture frames and number of shipments. Various combinations of the two cost drivers can yield zero operating income.

3-30 (15 min.) **Contribution margin, decision making.**

1.

Revenues		$500,000
Deduct variable costs:		
Cost of goods sold	$200,000	
Sales commissions	50,000	
Other operating costs	40,000	290,000
Contribution margin		$210,000

2. Contribution margin percentage $= \dfrac{\$210,000}{\$500,000} = 42\%$

3.

Incremental revenue (20% × $500,000) = $100,000		
Incremental contribution margin		
(42% × $100,000)		$42,000
Incremental fixed costs (advertising)		10,000
Incremental operating income		$32,000

If Mr. Schmidt spends $10,000 more on advertising, the operating income will increase by $32,000, converting an operating loss of $10,000 to an operating income of $22,000.

Proof (Optional):

Revenues (120% × $500,000)		$600,000
Cost of goods sold (40% of sales)		240,000
Gross margin		360,000
Operating costs:		
Salaries and wages	$150,000	
Sales commissions (10% of sales)	60,000	
Depreciation of equipment and fixtures	12,000	
Store rent	48,000	
Advertising	10,000	
Other operating costs:		
Variable ($\dfrac{\$40,000}{\$500,000} \times \$600,000$)	48,000	
Fixed	10,000	338,000
Operating income		$ 22,000

3-32 (15–20 min.) **Uncertainty, CVP analysis (chapter appendix).**

1.

Pay-per-view Audience (number of homes subscribing to the event) (1)	Probability (2)	Expected Audience (3) = (1)×(2)	Expected Payment to Foreman (4) = (3)×(25%×$16)
100,000	0.05	5,000	$ 20,000
200,000	0.10	20,000	80,000
300,000	0.30	90,000	360,000
400,000	0.35	140,000	560,000
500,000	0.15	75,000	300,000
1,000,000	0.05	50,000	200,000
Total		380,000	1,520,000

Fixed payment   2,000,000
Total expected payment to Foreman $3,520,000

2.
Selling price $ 16
Variable cost per subscribing home ($4 to Foreman + $2 to cable company)   6
Contribution margin per subscribing home $ 10
Fixed costs (Foreman, $2,000,000 + other costs, $1,000,000) $3,000,000

$$\text{Breakeven number of subscribing homes} = \frac{FC}{CMU} = \frac{\$3,000,000}{\$10} = 300,000 \text{ homes}$$

3.   Brady's expected audience size of 380,000 homes is more than 25% bigger than the breakeven audience size of 300,000 homes. So, if she is confident of the assumed probability distribution, she has a good margin of safety, and should proceed with her plans for the fight. She will only lose money if the pay-per-view audience is 100,000 or 200,000, which together have a 0.15 probability of occurring.

3-34   (30 min.) **CVP, target income, service firm.**

1.
Revenue per child	$600
Variable costs per child	200
Contribution margin per child	$400

$$\text{Breakeven quantity} = \frac{\text{Fixed costs}}{\text{Contribution margin per child}}$$

$$= \frac{\$5,600}{\$400} = 14 \text{ children}$$

2. $$\text{Target quantity} = \frac{\text{Fixed costs} + \text{Target operating income}}{\text{Contribution margin per child}}$$

$$= \frac{\$5,600 + \$10,400}{\$400} = 40 \text{ children}$$

3.
Increase in rent ($3,000 – $2,000)	$1,000
Field trips	1,000
Total increase in fixed costs	$2,000
Divide by the number of children enrolled	÷ 40
Increase in fee per child	$ 50

Therefore, the fee per child will increase from $600 to $650.

Alternatively,

$$\text{New contribution margin per child} = \frac{\$5,600 + \$2,000 + \$10,400}{40} = \$450$$

New fee per child = Variable costs per child + New contribution margin per child
$$= \$200 + \$450 = \$650$$

3-36 (30–40 min.)   **CVP analysis, income taxes.**

1.   Revenues – Variable costs – Fixed costs $= \dfrac{\text{Target net income}}{1 - \text{Tax rate}}$

Let X = Net income for 2005

$$20{,}000(\$25.00) - 20{,}000(\$13.75) - \$135{,}000 = \dfrac{X}{1 - 0.40}$$

$$\$500{,}000 - \$275{,}000 - \$135{,}000 = \dfrac{X}{0.60}$$

$$\$300{,}000 - \$165{,}000 - \$81{,}000 = X$$

$$X = \$54{,}000$$

Alternatively,

Operating income = Revenues – Variable costs – Fixed costs
$$= \$500{,}000 - \$275{,}000 - \$135{,}000 = \$90{,}000$$

Income taxes $= 0.40 \times \$90{,}000 = \$36{,}000$

Net income = Operating income – Income taxes
$$= \$90{,}000 - \$36{,}000 = \$54{,}000$$

2.   Let Q = Number of units to break even

$$\$25.00Q - \$13.75Q - \$135{,}000 = 0$$

$$Q = \$135{,}000 \div \$11.25 = 12{,}000 \text{ units}$$

3.   Let X = Net income for 2006

$$22{,}000(\$25.00) - 22{,}000(\$13.75) - (\$135{,}000 + \$11{,}250) = \dfrac{X}{1 - 0.40}$$

$$\$550{,}000 - \$302{,}500 - \$146{,}250 = \dfrac{X}{0.60}$$

$$\$101{,}250 = \dfrac{X}{0.60}$$

$$X = \$60{,}750$$

4.   Let Q = Number of units to break even with new fixed costs of $146,250

$$\$25.00Q - \$13.75Q - \$146{,}250 = 0$$

$$Q = \$146{,}250 \div \$11.25 = 13{,}000 \text{ units}$$

$$\text{Breakeven revenues} = 13{,}000 \times \$25.00 = \$325{,}000$$

5.   Let S = Required sales units to equal 2005 net income

$$\$25.00S - \$13.75S - \$146{,}250 = \dfrac{\$54{,}000}{0.60}$$

$$\$11.25S = \$236{,}250$$

$$S = 21{,}000 \text{ units}$$

$$\text{Revenues} = 21{,}000 \text{ units} \times \$25 = \$525{,}000$$

6.   Let A = Amount spent for advertising in 2006

$$\$550{,}000 - \$302{,}500 - (\$135{,}000 + A) = \dfrac{\$60{,}000}{0.60}$$

$$\$550{,}000 - \$302{,}500 - \$135{,}000 - A = \$100{,}000$$

$$\$550{,}000 - \$537{,}500 = A$$

$$A = \$12{,}500$$

3-38 (20–30 min.) **CVP analysis, shoe stores.**

1. CMU (SP – VCU = $30 – $21) $ 9.00
  a. Breakeven units (FC ÷ CMU = $360,000 ÷ $9 per unit)   40,000
  b. Breakeven revenues (Breakeven units × SP = 40,000 units × $30 per unit) $1,200,000

2. Pairs sold   35,000
  Revenues, 35,000 × $30 $1,050,000
  Total cost of shoes, 35,000 × $19.50   682,500
  Total sales commissions, 35,000 × $1.50   52,500
  Total variable costs   735,000
  Contribution margin   315,000
  Fixed costs   360,000
  Operating income (loss) $ (45,000)

3. Unit variable data (per pair of shoes)
  Selling price $ 30.00
  Cost of shoes   19.50
  Sales commissions   0
  Variable cost per unit $ 19.50
  Annual fixed costs
  Rent $ 60,000
  Salaries, $200,000 + $81,000   281,000
  Advertising   80,000
  Other fixed costs   20,000
  Total fixed costs $ 441,000

  CMU, $30 – $19.50 $ 10.50
  a. Breakeven units, $441,000 ÷ $10.50 per unit   42,000
  b. Breakeven revenues, 42,000 units × $30 per unit $1,260,000

4. Unit variable data (per pair of shoes)
  Selling price $ 30.00
  Cost of shoes   19.50
  Sales commissions   1.80
  Variable cost per unit $ 21.30
  Total fixed costs $ 360,000

  CMU, $30 – $21.30 $ 8.70
  a. Break even units = $360,000 ÷ $8.70 per unit   41,380 (rounded up)
  b. Break even revenues = 41,380 units × $30 per unit $1,241,400

5. Pairs sold   50,000
  Revenues (50,000 pairs × $30 per pair) $1,500,000
  Total cost of shoes (50,000 pairs × $19.50 per pair) $ 975,000
  Sales commissions on first 40,000 pairs (40,000 pairs × $1.50 per pair)   60,000
  Sales commissions on additional 10,000 pairs
   [10,000 pairs × ($1.50 + $0.30 per pair)]   18,000
  Total variable costs $1,053,000
  Contribution margin $ 447,000
  Fixed costs   360,000
  Operating income $ 87,000

Alternative approach:

Breakeven point in units = 40,000 pairs
Store manager receives commission of $0.30 on 10,000 (50,000 – 40,000) pairs.
Contribution margin per pair beyond breakeven point of 10,000 pairs equals $8.70 ($30 – $21 –$0.30) per pair.
Operating income = 10,000 pairs × $8.70 contribution margin per pair = $87,000.

3-40 (20 min.)   Alternative cost structures, sensitivity analysis.

	Requirement 1				Requirement 2			
	Fixed fee $2,000				Fixed fee $800			
	Percent of Revenues 0%				Percent of Revenues 15%			
Selling price	$ 200	$ 230	$ 275	$ 300	$ 200	$ 230	$ 275	$ 300
Demand	42	30	20	15	42	30	20	15
Cost per package	$ 120	$ 120	$ 120	$ 120	$ 120	$ 120	$ 120	$ 120
Revenues = Demand × SP	$8,400	$6,900	$5,500	$4,500	$8,400	$6,900	$5,500	$5,500
Package costs = $120 × Demand	5,040	3,600	2,400	1,800	5,040	3,600	2,400	2,400
Booth variable costs = Revenues × Percent of revenues	0	0	0	0	1,260	1,035	825	825
Contribution margin	3,360	3,300	3,100	2,700	2,100	2,265	2,275	2,275
Booth fixed fee	2,000	2,000	2,000	2,000	800	800	800	800
Operating income	$1,360	$1,300	$1,100	$ 700	$1,300	$1,465	$1,475	$1,475

1.   See section of table labeled Requirement 1 above. If Mary pays a fixed fee of $2,000 to rent the booth, she should sell the Do-All packages at $200 each in order to maximize operating income.

Contribution margin can also be calculated as contribution margin per unit × demand. For example, when selling price is $230, contribution margin per unit is $110 ($230 – $120) and contribution margin is $3,300 ($110 per unit × 30 units)

2.   See section of table labeled Requirement 2 above. If Mary pays a fixed fee of $800 plus 15% of revenues to rent the booth, she should sell the Do-All packages at $275 each in order to maximize operating income.

Contribution margin can also be calculated as contribution margin per unit × demand. For example, when selling price is $230, contribution margin per unit is $75.50 ($230 – $120 – 15% × $230) and contribution margin is $2,265 ($75.50 per unit × 30 units)

3-42 (30 min.) **CVP analysis, income taxes, sensitivity.**

1a. To break even, Almo Company must sell 500 units. This amount represents the point where revenues equal total costs.

Let Q denote the quantity of canopies sold.

$$
\begin{aligned}
\text{Revenue} &= \text{Variable costs} + \text{Fixed costs} \\
\$400Q &= \$200Q + \$100{,}000 \\
\$200Q &= \$100{,}000 \\
Q &= 500 \text{ units}
\end{aligned}
$$

Breakeven can also be calculated using contribution margin per unit.

Contribution margin per unit = Selling price – Variable cost per unit = $400 – $200 = $200

$$
\begin{aligned}
\text{Breakeven} &= \text{Fixed Costs} \div \text{Contribution margin per unit} \\
&= \$100{,}000 \div \$200 \\
&= 500 \text{ units}
\end{aligned}
$$

1b. To achieve its net income objective, Almo Company must sell 2,500 units. This amount represents the point where revenues equal total costs plus the corresponding operating income objective to achieve net income of $240,000.

$$
\begin{aligned}
\text{Revenue} &= \text{Variable costs} + \text{Fixed costs} + [\text{Net income} \div (1 - \text{Tax rate})] \\
\$400Q &= \$200Q + \$100{,}000 + [\$240{,}000 \div (1 - 0.4)] \\
\$400\,Q &= \$200Q + \$100{,}000 + \$400{,}000 \\
Q &= 2{,}500 \text{ units}
\end{aligned}
$$

2. To achieve its net income objective, Almo Company should select the first alternative where the sales price is reduced by $40, and 2,700 units are sold during the remainder of the year. This alternative results in the highest net income and is the only alternative that equals or exceeds the company's net income objective. Calculations for the three alternatives are shown below.

Alternative 1

$$
\begin{aligned}
\text{Revenues} &= (\$400 \times 350) + (\$360^{a} \times 2{,}700) = \$1{,}112{,}000 \\
\text{Variable costs} &= \$200 \times 3{,}050^{b} = \$610{,}000 \\
\text{Operating income} &= \$1{,}112{,}000 - \$610{,}000 - \$100{,}000 = \$402{,}000 \\
\text{Net income} &= \$402{,}000 \times (1 - 0.40) = \$241{,}200
\end{aligned}
$$

[a]$400 – $40; [b]350 units + 2,700 units.

Alternative 2

$$
\begin{aligned}
\text{Revenues} &= (\$400 \times 350) + (\$370^{c} \times 2{,}200) = \$954{,}000 \\
\text{Variable costs} &= (\$200 \times 350) + (\$190^{d} \times 2{,}200) = \$488{,}000 \\
\text{Operating income} &= \$954{,}000 - \$488{,}000 - \$100{,}000 = \$366{,}000 \\
\text{Net income} &= \$366{,}000 \times (1 - 0.40) = \$219{,}600
\end{aligned}
$$

[c]$400 – $30; [d]$200 – $10.

Alternative 3

$$\begin{aligned}
\text{Revenues} &= (\$400 \times 350) + (\$380^e \times 2{,}000) = \$900{,}000 \\
\text{Variable costs} &= \$200 \times 2{,}350^f = \$470{,}000 \\
\text{Operating income} &= \$900{,}000 - \$470{,}000 - \$90{,}000^g = \$340{,}000 \\
\text{Net income} &= \$340{,}000 \times (1 - 0.40) = \$204{,}000
\end{aligned}$$

$^e\$400 - (0.05 \times \$400) = \$400 - \$20$; $^f 350$ units $+ 2{,}000$ units; $^g\$100{,}000 - \$10{,}000$

3-44 (15–25 min.) **Sales mix, three products.**

1. Sales of A, B, and C are in ratio 20,000 : 100,000 : 80,000. So for every 1 unit of A, 5 (100,000 ÷ 20,000) units of B are sold, and 4 (80,000 ÷ 20,000) units of C are sold.

Let Q = Number of units of A to break even
  5Q = Number of units of B to break even
  4Q = Number of units of C to break even

Contribution margin – Fixed costs = Zero operating income

$$\begin{aligned}
\$3Q + \$2(5Q) + \$1(4Q) - \$255{,}000 &= 0 \\
\$17Q &= \$255{,}000 \\
Q &= 15{,}000 \ (\$255{,}000 \div \$17) \text{ units of A} \\
5Q &= 75{,}000 \text{ units of B} \\
4Q &= \underline{60{,}000} \text{ units of C} \\
\text{Total} &= \underline{\underline{150{,}000}} \text{ units}
\end{aligned}$$

2. Contribution margin:

A: 20,000 × $3	$ 60,000	
B: 100,000 × $2	200,000	
C: 80,000 × $1	80,000	
Contribution margin		$340,000
Fixed costs		255,000
Operating income		$ 85,000

3. Contribution margin

A: 20,000 × $3	$ 60,000	
B: 80,000 × $2	160,000	
C: 100,000 × $1	100,000	
Contribution margin		$320,000
Fixed costs		255,000
Operating income		$ 65,000

Let Q = Number of units of A to break even
  4Q = Number of units of B to break even
  5Q = Number of units of C to break even

Contribution margin − Fixed costs = Breakeven point

$$\$3Q + \$2(4Q) + \$1(5Q) - \$255,000 = 0$$

$$\$16Q = \$255,000$$

$$Q = 15,938 \ (\$255,000 \div \$16) \text{ units of A (rounded up)}$$

$$4Q = 63,752 \text{ units of B}$$

$$5Q = \underline{79,690} \text{ units of C}$$

$$\text{Total} = \underline{159,380} \text{ units}$$

Breakeven point increases because the new mix contains less of the higher contribution margin per unit, product B, and more of the lower contribution margin per unit, product C.

3-46 (20–25 min.) **Sales mix, two products.**

1. Let Q   = Number of units of Deluxe carrier to break even
       3Q   = Number of units of Standard carrier to break even

Revenues − Variable costs − Fixed costs = Zero operating income

$$\$20(3Q) + \$30Q - \$14(3Q) - \$18Q - \$1,200,000 = 0$$

$$\$60Q + \$30Q - \$42Q - \$18Q = \$1,200,000$$

$$\$30Q = \$1,200,000$$

$$Q = 40,000 \text{ units of Deluxe}$$

$$3Q = 120,000 \text{ units of Standard}$$

The breakeven point is 120,000 Standard units plus 40,000 Deluxe units, a total of 160,000 units.

2a.   Unit contribution margins are: Standard: $20 − $14 = $6; Deluxe: $30 − $18 = $12
       If only Standard carriers were sold, the breakeven point would be:
       $1,200,000 ÷ $6 = 200,000 units.
2b.   If only Deluxe carriers were sold, the breakeven point would be:
       $1,200,000 ÷ $12 = 100,000 units

3.   Operating income = Contribution margin of Standard + Contribution margin of Deluxe − Fixed costs
            = 180,000($6) + 20,000($12) − $1,200,000
            = $1,080,000 + $240,000 − $1,200,000
            = $120,000

Let Q   = Number of units of Deluxe product to break even
     9Q = Number of units of Standard product to break even

$$\$20(9Q) + \$30Q - \$14(9Q) - \$18Q - \$1,200,000 = 0$$

$$\$180Q + \$30Q - \$126Q - \$18Q = \$1,200,000$$

$$\$66Q = \$1,200,000$$

$$Q = 18,182 \text{ units of Deluxe (rounded up)}$$

$$9Q = 163,638 \text{ units of Standard}$$

3-18

The breakeven point is 163,638 Standard + 18,182 Deluxe, a total of 181,820 units.

The major lesson of this problem is that changes in the sales mix change breakeven points and operating incomes. In this example, the budgeted and actual total sales in number of units were identical, but the proportion of the product having the higher contribution margin declined. Operating income suffered, falling from $300,000 to $120,000. Moreover, the breakeven point rose from 160,000 to 181,820 units.

3-48 (30 min.) **Ethics, CVP analysis.**

1.
$$\text{Contribution margin percentage} = \frac{\text{Revenues} - \text{Variable costs}}{\text{Revenues}}$$

$$= \frac{\$5,000,000 - \$3,000,000}{\$5,000,000}$$

$$= \frac{\$2,000,000}{\$5,000,000} = 40\%$$

$$\text{Breakeven revenues} = \frac{\text{Fixed costs}}{\text{Contribution margin percentage}}$$

$$= \frac{\$2,160,000}{0.40} = \$5,400,000$$

2. If variable costs are 52% of revenues, contribution margin percentage equals 48% (100% − 52%)

$$\text{Breakeven revenues} = \frac{\text{Fixed costs}}{\text{Contribution margin percentage}}$$

$$= \frac{\$2,160,000}{0.48} = \$4,500,000$$

3.
Revenues	$5,000,000
Variable costs (0.52 × $5,000,000)	2,600,000
Fixed costs	2,160,000
Operating income	$ 240,000

4. Incorrect reporting of environmental costs with the goal of continuing operations is unethical. In assessing the situation, the specific "Standards of Ethical Conduct for Management Accountants" (described in Exhibit 1-7) that the management accountant should consider are listed below.

Competence
Clear reports using relevant and reliable information should be prepared. Preparing reports on the basis of incorrect environmental costs to make the company's performance look better than it is violates competence standards. It is unethical for Bush not to report environmental costs to make the plant's performance look good.

Integrity

The management accountant has a responsibility to avoid actual or apparent conflicts of interest and advise all appropriate parties of any potential conflict. Bush may be tempted to report lower environmental costs to please Lemond and Woodall and save the jobs of his colleagues. This action, however, violates the responsibility for integrity. The Standards of Ethical Conduct require the management accountant to communicate favorable as well as unfavorable information.

Objectivity

The management accountant's Standards of Ethical Conduct require that information should be fairly and objectively communicated and that all relevant information should be disclosed. From a management accountant's standpoint, underreporting environmental costs to make performance look good would violate the standard of objectivity.

Bush should indicate to Lemond that estimates of environmental costs and liabilities should be included in the analysis. If Lemond still insists on modifying the numbers and reporting lower environmental costs, Bush should raise the matter with one of Lemond's superiors. If after taking all these steps, there is continued pressure to understate environmental costs, Bush should consider resigning from the company and not engage in unethical behavior.

CHAPTER 4
JOB COSTING

4-2   In a *job-costing system,* costs are assigned to a distinct unit, batch, or lot of a product or service. In a *process-costing system,* the cost of a product or service is obtained by using broad averages to assign costs to masses of identical or similar units.

4-4   The seven steps in job costing are: (1) identify the job that is the chosen cost object, (2) identify the direct costs of the job, (3) select the cost-allocation bases to use for allocating indirect costs to the job, (4) identify the indirect costs associated with each cost-allocation base, (5) compute the rate per unit of each cost-allocation base used to allocate indirect costs to the job, (6) compute the indirect costs allocated to the job, and (7) compute the total cost of the job by adding all direct and indirect costs assigned to the job.

4-6   Three major source documents used in job-costing systems are (1) job cost record or job cost sheet, a document that records and accumulates all costs assigned to a specific job, starting when work begins (2) materials requisition record, a document that contains information about the cost of direct materials used on a specific job and in a specific department; and (3) labor-time record, a document that contains information about the labor time used on a specific job and in a specific department.

4-8   Two reasons for using an annual budget period are
  a. The numerator reason—the longer the time period, the less the influence of seasonal patterns, and
  b. The denominator reason—the longer the time period, the less the effect of variations in output levels on the allocation of fixed costs.

4-10   A house construction firm can use job cost information (a) to determine the profitability of individual jobs, (b) to assist in bidding on future jobs, and (c) to evaluate professionals who are in charge of managing individual jobs.

4-12   Debit entries to Work-in-Process Control represent increases in work in process. Examples of debit entries under normal costing are (a) direct materials used (credit to Materials Control), (b) direct manufacturing labor billed to job (credit to Wages Payable Control), and (c) manufacturing overhead allocated to job (credit to Manufacturing Overhead Allocated).

4-14   A company might use budgeted costs rather than actual costs to compute direct labor rates because it may be difficult to trace direct labor costs to jobs as they are completed (for example, because bonuses are only known at the end of the year).

4-16   (10 min) Job order costing, process costing.

a. Job costing
b. Process costing
c. Job costing
d. Process costing
e. Job costing
f. Process costing
g. Job costing
h. Job costing (but some process costing)
i. Process costing
j. Process costing
k. Job costing

l. Job costing
m. Process costing
n. Job costing
o. Job costing
p. Job costing
q. Job costing
r. Process costing
s. Job costing
t. Process costing
u. Job costing

4-18   (20 -30 min.)   Job costing, normal and actual costing.

1.
$$\text{Budgeted indirect-cost rate} = \frac{\text{Budgeted indirect costs}}{\text{Budgeted direct labor-hours}} = \frac{\$8,000,000}{160,000 \text{ hours}}$$

$$= \$50 \text{ per direct labor-hour}$$

$$\text{Actual indirect-cost rate} = \frac{\text{Actual indirect costs}}{\text{Actual direct labor-hours}} = \frac{\$6,888,000}{164,000 \text{ hours}}$$

$$= \$42 \text{ per direct labor-hour}$$

These rates differ because both the numerator and the denominator in the two calculations are different—one based on budgeted numbers and the other based on actual numbers.

2a.

	Laguna Model	Mission Model
Normal costing		
Direct costs		
Direct materials	$106,450	$127,604
Direct labor	36,276	41,410
	142,726	169,014
Indirect costs		
Assembly support ($50 × 900; $50 × 1,010)	45,000	50,500
Total costs	$187,726	$219,514

2b. Actual costing
Direct costs

Direct materials	$106,450	$127,604
Direct labor	36,276	41,410
	142,726	169,014
Indirect costs		
Assembly support ($42 × 900; $42 × 1,010)	37,800	42,420
Total costs	$180,526	$211,434

3.   Normal costing enables Anderson to report a job cost as soon as the job is completed, assuming that both the direct materials and direct labor costs are known at the time of use. Once the 900 direct labor-hours are known for the Laguna Model (June 2007), Anderson can compute the $187,726 cost figure using normal costing. Anderson can use this information to manage the costs of the Laguna Model job as well as to bid on similar jobs later in the year. In contrast, Anderson has to wait until the December 2007 year-end to compute the $180,526 cost of the Laguna Model using actual costing.

Although not required, the following overview diagram summarizes Anderson Construction's job-costing system.

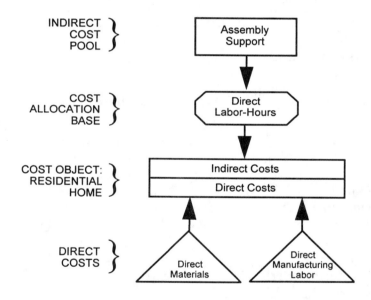

4-20 (20-30 min.)   **Job costing, accounting for manufacturing overhead, budgeted rates.**

1.   An overview of the product costing system is

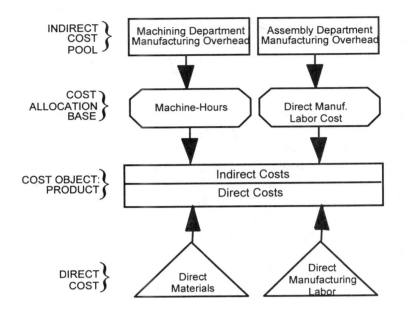

Budgeted manufacturing overhead divided by allocation base:

Machining overhead $\dfrac{\$1,800,000}{50,000}$ = $36 per machine-hour

Assembly overhead: $\dfrac{\$3,600,000}{\$2,000,000}$ = 180% of direct manuf. labor costs

2.

Machining department, 2,000 hours × $36	$72,000
Assembly department, 180% × $15,000	27,000
Total manufacturing overhead allocated to Job 494	$99,000

3.

	Machining	**Assembly**
Actual manufacturing overhead	$2,100,000	$ 3,700,000
Manufacturing overhead allocated,		
55,000 × $36	1,980,000	—
180% × $2,200,000	—	3,960,000
Underallocated (Overallocated)	$ 120,000	$ (260,000)

4-22 (15–20 min.) **Service industry, time period used to compute indirect cost rates.**

1.

	Jan–March	April–June	July–Sept	Oct–Dec	Total
Direct labor costs	$400,000	$280,000	$250,000	$270,000	$1,200,000
Variable costs as percentage of direct labor costs	90%	60%	60%	60%	
Variable overhead costs (Percentage × direct labor costs)	$360,000	$168,000	$150,000	$162,000	$ 840,000
Fixed overhead costs	300,000	300,000	300,000	300,000	1,200,000
Total overhead costs	$660,000	$468,000	$450,000	$462,000	$2,040,000
Total overhead costs as a percentage of direct labor costs	165%	167%	180%	171%	170%

	Budgeted Overhead Rate Used		
	Jan–March	July–Sept	Average
Job 332	Rate	Rate	Yearly Rate
Direct materials	$10,000	$10,000	$10,000
Direct labor costs	6,000	6,000	6,000
Overhead allocated (variable + fixed) (165%; 180%; 170% of $6,000)	9,900	10,800	10,200
Full cost of Job 332	$25,900	$26,800	$26,200

(a)   The full cost of Job 332, using the budgeted overhead rate of 165% for January–March, is $25,900.

(b)   The full cost of Job 332, using the budgeted overhead rate of 180% for July–September, is $26,800.

(c)   The full cost of Job 332, using the annual budgeted overhead rate of 170%, is $26,200.

2.

Budgeted fixed overhead rate based on annual fixed overhead costs and annual direct labor costs = $1,200,000 ÷ $1,200,000 = 100%

	Budgeted Variable Overhead Rate Used	
	January–March	July–Sept
Job 332	rate	rate
Direct materials	$10,000	$10,000
Direct labor costs	6,000	6,000
Variable overhead allocated (90%; 60%; of $6,000)	5,400	3,600
Fixed overhead allocated (100% of $6,000)	6,000	6,000
Full cost of Job 332	$27,400	$25,600

(a)   The full cost of Job 332, using the budgeted variable overhead rate of 90% for January–March and an annual fixed overhead rate of 100%, is $27,400.

(b)   The full cost of Job 332, using the budgeted variable overhead rate of 60% for July–September and an annual fixed overhead rate of 100%, is $25,600.

3.   If Printers, Inc. sets prices at a markup of costs, then prices based on costs calculated as in Requirement 2 (rather than as in Requirement 1) would be more effective in deterring clients from sending in last-minute, congestion-causing orders in the January–March time frame. In this calculation, more variable manufacturing overhead costs are allocated to jobs in the first quarter, reflecting the larger costs of that quarter caused by higher overtime and facility and machine maintenance. This method better captures the cost of congestion during the first quarter.

4-24   (35–45 min.)   **Job costing, journal entries.**

Some instructors may also want to assign Exercise 4-25. It demonstrates the relationships of the general ledger to the underlying subsidiary ledgers and source documents.

1.   An overview of the product costing system is:

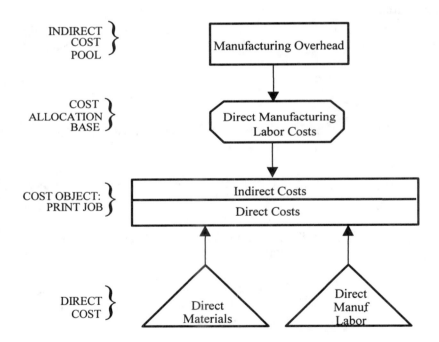

2. & 3.

This answer assumes COGS given of $4,020 does not include the writeoff of overallocated manufacturing overhead.

2. (1) Materials Control   800
            Accounts Payable Control   800
    (2) Work-in-Process Control   710
            Materials Control   710
    (3) Manufacturing Overhead Control   100
            Materials Control   100
    (4) Work-in-Process Control   1,300
         Manufacturing Overhead Control   900
            Wages Payable Control   2,200
    (5) Manufacturing Overhead Control   400
         Accumulated Depreciation—buildings and
            manufacturing equipment   400
    (6) Manufacturing Overhead Control   550
            Miscellaneous accounts   550
    (7) Work-in-Process Control   2,080
            Manufacturing Overhead Allocated   2,080
            ($1.60 \times \$1,300 = \$2,080$)
    (8) Finished Goods Control   4,120
            Work-in-Process Control   4,120
    (9) Accounts Receivable Control (or Cash)   8,000
            Revenues   8,000
    (10) Cost of Goods Sold   4,020
            Finished Goods Control   4,020
    (11) Manufacturing Overhead Allocated   2,080
         Manufacturing Overhead Control   1,950
         Cost of Goods Sold   130

3.

Materials Control

Bal. 12/31/2006	100	(2)	Issues	710
(1) Purchases	800	(3)	Issues	100
Bal. 12/31/2007	90			

Work-in-Process Control

Bal. 12/31/2006	60	(8)Goods completed	4,120
(2) Direct materials	710		
(4) Direct manuf. labor	1,300		
(7) Manuf. overhead allocated	2,080		
Bal. 12/31/2007	30		

Finished Goods Control

Bal. 12/31/2006	500	(10) Goods sold	4,020
(8) Goods completed	4,120		
Bal. 12/31/2007	600		

Cost of Goods Sold

(10) Goods sold	4,020	(11) Adjust for over-allocation	130
Bal. 12/31/2007	3,890		

Manufacturing Overhead Control

(3) Indirect materials	100	(11) To close	1,950
(4) Indirect manuf. labor	900		
(5) Depreciation	400		
(6) Miscellaneous	550		
Bal.	0		

Manufacturing Overhead Allocated

(11) To close	2,080	(7) Manuf. overhead allocated	2,080
		Bal.	0

4-26 (45 min.) **Job costing, journal entries.**

Some instructors may wish to assign Problem 4-24. It demonstrates the relationships of journal entries, general ledger, subsidiary ledgers, and source documents.

1.   An overview of the product-costing system is

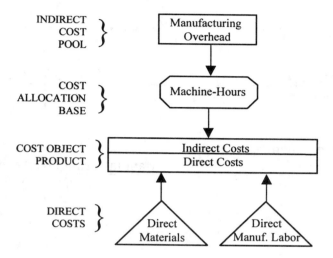

2.   Amounts in millions.

(1)	Materials Control	150	
	Accounts Payable Control		150
(2)	Work-in-Process Control	145	
	Materials Control		145
(3)	Manufacturing Department Overhead Control	10	
	Materials Control		10
(4)	Work-in-Process Control	90	
	Wages Payable Control		90
(5)	Manufacturing Department Overhead Control	30	
	Wages Payable Control		30
(6)	Manufacturing Department Overhead Control	19	
	Accumulated Depreciation		19
(7)	Manufacturing Department Overhead Control	9	
	Various liabilities		9
(8)	Work-in-Process Control	63	
	Manufacturing Overhead Allocated		63
(9)	Finished Goods Control	294	
	Work-in-Process Control		294
(10a)	Cost of Goods Sold	292	
	Finished Goods Control		292
(10b)	Accounts Receivable Control (or Cash)	400	
	Revenues		400

The posting of entries to T-accounts is as follows:

Materials Control			
Bal.	12	(2)	145
(1)	150	(3)	10

Work-in-Process Control			
Bal.	2	(9)	294
(2)	145		
(4)	90		
(8)	63		
Bal.	6		

Finished Goods Control			
Bal.	6	(10a)	292
(9)	294		

Cost of Goods Sold			
(10a)	292		
(11)	5		

Manufacturing Department Overhead Control			
(3)	10	(11)	68
(5)	30		
(6)	19		
(7)	9		

Manufacturing Overhead Allocated			
(11)	63	(8)	63

Accounts Payable Control			
		(1)	150

Wages Payable Control			
		(4)	90
		(5)	30

Accumulated Depreciation			
		(6)	19

Various Liabilities			
		(7)	9

Accounts Receivable Control			
(10b)	400		

Revenues			
		(10b)	400

The ending balance of Work-in-Process Control is $6.

3. (11) Manufacturing Overhead Allocated   63
         Cost of Goods Sold   5
              Manufacturing Department Overhead Control   68

Entry posted to T-accounts in Requirement 2.

4-10

4-28 (20–30 min.) **Job costing; actual, normal, and variation from normal costing.**

1. Actual direct cost rate for professional labor = $58 per professional labor-hour

$$\text{Actual indirect cost rate} = \frac{\$744,000}{15,500 \text{ hours}} = \$48 \text{ per professional labor-hour}$$

$$\begin{array}{l} \text{Budgeted direct cost rate} \\ \text{for professional labor} \end{array} = \frac{\$960,000}{16,000 \text{ hours}} = \$60 \text{ per professional labor-hour}$$

$$\text{Budgeted indirect cost rate} = \frac{\$720,000}{16,000 \text{ hours}} = \$45 \text{ per professional labor-hour}$$

	(a) Actual Costing	(b) Normal Costing	(c) Variation of Normal Costing
Direct-Cost Rate	$58 (Actual rate)	$58 (Actual rate)	$60 (Budgeted rate)
Indirect-Cost Rate	$48 (Actual rate)	$45 (Budgeted rate)	$45 (Budgeted rate)

2.

	(a) Actual Costing	(b) Normal Costing	(c) Variation of Normal Costing
Direct Costs	$58 × 120 = $ 6,960	$58 × 120 = $ 6,960	$60 × 120 = $ 7,200
Indirect Costs	48 × 120 = 5,760	45 × 120 = 5,400	45 × 120 = 5,400
Total Job Costs	$12,720	$12,360	$12,600

All three costing systems use the actual professional labor time of 120 hours. The budgeted 110 hours for the Pierre Enterprises audit job is not used in job costing. However, Chirac may have used the 110 hour number in bidding for the audit.

The actual costing figure of $12,720 exceeds the normal costing figure of $12,360 because the actual indirect-cost rate ($48) exceeds the budgeted indirect-cost rate ($45). The normal costing figure of $12,360 is less than the variation of normal costing (based on budgeted rates for direct costs) figure of $12,600, because the actual direct-cost rate ($58) is less than the budgeted direct-cost rate ($60).

Although not required, the following overview diagram summarizes Chirac's job-costing system.

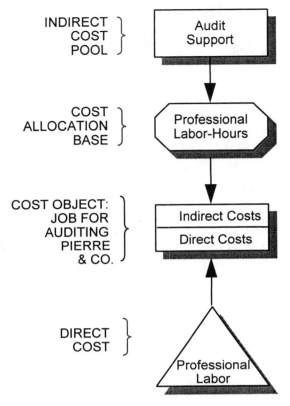

4-30 (20–30 min) **Job costing, accounting for manufacturing overhead, budgeted rates.**

1. An overview of the job-costing system is:

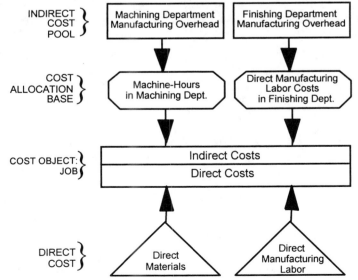

2. Budgeted manufacturing overhead divided by allocation base:

    a. Machining Department:

$$\frac{\$10,000,000}{200,000} = \$50 \text{ per machine-hour}$$

    b. Finishing Department:

$$\frac{\$8,000,000}{\$4,000,000} = 200\% \text{ of direct manufacturing labor costs}$$

3.
Machining Department overhead, $50 × 130 hours	$6,500
Finishing Department overhead, 200% of $1,250	2,500
Total manufacturing overhead allocated	$9,000

4. Total costs of Job 431:

Direct costs:		
Direct materials—Machining Department	$14,000	
—Finishing Department	3,000	
Direct manufacturing labor —Machining Department	600	
—Finishing Department	1,250	$18,850
Indirect costs:		
Machining Department overhead, $50 × 130	$6,500	
Finishing Department overhead, 200% of $1,250	2,500	9,000
Total costs		$27,850

The per-unit product cost of Job 431 is $27,850 ÷ 200 units = $139.25 per unit

The point of this part is (a) to get the definitions straight and (b) to underscore that overhead is allocated by multiplying the actual amount of the allocation base by the budgeted rate.

5.

	Machining	Finishing
Manufacturing overhead incurred (actual)	$11,200,000	$7,900,000
Manufacturing overhead allocated		
220,000 hours × $50	11,000,000	
200% of $4,100,000		8,200,000
Underallocated manufacturing overhead	$ 200,000	
Overallocated manufacturing overhead		$ 300,000

Total overallocated overhead = $300,000 – $200,000 = $100,000

6.   A homogeneous cost pool is one where all costs have the same or a similar cause-and-effect or benefits-received relationship with the cost-allocation base. Solomon likely assumes that all its manufacturing overhead cost items are not homogeneous. Specifically, those in the Machining Department have a cause-and-effect relationship with machine-hours, while those in the Finishing Department have a cause-and-effect relationship with direct manufacturing labor costs. Solomon believes that the benefits of using two cost pools (more accurate product costs and better ability to manage costs) exceeds the costs of implementing a more complex system.

4-32   (25–30 min.) **Service industry, job costing, two direct- and indirect-cost categories, law firm (continuation of 4-31).**

Although not required, the following overview diagram is helpful to understand Keating's job-costing system.

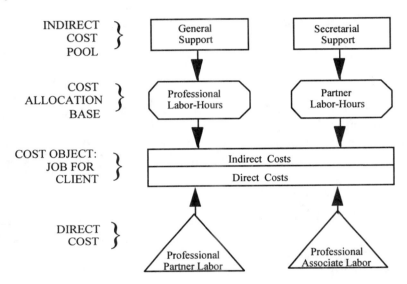

1.

	Professional Partner Labor	**Professional Associate Labor**
Budgeted compensation per professional	$ 200,000	$80,000
Divided by budgeted hours of billable time per professional	÷1,600	÷1,600
Budgeted direct-cost rate	$125 per hour*	$50 per hour†

*Can also be calculated as $\dfrac{\text{Total budgeted partner labor costs}}{\text{Total budgeted partner labor - hours}} = \dfrac{\$200,000 \times 5}{1,600 \times 5} = \dfrac{\$1,000,000}{8,000} = \$125$

†Can also be calculated as $\dfrac{\text{Total budgeted associate labor costs}}{\text{Total budgeted associate labor - hours}} = \dfrac{\$80,000 \times 20}{1,600 \times 20} = \dfrac{\$1,600,000}{32,000} = \$50$

2.

	General Support	**Secretarial Support**
Budgeted total costs	$1,800,000	$400,000
Divided by budgeted quantity of allocation base	÷ 40,000 hours	÷ 8,000 hours
Budgeted indirect cost rate	$45 per hour	$50 per hour

3.

	Richardson		Punch	
Direct costs:				
Professional partners, $125 × 60; $125 × 30	$7,500		$3,750	
Professional associates, $50 × 40; $50 × 120	2,000		6,000	
Direct costs		$ 9,500		$ 9,750
Indirect costs:				
General support, $45 × 100; $45 × 150	4,500		6,750	
Secretarial support, $50 × 60; $50 × 30	3,000		1,500	
Indirect costs		7,500		8,250
Total costs		$17,000		$18,000

4.

	Richardson	Punch
Single direct - Single indirect (from Problem 4-31)	$12,000	$18,000
Multiple direct – Multiple indirect (from requirement 3 of Problem 4-32)	17,000	18,000
Difference	$5,000 undercosted	no change

The Richardson and Punch jobs differ in their use of resources. The Richardson job has a mix of 60% partners and 40% associates, while Punch has a mix of 20% partners and 80% associates. Thus, the Richardson job is a relatively high user of the more costly partner-related resources (both direct partner costs and indirect partner secretarial support). The refined-costing system in Problem 4-32 increases the reported cost in Problem 4-31 for the Richardson job by 41.7% (from $12,000 to $17,000).

4-34 (15 min.) **Normal costing, overhead allocation, working backward.**

1.a.   Manufacturing overhead allocated $= 200\% \times$ Direct manufacturing labor cost

$\$3,600,000 = 2 \times$ Direct manufacturing labor cost

Direct manufacturing labor cost $= \dfrac{\$3,600,000}{2} = \$1,800,000$

b.
$$\text{Total manufacturing cost} = \text{Direct material used} + \text{Direct manufacturing labor cost} + \text{Manufacturing overhead allocated}$$

$\$8,000,000 = $ Direct material used $+ \$1,800,000 + \$3,600,000$

Direct material used $= \$2,600,000$

2. $$\frac{\text{Work in Process}}{1/1/2007} + \text{Total manufacturing cost} =$$

$$\text{Cost of goods manufactured} + \frac{\text{Work in Process}}{1/1/2007}$$

Denote Work in Process on 12/31/2007 by X

$320,000 + \$8,000,000 = \$7,920,000 + X$

$X = \$400,000$

4-36 (35 min.) **General ledger relationships, under- and overallocation.**

The solution assumes all materials used are <u>direct</u> materials. A summary of the T-accounts for Needham Company before adjusting for under- or overallocation of overhead follows:

Direct Materials Control			
1-1-2006	30,000	Material used for	
Purchases	400,000	manufacturing	380,000
12-31-2006	50,000		

Work-in-Process Control			
1-1-2006	20,000	Transferred to	
Direct materials	380,000	finished goods	940,000
Direct manuf. Labor	360,000		
Manuf. overhead Allocated	480,000		
12-31-2006	300,000		

Finished Goods Control			
1-1-2006	10,000	Cost of goods	
Transferred in from WIP	940,000	sold	900,000
12-31-2006	50,000		

Cost of Goods Sold		
Finished goods Sold	900,000	

Manufacturing Overhead Control	
Manufacturing Overhead Costs	540,000

Manufacturing Overhead Allocated	
Manufacturing overhead allocated to work in process	480,000

1.   From Direct Materials Control T-account,
Direct materials issued to production = $380,000 that appears as a credit.

2. $$\text{Direct manufacturing labor-hours} = \frac{\text{Direct manufacturing labor costs}}{\text{Direct manufacturing wage rate per hour}}$$

$$= \frac{\$360,000}{\$15 \text{ per hour}} = 24,000 \text{ hours}$$

$$\text{Manufacturing overhead allocated} = \frac{\text{Direct manufacturing}}{\text{labor hours}} \times \frac{\text{Manufacturing}}{\text{overhead rate}}$$

$$= 24,000 \text{ hours} \times \$20 = \$480,000$$

3. From the debit entry to Finished Goods T-account,
   Cost of jobs completed and transferred from WIP   = $940,000

4. From Work-in-Process T-account,
   Work in process inventory
   on 12/31/2006   = $20,000 + $380,000 + $360,000 + $480,000 − $940,000

   = $300,000

5. From the credit entry to Finished Goods Control T-account, Cost of goods sold (before proration) = $900,000

6. $$\text{Manufacturing overhead underallocated} = \text{Debits to Manufacturing Overhead Control} - \text{Credit to Manufacturing Overhead Allocated}$$
   = $540,000 − $480,000
   = $60,000 underallocated

7. a. Write-off to Cost of Goods Sold will increase (debit) Cost of Goods Sold by $60,000. Hence, Cost of Goods Sold = $900,000 + $60,000 = $960,000.
   b. Proration based on ending balances (before proration) in Work in Process, Finished Goods, and Cost of Goods Sold.

   Account balances in each account after proration follows:

Account (1)	Account Balance (Before Proration) (2)		Proration of $60,000 Underallocated Manufacturing Overhead (3)	Account Balance (After Proration) (4)=(2)+(3)
Work in Process	$ 300,000	(24%)	0.24 × $60,000 = $14,400	$ 314,400
Finished Goods	50,000	(4%)	0.04 × $60,000 = 2,400	52,400
Cost of Goods Sold	900,000	(72%)	0.72 × $60,000 = 43,200	943,200
	$1,250,000	100%	$60,000	$1,310,000

8. Needham's operating income using write-off to Cost of Goods Sold and Proration based on ending balances (before proration) follows:

	Write-off to Cost of Goods Sold	Proration Based on Ending Balances
Revenues	$1,090,000	$1,090,000
Cost of goods sold	960,000	943,200
Gross margin	130,000	146,800
Marketing and distribution costs	140,000	140,000
Operating income/(loss)	$ (10,000)	$ 6,800

9.   If the purpose is to report the most accurate inventory and cost of goods sold figures, the preferred method is to prorate based on the manufacturing overhead allocated component in the inventory and cost of goods sold accounts. Proration based on the balances in Work in Process, Finished Goods, and Cost of Goods Sold will equal the proration based on the manufacturing overhead allocated component if the proportions of direct costs to manufacturing overhead costs are constant in the Work in Process, Finished Goods and Cost of Goods Sold accounts. Even if this is not the case, the prorations based on Work in Process, Finished Goods, and Cost of Goods Sold will better approximate the results if actual cost rates had been used rather than the write-off to Cost of Goods Sold method.

Another consideration in Needham's decision about how to dispose of underallocated manufacturing overhead is the effects on operating income. The write-off to Cost of Goods Sold will lead to an operating loss. Proration based on the balances in Work in Process, Finished Goods, and Cost of Goods Sold will help Needham avoid the loss and show an operating income.

The main merit of the write-off to Cost of Goods Sold method is its simplicity. However, accuracy and the effect on operating income favor the preferred and recommended proration approach.

4-38 (15 min.) **General ledger relationships, under- and overallocation, service industry.**

1. 1. Jobs-in-Process Control   150,000
          Cash Control   150,000

    2. Direct Professional Labor Control   1,500,000
          Cash Control   1,500,000

    3. Jobs-in-Process Control   1,450,000
          Direct Professional Labor Costs Charged to Jobs   1,450,000

    4. Engineering Support Overhead Control   1,140,000
          Cash Control   1,140,000

    5. Jobs-in-Process Control   1,160,000
          Engineering Support Overhead Allocated   1,160,000

    6. Cost of Jobs Billed   2,500,000
          Jobs-in-Process Control   2,500,000

    7. Accounts Receivable   3,500,000
          Revenues   3,500,000

2. Direct Professional Labor Costs Charged to Jobs   1,450,000
    Engineering Support Overhead Allocated   1,160,000
    Cost of Jobs Billed   30,000
       Direct Professional Labor Control   1,500,000
       Engineering Support Overhead Control   1,140,000

3. Revenues $3,500,000
    Cost of Jobs Billed ($2,500,000 + $30,000)   2,530,000
    Gross Margin $ 970,000
    Gross Margin percentage = $970,000 ÷ $3,500,000 =   27.7%

4-40   (20 min.)   **Job costing, contracting, ethics.**

1.   Direct manufacturing costs:

Direct materials	$25,000	
Direct manufacturing labor	6,000	$31,000
Indirect manufacturing costs,		
150% × $6,000		9,000
Total manufacturing costs		$40,000

Aerospace bills the Navy $52,000 ($40,000 × 130%) for 100 X7 seats or $520 ($52,000 ÷ 100) per X7 seat.

2.   Direct manufacturing costs:

Direct materials		
Direct manufacturing labor[a]	$25,000	
Indirect manufacturing costs,	5,000	$30,000
150% × $5,000		
Total manufacturing costs		7,500
		$37,500

[a]$6,000 – $400 ($25 × 16) setup – $600 ($50 × 12) design

Aerospace should have billed the Navy $48,750 ($37,500 × 130%) for 100 X7 seats or $487.50 ($48,750 ÷ 100) per X7 seat.

3.   The problems the letter highlights (assuming it is correct) include the following:

a. Costs included that should be excluded (design costs)
b. Costs double-counted (setup included as both a direct cost and in an indirect cost pool)
c. Possible conflict of interest in Aerospace Comfort purchasing materials from a family-related company

Steps the Navy could undertake include the following:

(i) Use only contractors with a reputation for ethical behavior as well as quality products or services.
(ii) Issue guidelines detailing acceptable and unacceptable billing practices by contractors. For example, prohibiting the use of double-counting cost allocation methods by contractors.
(iii)Issue guidelines detailing acceptable and unacceptable procurement practices by contractors. For example, if a contractor purchases from a family-related company, require that the contractor obtain quotes from at least two other bidders.
(iv)Employ auditors who aggressively monitor the bills submitted by contractors.
(v) Ask contractors for details regarding determination of costs.

CHAPTER 5
ACTIVITY-BASED COSTING AND ACTIVITY-BASED MANAGEMENT

5-2 Overcosting may result in competitors entering a market and taking market share for products that a company erroneously believes are low-margin or even unprofitable.

Undercosting may result in companies selling products on which they are in fact losing money, when they erroneously believe them to be profitable.

5-4 An activity-based approach refines a costing system by focusing on individual activities as the fundamental cost objects. It uses the cost of these activities as the basis for assigning costs to other cost objects such as products or services.

5-6 It is important to classify costs into a cost hierarchy because costs in different cost pools relate to different cost-allocation bases and not all cost-allocation bases are unit-level. For example, an allocation base like setup hours is a batch-level allocation base, and design hours is a product-sustaining base, both insensitive to the number of units in a batch or the number of units of product produced. If costs were not classified into a cost hierarchy, the alternative would be to consider all costs as unit-level costs, leading to misallocation of those costs that are not unit-level costs.

5-8 Four decisions for which ABC information is useful are
1. pricing and product mix decisions,
2. cost reduction and process improvement decisions,
3. product design decisions, and
4. decisions for planning and managing activities.

5-10 "Tell-tale" signs that indicate when ABC systems are likely to provide the most benefits are as follows:
1. Significant amounts of indirect costs are allocated using only one or two cost pools.
2. All or most indirect costs are identified as output-unit-level costs (i.e., few indirect costs are described as batch-level, product-sustaining, or facility-sustaining costs).
3. Products make diverse demands on resources because of differences in volume, process steps, batch size, or complexity.
4. Products that a company is well suited to make and sell show small profits, whereas products that a company is less suited to produce and sell show large profits.
5. Operations staff has significant disagreements with the accounting staff about the costs of manufacturing and marketing products and services.

5-12 No, ABC systems apply equally well to service companies such as banks, railroads, hospitals, and accounting firms, as well merchandising companies such as retailers and distributors.

5-14 Increasing the number of indirect-cost pools does NOT guarantee increased accuracy of product or service costs. If the existing cost pool is already homogeneous, increasing the number of cost pools will not increase accuracy. If the existing cost pool is not homogeneous, accuracy will increase only if the increased cost pools themselves increase in homogeneity vis-a-vis the single cost pool.

5-16 (20 min.) **Cost hierarchy.**

1. a. Indirect manufacturing labor costs of $1,000,000 support direct manufacturing labor and are output unit-level costs. Direct manufacturing labor generally increases with output units, and so will the indirect costs to support it.

    b. Batch-level costs are costs of activities that are related to a group of units of a product rather than each individual unit of a product. Purchase order-related costs (including costs of receiving materials and paying suppliers) of $500,000 relate to a group of units of product and are batch-level costs.

    c. Cost of indirect materials of $250,000 generally changes with labor hours or machine hours which are unit-level costs. Therefore, indirect material costs are output unit-level costs.

    d. Setup costs of $600,000 are batch-level costs because they relate to a group of units of product produced after the machines are set up.

    e. Costs of designing processes, drawing process charts, and making engineering changes for individual products, $800,000, are product-sustaining because they relate to the costs of activities undertaken to support individual products regardless of the number of units or batches in which the product is produced.

    f. Machine-related overhead costs (depreciation and maintenance) of $1,100,000 are output unit-level costs because they change with the number of units produced.

    g. Plant management, plant rent, and insurance costs of $900,000 are facility-sustaining costs because the costs of these activities cannot be traced to individual products or services but support the organization as a whole.

2. The complex boom box made in many batches will use significantly more batch-level overhead resources compared to the simple boom box that is made in a few batches. In addition, the complex boom box will use more product-sustaining overhead resources because it is complex. Because each boom box requires the same amount of machine-hours, both the simple and the complex boom box will be allocated the same amount of overhead costs per boom box if Teledor uses only machine-hours to allocate overhead costs to boom boxes. As a result, the complex boom box will be undercosted (it consumes a relatively high level of resources but is reported to have a relatively low cost) and the simple boom box will be overcosted (it consumes a relatively low level of resources but is reported to have a relatively high cost).

3. Using the cost hierarchy to calculate activity-based costs can help Teledor to identify both the costs of individual activities and the cost of activities demanded by individual products. Teledor can use this information to manage its business in several ways:

    a. Pricing and product mix decisions. Knowing the resources needed to manufacture and sell different types of boom boxes can help Teledor to price the different boom boxes and also identify which boom boxes are more profitable. It can then emphasize its more profitable products.

    b. Teledor can use information about the costs of different activities to improve processes and reduce costs of the different activities. Teledor could have a target of reducing costs of activities (setups, order processing, etc.) by, say, 3% and constantly seek to eliminate activities and costs (such as engineering changes) that its customers perceive as not adding value.

c. Teledor management can identify and evaluate new designs to improve performance by analyzing how product and process designs affect activities and costs.

d. Teledor can use its ABC systems and cost hierarchy information to plan and manage activities. What activities should be performed in the period and at what cost?

5-18 (15 min.) **Alternative allocation bases for a professional services firm.**

1.

| Client (1) | Direct Professional Time | | | Support Services | | Amount Billed to Client |
	Rate per Hour (2)	Number of Hours (3)	Total (4) = (2) × (3)	Rate (5)	Total (6) = (4) × (5)	(7) = (4) + (6)
SEATTLE DOMINION						
Wolfson	$500	15	$7,500	30%	$2,250	$ 9,750
Brown	120	3	360	30	108	468
Anderson	80	22	1,760	30	528	2,288
						$12,506
TOKYO ENTERPRISES						
Wolfson	$500	2	$1,000	30%	$300	$1,300
Brown	120	8	960	30	288	1,248
Anderson	80	30	2,400	30	720	3,120
						$5,668

2.

Client (1)	Direct Professional Time			Support Services		Amount Billed to Client (7) = (4) + (6)
	Rate per Hour (2)	Number of Hours (3)	Total (4) = (2) × (3)	Rate per Hour (5)	Total (6) = (3) × (5)	
SEATTLE DOMINION						
Wolfson	$500	15	$7,500	$50	$ 750	$ 8,250
Brown	120	3	360	50	150	510
Anderson	80	22	1,760	50	1,100	2,860
						$11,620
TOKYO ENTERPRISES						
	$500	2	$1,000	$50	$ 100	$1,100
Wolfson	120	8	960	50	400	1,360
Brown	80	30	2,400	50	1,500	3,900
Anderson						$6,360

	Requirement 1	Requirement 2
Seattle Dominion	$12,506	$11,620
Tokyo Enterprises	5,668	6,360
	$18,174	$17,980

Both clients use 40 hours of professional labor time. However, Seattle Dominion uses a higher proportion of Wolfson's time (15 hours), which is more costly. This attracts the highest support-services charge when allocated on the basis of direct professional labor costs.

3.   Assume that the Wolfson Group uses a cause-and-effect criterion when choosing the allocation base for support services. You could use several pieces of evidence to determine whether professional labor costs or hours is the driver of support-service costs:

a. *Interviews with personnel.* For example, staff in the major cost categories in support services could be interviewed to determine whether Wolfson requires more support per hour than, say, Anderson. The professional labor costs allocation base implies that an hour of Wolfson's time requires 6.25 ($500 ÷ $80) times more support-service dollars than does an hour of Anderson's time.

b. *Analysis of tasks undertaken for selected clients.* For example, if computer-related costs are a sizable part of support costs, you could determine if there was a systematic relationship between the percentage involvement of professionals with high billing rates on cases and the computer resources consumed for those cases.

5-20 (10–15 min.) **ABC, process costing.**

Rates per unit cost driver.

Activity	Cost Driver	Rate
Machining	Machine-hours	$375,000 ÷ (25,000 + 50,000) = $5 per machine-hour
Set up	Production runs	$120,000 ÷ (50 + 50) = $1,200 per production run
Inspection	Inspection-hours	$105,000 ÷ (1,000 + 500) = $70 per inspection-hour

Overhead cost per unit:

	Mathematical	Financial
Machining: $5 × 25,000; 50,000	$125,000	$250,000
Set up: $1,200 × 50; $1,200 × 50	60,000	60,000
Inspection: $70 × 1,000; $70 × 500	70,000	35,000
Total manufacturing overhead costs	$255,000	$345,000
Divide by number of units	÷ 50,000	÷100,000
Manufacturing overhead cost per unit	$ 5.10	$ 3.45

2.

	Mathematical	Financial
Manufacturing cost per unit:		
Direct materials		
$150,000 ÷ 50,000	$3.00	
$300,000 ÷ 100,000		$3.00
Direct manufacturing labor		
$50,000 ÷ 50,000	1.00	
$100,000 ÷ 100,000		1.00
Manufacturing overhead (from requirement 1)	5.10	3.45
Manufacturing cost per unit	$9.10	$7.45

5-22 (25 min.) **Allocation of costs to activities, unused capacity.**

1.

	Percentage of Costs Used by Each Activity				
Indirect Resources	**Academic Instruction**	**Administration**	**Sports Training**	**Community relationships**	**2006 Expenditures**
Teachers' salaries and benefits	60%	20%	8%	12%	$4,000,000
Principals' salaries and benefits	10%	60%	5%	25%	400,000
Facilities cost	35%	15%	45%	5%	2,600,000
Office staff salaries and benefits	5%	60%	10%	25%	300,000
Sports program staff salaries and benefits	35%	10%	45%	10%	500,000
					$7,800,000

	Actual Resource Cost Used by Each Activity				
Indirect Resources	**Academic Instruction**	**Administration**	**Sports Training**	**Community Relationships**	**2006 Expenditures**
Teachers' salaries and benefits	$2,400,000	$800,000	$320,000	$480,000	$4,000,000
Principals' salaries and benefits	40,000	240,000	20,000	$100,000	400,000
Facilities cost	910,000	390,000	1,170,000	$130,000	2,600,000
Office staff salaries and benefits	15,000	180,000	30,000	$ 75,000	300,000
Sports program staff salaries and benefits	175,000	50,000	225,000	$ 50,000	500,000
Total	$3,540,000	$1,660,000	$1,765,000	$835,000	$7,800,000
No. of students	500	500	500	500	500
Percent of total cost by activity	45%	21%	23%	11%	100%
Cost per student	$7,080	$ 3,320	$3,530	$1,670	$15,600

The overall cost of educating each student is $15,600. Of this, $7,080 (or 45%) is spent on academic instruction and $3,320 (or 21%) is spent on administration.

2. Cost of ice hockey program $ 300,000
    Total cost of activities without ice hockey program = $7,800,000 – $300,000 = $7,500,000
    Per student cost of educational program without hockey = $7,500,000 ÷ 500 = $ 15,000

3. Net cost of ice hockey program with $1,000 fee = $300,000 – (30 × $1,000) = $ 270,000
    Total cost of activities with ice hockey program fee = $7,500,000 + $270,000 = $7,770,000
    Per student cost of educational program with hockey fee = $7,770,000 ÷ 500 = $ 15,540

Charging a fee helps a bit but the net cost of the ice hockey program is still high and significantly increases the cost of educating each student

4.

Academic instruction capacity	600	students

Cost of academic instruction activity
(from requirement 1 calculations) $3,540,000

Cost of academic instruction per student at full utilization =
$3,540,000 ÷ 600 $ 5,900

Academic instruction resource costs used by current student
population = 500 × $5,900 = $2,950,000

Cost of excess academic instruction capacity =
$3,540,000 − $2,950,000 = $ 590,000

Most of the costs at Harmon school are fixed in the short-run. So, Smith must try to recruit more students to the school. If, in the long run, it seems like the student population is going to be stable at around 500, he should plan how some of the excess capacity can be cut back so that the fixed school capacity is better utilized, that is, he should work to reduce the cost of excess capacity. One problem with that plan is that "cutting excess academic instruction capacity" may eventually mean reducing the number of sections in each grade and letting teachers go, and if this involves the loss of experienced teachers, that could cause long-term damage to the school.

Unrelated to the excess capacity issue, but with the aim of improving the school's economics, he should consider doing away with expensive activities like the ice hockey program which raises the cost per student substantially, even after a large fee is charged from students who choose to play the sport.

5-24 (15–20 min.) **ABC, wholesale, customer profitability.**

	Chain			
	1	**2**	**3**	**4**
Gross sales	$50,000	$30,000	$100,000	70,000
Sale returns	10,000	5,000	7,000	6,000
Net sales	40,000	25,000	93,000	64,000
Cost of goods sold (80%)	32,000	20,000	74,400	51,200
Gross margin	8,000	5,000	18,600	12,800
Customer-related costs:				
Regular orders				
$20 × 40; 150; 50; 70	800	3,000	1,000	1,400
Rush orders				
$100 × 10; 50; 10; 30	1,000	5,000	1,000	3,000
Returned items				
$10 × 100; 26; 60; 40	1,000	260	600	400
Catalogs and customer support	1,000	1,000	1,000	1,000
Customer related costs	3,800	9,260	3,600	5,800
Contribution (loss) margin	$ 4,200	$ (4,260)	$ 15,000	$ 7,000
Contribution (loss) margin as				
percentage of gross sales	8.4%	(14.2%)	15.0%	10.0%

The analysis indicates that customers' profitability (loss) contribution varies widely from (14.2%) to 15.0%. Immediate attention to Chain 2 is required which is currently showing a loss contribution. The chain has a disproportionate number of both regular orders and rush orders. Villeagas should work with the management of Chain 2 to find ways to reduce the number of orders, while maintaining or increasing the sales volume. If this is not possible, Villeagas should consider dropping Chain 2, if it can save the customer-related costs.

Chain 1 has a disproportionate number of the items returned as well as sale returns. The causes of these should be investigated so that the profitability contribution of Chain 1 could be improved.

5-26 (20–25 min.) **Activity-based costing, job-costing system.**

1.   An overview of the activity-based job-costing system is:

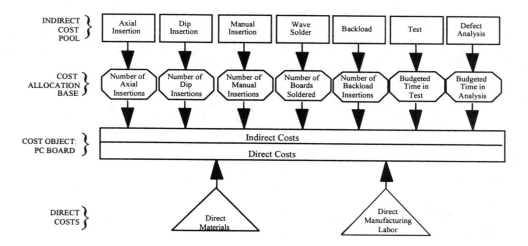

2.

Activity Area	Indirect Manufacturing Costs Allocated		
1. Axial insertion	$ 0.08	× 45	= $ 3.60
2. Dip insertion	0.25	× 24	= 6.00
3. Manual insertion	0.50	× 11	= 5.50
4. Wave solder	3.50	× 1	= 3.50
5. Backload	0.70	× 6	= 4.20
6. Test	90.00	× .25	= 22.50
7. Defect analysis	80.00	× .10	= 8.00
Total			$53.30

Direct manufacturing costs:		
Direct materials	$75.00	
Direct manufacturing labor	15.00	$ 90.00
Indirect manufacturing costs:		
Manufacturing overhead (see above)		53.30
Total manufacturing costs		$143.30

3.   The manufacturing manager likely would find the ABC job-costing system useful in cost management. Unlike direct manufacturing labor costs, the seven indirect cost pools are systematically linked to the activity areas at the plant. The result is more accurate product costing. Productivity measures can be developed that directly link to the management accounting system.

    Marketing managers can use ABC information to price jobs as well as to advise customers about how selecting different product features will affect price.

5-28 (15 min.) **Job costing with single direct-cost category, single indirect-cost pool, law firm.**

1.   Pricing decisions at Wigan Associates are heavily influenced by reported cost numbers. Suppose Wigan is bidding against another firm for a client with a job similar to that of Widnes Coal. If the costing system overstates the costs of these jobs, Wigan may bid too high and fail to land the client. If the costing system understates the costs of these jobs, Wigan may bid low, land the client, and then lose money in handling the case.

2.

	Widnes Coal	St. Helen's Glass	Total
Direct professional labor, $70 × 104; $70 × 96	$ 7,280	$ 6,720	$14,000
Indirect costs allocated, $105 × 104; $105 × 96	10,920	10,080	21,000
Total costs to be billed	$18,200	$16,800	$35,000

5-30 (30 min.) **Job costing with multiple direct-cost categories, multiple indirect-cost pools, law firm (continuation of 5-28 and 5-29).**

1.

	Widnes Coal	St. Helen's Glass	Total
Direct costs:			
Partner professional labor, $100 × 24; $100 × 56	$ 2,400	$ 5,600	$ 8,000
Associate professional labor, $50 × 80; $50 × 40	4,000	2,000	6,000
Research support labor	1,600	3,400	5,000
Computer time	500	1,300	1,800
Travel and allowances	600	4,400	5,000
Telephones/faxes	200	1,000	1,200
Photocopying	250	750	1,000
Total direct costs	9,550	18,450	28,000
Indirect costs allocated:			
Indirect costs for partners, $57.50 × 24; $57.50 × 56	1,380	3,220	4,600
Indirect costs for associates, $20 × 80; $20 × 40	1,600	800	2,400
Total indirect costs	2,980	4,020	7,000
Total costs to be billed	$12,530	$22,470	$35,000

Comparison	Widnes Coal	St. Helen's Glass	Total
Single direct cost/			
Single indirect cost pool	$18,200	$16,800	$35,000
Multiple direct costs/			
Single indirect cost pool	$14,070	$20,930	$35,000
Multiple direct costs/			
Multiple indirect cost pools	$12,530	$22,470	$35,000

The higher the percentage of costs directly traced to each case, and the greater the number of homogeneous indirect cost pools linked to the cost drivers of indirect costs, the more accurate the product cost of each individual case.

The Widnes and St. Helen's cases differ in how they use "resource areas" of Wigan Associates:

	Widnes Coal	St. Helen's Glass
Partner professional labor	30.0%	70.0%
Associate professional labor	66.7	33.3
Research support labor	32.0	68.0
Computer time	27.8	72.2
Travel and allowances	12.0	88.0
Telephones/faxes	16.7	83.3
Photocopying	25.0	75.0

The Widnes Coal case makes relatively low use of the higher-cost partners but relatively higher use of the lower-cost associates than does St. Helen's Glass. As a result, it also uses less of the higher indirect costs required to support partners compared to associates. The Widnes Coal case also makes relatively lower use of the support labor, computer time, travel, phones/faxes, and photocopying resource areas than does the St. Helen's Glass case.

2. The specific areas where the multiple direct/multiple indirect (MD/MI) approach can provide better information for decisions at Wigan Associates include:

Pricing and product (case) emphasis decisions. In a bidding situation using single direct/single indirect (SD/SI) or multiple direct/single indirect (MD/SI) data, Wigan may win bids for legal cases on which it will subsequently lose money. It may also not win bids on which it would make money with a lower-priced bid.

From a strategic viewpoint, SD/SI or MD/SI exposes Wigan Associates to cherry-picking by competitors. Other law firms may focus exclusively on Widnes Coal-type cases and take sizable amounts of "profitable" business from Wigan Associates. MD/MI reduces the likelihood of Wigan Associates losing cases on which it would have made money.

Client relationships. MD/MI provides a better "road map" for clients to understand how costs are accumulated at Wigan Associates. Wigan can use this road map when meeting with clients to plan the work to be done on a case *before* it commences. Clients can negotiate ways to get a lower-cost case from Wigan, given the information in MD/MI—for example, (a) use a higher proportion of associate labor time and a lower proportion of a partner time, and (b) use fax machines more and air travel less. If clients are informed in advance how costs will be accumulated, there is less likelihood of disputes about bills submitted to them *after* the work is done.

Cost control. The MD/MI approach better highlights the individual cost areas at Wigan Associates than does the SD/SI or MD/SI approaches:

	MD/MI	SD/SI	MD/SI
Number of direct cost categories	7	1	7
Number of indirect cost categories	2	1	1
Total	9	2	8

MD/MI is likely to promote better cost-control practices than SD/SI or MD/SI, as the nine cost categories in MD/MI give Wigan a better handle on how to effectively manage different categories of both direct and indirect costs.

5-32 (30 min.) **Plantwide versus department overhead cost rates.**

1.

	Molding	Component	Assembly	Total
	Amounts (in thousands)			
Manufacturing department overhead	$21,000	$16,200	$22,600	$59,800
Service departments:				
Power				18,400
Maintenance				4,000
Total budgeted plantwide overhead				$82,200
Budgeted direct manufacturing labor-hours (DMLH):				
Molding				500
Component				2,000
Assembly				1,500
Total budgeted DMLH				4,000

$$\text{Plantwide overhead rate} = \frac{\text{Budgeted plantwide overheard}}{\text{Budgeted DMLH}}$$

$$= \frac{\$82,200}{4,000} = \$20.55 \text{ per DMLH}$$

2. The department overhead cost rates are shown in Solution Exhibit 5-32

3. MumsDay Corporation should use department rates to allocate plant overhead because: (1) the cost drivers of resources used in each department differ and (2) the departments do not use resources from the support departments in the same proportion. Hence, department rates better capture cause-and-effect relationships at MumsDay than does a plantwide rate.

4. MumsDay should further subdivide the department cost pools into activity-cost pools if (a) significant costs are incurred on *different* activities within the department, (b) the different activities have different cost drivers, and (c) different products use different activities in different proportions.

SOLUTION EXHIBIT 5-32

	Departments (in thousands)				
	Service			Manufacturing	
	Power	Maintenance	Molding	Component	Assembly
2 (a)					
Departmental overhead costs	$18,400	$4,000	$21,000	$16,200	$22,600
Allocation of maintenance costs (direct method)					
$4,000 × 90/125, 25/125, 10/125		(4,000)	2,880	800	320
Allocation of power costs					
$18,400 × 360/800, 320/800, 120/800	(18,400)	____	8,280	7,360	2,760
Total budgeted overhead of manufacturing departments	$ 0	$ 0	$32,160	$24,360	$25,680
2 (b) Allocation Base			875 MH	2,000 DMLH	1,500 DMLH
Budgeted Rate (Budgeted overhead ÷ Alloc. Base)			$36.75/MH	$12.18/DMLH	$17.12/DMLH

5-14

5-34 (30–40 min.)   **Activity-based costing, merchandising.**

1.

	General Supermarket Chains	Drugstore Chains	Mom-and-Pop Single Stores	Total
Revenues[a]	$3,708,000	$3,150,000	$1,980,000	$8,838,000
Cost of goods sold[b]	3,600,000	3,000,000	1,800,000	8,400,000
Gross margin	$ 108,000	$ 150,000	$ 180,000	$ 438,000
Other operating costs				301,080
Operating income				$ 136,920
Gross margin %	2.91%	4.76%	9.09%	

[a]($30,900 × 120); ($10,500 × 300); ($1,980 × 1,000)
[b]($30,000 × 120); ($10,000 × 300); ($1,800 × 1,000)

The gross margin of Pharmacare, Inc., was 4.96% ($438,000 ÷ $8,838,000). The operating income margin of Pharmacare, Inc., was 1.55% ($136,920 ÷ $8,838,000).

2.   The per-unit cost driver rates are:

    1. Customer purchase order processing,
       $80,000 ÷ 2,000 (140 + 360 + 1,500) orders   = $40 per order
    2. Line item ordering,
       $63,840 ÷ 21,280 (1,960 + 4,320 + 15,000) line items   = $ 3 per line item
    3. Store delivery,
       $71,000 ÷ 1,420 (120 + 300 + 1,000) deliveries   = $50 per delivery
    4. Cartons shipped,
       $76,000 ÷ 76,000 (36,000 + 24,000 + 16,000) cartons   = $ 1 per carton
    5. Shelf-stocking,
       $10,240 ÷ 640 (360 + 180 + 100) hours   = $16 per hour

3. The activity-based costing of each distribution market for August 2005 is:

	General Supermarket Chains	Drugstore Chains	Mom-and-Pop Single Stores
1. Customer purchase order processing, ($40 × 140; 360; 1,500)	$ 5,600	$14,400	$ 60,000
2. Line item ordering, ($3 × (140 × 14; 360 × 12; 1,500 × 10))	5,880	12,960	45,000
3. Store delivery, ($50 × 120, 300, 1,000)	6,000	15,000	50,000
4. Cartons shipped, ($1 × (120 × 300; 300 × 80; 1,000 × 16))	36,000	24,000	16,000
5. Shelf-stocking, ($16 × (120 × 3; 300 × 0.6; 1,000 × 0.1))	5,760	2,880	1,600
	$59,240	$69,240	$172,600

The revised operating income statement is:

	General Supermarket Chains	Drugstore Chains	Mom-and-Pop Single Stores	Total
Revenues	$3,708,000	$3,150,000	$1,980,000	$8,838,000
Cost of goods sold	3,600,000	3,000,000	1,800,000	8,400,000
Gross margin	108,000	150,000	180,000	438,000
Operating costs	59,240	69,240	172,600	301,080
Operating income	$ 48,760	$ 80,760	$ 7,400	$ 136,920
Operating income margin 1.31%		2.56%	0.37%	1.55%

4. The ranking of the three markets are:

Using Gross Margin		**Using Operating Income**	
1. Mom-and-Pop Single Stores	9.09%	1. Drugstore Chains	2.56%
2. Drugstore Chains	4.76%	2. General Supermarket Chains	1.31%
3. General Supermarket Chains	2.91%	3. Mom-and-Pop Single Stores	0.37%

The activity-based analysis of costs highlights how the Mom-and-Pop Single Stores use a larger amount of Pharmacare's resources per revenue dollar than do the other two markets. The ratio of the operating costs to revenues across the three markets is:

General Supermarket Chains	1.60%	($59,240 ÷ $3,708,000)
Drugstore Chains	2.20%	($69,240 ÷ $3,150,000)
Mom-and-Pop Single Stores	8.72%	($172,600 ÷ $1,980,000)

This is a classic illustration of the maxim that "all revenue dollars are not created equal." The analysis indicates that the Mom-and-Pop Single Stores are the least profitable market. Pharmacare should work to increase profits in this market through: (1) a possible surcharge, (2) decreasing the number of orders, (3) offering discounts for quantity purchases, etc.

Other issues for Pharmacare to consider include

a. *Choosing the appropriate cost drivers for each area.* The problem gives a cost driver for each chosen activity area. However, it is likely that over time further refinements in cost drivers would occur. For example, not all store deliveries are equally easy to make, depending on parking availability, accessibility of the storage/shelf space to the delivery point, etc. Similarly, not all cartons are equally easy to deliver—their weight, size, or likely breakage component are factors that can vary across carton types.

b. *Developing a reliable data base on the chosen cost drivers.* For some items, such as the number of orders and the number of line items, this information likely would be available in machine readable form at a high level of accuracy. Unless the delivery personnel have hand-held computers that they use in a systematic way, estimates of shelf-stocking time are likely to be unreliable. Advances in information technology likely will reduce problems in this area over time.

c. *Deciding how to handle costs that may be common across several activities.* For example, (3) store delivery and (4) cartons shipped to stores have the common cost of the same trip. Some organizations may treat (3) as the primary activity and attribute only incremental costs to (4). Similarly, (1) order processing and (2) line item ordering may have common costs.

d. *Behavioral factors are likely to be a challenge to Flair.* He must now tell those salespeople who specialize in Mom-and-Pop accounts that they have been less profitable than previously thought.

5-36 (40 min.) ABC, health care.

1a.
$$\text{Medical supplies rate} = \frac{\text{Medical supplies costs}}{\text{Total number of patient - years}} = \frac{\$300,000}{150}$$
$$= \$2,000/\text{patient-year}$$

$$\text{Rent and clinic maintenance rate} = \frac{\text{Rent and clinic maint. costs}}{\text{Total amount of square feet of space}} = \frac{\$180,000}{30,000}$$
$$= \$6 \text{ per square foot}$$

$$\text{Admin. cost rate for patient-charts food and laundry} = \frac{\text{Admin. costs to manage patient charts, food, laundry}}{\text{Total number of patient - years}} = \frac{\$600,000}{150}$$
$$= \$4,000/\text{patient-year}$$

$$\text{Laboratory services rate} = \frac{\text{Laboratory services costs}}{\text{Total number of laboratory tests}} = \frac{\$100,000}{2,500}$$
$$= \$40 \text{ per test}$$

These cost drivers are chosen as the ones that best match the descriptions of why the costs arise. Other answers are acceptable, provided that clear explanations are given.

1b.   Activity-based costs for each program and cost per patient-year of the alcohol and drug program follow:

	Alcohol	Drug	After-Care
Direct labor			
Physicians at $150,000 × 0; 4; 0	—	$ 600,000	—
Psychologists at $75,000 × 6; 4; 8	$450,000	300,000	$600,000
Nurses at $30,000 × 4; 6; 10	120,000	180,000	300,000
Direct labor costs	570,000	1,080,000	900,000
Medical supplies[1] $2,000 × 40; 50; 60	80,000	100,000	120,000
Rent and clinic maintenance[2]			
$6 × 9,000; 9,000; 12,000	54,000	54,000	72,000
Administrative costs to manage patient charts, food, and laundry[3]			
$4,000 × 40; 50; 60	160,000	200,000	240,000
Laboratory services[4] $40 × 400; 1,400; 700	16,000	56,000	28,000
Total costs	$880,000	$1,490,000	$1,360,000

Cost per patient-year $\dfrac{\$880,000}{40} = \$22,000$ $\dfrac{\$1,490,000}{50} = \$29,800$

[1] Allocated using patient-years
[2] Allocated using square feet of space
[3] Allocated using patient-years
[4] Allocated using number of laboratory tests

1c.   The ABC system more accurately allocates costs because it identifies better cost drivers. The ABC system chooses cost drivers for overhead costs that have a cause-and-effect relationship between the cost drivers and the costs. Of course, Clayton should continue to evaluate if better cost drivers can be found than the ones they have identified so far.

By implementing the ABC system, Clayton can gain a more detailed understanding of costs and cost drivers. This is valuable information from a cost management perspective. The system can yield insight into the efficiencies with which various activities are performed. Clayton can then examine if redundant activities can be eliminated. Clayton can study trends and work toward improving the efficiency of the activities.

In addition, the ABC system will help Clayton determine which programs are the most costly to operate. This will be useful in making long-run decisions as to which programs to offer or emphasize. The ABC system will also assist Clayton in setting prices for the programs that more accurately reflect the costs of each program.

2.   The concern with using costs per patient-year as the rule to allocate resources among its programs is that it emphasizes "input" to the exclusion of "outputs" or effectiveness of the programs. After-all, Clayton's goal is to cure patients while controlling costs, not minimize costs per-patient year. The problem, of course, is measuring outputs.

Unlike many manufacturing companies, where the outputs are obvious because they are tangible and measurable, the outputs of service organizations are more difficult to measure. Examples are "cured" patients as distinguished from "processed" or "discharged" patients, "educated" as distinguished from "partially educated" students, and so on.

5-38 (40–50 min.) **Activity-based job costing, unit-cost comparisons.**

An overview of the product-costing system is:

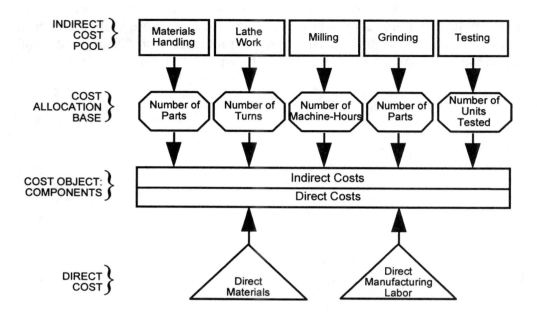

1.

	Job Order 410		Job Order 411	
Direct manufacturing cost				
Direct materials	$9,700		$59,900	
Direct manufacturing labor				
$30 × 25; $30 × 375	750	$10,450	11,250	$ 71,150
Indirect manufacturing cost				
$115 × 25; $115 × 375		2,875		43,125
Total manufacturing cost		$13,325		$114,275
Number of units		÷ 10		÷ 200
Manufacturing cost per unit		$ 1,332.50		$ 571.375

2.

	Job Order 410		Job Order 411	
Direct manufacturing cost				
Direct materials	$9,700		$59,900	
Direct manufacturing labor				
$30 × 25; $30 × 375	750	$10,450	11,250	$ 71,150
Indirect manufacturing cost				
Materials handling				
$0.40 × 500; $0.40 × 2,000	200		800	
Lathe work				
$0.20 × 20,000; $0.20 × 60,000	4,000		12,000	
Milling				
$20.00 × 150; $20.00 × 1,050	3,000		21,000	
Grinding				
$0.80 × 500; $0.80 × 2,000	400		1,600	
Testing				
$15.00 × 10; $15.00 × 200	150	7,750	3,000	38,400
Total manufacturing cost		$18,200		$109,550
Number of units		÷ 10		÷ 200
Manufacturing cost per unit		$ 1,820		$ 547.75

3.

	Job Order 410	Job Order 411
Number of units in job	10	200
Costs per unit with prior costing system	$1,332.50	$571.375
Costs per unit with activity-based costing	1,820.00	547.750

Job order 410 has an increase in reported unit cost of 36.6% [($1,820 − $1,332.50) ÷ $1,332.50], while job order 411 has a decrease in reported unit cost of 4.1% [($547.75 − $571.375) ÷ $571.375].

A common finding when activity-based costing is implemented is that low-volume products have increases in their reported costs while high-volume products have decreases in their reported cost. This result is also found in requirements 1 and 2 of this problem. Costs such as materials-handling costs vary with the number of parts handled (a function of batches and complexity of products) rather than with direct manufacturing labor-hours, an output-unit level cost driver, which was the only cost driver in the previous job-costing system.

The product cost figures computed in requirements 1 and 2 differ because
- a. the job orders differ in the way they use each of five activity areas, and
- b. the activity areas differ in their indirect cost allocation bases (specifically, each area does not use the direct manufacturing labor-hours indirect cost allocation base).

The following table documents how the two job orders differ in the way they use each of the five activity areas included in indirect manufacturing costs:

| Activity Area | Usage Based on Analysis of Activity Area Cost Drivers | | Usage Assumed with Direct Manuf. Labor-Hours as Application Base | |
	Job Order 410	Job Order 411	Job Order 410	Job Order 411
Materials handling	20.0%	80.0%	6.25%	93.75%
Lathe work	25.0	75.0	6.25	93.75
Milling	12.5	87.5	6.25	93.75
Grinding	20.0	80.0	6.25	93.75
Testing	4.8	95.2	6.25	93.75

The differences in product cost figures might be important to Tracy Corporation for product pricing and product emphasis decisions. The activity-based accounting approach indicates that job order 410 is being undercosted while job order 411 is being overcosted. Tracy Corporation may erroneously push job order 410 and deemphasize job order 411. Moreover, by its actions, Tracy Corporation may encourage a competitor to enter the market for job order 411 and take market share away from it.

4.   Information from the ABC system can also help Tracy manage its business better in several ways.
   a. *Product design.* Product designers at Tracy Corporation likely will find the numbers in the activity-based costing approach more believable and credible than those in the simple system. In a machine-paced manufacturing environment, it is unlikely that direct labor-hours would be the major cost driver. Activity-based costing provides more credible signals to product designers about the ways the costs of a product can be reduced—for example, use fewer parts, require fewer turns on the lathe, and reduce the number of machine-hours in the milling area.
   b. *Cost management.* Tracy can reduce the cost of jobs both by making process improvements that reduce the activities that need to be done to complete jobs and by reducing the costs of doing the activities.
   c. *Cost planning.* ABC provides a more refined model to forecast costs and to explain why actual costs differ from budgeted costs.

5-40 (40–60 min.) **Activity-based costing, cost hierarchy.**

This solution is adapted from the CMA suggested solution.

1a. Budgeted manufacturing overhead rate = $\dfrac{\text{Budgeted manufacturing overhead}}{\text{Budgeted direct labor cost}}$

$$= \dfrac{\$3,000,000}{\$600,000}$$

$$= \$5 \text{ per direct labor-dollar}$$

1b.

	Mauna Loa	**Malaysian**
Direct cost		
Direct materials	$4.20	$3.20
Direct labor	0.30	0.30
	4.50	3.50
Indirect cost		
Manufacturing overhead		
($0.30 × 5.00)	1.50	1.50
Total cost	$6.00	$5.00

Budgeted selling prices per pound:
   Mauna Loa ($6.00 × 1.30)   = $7.80
   Malaysian ($5.00 × 1.30)   = $6.50

2.   The total budgeted unit cost per pound is:

Mauna Loa Coffee			**Malaysian Coffee**		
Direct cost per unit			Direct cost per unit		
Direct materials	$4.20		Direct materials	$3.20	
Direct labor	0.30	$4.50	Direct labor	0.30	$3.50
Manufacturing overhead per unit			Manufacturing overhead per unit		
Purchase orders			Purchase orders		
(4 orders × $500 ÷ 100,000 lbs.)	0.02		(4 orders × $500 ÷ 2,000 lbs.)	1.00	
Material handling			Material handling		
(30 setups × $400 ÷ 100,000 lbs.)	0.12		(12 setups × $400 ÷ 2,000 lbs.)	2.40	
Quality control			Quality control		
(10 batches × $240 ÷ 100,000 lbs.)	0.02		(4 batches × $240 ÷ 2,000 lbs.)	0.48	
Roasting			Roasting		
(1,000 hours × $10 ÷ 100,000 lbs.)	0.10		(20 hours × $10 ÷ 2,000 lbs.)	0.10	
Blending			Blending		
(500 hours × $10 ÷ 100,000 lbs.)	0.05		(10 hours × $10 ÷ 2,000 lbs.)	0.05	
Packaging			Packaging		
(100 hours × $10 ÷ 100,000 lbs.)	0.01	0.32	(2 hours × $10 ÷ 2,000 lbs.)	0.01	4.04
Total cost per unit		$4.82	Total cost per unit		$7.54

The comparative cost numbers are:

	Mauna Loa	Malaysian
Requirement 1	$6.00	$5.00
Requirement 2	4.82	7.54

The ABC system in requirement 2 reports a decreased cost for the high-volume Mauna Loa and an increased cost for the low-volume Malaysian.

3.   The traditional costing approach leads to cross-subsidization between the two products. With the traditional approach, the high-volume Mauna Loa is overcosted, while the low-volume Malaysian is undercosted. The ABC system indicates that Mauna Loa is profitable and should be emphasized.

    Pricing of Mauna Loa can be reduced to make it more competitive. In contrast, Malaysian should be priced at a much higher level if the strategy is to cover the current period's cost. Coffee Bean may wish to have lower margins with its low-volume products in an attempt to build up volume.

CHAPTER 6
MASTER BUDGET AND RESPONSIBILITY ACCOUNTING

6-2 The *master budget* expresses management's operating and financial plans for a specified period (usually a fiscal year) and includes a set of budgeted financial statements. It is the initial plan of what the company intends to accomplish in the period.

6-4 We agree that budgeted performance is a better criterion than past performance for judging managers, because inefficiencies included in past results can be detected and eliminated in budgeting. Also, future conditions may be expected to differ from the past, and these can also be factored into budgets.

6-6 In many organizations, budgets impel managers to plan. Without budgets, managers drift from crisis to crisis. Research also shows that budgets can motivate managers to meet targets and improve their performance. Thus, many top managers believe that budgets meet the cost-benefit test.

6-8 The steps in preparing an operating budget are as follows:
1. Prepare the revenues budget
2. Prepare the production budget (in units)
3. Prepare the direct material usage budget and direct material purchases budget
4. Prepare the direct manufacturing labor budget
5. Prepare the manufacturing overhead budget
6. Prepare the ending inventories budget
7. Prepare the cost of goods sold budget
8. Prepare the nonmanufacturing costs budget
9. Prepare the budgeted income statement

6-10 Sensitivity analysis adds an extra dimension to budgeting. It enables managers to examine how budgeted amounts change with changes in the underlying assumptions. This assists managers in monitoring those assumptions that are most critical to a company in attaining its budget and allows them to make timely adjustments to plans when appropriate.

6-12 Nonoutput-based cost drivers can be incorporated into budgeting by the use of activity-based budgeting (ABB). ABB focuses on the budgeted cost of activities necessary to produce and sell products and services. Nonoutput-based cost drivers, such as the number of part numbers, number of batches, and number of new products can be used with ABB.

6-14 Budgeting in multinational companies may involve budgeting in several different foreign currencies. Further, management accountants must translate operating performance into a single currency for reporting to shareholders, by budgeting for exchange rates. Managers and accountants must understand the factors that impact exchange rates, and where possible, plan financial strategies to limit the downside of unexpected unfavorable moves in currency valuations. In developing budgets for operations in different countries, they must also have good understanding of political, legal and economic issues in those countries.

6-16 (15 min.) **Sales budget, service setting.**

1.

McGrath & Sons	2006 Volume	At 2006 Selling Prices	Expected 2007 Change in Volume	Expected 2007 Volume
Radon Tests	11,000	$250	+5%	11,550
Lead Tests	15,200	$200	-10%	13,680

McGrath & Sons Sales Budget
For the Year Ended December 31, 2007

	Selling Price	Units Sold	Total Revenues
Radon Tests	$250	11,550	$2,887,500
Lead Tests	$200	13,680	2,736,000
			$5,623,500

2.

McGrath & Sons	2006 Volume	Planned 2007 Selling Prices	Expected 2007 Change in Volume	Expected 2007 Volume
Radon Tests	11,000	$250	+5%	11,550
Lead Tests	15,200	$190	-5%	14,440

McGrath & Sons Sales Budget
For the Year Ended December 31, 2007

	Selling Price	Units Sold	Total Revenues
Radon Tests	$250	11,550	$2,887,500
Lead Tests	$190	14,440	2,743,600
			$5,631,100

Expected revenues at the new 2007 prices are $5,631,100, which are greater than the expected 2007 revenues of $5,623,500 if the prices are unchanged. So, if the goal is to maximize sales revenue and if Jim McGrath's forecasts are reliable, the company should lower its price for a lead test in 2007.

6-18 (5 min.) **Direct materials purchases budget.**

Direct materials to be used in production (bottles)	1,500,000
Add target ending direct materials inventory (bottles)	50,000
Total requirements (bottles)	1,550,000
Deduct beginning direct materials inventory (bottles)	20,000
Direct materials to be purchased (bottles)	1,530,000

6-20 (30 min.) **Revenues and production budget.**

1.

	Selling Price	Units Sold	Total Revenues
12-ounce bottles	$0.25	4,800,000[a]	$1,200,000
4-gallon units	1.50	1,200,000[b]	1,800,000
			$3,000,000

[a] 400,000 × 12 months = 4,800,000
[b] 100,000 × 12 months = 1,200,000

2.

Budgeted unit sales (12-ounce bottles)	4,800,000
Add target ending finished goods inventory	600,000
Total requirements	5,400,000
Deduct beginning finished goods inventory	900,000
Units to be produced	4,500,000

3.
$$\text{Beginning inventory} = \text{Budgeted sales} + \text{Target ending inventory} - \text{Budgeted production}$$
$$= 1,200,000 + 200,000 - 1,300,000$$
$$= 100,000 \text{ 4-gallon units}$$

6-22 (15–20 min.) **Revenues, production, and purchases budget.**

1.   800,000 motorcycles × 400,000 yen = 320,000,000,000 yen

2.

Budgeted sales (motorcycles)	800,000
Add target ending finished goods inventory	100,000
Total requirements	900,000
Deduct beginning finished goods inventory	120,000
Units to be produced	780,000

3.

Direct materials to be used in production, 780,000 × 2 (wheels)	1,560,000
Add target ending direct materials inventory	30,000
Total requirements	1,590,000
Deduct beginning direct materials inventory	20,000
Direct materials to be purchased (wheels)	1,570,000
Cost per wheel in yen	16,000
Direct materials purchase cost in yen	25,120,000,000

Note the relatively small inventory of wheels. In Japan, suppliers tend to be located very close to the major manufacturer. Inventories are controlled by just-in-time and similar systems. Indeed, some direct materials inventories are almost nonexistent.

6-24 (20–30 min.) **Activity-based budgeting.**

1.   This question links to the ABC example used in the Problem for Self-Study in Chapter 5 and to Question 5-23 (ABC, retail product-line profitability).

Activity	Cost Hierarchy	Soft Drinks	Fresh Produce	Packaged Food	Total
Ordering					
$90 × 14; 24; 14	Batch-level	$1,260	$ 2,160	$1,260	$ 4,680
Delivery					
$82 × 12; 62; 19	Batch-level	984	5,084	1,558	7,626
Shelf-stocking	Output-unit-level				
$21 × 16; 172; 94		336	3,612	1,974	5,922
Customer support	Output-unit-level				
$0.18 × 4,600; 34,200; 10,750		828	6,156	1,935	8,919
Total budgeted indirect costs		$3,408	$17,012	$6,727	$27,147
Percentage of total indirect costs (subject to rounding)		13%	63%	25%	

2.   Refer to the last row of the table in requirement 1. Fresh produce, which probably represents the smallest portion of COGS, is the product category that consumes the largest share (63%) of the indirect resources. Fresh produce demands the highest level of ordering, delivery, shelf-stocking and customer support resources of all three product categories—it has to be ordered, delivered and stocked in small, perishable batches, and supermarket customers often ask for a lot of guidance on fresh produce items.

3.   An ABB approach recognizes how different products require different mixes of support activities. The relative percentage of how each product area uses the cost driver at each activity area is:

Activity	Cost Hierarchy	Soft Drinks	Fresh Produce	Packaged Food	Total
Ordering	Batch-level	27%	46%	27%	100%
Delivery	Batch-level	13	67	20	100
Shelf-stocking	Output-unit-level	6	61	33	100
Customer support	Output-unit-level	9	69	22	100

By recognizing these differences, FS managers are better able to budget for different unit sales levels and different mixes of individual product-line items sold. Using a single cost driver (such as COGS) assumes homogeneity in the use of indirect costs (support activities) across product lines which does not occur at FS. Other benefits cited by managers include: (1) better identification of resource needs, (2) clearer linking of costs with staff responsibilities, and (3) identification of budgetary slack.

6-26 (15 min.) **Responsibility and controllability.**

1. (a) Salesman
   (b) VP of Sales
   Permit the salesman to offer a reasonable discount to customers, but require that he clear bigger discounts with the VP. Also, base his bonus/performance evaluation not just on revenues generated, but also on margins (or, ability to meet budget).

2. (a) VP of Sales
   (b) VP of Sales
   VP of Sales should compare budgeted sales with actuals, and ask for an analysis of all the sales during the quarter. Discuss with salespeople why so many discounts are being offered—are they really needed to close each sale. Are our prices too high (i.e., uncompetitive)?

3. (a) Manager, Shipping department
   (b) Manager or Director of Operations (including shipping)
   Shipping department manager must report delays more regularly and request additional capacity in a timely manner. Operations manager should ask for a review of shipping capacity utilization, and consider expanding the department.

4. (a) HR department
   (b) Production supervisor
   The production supervisor should devise his or her own educational standards that all new plant employees are held to before they are allowed to work on the plant floor. Offer remedial in-plant training to those workers who show promise. Be very specific about the types of skills required when using the HR department to hire plant workers. Test the workers periodically for required skills.

5. (a) Production supervisor
   (b) Production supervisor
   Get feedback from the workers, analyze it, and act on it. Get extra coaching and training from experienced mentors.

6. (a) Maintenance department
   (b) Production supervisor
   First, get the requisite maintenance done on the machines. Make sure that the maintenance department head clearly understands the repercussions of poor maintenance. Discuss and establish maintenance standards that must be met (frequency of maintenance and tolerance limits, for example). Test and keep a log of the maintenance work.

6-28 (40 min.) **Budget schedules for a manufacturer.**

a.   Revenues Budget

	Executive Line	Chairman Line	Total
Units sold	740	390	
Selling price	$ 1,020	$ 1,600	
Budgeted revenues	$754,800	$624,000	$1,378,800

b.   Production Budget in Units

	Executive Line	Chairman Line
Budgeted unit sales	740	390
Add budgeted ending fin. goods inventory	30	15
Total requirements	770	405
Deduct beginning fin. goods. inventory	20	5
Budgeted production	750	400

c.   Direct Materials Usage Budget (units)

	Oak	Red Oak	Oak Legs	Red Oak Legs	Total
Executive Line:					
1. Budgeted input per f.g. unit	16	–	4	–	
2. Budgeted production	750	–	750	–	
3. Budgeted usage (1 × 2)	12,000	–	3,000	–	
Chairman Line:					
4. Budgeted input per f.g. unit	–	25	–	4	
5. Budgeted production	–	400	–	400	
6. Budgeted usage (4 × 5)	–	10,000	–	1,600	
7. Total direct materials usage (3 + 6)	12,000	10,000	3,000	1,600	
Direct Materials Cost Budget					
8. Beginning inventory	320	150	100	40	
9. Unit price (FIFO)	$18	$23	$11	$17	
10. Cost of DM used from beginning inventory (8 × 9)	$5,760	$3,450	$1,100	$680	$10,990
11. Materials to be used from purchases (7 – 8)	11,680	9,850	2,900	1,560	
12. Cost of DM in March	$20	$25	$12	$18	
13. Cost of DM purchased and used in March (11 × 12)	$233,600	$246,250	$34,800	$28,080	$542,730
14. Direct materials to be used (10 + 13)	$239,360	$249,700	$35,900	$28,760	$553,720

Direct Materials Purchases Budget

	Oak	Red Oak	Oak Legs	Red Oak Legs	Total
Budgeted usage (from line 7)	12,000	10,000	3,000	1,600	
Add target ending inventory	192	200	80	44	
Total requirements	12,192	10,200	3,080	1,644	
Deduct beginning inventory	320	150	100	40	
Total DM purchases	11,872	10,050	2,980	1,604	
Purchase price (March)	$20	$25	$12	$18	
Total purchases	$237,440	$251,250	$35,760	$28,872	$553,322

d. Direct Manufacturing Labor Budget

	Output Units Produced	Direct Manuf. Labor-Hours per Output Unit	Total Hours	Hourly Rate	Total
Executive Line	750	3	2,250	$30	$ 67,500
Chairman Line	400	5	2,000	$30	60,000
			4,250		$127,500

e. Manufacturing Overhead Budget

Variable manufacturing overhead costs (4,250 × $35)	$148,750
Fixed manufacturing overhead costs	42,500
Total manufacturing overhead costs	$191,250

$$\text{Total manuf. overhead cost per hour} = \frac{\$191,250}{4,250} = \$45 \text{ per direct manufacturing labor-hour}$$

$$\text{Fixed manuf. overhead cost per hour} = \frac{\$42,500}{4,250} = \$10 \text{ per direct manufacturing labor-hour}$$

f. Computation of unit costs of ending inventory of finished goods

	Executive Line	Chairman Line
Direct materials		
Oak top ($20 × 16, 0)	$320	$ 0
Red oak ($25 × 0, 25)	0	625
Oak legs ($12 × 4, 0)	48	0
Red oak legs ($18 × 0, 4)	0	72
Direct manufacturing labor ($30 × 3, 5)	90	150
Manufacturing overhead		
Variable ($35 × 3, 5)	105	175
Fixed ($10 × 3, 5)	30	50
Total manufacturing cost	$593	$1,072

Ending Inventories Budget

	Cost per Unit	Units	Total
Direct Materials			
Oak top	$ 20	192	$ 3,840
Red oak top	25	200	5,000
Oak legs	12	80	960
Red oak legs	18	44	792
			10,592
Finished Goods			
Executive	593	30	17,790
Chairman	1,072	15	16,080
			33,870
Total			$44,462

g. Cost of goods sold budget

Budgeted finished goods inventory, March 1, 2006 ($10,480 + $4,850)		$ 15,330
Direct materials used (from Dir. materials purch. budget)	$553,720	
Direct manufacturing labor (Dir. manuf. labor budget)	127,500	
Manufacturing overhead (Manuf. overhead budget)	191,250	
Cost of goods manufactured		872,470
Cost of goods available for sale		887,800
Deduct ending finished goods inventory, March 31, 2006 (Inventories budget)		33,870
Cost of goods sold		$853,930

2. Areas where continuous improvement might be incorporated into the budgeting process:
(a) Direct materials. Either an improvement in usage or price could be budgeted. For example, the budgeted usage amounts could be related to the maximum improvement (current usage – minimum possible usage) of 1 square foot for either desk:
- Executive: 16 square feet – 15 square feet minimum = 1 square foot
- Chairman: 25 square feet – 24 square feet minimum = 1 square foot

Thus, a 1% reduction target per month could be:
- Executive: 15 square feet + $(0.99 \times 1) = 15.99$
- Chairman: 24 square feet + $(0.99 \times 1) = 24.99$

Some students suggested the 1% be applied to the 16 and 25 square-foot amounts. This can be done so long as after several improvement cycles, the budgeted amount is not less than the minimum desk requirements.
(b) Direct manufacturing labor. The budgeted usage of 3 hours/5 hours could be continuously revised on a monthly basis. Similarly, the manufacturing labor cost per hour of $30 could be continuously revised down. The former appears more feasible than the latter.
(c) Variable manufacturing overhead. By budgeting more efficient use of the allocation base, a signal is given for continuous improvement. A second approach is to budget continuous improvement in the budgeted variable overhead cost per unit of the allocation base.
(d) Fixed manufacturing overhead. The approach here is to budget for reductions in the year-to-year amounts of fixed overhead. If these costs are appropriately classified as fixed, then they are more difficult to adjust down on a monthly basis.

6-30 (30–40 min.) **Revenue and production budgets.**

This is a routine budgeting problem. The key to its solution is to compute the correct *quantities* of finished goods and direct materials. Use the following general formula:

$$\begin{pmatrix} \text{Budgeted} \\ \text{production} \\ \text{or purchases} \end{pmatrix} = \begin{pmatrix} \text{Target} \\ \text{ending} \\ \text{inventory} \end{pmatrix} + \begin{pmatrix} \text{Budgeted} \\ \text{sales or} \\ \text{materials used} \end{pmatrix} - \begin{pmatrix} \text{Beginning} \\ \text{inventory} \end{pmatrix}$$

1.
Scarborough Corporation
Revenue Budget for 2007

	Units	Price	Total
Thingone	60,000	$165	$ 9,900,000
Thingtwo	40,000	250	10,000,000
Budgeted revenues			$19,900,000

2.
Scarborough Corporation
Production Budget (in units) for 2007

	Thingone	Thingtwo
Budgeted sales in units	60,000	40,000
Add target finished goods inventories, December 31, 2007	25,000	9,000
Total requirements	85,000	49,000
Deduct finished goods inventories, January 1, 2007	20,000	8,000
Units to be produced	65,000	41,000

3.
Scarborough Corporation
Direct Materials Purchases Budget (in quantities) for 2007

	Direct Materials		
	A	B	C
Direct materials to be used in production			
• Thingone (budgeted production of 65,000 units times 4 lbs. of A, 2 lbs. of B)	260,000	130,000	--
• Thingtwo (budgeted production of 41,000 units times 5 lbs. of A, 3 lbs. of B, 1 lb. of C)	205,000	123,000	41,000
Total	465,000	253,000	41,000
Add target ending inventories, December 31, 2007	36,000	32,000	7,000
Total requirements in units	501,000	285,000	48,000
Deduct beginning inventories, January 1, 2007	32,000	29,000	6,000
Direct materials to be purchased (units)	469,000	256,000	42,000

4.

Scarborough Corporation
Direct Materials Purchases Budget (in dollars) for 2007

	Budgeted Purchases (Units)	Expected Purchase Price per unit	Total
Direct material A	469,000	$12	$5,628,000
Direct material B	256,000	5	1,280,000
Direct material C	42,000	3	126,000
Budgeted purchases			$7,034,000

5.

Scarborough Corporation
Direct Manufacturing Labor Budget (in dollars) for 2007

	Budgeted Production (Units)	Direct Manufacturing Labor-Hours per Unit	Total Hours	Rate per Hour	Total
Thingone	65,000	2	130,000	$12	$1,560,000
Thingtwo	41,000	3	123,000	16	1,968,000
Total					$3,528,000

6.

Scarborough Corporation
Budgeted Finished Goods Inventory
at December 31, 2007

Thingone:
  Direct materials costs:
    A, 4 pounds × $12 $48
    B, 2 pounds × $5   10 $ 58
  Direct manufacturing labor costs,
    2 hours × $12   24
  Manufacturing overhead costs at $20 per direct
    manufacturing labor-hour (2 hours × $20)   40
  Budgeted manufacturing costs per unit $122
  Finished goods inventory of Thingone
    $122 × 25,000 units $3,050,000
Thingtwo:
  Direct materials costs:
    A, 5 pounds × $12 $60
    B, 3 pounds × $5   15
    C, 1 each × $3   3 $ 78
  Direct manufacturing labor costs,
    3 hours × $16   48
  Manufacturing overhead costs at $20 per direct
    manufacturing labor-hour (3 hours × $20)   60
  Budgeted manufacturing costs per unit $186
  Finished goods inventory of Thingtwo
    $186 × 9,000 units   1,674,000
Budgeted finished goods inventory, December 31, 2007 $4,724,000

6-32 (15 min.) **Responsibility of purchasing agent.**

The time lost in the plant should be charged to the purchasing department. The plant manager probably should not be asked to underwrite a loss due to failure of delivery over which he had no supervision. Although the purchasing agent may feel that he has done everything he possibly could, he must realize that, in the whole organization, he is *the one* who is in the best position to evaluate the situation. He receives an assignment. He may accept it or reject it. But if he accepts, he must perform. If he fails, the damage is evaluated. Everybody makes mistakes. The important point is to avoid making too many mistakes and also to understand fully that the extensive control reflected in responsibility accounting is the necessary balance to the great freedom of action that individual executives are given.

Discussions of this problem have again and again revealed a tendency among students (and among accountants and managers) to "fix the blame"—as if the variances arising from a responsibility accounting system should pinpoint misbehavior and provide answers. The point is that no accounting system or variances can provide answers. However, variances can lead to questions. In this case, in deciding where the penalty should be assigned, the student might inquire who should be asked—not who should be blamed.

Classroom discussions have also raised the following diverse points:
(a) Is the railroad company liable?
(b) Costs of idle time are usually routinely charged to the production department. Should the information system be fine-tuned to reallocate such costs to the purchasing department?
(c) How will the purchasing managers behave in the future regarding willingness to take risks?

The text emphasizes the following: Beware of overemphasis on controllability. For example, a time-honored theme of management is that responsibility should not be given without accompanying authority. Such a guide is a useful first step, but responsibility accounting is more far-reaching. The basic focus should be on information or knowledge, not on control. The key question is: Who is the best informed? Put another way, "Who is the person who can tell us the most about the specific item, regardless of ability to exert personal control?"

6-34 (60 min.) **Comprehensive operating budget, budgeted balance sheet.**

1. **Schedule 1: Revenues Budget for the Year Ended December 31, 2007**

	Units	Selling Price	Total Revenues
Snowboards	1,000	$450	$450,000

2. **Schedule 2: Production Budget (in Units) for the Year Ended December 31, 2007**

	Snowboards
Budgeted unit sales (Schedule 1)	1,000
Add target ending finished goods inventory	200
Total requirements	1,200
Deduct beginning finished goods inventory	100
Units to be produced	1,100

3. **Schedule 3A: Direct Materials Usage Budget for the Year Ended December 31, 2007**

	Wood	Fiberglass	Total

Physical Units Budget

Wood: 1,100 × 5.00 b.f.	5,500	
Fiberglass: 1,100 × 6.00 yards		6,600
To be used in production	5,500	6,600

Cost Budget

Available from beginning inventory			
Wood: 2,000 b.f. × $28.00	$ 56,000		
Fiberglass: 1,000 b.f. × $4.80		$ 4,800	
To be used from purchases this period			
Wood: (5,500 − 2,000) × $30.00	105,000		
Fiberglass: (6,600 − 1,000) × $5.00		28,000	
Total cost of direct materials to be used	$161,000	$32,800	$193,800

Schedule 3B: Direct Materials Purchases Budget for the Year Ended December 31, 2007

	Wood	Fiberglass	Total
Physical Units Budget			
Production usage (from Schedule 3A)	5,500	6,600	
Add target ending inventory	1,500	2,000	
Total requirements	7,000	8,600	
Deduct beginning inventory	2,000	1,000	
Purchases	5,000	7,600	
Cost Budget			
Wood: 5,000 × $30.00	$150,000		
Fiberglass: 7,600 × $5.00)		$38,000	
Purchases	$150,000	$38,000	$188,000

4. **Schedule 4: Direct Manufacturing Labor Budget for the Year Ended December 31, 2007**

Labor Category	Cost Driver Units	DML Hours per Driver Unit	Total Hours	Wage Rate	Total
Manufacturing labor	1,100	5.00	5,500	$25.00	$137,500

5. **Schedule 5: Manufacturing Overhead Budget for the Year Ended December 31, 2007**

	At Budgeted Level of 5,500 Direct Manufacturing Labor-Hours
Variable manufacturing overhead costs ($7.00 × 5,500)	$ 38,500
Fixed manufacturing overhead costs	66,000
Total manufacturing overhead costs	$104,500

6. Budgeted manufacturing overhead rate: $\dfrac{\$104,500}{5,500} = \$19.00$ per hour

7. Budgeted manufacturing overhead cost per output unit: $\dfrac{\$104,500}{1,100} = \$95.00$ per output unit

8. **Schedule 6A: Computation of Unit Costs of Manufacturing Finished Goods in 2007**

	Cost per Unit of Input[a]	Inputs[b]	Total
Direct materials			
Wood	$30.00	5.00	$150.00
Fiberglass	5.00	6.00	30.00
Direct manufacturing labor	25.00	5.00	125.00
Total manufacturing overhead			95.00
			$400.00

[a]cost is per board foot, yard or per hour
[b]inputs is the amount of each input per board

9. **Schedule 6B: Ending Inventories Budget, December 31, 2007**

	Units	Cost per Unit	Total
Direct materials			
Wood	1,500	$ 30.00	$ 45,000
Fiberglass	2,000	5.00	10,000
Finished goods			
Snowboards	200	400.00	80,000
Total Ending Inventory			$135,000

10. **Schedule 7: Cost of Goods Sold Budget for the Year Ended December 31, 2007**

	From Schedule		Total
Beginning finished goods inventory			
January 1, 2004, $374.80 × 100	Given		$ 37,480
Direct materials used	3A	$193,800	
Direct manufacturing labor	4	137,500	
Manufacturing overhead	5	104,500	
Cost of goods manufactured			435,800
Cost of goods available for sale			473,280
Deduct ending finished goods			
inventory, December 31, 2007	6B		80,000
Cost of goods sold			$393,280

11. **Budgeted Income Statement for Slopes for the Year Ended December 31, 2007**

Revenues	Schedule 1		$450,000
Cost of goods sold	Schedule 7		393,280
Gross margin			56,720
Operating costs			
Variable marketing costs ($250 × 30)		$ 7,500	
Fixed nonmanufacturing costs		30,000	37,500
Operating income			$ 19,220

12. **Budgeted Balance Sheet for Slopes as of December 31, 2007**

Cash		$ 10,000
Inventory	Schedule 6B	135,000
Property, plant, and equipment (net)		850,000
Total assets		$995,000
Current liabilities		$ 17,000
Long-term liabilities		178,000
Stockholders' equity		800,000
Total liabilities and stockholders' equity		$995,000

6-36 (30 min.) **Cash budget, fill in the blanks, chapter appendix.**

	Quarters				Year as a
	I	II	III	IV	Whole
Cash balance, beginning	$ 15,000	$ 32,000	$ 15,000	$ 50,000	$ 15,000
Add receipts					
Collections from customers	385,000	315,000	295,000	365,000	1,360,000
Total cash available for needs	400,000	347,000	310,000	415,000	1,375,000
Deduct disbursements					
Direct materials	175,000	125,000	110,000	155,000	565,000
Payroll	125,000	110,000	95,000	118,000	448,000
Other costs	50,000	45,000	40,000	49,000	184,000
Machinery purchase	0	85,000	0	0	85,000
Interest costs (bond)	3,000	3,000	3,000	3,000	12,000
Income taxes	15,000	14,000	12,000	20,000	61,000
Total disbursements	368,000	382,000	260,000	345,000	1,355,000
Minimum cash balance desired	15,000	15,000	15,000	15,000	15,000
Total cash needed	383,000	397,000	275,000	360,000	1,370,000
Cash excess (deficiency)	17,000	(50,000)	35,000	55,000	5,000
Financing					
Borrowing (at beginning)	0	50,000	0	0	50,000
Repayment (at end)	0	0	0	(50,000)	(50,000)
Interest (at 12% per annum)	0	0	0	(4,500)	(4,500)
Total effects of financing	0	50,000	0	(54,500)	(4,500)
Cash balance, ending	$ 32,000	$ 15,000	$ 50,000	$ 15,500	$ 15,500

Note that the short-term loan is only repaid when it can be paid in full and after maintaining the minimum balance. The interest on the loan is only paid at the time the loan is repaid.

6-38 (60–75 min.) **Comprehensive budget, fill in schedules.**

1.

Schedule A
Budgeted Monthly Cash Receipts

Item	September	October	November	December
Total sales	$40,000	$48,000	$60,000	$80,000
Credit sales (25% of total sales)	10,000	12,000	15,000	20,000
Cash sales (total sales – credit sales)	$30,000	$36,000	$45,000	$60,000
Receipts:				
Cash sales		$36,000	$45,000	$60,000
Collections on accounts receivable (past month's credit sales)		10,000	12,000	15,000
Total		$46,000	$57,000	$75,000

Schedule B
Budgeted Monthly Cash Disbursements for Purchases

Item	October	November	December	4th Quarter
Purchases (70% of next month's anticipated sales)	$42,000	$56,000	$25,200	$123,200
Deduct 2% cash discount	840	1,120	504	2,464
Disbursements	$41,160	$54,880	$24,696	$120,736

Schedule C
Budgeted Monthly Cash Disbursements for Operations

Item	October	November	December	4th Quarter
Salaries and wages (15% of total monthly sales)	$7,200	$ 9,000	$12,000	$28,200
Rent (5% of total monthly sales)	2,400	3,000	4,000	9,400
Other cash operating costs (4% of total monthly sales)	1,920	2,400	3,200	7,520
Total disbursements for operations	$11,520	$14,400	$19,200	$45,120

Schedule D
Budgeted Total Monthly Cash Disbursements

Item	October	November	December	4th Quarter
Purchases (from Schedule B)	$41,160	$54,880	$24,696	$120,736
Cash operating costs (from Schedule C)	11,520	14,400	19,200	45,120
Light fixtures	600	400	-	1,000
Total disbursements	$53,280	$69,680	$43,896	$66,856

Schedule E
Budgeted Cash Receipts and Disbursements

Item	October	November	December	4th Quarter
Total receipts (from Schedule A)	$ 46,000	$57,000	$75,000	$178,000
Total disbursements (from Schedule D)	53,280	69,680	43,896	166,856
Net cash increase (decrease)	$ (7,280)	$(12,680)	$31,104	$ 11,144

Schedule F
Financing Required

Item	September	October	November	December	4th Quarter
Beginning cash balance (prior month's ending cash balance)		$12,000	$ 8,720	$ 8,040	$12,000
Net cash increase (decrease) (from Schedule E)		(7,280)	(12,680)	31,104	11,144
Cash position before borrowing		4,720	(3,960)	39,144	23,144
Minimum cash balance required		(8,000)	(8,000)	(8,000)	(8,000)
Cash excess (deficiency)		(3,280)	(11,960)	31,144	15,144
Borrowing required (multiples of $1,000)		4,000	12,000	-	16,000
Interest payments				(540)*	(540)
Borrowing repaid				(16,000)	(16,000)
Ending cash balance	$12,000	$ 8,720	$ 8,040	$22,604	$22,604

*Interest computation:

	$ 4,000 @ 18% for 3 months	=	$180
	$12,000 @ 18% for 2 months	=	360
	Total interest expense		$540

2.   Short-term, self-liquidating financing is best. The schedules clearly demonstrate the mechanics of a self-liquidating loan. The need for such a loan arises because of the seasonal nature of many businesses. When sales soar, the payroll and suppliers must be paid in cash. The basic source of cash is proceeds from sales. However, the credit extended to customers creates a lag between the sale and the collection of cash. When the cash is collected, it in turn may be used to repay the loan. The amount of the loan and the timing of the repayment are heavily dependent on the credit terms that pertain to both the purchasing and selling functions of the business. In seasonal businesses, the squeeze on cash is often heaviest in the months of peak sales and is lightest in the months of low sales.

3.

Newport Stationery Store
Budgeted Income Statement
for Quarter Ending December 31, 2007

Revenues (Schedule A)		$188,000
Cost of goods sold (70% of revenues)*		131,600
Gross margin		56,400
Operating costs		
Salaries and wages (Schedule C)	$28,200	
Rent (Schedule C)	9,400	
Other cash operating costs (Schedule C)	7,520	
Depreciation ($1,000 × 3 months)	3,000	48,120
Operating income		8,280
Deduct interest expense (Schedule F)		(540)
Add purchase discounts (Schedule B)		2,464
Net income before taxes		$10,204

*Note: Ending inventory and proof of cost of goods sold:

Inventory, September 30	$ 63,600	
Add purchases—Schedule B	123,200	$186,800
Deduct inventory, December 31:		
Basic inventory	30,000	
December purchases—Schedule B	25,200	55,200
Cost of goods sold		$131,600

Newport Stationery Store
Balance Sheet as of December 31, 2007

Assets		
Current assets		
Cash (Schedule F)		$ 22,604
Accounts receivable (December credit sales from Schedule A)		20,000
Inventory (buffer inventory $30,000 + Dec. purchases from Sch. B $25,200)		55,200
Total current assets		$ 97,804
Equipment and fixtures		
Equipment— net		
($100,000 Sept 30 balance – $3,000 depreciation for quarter)	$ 97,000	
Fixtures (Schedule D)	1,000	98,000
Total		$195,804
Liabilities and Owner's Equity		
Liabilities		None
Owners' Equity*		$195,804
		$195,804

*Owners' equity, September 30:

$12,000 + $10,000 + $63,600 + $100,000 (all given)	$185,600	
Net income, quarter ended December 31	10,204	
Owners' equity, December 31	$195,804	

4.   All of the transactions have been simplified—for example, no bad debts are considered. Also, many businesses face wide fluctuations of cash flows within a month. For example, perhaps customer receipts lag and are bunched together near the end of a month, and disbursements are due evenly throughout the month, or are bunched near the beginning of the month. Cash needs would then need to be evaluated on a weekly and, perhaps a daily basis, rather than on a monthly basis.

6-40   (60 min.)   Comprehensive Review of Budgeting, Cash Budgeting, Chapter Appendix.

a.   **Schedule 1: Revenues Budget for the Year Ended December 31, 2005**

	Units (Lots)	Selling Price	Total Sales
Lemonade	1,080	$9,000	$ 9,720,000
Diet Lemonade	540	8,500	4,590,000
Total			$14,310,000

b.   **Schedule 2: Production Budget in Units for the Year Ended December 31, 2005**

	Products	
	Lemonade	Diet Lemonade
Budgeted unit sales (Schedule 1)	1,080	540
Add target ending finished goods inventory	20	10
Total requirements	1,100	550
Deduct beginning finished goods inventory	100	50
Units to be produced	1,000	500

c. **Schedule 3A: Direct Materials Usage Budget in Units and Dollars for the Year Ended December 31, 2005**

	Syrup-Lemon.	Syrup-Diet Lem.	Containers	Packaging	Total
Units of direct materials to be used for production of Lemonade (1,000 lots × 1)	1,000		1,000	1,000	
Units of direct materials to be used for production of Diet Lemonade (500 lots × 1)		500	500	500	
Total direct materials to be used (in units)	1,000	500	1,500	1,500	
Units of direct materials to be used from beginning inventory (under FIFO)	80	70	200	400	
Multiply by cost per unit of beginning inventory	$ 1,100	$ 1,000	$ 950	$ 900	
Cost of direct materials to be used from beginning inventory (a)	$ 88,000	$ 70,000	$ 190,000	$ 360,000	$ 708,000
Units of direct materials to be used from purchases (1,000 – 80; 500 – 70; 1,500 – 200; 1,500 – 400)	920	430	1,300	1,100	
Multiply by cost per unit of purchased materials	$ 1,200	$ 1,100	$ 1,000	$ 800	
Cost of direct materials to be used from purchases (b)	$1,104,000	$473,000	$1,300,000	$ 880,000	3,757,000
Total cost of direct materials to be used (a + b)	$1,192,000	$543,000	$1,490,000	$1,240,000	$4,465,000

d. **Schedule 3B: Direct Materials Purchases Budget in Units and Dollars for the Year Ended December 31, 2005**

	Syrup-Lemon	Syrup-Diet Lem.	Containers	Packaging	Total
Direct materials to be used in production (in units) from Schedule 3A	1,000	500	1,500	1,500	
Add target ending direct materials inventory in units	30	20	100	200	
Total requirements in units	1,030	520	1,600	1,700	
Deduct beginning direct materials inventory in units	80	70	200	400	
Units of direct materials to be purchased	950	450	1,400	1,300	
Multiply by cost/unit of purchased materials	$1,200	$1,100	$1,000	$800	
Direct materials purchase costs	$1,140,000	$495,000	$1,400,000	$1,040,000	$4,075,000

e. **Schedule 4: Direct Manufacturing Labor Budget for the Year Ended December 31, 2005**

	Output Units Produced (Schedule 2)	Direct Manufacturing Labor Hours per Unit	Total Hours	Hourly Rate	Total
Lemonade	1,000	20	20,000	$25	$500,000
Diet Lemonade	500	20	10,000	25	250,000
Total			30,000		$750,000

f. **Schedule 5: Manufacturing Overhead Costs Budget for the Year Ended December 31, 2005**

Variable manufacturing overhead costs:	
Lemonade [$600 × 2 hours per lot × 1,000 lots (Schedule 2)]	$1,200,000
Diet Lemonade [$600 × 2 hours per lot × 500 lots (Schedule 2)]	600,000
Variable manufacturing overhead costs	1,800,000
Fixed manufacturing overhead costs	1,200,000
Total manufacturing overhead costs	$3,000,000

Fixed manufacturing overhead per bottling hour = $1,200,000 ÷ 3,000 = $400. Note that the total number of bottling hours is 3,000 hours: 2,000 hours for Lemonade (2 hours per lot × 1,000 lots) plus 1,000 hours for Diet Lemonade (2 hours per lot × 500 lots).

g. **Schedule 6A: Ending Finished Goods Inventory Budget as of December 31, 2005**

	Units (Lots)	Cost per Unit (Lot)		Total
Direct materials:				
Syrup for Lemonade	30	$1,200	$ 36,000	
Syrup for Diet Lemonade	20	1,100	22,000	
Containers	100	1,000	100,000	
Packaging	200	800	160,000	$318,000

	Units	Cost per Unit		
Finished goods:				
Lemonade	20	$5,500*	$110,000	
Diet Lemonade	10	5,400*	54,000	164,000
Total ending inventory				$482,000

*See Schedule 6B

Schedule 6B: Computation of Unit Costs of Manufacturing Finished Goods For the Year Ended December 31, 2005

	Cost per Unit (Lot) or Hour of Input	Lemonade Inputs in Units (Lots) or Hours	Amount	Diet Lemonade Inputs in Units (Lots) or Hours	Amount
Syrup			$1,200		$1,100
Containers			1,000		1,000
Packaging			800		800
Direct manufacturing labor	$ 25	20	500	20	500
Variable manufacturing overhead*	600	2	1,200	2	1,200
Fixed manufacturing overhead*	400	2	800	2	800
Total			$5,500		$5,400

*Variable manufacturing overhead varies with bottling hours (2 hours per lot for both Lemonade and Diet Lemonade). Fixed manufacturing overhead is allocated on the basis of bottling hours at the rate of $400 per bottling hour calculated in Schedule 5.

h. **Schedule 7: Cost of Goods Sold Budget for the Year Ended December 31, 2005**

	From Schedule		Total
Beginning finished goods inventory, January 1, 2005	Given*		$ 790,000
Direct materials used	3A	$4,465,000	
Direct manufacturing labor	4	750,000	
Manufacturing overhead	5	3,000,000	
Cost of goods manufactured			8,215,000
Cost of goods available for sale			9,005,000
Deduct ending finished goods inventory, December 31, 2005	6A		164,000
Cost of goods sold			$8,841,000

*Given in description of basic data and requirements (Lemonade, $5,300 × 100; diet Lemonade, $5,200 × 50)

i. **Schedule 8: Marketing Costs Budget for the Year Ended December 31, 2005**
Marketing costs, 12% × Revenues, $14,310,000 $1,717,200

j. **Schedule 9: Distribution Costs Budget for the Year Ended December 31, 2005**
Distribution costs, 8% × Revenues, $14,310,000 $1,144,800

k. **Schedule 10: Administration Costs Budget for the Year Ended December 31, 2005**
Administration costs, 10% × Cost of goods
manufactured, $8,215,000 $ 821,500

l. **Budgeted Income Statement for the Year Ended December 31, 2005**

Sales	Schedule 1		$14,310,000
Cost of goods sold	Schedule 7		8,841,000
Gross margin			5,469,000
Operating costs:			
Marketing costs	Schedule 8	$1,717,200	
Distribution costs	Schedule 9	1,144,800	
Administration costs	Schedule 10	821,500	
Total operating costs			3,683,500
Operating income			$ 1,785,500
Income tax expense	Given		625,000
Net income			$ 1,160,500

m. **Schedule 11: Collections from Customers**

Budgeted Revenue for 2005	Schedule 1	$14,310,000
Add collections from beginning		
accounts receivable balance	Given	550,000
		14,860,000
Deduct ending accounts receivable		
balance	Given	600,000
Collections from customers		$14,260,000

Schedule 12: Direct Materials Disbursements

Budgeted direct material purchase		
costs for 2005	Schedule 3B	$ 4,075,000
Add payment for beginning accounts		
payable balance	Given	300,000
		4,375,000
Deduct ending accounts payable		
balance	Given	400,000
Disbursements for direct materials		$ 3,975,000

Schedule 13: Variable Manufacturing Overhead Disbursements

Variable Manufacturing Overhead:		
Lemonade (1,000 × $600 × 2)	Schedule 5	$ 1,200,000
Diet Lemonade (500 × $600 × 2)	Schedule 5	600,000
Total		$ 1,800,000

Schedule 14: Fixed Manufacturing Overhead Disbursements

Budgeted fixed manufacturing overhead	Schedule 5	$ 1,200,000
Deduct depreciation	Given	400,000
Cash disbursements for fixed overhead		$ 800,000

Cash Budget
December 31, 2005

Cash balance, beginning	Given	$	100,000
Add receipts			
Collections from customers	Schedule 11		14,260,000
Total cash available for needs			$14,360,000
Deduct disbursements			
Direct materials	Schedule 12	$	3,975,000
Direct manufacturing labor	Schedule 4		750,000
Variable manufacturing overhead	Schedule 13		1,800,000
Fixed manufacturing overhead	Schedule 14		800,000
Equipment purchase	Given		1,350,000
Marketing costs	Schedule 8		1,717,200
Distribution costs	Schedule 9		1,144,800
Administration costs	Schedule 10		821,500
Income tax expense	Given		625,000
Total disbursements			$12,983,500
Cash excess (deficiency)			$ 1,376,500
Financing			
Borrowing			0
Repayment			0
Interest			0
Total effects of financing			0
Cash balance ending			$ 1,376,500

CHAPTER 7
FLEXIBLE BUDGETS, DIRECT-COST VARIANCES, AND MANAGEMENT CONTROL

7-2   Two sources of information about budgeted amounts are (a) past amounts and (b) detailed engineering studies.

7-3   The key difference is the output level used to set the budget. A *static budget* is based on the level of output planned at the *start of the budget period*. A *flexible budget* is developed using budgeted revenues or cost amounts based on the actual output level in the budget period. The actual level of output is not known until the *end of the budget period*.

7-6   The steps in developing a flexible budget are:
Step 1: Identify the actual quantity of output.
Step 2: Calculate the flexible budget for revenues based on budgeted selling price and actual quantity of output.
Step 3: Calculate the flexible budget for costs based on budgeted variable cost per output unit, actual quantity of output, and budgeted fixed costs.

7-8   A manager should subdivide the flexible-budget variance for direct materials into a price variance (that reflects the difference between actual and budgeted prices of direct materials) and an efficiency variance (that reflects the difference between the actual and budgeted quantities of direct materials used to produce actual output). The individual causes of these variances can then be investigated, recognizing possible interdependencies across these individual causes.

7-10   Some possible reasons for an unfavorable direct manufacturing labor efficiency variance are the hiring and use of underskilled workers; inefficient scheduling of work so that the workforce was not optimally occupied; poor maintenance of machines resulting in a high proportion of non-value-added labor; unrealistic time standards. Each of these factors would result in actual direct manufacturing labor-hours being higher than indicated by the standard work rate.

7-12   An individual business function, such as production, is interdependent with other business functions. Factors outside of production can explain why variances arise in the production area. For example:
- poor design of products or processes can lead to a sizable number of defects,
- marketing personnel making promises for delivery times that require a large number of rush orders can create production-scheduling difficulties, and
- purchase of poor-quality materials by the purchasing manager can result in defects and waste.

7-14   Variances can be calculated at the activity level as well as at the company level. For example, a price variance and an efficiency variance can be computed for an activity area.

7-16 (20–30 min.) Flexible budget.

	Actual Results (1)	Flexible-Budget Variances (2) = (1) – (3)	Flexible Budget (3)	Sales-Volume Variances (4) = (3) – (5)	Static Budget (5)
Units sold	2,800[g]	0	2,800	200 U	3,000[g]
Revenues	$313,600[a]	$ 5,600 F	$308,000[b]	$22,000 U	$330,000[c]
Variable costs	229,600[d]	22,400 U	207,200[e]	14,800 F	222,000[f]
Contribution margin	84,000	16,800 U	100,800	7,200 U	108,000
Fixed costs	50,000[g]	4,000 F	54,000[g]	0	54,000[g]
Operating income	$ 34,000	$12,800 U	$ 46,800	$ 7,200 U	$ 54,000

$12,800 U $ 7,200 U

Total flexible-budget variance   Total sales-volume variance

$20,000 U

Total static-budget variance

[a] $112 × 2,800 = $313,600

[b] $110 × 2,800 = $308,000

[c] $110 × 3,000 = $330,000

[d] Given. Unit variable cost = $229,600 ÷ 2,800 = $82 per tire

[e] $74 × 2,800 = $207,200

[f] $74 × 3,000 = $222,000

[g] Given

2. The key information items are:

	Actual	Budgeted
Units	2,800	3,000
Unit selling price	$ 112	$ 110
Unit variable cost	$ 82	$ 74
Fixed costs	$50,000	$54,000

The total static-budget variance in operating income is $20,000 U. There is both an unfavorable total flexible-budget variance ($12,800) and an unfavorable sales-volume variance ($7,200).

The unfavorable sales-volume variance arises solely because actual units manufactured and sold were 200 less than the budgeted 3,000 units. The unfavorable flexible-budget variance of $12,800 in operating income is due primarily to the $8 increase in unit variable costs. This increase in unit variable costs is only partially offset by the $2 increase in unit selling price and the $4,000 decrease in fixed costs.

7-18 (25–30 min.) **Flexible-budget preparation and analysis.**

1. Variance Analysis for Bank Management Printers for September 2007

Level 1 Analysis

	Actual Results (1)	Static-Budget Variances (2) = (1) − (3)	Static Budget (3)
Units sold	12,000	3,000 U	15,000
Revenue	$252,000[a]	$ 48,000 U	$300,000[c]
Variable costs	84,000[d]	36,000 F	120,000[f]
Contribution margin	168,000	12,000 U	180,000
Fixed costs	150,000	5,000 U	145,000
Operating income	$ 18,000	$ 17,000 U	$ 35,000

$17,000 U
Total static-budget variance

2. *Level 2 Analysis*

	Actual Results (1)	Flexible-Budget Variances (2) = (1) − (3)	Flexible Budget (3)	Sales Volume Variances (4) = (3) − (5)	Static Budget (5)
Units sold	12,000	0	12,000	3,000 U	15,000
Revenue	$252,000[a]	$12,000 F	$240,000[b]	$60,000 U	$300,000[c]
Variable costs	84,000[d]	12,000 F	96,000[e]	24,000 F	120,000[f]
Contribution margin	168,000	24,000 F	144,000	36,000 U	180,000
Fixed costs	150,000	5,000 U	145,000	0	145,000
Operating income	$ 18,000	$19,000 F	$ (1,000)	$36,000 U	$ 35,000

$19,000 F
Total flexible-budget variance

$36,000 U
Total sales-volume variance

$17,000 U
Total static-budget variance

[a] 12,000 × $21 = $252,000   [d] 12,000 × $7 = $ 84,000
[b] 12,000 × $20 = $240,000   [e] 12,000 × $8 = $ 96,000
[c] 15,000 × $20 = $300,000   [f] 15,000 × $8 = $120,000

3. Level 2 analysis provides a breakdown of the static-budget variance into a flexible-budget variance and a sales-volume variance. The primary reason for the static-budget variance being unfavorable ($17,000 U) is the reduction in unit volume from the budgeted 15,000 to an actual 12,000. One explanation for this reduction is the increase in selling price from a budgeted $20 to an actual $21. Operating management was able to reduce variable costs by $12,000 relative to the flexible budget. This reduction could be a sign of efficient management. Alternatively, it could be due to using lower quality materials (which in turn adversely affected unit volume).

7-20

1. and 2.

Performance Report, June 2007

	Actual (1)	Flexible Budget Variances (2) = (1) − (3)		Flexible Budget (3)	Sales Volume Variances (4) = (3) − (5)		Static Budget (5)	Static Budget Variance (6) = (1) − (5)		Static Budget Variance as % of Static Budget (7) = (6) ÷ (5)
Units (pounds)	525,000	−		525,000	25,000	F	500,000	25,000	F	5.0%
Revenues	$3,360,000	$ 52,500	U	$3,412,500[a]	$162,500	F	$3,250,000	$110,000	F	3.4%
Variable mfg. costs	1,890,000	52,500	U	1,837,500[b]	87,500	U	1,750,000	140,000	U	8.0%
Contribution margin	$1,470,000	$105,000	U	$1,575,000	$ 75,000	F	$1,500,000	$ 30,000	U	2.0%

$105,000 U $ 75,000 F

Flexible-budget variance   Sales-volume variance

$30,000 U

Static-budget variance

[a] Budgeted selling price = $3,250,000 ÷ 500,000 lbs = $6.50 per lb.
Flexible-budget revenues = $6.50 per lb. × 525,000 lbs. = $3,412,500

[b] Budgeted variable mfg. cost per unit = $1,750,000 ÷ 500,000 lbs. = $3.50
Flexible-budget variable mfg. costs = $3.50 per lb. × 525,000 lbs. = $1,837,500

7-4

3.   The selling price variance, caused solely by the difference in actual and budgeted selling price, is the flexible-budget variance in revenues = $52,500 U.

4.   The flexible-budget variances show that for the actual sales volume of 525,000 pounds, selling prices were lower and costs per pound were higher. The favorable sales volume variance in revenues (because more pounds of ice cream were sold than budgeted) helped offset the unfavorable variable cost variance and shored up the results in June 2007. Levine should be more concerned because the small static-budget variance in contribution margin of $30,000 U is actually made up of a favorable sales-volume variance in contribution margin of $75,000, an unfavorable selling-price variance of $52,500 and an unfavorable variable manufacturing costs variance of $52,500. Levine should analyze why each of these variances occurred and the relationships among them. Could the efficiency of variable manufacturing costs be improved? Did the sales volume increase because of a decrease in selling price or because of growth in the overall market? Analysis of these questions would help Levine decide what actions he should take.

7-24 (30 min.) **Direct materials and direct manufacturing labor variances.**

1.

June 2007	Actual Results (1)	Price Variance (2) = (1)–(3)		Actual Quantity × Budgeted Price (3)	Efficiency Variance (4) = (3) – (5)		Flexible Budget (5)
Units	550						550
Direct materials	$12,705.00	$1,815.00	U	$10,890.00[a]	$990.00	U	$9,900.00[b]
Direct manuf. labor	$ 8,464.50	$ 104.50	U	$ 8,360.00[c]	$440.00	F	$8,800.00[d]
Total price variance		$1,919.50	U				
Total efficiency variance					$550.00	U	

[a] 7,260 meters × $1.50 per meter = $10,890
[b] 550 lots × 12 meters per lot × $1.50 per meter = $9,900
[c] 1,045 hours × $8.00 per hour = $8,360
[d] 550 lots × 2 hours per lot × $8 per hour = $8,800

Total flexible-budget variance for both inputs = $1,919.50U + $550U = $2,469.50U
Total flexible-budget cost of direct materials and direct manuf. labor = $9,900 + $8,800 = $18,700
Total flexible-budget variance as % of total flexible-budget costs = $2,469.50 ÷ $18,700 = 13.21%

2.

June 2008	Actual Results (1)	Price Variance (2) = (1) – (3)		Actual Quantity × Budgeted Price (3)	Efficiency Variance (4) = (3) – (5)		Flexible Budget (5)
Units	550						550
Direct materials	$11,828.36[a]	$1,156.16	U	$10,672.20[b]	$772.20	U	$9,900.00[c]
Direct manuf. labor	$ 8,295.21[d]	$ 102.41	U	$ 8,192.80[e]	$607.20	F	$8,800.00[c]
Total price variance		$1,258.57	U				
Total efficiency variance					$165.00	U	

[a] Actual dir. mat. cost, June 2008 = Actual dir. mat. cost, June 2007 × 0.98 × 0.95 = $12,705 × 0.98 × 0.95 = $11.828.36
  Alternatively, actual dir. mat. cost, June 2008
  = (Actual dir. mat. quantity used in June 2007 × 0.98) × (Actual dir. mat. price in June 2007 × 0.95)
  = (7,260 meters × 0.98) × ($1.75/meter × 0.95)
  = 7,114.80 × 1.6625 = $11,828.36
[b] (7,260 meters × 0.98) × $1.50 per meter = $10,672.20
[c] Unchanged from 2007.
[d] Actual dir. manuf. labor cost, June 2008 = Actual dir. manuf. cost June 2007 × 0.98 = $8,464.50 × 0.98 = $8,295.21
  Alternatively, actual dir. manuf. labor cost, June 2008
  = (Actual dir. manuf. labor quantity used in June 2007 × 0.98) × Actual dir. manuf. labor price in 2007
  = (1,045 hours × 0.98) × $8.10 per hour
  = 1,024.10 hours × $8.10 per hour = $8,295.21
[e] (1,045 hours × 0.98) × $8.00 per hour = $8,192.80

Total flexible-budget variance for both inputs = $1,258.57U + $165U = $1,423.57U
Total flexible-budget cost of direct materials and direct labor = $9,900 + $8,800 = $18,700
Total flexible-budget variance as % of total flexible-budget costs = $1,423.57 ÷ $18,700 = 7.61%

3.   Efficiencies have improved in the direction indicated by the production manager—but, it is unclear whether they are a trend or a one-time occurrence. Also, overall, variances are still 7.6% of flexible input budget. GloriaDee should continue to use the new material, especially in light of its superior quality and feel, but it may want to keep the following points in mind:

- The new material costs substantially more than the old ($1.75 in 2007 and $1.6625 in 2008 vs. $1.50 per meter). Its price is unlikely to come down even more within the coming year. Standard material price should be re-examined and possibly changed.
- GloriaDee should continue to work to reduce direct materials and direct manufacturing labor content. The reductions from June 2007 to June 2008 are a good development and should be encouraged.

7-26 (20 min.) **Continuous improvement (continuation of 7-25).**

1.   Standard quantity input amounts per output unit are:

	Direct Materials (pounds)	Direct Manufacturing Labor (hours)
January	10.0000	0.5000
February (Jan. × 0.997)	9.9700	0.4985
March (Feb. × 0.997)	9.9401	0.4970

2.   The answer to requirement 1 of Question 7-25 is identical except for the flexible- budget amount.

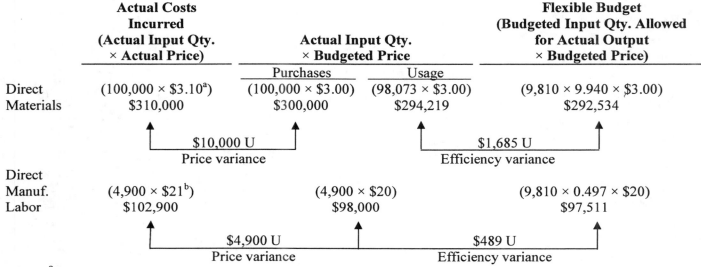

ª $310,000 ÷ 100,000 = $3.10
ᵇ $102,900 ÷ 4,900 = $21

Using continuous improvement standards sets a tougher benchmark. The efficiency variances for January (from Exercise 7-25) and March (from Exercise 7-26) are:

	January	March
Direct materials	$ 81 F	$1,685 U
Direct manufacturing labor	$100 F	$ 489 U

Note that the question assumes the continuous improvement applies only to quantity inputs. An alternative approach is to have continuous improvement apply to budgeted input cost per output unit ($30 for direct materials in January and $10 for direct manufacturing labor in January). This approach is more difficult to incorporate in a Level 2 variance analysis, because Level 2 requires separate amounts for quantity inputs and the cost per input.

7-28 (15–25 min.) **Journal entries and T-accounts (continuation of 7-27).**

Requirement 1 from Exercise 7-27:

a. Direct Materials Control   370,000
    Direct Materials Price Variance   7,400
      Accounts Payable Control   377,400
    To record purchase of direct materials.

b. Work-in-Process Control   400,000
      Direct Materials Efficiency Variance   30,000
      Direct Materials Control   370,000
    To record direct materials used.

c. Work-in-Process Control   200,000
      Direct Manufacturing Labor Price Variance   3,600
      Direct Manufacturing Labor Efficiency Variance   20,000
      Wages Payable Control   176,400
    To record liability for and allocation of direct labor costs.

Direct Materials Control		Direct Materials Price Variance		Direct Materials Efficiency Variance	
(a) 370,000	(b) 370,000	(a) 7,400			(b) 30,000

Work-in-Process Control		Direct Manufacturing Labor Price Variance		Direct Manuf. Labor Efficiency Variance	
(b) 400,000			(c) 3,600		(c) 20,000
(c) 200,000					

Wages Payable Control		Accounts Payable Control	
	(c) 176,400		377,400 (a)

Requirement 2 from Exercise 7-27:
The following journal entries pertain to the measurement of price and efficiency variances when 60,000 sq. yds. of direct materials are purchased:

a1. Direct Materials Control   600,000
    Direct Materials Price Variance   12,000
      Accounts Payable Control   612,000
    To record direct materials purchased.

a2. Work-in-Process Control   400,000
      Direct Materials Control   370,000
      Direct Materials Efficiency Variance   30,000
    To record direct materials used.

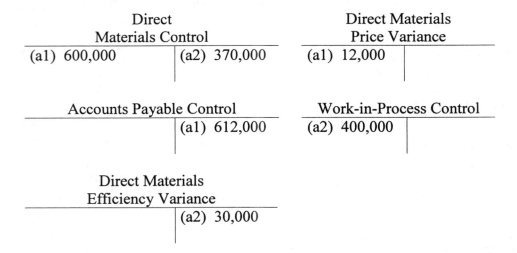

	Direct Materials Control		Direct Materials Price Variance	
(a1) 600,000	(a2) 370,000	(a1) 12,000	

	Accounts Payable Control		Work-in-Process Control	
	(a1) 612,000	(a2) 400,000	

	Direct Materials Efficiency Variance
	(a2) 30,000

The T-account entries related to direct manufacturing labor are the same as in requirement 1. The difference between standard costing and normal costing for direct cost items is:

	Standard Costs	Normal Costs
Direct Costs	Standard price(s) × Standard input allowed for actual outputs achieved	Actual price(s) × Actual input

These journal entries differ from the *normal costing* entries because Work-in-Process Control is no longer carried at "actual" costs. Furthermore, Direct Materials Control is carried at standard unit prices rather than actual unit prices. Finally, variances appear for direct materials and direct manufacturing labor under *standard costing* but not under *normal costing*.

7-30 (45–50 min.) **Activity-based costing, flexible-budget variances for finance-function activities.**

1. *Receivables*
    Receivables is an output unit level activity. Its flexible-budget variance can be calculated as follows:

$$\text{Flexible-budget variance} = \text{Actual costs} - \text{Flexible-budget costs}$$
$$= (\$0.75 \times 948,000) - (\$0.639 \times 948,000)$$
$$= \$711,000 - \$605,772$$
$$= \$105,228 \text{ U}$$

Payables
Payables is a batch level activity.

		Static-budget Amounts	Actual Amounts
a.	Number of deliveries	1,000,000	948,000
b.	Batch size (units per batch)	5	4.468
c.	Number of batches (a ÷ b)	200,000	212,175
d.	Cost per batch	$2.90	$2.80
e.	Total payables activity cost (c × d)	$580,000	$594,090

Step 1: The number of batches in which payables should have been processed
     = 948,000 actual units ÷ 5 budgeted units per batch
     = 189,600 batches

Step 2: The flexible-budget amount for payables
     = 189,600 batches × $2.90 budgeted cost per batch
     = $549,840

The flexible-budget variance can be computed as follows:

$$\begin{aligned}\text{Flexible-budget variance} &= \text{Actual costs} - \text{Flexible-budget costs} \\ &= (212,175 \times \$2.80) - (189,600 \times \$2.90) \\ &= \$594,090 - \$549,840 = \$44,250 \text{ U}\end{aligned}$$

Travel expenses
Travel expenses is a batch level activity.

		Static-Budget Amounts	Actual Amounts
a.	Number of deliveries	1,000,000	948,000
b.	Batch size (units per batch)	500	501.587
c.	Number of batches (a ÷ b)	2,000	1,890
d.	Cost per batch	$7.60	$7.40
e.	Total travel expenses activity cost (c × d)	$15,200	$13,986

Step 1: The number of batches in which the travel expense should have been processed
  = 948,000 actual units ÷ 500 budgeted units per batch
  = 1,896 batches

Step 2: The flexible-budget amount for travel expenses
  = 1,896 batches × \$7.60 budgeted cost per batch
  = \$14,410

The flexible budget variance can be calculated as follows:

Flexible budget variance = Actual costs − Flexible-budget costs
  = (1,890 × \$7.40) − (1,896 × \$7.60)
  = \$13,986 − \$14,410 = \$424 F

2.   The flexible budget variances can be subdivided into price and efficiency variances.

$$\text{Price variance} = \left[\begin{array}{c} \text{Actual price} \\ \text{of input} \end{array} - \begin{array}{c} \text{Budgeted price} \\ \text{of input} \end{array} \right] \times \begin{array}{c} \text{Actual quantity} \\ \text{of input} \end{array}$$

$$\text{Efficiency variance} = \left[\begin{array}{c} \text{Actual quantity} \\ \text{of input used} \end{array} - \begin{array}{c} \text{Budgeted quantity of} \\ \text{input allowed for} \\ \text{actual output} \end{array} \right] \times \begin{array}{c} \text{Budgeted price} \\ \text{of input} \end{array}$$

Receivables
Price Variance   = (\$0.750 − \$0.639) × 948,000
                     = \$105,228 U
Efficiency variance = (948,000 − 948,000) × \$0.639
                     = \$0

Payables
Price variance   = (\$2.80 − \$2.90) × 212,175
                     = \$21,218 F
Efficiency variance = (212,175 − 189,600) × \$2.90
                     = \$65,468 U

Travel expenses
Price variance   = (\$7.40 − \$7.60) × 1,890
                     = \$378 F
Efficiency variance = (1,890 − 1,896) × \$7.60
                     = \$46F

7-32 (30 min.) **Flexible budget, direct materials and direct manufacturing labor variances.**

1.

	Actual Results (1)	Flexible-Budget Variances (2) = (1) – (3)	Flexible Budget (3)	Sales-Volume Variances (4) = (3) – (5)	Static Budget (5)
Units sold	6,000[a]	0	6,000	1,000 F	5,000[a]
Direct materials	$ 594,000	$ 6,000 F	$ 600,000[b]	$100,000 U	$ 500,000[c]
Direct manufacturing labor	950,000[a]	10,000 F	960,000[d]	160,000 U	800,000[e]
Fixed costs	1,005,000[a]	5,000 U	1,000,000[a]	0	1,000,000[a]
Total costs	$2,549,000	$11,000 F	$2,560,000	$260,000 U	$2,300,000

$11,000 F $260,000 U

▲ Flexible-budget variance   Sales-volume variance ▲

$249,000 U

Static-budget variance

[a] Given
[b] $100 × 6,000 = $600,000
[c] $100 × 5,000 = $500,000

[d] $160 × 6,000 = $960,000
[e] $160 × 5,000 = $800,000

2.

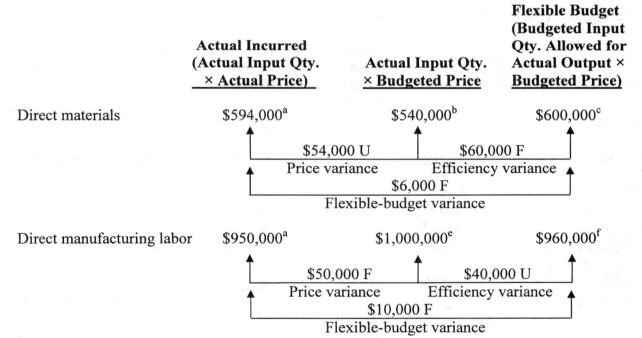

	Actual Incurred (Actual Input Qty. × Actual Price)	Actual Input Qty. × Budgeted Price	Flexible Budget (Budgeted Input Qty. Allowed for Actual Output × Budgeted Price)
Direct materials	$594,000[a]	$540,000[b]	$600,000[c]

$54,000 U $60,000 F

Price variance   Efficiency variance

$6,000 F

Flexible-budget variance

Direct manufacturing labor	$950,000[a]	$1,000,000[e]	$960,000[f]

$50,000 F $40,000 U

Price variance   Efficiency variance

$10,000 F

Flexible-budget variance

[a] 54,000 pounds × $11/pound = $594,000
[b] 54,000 pounds × $10/pound = $540,000
[c] 6,000 statues × 10 pounds/statue × $10/pound = 60,000 pounds × $10/pound = $600,000
[d] 25,000 pounds × $38/pound = $950,000
[e] 25,000 pounds × $40/pound = $1,000,000
[f] 6,000 statues × 4 hours/statue × $40/hour = 24,000 hours × $40/hour = $960,000

7-34 (60 min.) **Comprehensive variance analysis, responsibility issues.**

1a.　Actual selling price　= $82.00
　　Budgeted selling price = $80.00
　　Actual sales volume = 4,850 units
　　Selling price variance　= (Actual sales price − Budgeted sales price) × Actual sales volume
　　= ($82 − $80) × 4,850 = $9,700 Favorable

1b.　Development of Flexible Budget

		Budgeted Unit Amounts	Actual Volume	Flexible Budget Amount
Revenues		$80.00	4,850	$388,000
Variable costs				
DM–Frames	$2.20/oz. × 3.00 oz.	6.60[a]	4,850	32,010
DM–Lenses	$3.10/oz. × 6.00 oz.	18.60[b]	4,850	90,210
Direct manuf. labor	$15.00/hr. × 1.20 hrs.	18.00[c]	4,850	87,300
Total variable manufacturing costs				$209,520
Fixed manufacturing costs				75,000
Total manufacturing costs				284,520
Gross margin				$103,480

[a]$33,000 ÷ 5,000 units; [b]$93,000 ÷ 5,000 units; [c]$90,000 ÷ 5,000 units

	Actual Results (1)	Flexible- Budget Variances (2)=(1)-(3)	Flexible Budget (3)	Sales - Volume Variance (4)=(3)-(5)	Static Budget (5)
Units sold	4,850		4,850		5,000
Revenues	$397,700	$ 9,700 F	$388,000	$ 12,000 U	$400,000
Variable costs					
DM–frames	37,248	5,238 U	32,010	990 F	33,000
DM–lens	100,492	10,282 U	90,210	2,790 F	93,000
Direct labor	96,903	9,603 U	87,300	2,700 F	90,000
Total variable costs	234,643	25,123 U	209,520	6,480 F	216,000
Fixed manuf. costs	72,265	2,735 F	75,000	0	75,000
Total costs	306,908	22,388 U	284,520	6,480 F	291,000
Gross margin	$ 90,792	$12,688 U	$103,480	$ 5,520 U	$109,000

Level 2　　　　　　$12,688 U　　　　　　$ 5,520 U
　　　　　Flexible-budget variance　　　Sales-volume variance

Level 1　　　　　　　　　　　$18,208 U
　　　　　　　　　　　Static-budget variance

1c.   Price and Efficiency Variances

DM–Frames–Actual ounces used = 3.20 per unit × 4,850 units = 15,520 oz.
Price per oz. = $37,248 ÷ 15,520 = $2.40
DM–Lenses–Actual ounces used = 7.00 per unit × 4,850 units = 33,950 oz.
Price per oz. = $100,492 ÷ 33,950 = $2.96
Direct Labor–Actual labor hours = $96,903 ÷ 14.80 = 6,547.5 hours
Labor hours per unit = 6,547.5 ÷ 4,850 units = 1.35 hours per unit

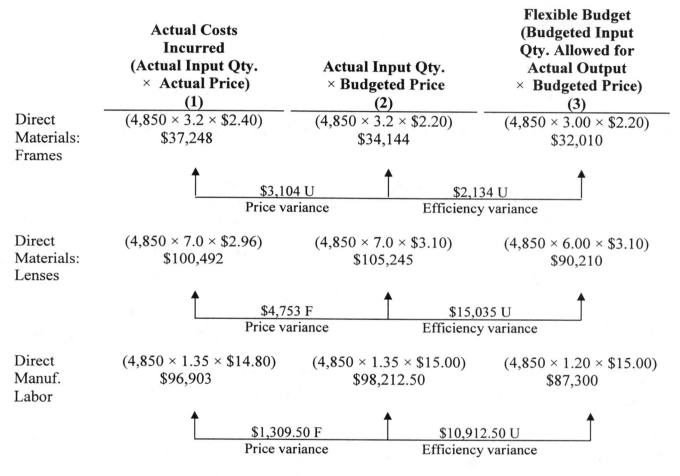

	Actual Costs Incurred (Actual Input Qty. × Actual Price) (1)	Actual Input Qty. × Budgeted Price (2)	Flexible Budget (Budgeted Input Qty. Allowed for Actual Output × Budgeted Price) (3)
Direct Materials: Frames	(4,850 × 3.2 × $2.40) $37,248	(4,850 × 3.2 × $2.20) $34,144	(4,850 × 3.00 × $2.20) $32,010
	$3,104 U — Price variance	$2,134 U — Efficiency variance	
Direct Materials: Lenses	(4,850 × 7.0 × $2.96) $100,492	(4,850 × 7.0 × $3.10) $105,245	(4,850 × 6.00 × $3.10) $90,210
	$4,753 F — Price variance	$15,035 U — Efficiency variance	
Direct Manuf. Labor	(4,850 × 1.35 × $14.80) $96,903	(4,850 × 1.35 × $15.00) $98,212.50	(4,850 × 1.20 × $15.00) $87,300
	$1,309.50 F — Price variance	$10,912.50 U — Efficiency variance	

2.   Possible explanations for price variances are:
(a) Purchasing and labor negotiations.
(b) Quality of frames and lenses purchased.
(c) Standards set incorrectly.

Possible explanations for efficiency variance are:
(a) Higher materials usage due to lower quality frames and lenses purchased at lower price.
(b) Lesser trained workers hired at lower rates result in higher materials usage and lower labor efficiency.
(c) Standards set incorrectly.

7-36 (30 min.) **Level 2 variance analysis, solve for unknowns.**

1. Budgeted selling price $= \dfrac{\$4,800,000}{600,000} = \$\ 8.00$ per cap

    Actual selling price $= \dfrac{\$5,000,000}{500,000} = \$10.00$ per cap

2. Budgeted variable cost per unit $= \dfrac{\$1,800,000}{600,000} = \$3.00$ per unit

    Actual variable cost per unit $= \dfrac{\$1,400,000}{500,000} = \$2.80$ per unit

Level 2 Flexible-budget-based Variance Analysis for Homerun Headgear for Year Ended December 2006

	Actual Results (1)	Flexible-Budget Variances (2)=(1)–(3)	Flexible Budget (3)	Sales - Volume Variance (4)=(3)–(5)	Static Budget (5)
Units sold	500,000	0	500,000	100,000 U	600,000
Revenues (sales)	$5,000,000	$1,000,000 F	$4,000,000	$800,000 U	$4,800,000
Variable costs	1,400,000	100,000 F	1,500,000	300,000 F	1,800,000
Contribution margin	3,600,000	1,100,000 F	2,500,000	500,000 U	3,000,000
Fixed costs	1,150,000	150,000 U	1,000,000	0	1,000,000
Operating income	$2,450,000	$ 950,000 F	$1,500,000	$500,000 U	$2,000,000

$950, 000$ F
Total flexible-budget variance

$500, 000$ U
Total sales-volume variance

$450, 000$ F
Total static-budget variance

3. Flexible-budget operating income = $1,500,000

4. Flexible-budget variance for operating income = $950,000 F

5. Sales-volume variance for operating income = $500,000 U

6. Static-budget variance for operating income = $450,000 F

7-38 (20–30 min.) **Direct materials and manufacturing labor variances, solving unknowns.**

All given items are designated by an asterisk.

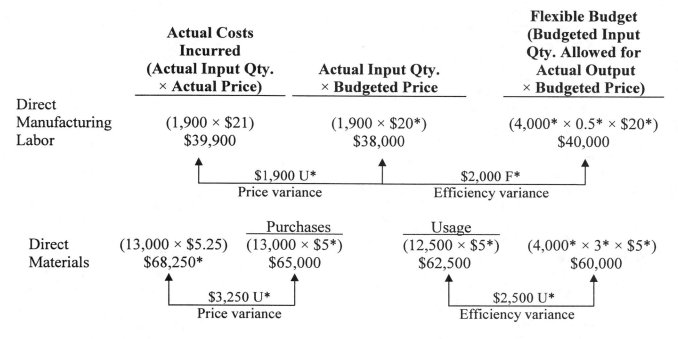

	Actual Costs Incurred (Actual Input Qty. × Actual Price)	Actual Input Qty. × Budgeted Price		Flexible Budget (Budgeted Input Qty. Allowed for Actual Output × Budgeted Price)
Direct Manufacturing Labor	(1,900 × $21) $39,900	(1,900 × $20*) $38,000		(4,000* × 0.5* × $20*) $40,000

$1,900 U* Price variance $2,000 F* Efficiency variance

		Purchases	Usage	
Direct Materials	(13,000 × $5.25) $68,250*	(13,000 × $5*) $65,000	(12,500 × $5*) $62,500	(4,000* × 3* × $5*) $60,000

$3,250 U* Price variance $2,500 U* Efficiency variance

1. 4,000 units × 0.5 hours/unit = 2,000 hours

2. Flexible budget – Efficiency variance = $40,000 – $2,000 = $38,000
   Actual dir. manuf. labor hours = $38,000 ÷ Budgeted price of $20/hour = 1,900 hours

3. $38,000 + Price variance, $1,900 = $39,900, the actual direct manuf. labor cost
   Actual rate = Actual cost ÷ Actual hours = $39,000 ÷ 1,900 hours = $21/hour (rounded)

4. Standard qty. of direct materials = 4,000 units × 3 pounds/unit = 12,000 pounds

5. Flexible budget + Dir. matls. effcy. var. = $60,000 + $2,500 = $62,500
   Actual quantity of dir. matls. used = $62,500 ÷ Budgeted price per lb
   = $62,500 ÷ $5/lb = 12,500 lbs

6. Actual cost of direct materials, $68,250 – Price variance, $3,250 = $65,000
   Actual qty. of direct materials purchased = $65,000 ÷ Budgeted price, $5/lb = 13,000 lbs.

7. Actual direct materials price = $68,250 ÷ 13,000 lbs = $5.25 per lb.

7-40 (60 min.) **Comprehensive variance analysis review**.

Actual Results

Units sold (80% × 1,500,000)	1,200,000
Selling price per unit	$3.70
Revenues (1,200,000 × $3.70)	$4,440,000
Direct materials purchased and used:	
Direct materials per unit	$0.80
Total direct materials cost (1,200,000 × $0.80)	$960,000
Direct manufacturing labor:	
Actual manufacturing rate per hour	$15
Labor productivity per hour in units	250
Manufacturing labor-hours of input (1,200,000 ÷ 250)	4,800
Total direct manufacturing labor costs (4,800 × $15)	$72,000
Direct marketing costs:	
Direct marketing cost per unit	$0.30
Total direct marketing costs (1,200,000 × $0.30)	$360,000
Fixed costs ($900,000 – $30,000)	$870,000

Static Budgeted Amounts

Units sold	1,500,000
Selling price per un	$4.00
Revenues (1,500,000 × $4.00)	$6,000,000
Direct materials purchased and used:	
Direct materials per unit	$0.85
Total direct materials costs (1,500,000 × $0.85)	$1,275,000
Direct manufacturing labor:	
Direct manufacturing rate per hour	$15.00
Labor productivity per hour in units	300
Manufacturing labor-hours of input (1,500,000 ÷ 300)	5,000
Total direct manufacturing labor cost (5,000 × $15.00)	$75,000
Direct marketing costs:	
Direct marketing cost per unit	$0.30
Total direct marketing cost (1,500,000 × $0.30)	$450,000
Fixed costs	$900,000

1.

	Actual Results	Static-Budget Amounts
Revenues	$4,440,000	$6,000,000
Variable costs		
Direct materials	$ 960,000	$1,275,000
Direct manufacturing labor	72,000	75,000
Direct marketing costs	360,000	450,000
Total variable costs	1,392,000	1,800,000
Contribution margin	3,048,000	4,200,000
Fixed costs	870,000	900,000
Operating income	$2,178,000	$3,300,000

2.

Actual operating income	$2,178,000
Static-budget operating income	3,300,000
Total static-budget variance	$1,122,000 U

Level 2 Flexible-budget-based Variance Analysis

	Actual Results	Flexible-Budget Variances	Flexible Budget	Sales-Volume Variances	Static Budget
Units sold	1,200,000	0	1,200,000	300,000	1,500,000
Revenues	$4,440,000	$360,000 U	$4,800,000	$1,200,000 U	$6,000,000
Variable costs					
Direct materials	960,000	60,000 F	1,020,000	255,000 F	1,275,000
Direct manuf. labor	72,000	12,000 U	60,000	15,000 F	75,000
Direct marketing costs	360,000	0	360,000	90,000 F	450,000
Total variable costs	1,392,000	48,000 F	1,440,000	360,000 F	1,800,000
Contribution margin	3,048,000	312,000 U	3,360,000	840,000 U	4,200,000
Fixed costs	870,000	30,000 F	900,000	0	900,000
Operating income	$2,178,000	$282,000 U	$2,460,000	$ 840,000 U	$3,300,000

$282, 000 U

Total flexible-budget variance

$840, 000 U

Total sales-volume variance

$1,122,000 U

Total static-budget variance

3.   Flexible-budget operating income = $2,460,000.

4.   Flexible-budget variance for operating income = $282,000U.

5.   Sales-volume variance for operating income = $840,000U.

Level 3 Analysis of Direct Manufacturing Labor flexible-budget variance

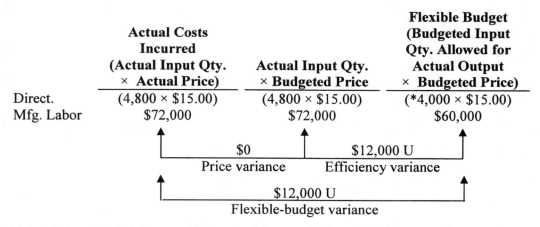

	Actual Costs Incurred (Actual Input Qty. × Actual Price)	Actual Input Qty. × Budgeted Price	Flexible Budget (Budgeted Input Qty. Allowed for Actual Output × Budgeted Price)
Direct. Mfg. Labor	(4,800 × $15.00) $72,000	(4,800 × $15.00) $72,000	(*4,000 × $15.00) $60,000

$0

Price variance

$12,000 U

Efficiency variance

$12,000 U

Flexible-budget variance

* 1,200,000 units ÷ 300 direct manufacturing labor standard productivity rate per hour.

6.   DML price variance = $0; DML efficiency variance = $12,000U

7.   DML   flexible-budget   variance   = $12,000U

7-42 (30 min.) **Comprehensive variance analysis.**

1. Computing unit selling prices and unit costs of inputs:

    Actual selling price   = $3,555,000 ÷ 450,000
                               = $7.90

    Budgeting selling price   = $3,200,000 ÷ 400,000
                               = $8.00

$$\text{Selling-price variance} = \left(\begin{array}{c} \text{Actual} \\ \text{selling price} \end{array} - \begin{array}{c} \text{Budgeted} \\ \text{selling price} \end{array} \right) \times \begin{array}{c} \text{Actual} \\ \text{units sold} \end{array}$$

                                     =   ($7.90/unit – $8.00/unit)   ×   450,000 units

                                     = $45,000 U

2., 3., and 4.

The actual and budgeted unit costs are:

	Actual	**Budgeted**
Direct materials		
Cookie mix	$0.02 ($93,000 ÷ 4,650,000)	$0.02
Milk chocolate	0.20 ($532,000 ÷ 2,660,000)	0.15
Almonds	0.50 ($240,000 ÷ 480,000)	0.50
Direct manuf. labor		
Mixing	14.40 ($108,000 ÷ 450,000 × 60)	14.40
Baking	18.00 ($240,000 ÷ 800,000 × 60)	18.00

The actual output achieved is 450,000 pounds of chocolate nut supreme.

The direct cost price and efficiency variances are:

	Actual Costs Incurred (Actual Input Qty. × Actual Price) (1)	Price Variance (2)=(1)–(3)	Actual Input Qty. × Budgeted Price (3)	Efficiency Variance (4)=(3)–(5)	Flex. Budget (Budgeted Input Qty. Allowed for Actual Output × Budgeted Price) (5)
Direct materials					
Cookie mix	$ 93,000	$ 0	$ 93,000[a]	$ 3,000 U	$ 90,000[f]
Milk chocolate	532,000	133,000 U	399,000[b]	61,500 U	337,500[g]
Almonds	240,000	0	240,000[c]	15,000 U	225,000[h]
	$865,000	$133,000 U	$732,000	$79,500 U	$652,500
Direct manuf. labor costs					
Mixing	$108,000	$ 0	$108,000[d]	$ 0	$108,000[i]
Baking	240,000	0	240,000[e]	30,000 F	270,000[j]
	$348,000	$ 0	$348,000	$30,000 F	$378,000

[a] $0.02 × 4,650,000 = $93,000

[b] $0.15 × 2,660,000 = $399,000

[c] $0.50 × 480,000 = $240,000

[d] $14.40/hr. × (450,000 min. ÷ 60 min./hr.) = $108,000

[e] $18.00/hr. × (800,000 min. ÷ 60 min./hr.) = $240,000

[f] $0.02 × 10 × 450,000 = $90,000

[g] $0.15 × 5 × 450,000 = $337,500

[h] $0.50 × 1 × 450,000 = $225,000

[i] $14.40 × (450,000 ÷ 60) = $108,000

[j] $18.00 × (450,000 ÷ 30) = $270,000

Comments on the variances include

- Selling price variance. This may arise from a proactive decision to reduce price to expand market share or from a reaction to a price reduction by a competitor. It could also arise from unplanned price discounting by salespeople.

- Material price variance. The $0.05 increase in the price per ounce of milk chocolate could arise from uncontrollable market factors or from poor contract negotiations by Aunt Molly's.

- Material efficiency variance. For all three material inputs, usage is greater than budgeted. Possible reasons include lower quality inputs, use of lower quality workers, and the mixing and baking equipment not being maintained in a fully operational mode. The higher price per ounce of milk chocolate (and perhaps higher quality of milk chocolate) did not reduce the quantity of milk chocolate used to produce actual output.

- Labor efficiency variance. The favorable efficiency variance for baking could be due to workers eliminating nonvalue-added steps in production.

7-44 (30 min.) **Price and efficiency variances, problems in standard setting, benchmarking.**

1. Budgeted direct materials input per shirt = 400 rolls ÷ 4,000 shirts= 0.10 roll of cloth
    Budgeted direct manufacturing. labor-hours per shirt (1,000 hours ÷ 4,000 shirts) = 0.25 hours
    Budgeted direct materials cost ($20,000 ÷ 400) = $50 per roll
    Budgeted direct manufacturing labor cost per hour ($18,000 ÷ 1,000) = $18 per hour
    Actual output achieved = 4,488 shirts

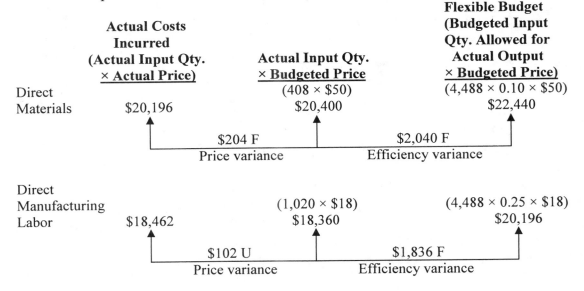

2. Actions employees may have taken include:
    (a) Adding steps that are not necessary in working on a shirt.
    (b) Taking more time on each step than is necessary.
    (c) Creating problem situations so that the budgeted amount of average downtime will be overstated.
    (d) Creating defects in shirts so that the budgeted amount of average rework will be overstated.
    Employees may take these actions for several possible reasons.
    (a) They may be paid on a piece-rate basis with incentives for above-budgeted production.
    (b) They may want to create a relaxed work atmosphere, and a less demanding standard can reduce stress.
    (c) They have a "them vs. us" mentality rather than a partnership perspective.
    (d) They may want to gain all the benefits that ensue from superior performance (job security, wage rate increases) without putting in the extra effort required.
This behavior is unethical if it is deliberately designed to undermine the credibility of the standards used at Savannah Fashions.

3.   If Anderson does nothing about standard costs, his behavior will violate the "Standards of Ethical Conduct for Management Accountants." In particular, he would be violating the
        (a) standards of competence, by not performing technical duties in accordance with relevant standards;
        (b) standards of integrity, by passively subverting the attainment of the organization's objective to control costs; and
        (c) standards of objectivity, by not communicating information fairly and not disclosing all relevant cost information.

4.   Anderson should discuss the situation with Fenton and point out that the standards are lax and that this practice is unethical. If Fenton does not agree to change, Anderson should escalate the issue up the hierarchy in order to effect change. If organizational change is not forthcoming, Anderson should be prepared to resign rather than compromise his professional ethics.

5.   Main pros of using Benchmarking Clearing House information to compute variances are
        (a) Highlights to Savannah in a direct way how it may or may not be cost-competitive.
        (b) Provides a "reality check" to many internal positions about efficiency or effectiveness.

      Main cons are
        (a) Savannah may not be comparable to companies in the database.
        (b) Cost data about other companies may not be reliable.
        (c) Cost of Benchmarking Clearing House reports.

CHAPTER 8
FLEXIBLE BUDGETS, OVERHEAD COST VARIANCES, AND MANAGEMENT CONTROL

8-2　At the start of an accounting period, a larger percentage of fixed overhead costs are locked-in than is the case with variable overhead costs. When planning fixed overhead costs, a company must choose the appropriate level of capacity or investment that will benefit the company over a long time. This is a strategic decision.

8-4　Steps in developing a budgeted variable-overhead cost rate are:
1. Choose the period to be used for the budget,
2. Select the cost-allocation bases to use in allocating variable overhead costs to the output produced,
3. Identify the variable overhead costs associated with each cost-allocation base, and
4. Compute the rate per unit of each cost-allocation base used to allocate variable overhead costs to output produced.

8-6　Possible reasons for a favorable variable-overhead efficiency variance are:
- Workers more skillful in using machines than budgeted,
- Production scheduler was able to schedule jobs better than budgeted, resulting in lower-than-budgeted machine-hours,
- Machines operated with fewer slowdowns than budgeted, and
- Machine time standards were overly lenient.

8-8　Steps in developing a budgeted fixed-overhead rate are
1. Choose the period to use for the budget,
2. Select the cost-allocation base to use in allocating fixed overhead costs to output produced,
3. Identify the fixed-overhead costs associated with each cost-allocation base, and
4. Compute the rate per unit of each cost-allocation base used to allocate fixed overhead costs to output produced.

8-10　For planning and control purposes, fixed overhead costs are a lump sum amount that is not controlled on a per-unit basis. In contrast, for inventory costing purposes, fixed overhead costs are allocated to products on a per-unit basis.

8-12 A strong case can be made for writing off an unfavorable production-volume variance to cost of goods sold. The alternative is prorating it among inventories and cost of goods sold, but this would "penalize" the units produced (and in inventory) for the cost of unused capacity, i.e., for the units *not* produced. But, if we take the view that the denominator level is a "soft" number—i.e., it is only an estimate, and it is never expected to be reached exactly, then it makes more sense to prorate the production volume variance—whether favorable or not—among the inventory stock and cost of goods sold. Prorating a favorable variance is also more conservative: it results in a lower operating income than if the favorable variance had all been written off to cost of goods sold. Finally, prorating also dampens the efficacy of any steps taken by company management to manage operating income through manipulation of the production volume variance. In sum, a production-volume variance need not always be written off to cost of goods sold.

8-14 Interdependencies among the variances could arise for the spending and efficiency variances. For example, if the chosen allocation base for the variable overhead efficiency variance is only one of several cost drivers, the variable overhead spending variance will include the effect of the other cost drivers. As a second example, interdependencies can be induced when there are misclassifications of costs as fixed when they are variable, and vice versa.

8-16 (20 min.) **Variable manufacturing overhead, variance analysis.**

1.

Actual Costs Incurred Actual Input Qty. × Actual Rate (1)	Actual Input Qty. × Budgeted Rate (2)	Flexible Budget: Budgeted Input Qty. Allowed for Actual Output × Budgeted Rate (3)	Allocated: Budgeted Input Qty. Allowed for Actual Output × Budgeted Rate (4)
(4,536 × $11.50) $52,164	(4,536 × $12) $54,432	(4 × 1,080 × $12) $51,840	(4 × 1,080 × $12) $51,840

$2,268 F Spending variance $2,592 U Efficiency variance   Never a variance

$324 U Flexible-budget variance   Never a variance

2. Esquire had a favorable spending variance of $2,268 because the actual variable overhead rate was $11.50 per direct manufacturing labor-hour versus $12 budgeted. It had an unfavorable efficiency variance of $2,592 U because each suit averaged 4.2 labor-hours (4,536 hours ÷ 1,080 suits) versus 4.0 budgeted labor-hours.

8-18 (30 min.) **Variable manufacturing overhead variance analysis.**

1. Denominator level = (3,200,000 × 0.02 hours) = 64,000 hours

2.

	Actual Results	Flexible Budget Amounts
1. Output units (baguettes)	2,800,000	2,800,000
2. Direct manufacturing labor-hours	50,400	56,000[a]
3. Labor-hours per output unit (2 ÷1)	0.018	0.020
4. Variable manuf. overhead (MOH) costs	$680,400	$560,000
5. Variable MOH per labor-hour (4 ÷2)	$13.50	$10
6. Variable MOH per output unit (4 ÷1)	$0.243	$0.200

[a]2,800,000 × 0.020= 56,000 hours

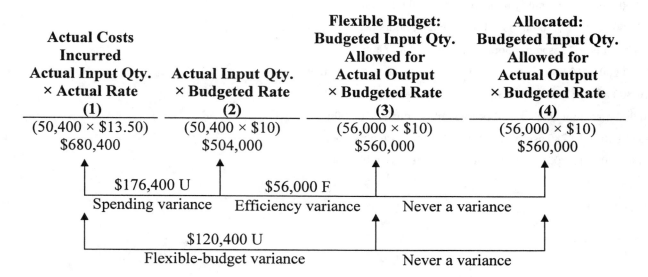

Actual Costs Incurred Actual Input Qty. × Actual Rate (1)	Actual Input Qty. × Budgeted Rate (2)	Flexible Budget: Budgeted Input Qty. Allowed for Actual Output × Budgeted Rate (3)	Allocated: Budgeted Input Qty. Allowed for Actual Output × Budgeted Rate (4)
(50,400 × $13.50) $680,400	(50,400 × $10) $504,000	(56,000 × $10) $560,000	(56,000 × $10) $560,000

$176,400 U
Spending variance

$56,000 F
Efficiency variance

Never a variance

$120,400 U
Flexible-budget variance

Never a variance

3. Spending variance of $176,400U. It is unfavorable because variable manufacturing overhead was 35% higher than planned. A possible explanation could be an increase in energy rates relative to the rate per standard labor-hour assumed in the flexible budget.

Efficiency variance of $56,000F. It is favorable because the actual number of direct manufacturing labor-hours required was lower than the number of hours in the flexible budget. Labor was more efficient in producing the baguettes than management had anticipated in the budget. This could occur because of improved morale in the company, which could result from an increase in wages or an improvement in the compensation scheme.

Flexible-budget variance of $120,400U. It is unfavorable because the favorable efficiency variance was not large enough to compensate for the large unfavorable spending variance.

8-20 (30–40 min.) **Manufacturing overhead, variance analysis.**

1.   The summary information is:

Zircon (March 2007)	Actual	Flexible Budget	Static Budget
Outputs units (number of assembled CardioX)	5,400	5,400	5,000
Hours of assembly time	10,280	10,800[c]	10,000[a]
Assembly hours per CardioX unit	1.90[b]	2.00	2.00
Variable overhead costs per hour of assembly time	$ 30.20[d]	$ 30.00	$ 30.00
Variable overhead costs	$310,500	$324,000[e]	$300,000[f]
Fixed overhead costs	$514,000	$480,000	$480,000
Fixed overhead costs per hour of assembly time	$ 50.00[g]		$ 48.00[h]

[a] 5,000 units × 2 assembly hours per unit = 10,000 hours

[b] 10,280 hours ÷ 5,400 units = 1.90 assembly hours per unit

[c] 5,400 units × 2 assembly hours per unit = 10,800 hours

[d] $310,500 ÷ 10,280 assembly hours = $30.20 per assembly hour

[e] 10,800 assembly hours × $30 per assembly hour = $324,000

[f] 10,000 assembly hours × $30 per assembly hour = $300,000

[g] $514,000 ÷ 10,280 assembly hours = $50 per assembly hour

[h] $480,000 ÷ 10,000 assembly hours = $48 per assembly hour

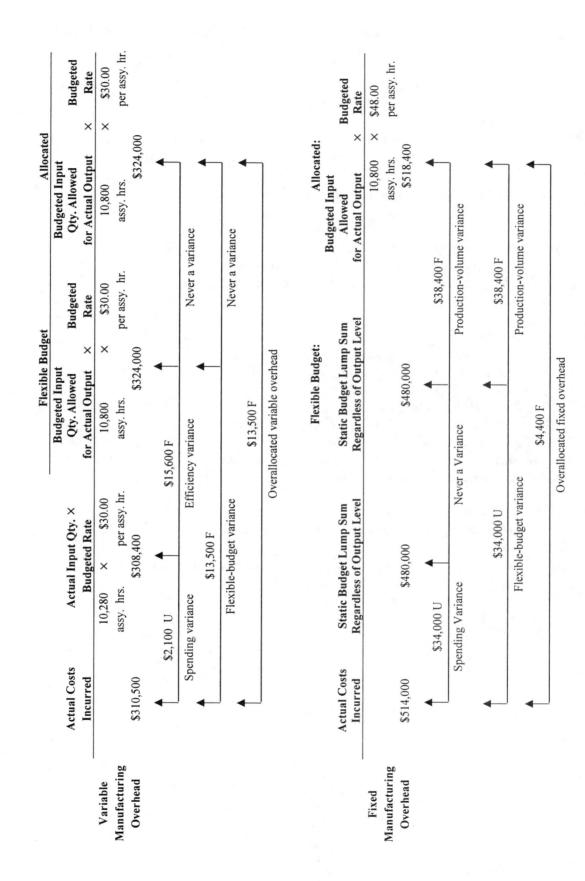

Variable Manufacturing Overhead

	Actual Costs Incurred	Actual Input Qty. × Budgeted Rate		Flexible Budget Budgeted Input Qty. Allowed for Actual Output		Budgeted Rate		Allocated Budgeted Input Qty. Allowed for Actual Output		Budgeted Rate
	$310,500	10,280 assy. hrs.	× $30.00 per assy. hr.	10,800 assy. hrs.	×	$30.00 per assy. hr.		10,800 assy. hrs.	×	$30.00 per assy. hr.
			$308,400		$324,000				$324,000	

$2,100 U
Spending variance

$15,600 F
Efficiency variance

Never a variance

$13,500 F
Flexible-budget variance

$13,500 F
Never a variance

Overallocated variable overhead

Fixed Manufacturing Overhead

	Actual Costs Incurred	Static Budget Lump Sum Regardless of Output Level	Flexible Budget: Static Budget Lump Sum Regardless of Output Level	Allocated: Budgeted Input Allowed for Actual Output		Budgeted Rate
	$514,000	$480,000	$480,000	10,800 assy. hrs.	×	$48.00 per assy. hr.
					$518,400	

$34,000 U
Spending Variance

Never a Variance

$38,400 F
Production-volume variance

$34,000 U
Flexible-budget variance

$38,400 F
Production-volume variance

$4,400 F
Overallocated fixed overhead

8-5

The summary analysis is:

	Spending Variance	Efficiency Variance	Production-Volume Variance
Variable Manufacturing Overhead	$2,100 U	$15,600 F	Never a variance
Fixed Manufacturing Overhead	$34,000 U	Never a variance	$38,400 F

2.   **Variable Manufacturing Costs and Variances**

a. Variable Manufacturing Overhead Control   310,500
    Accounts Payable Control and various other accounts   310,500
To record actual variable manufacturing overhead costs incurred.

b. Work-in-Process Control   324,000
    Variable Manufacturing Overhead Allocated   324,000
To record variable manufacturing overhead allocated.

c. Variable Manufacturing Overhead Allocated   324,000
    Variable Manufacturing Overhead Spending Variance   2,100
      Variable Manufacturing Overhead Control   310,500
      Variable Manufacturing Overhead Efficiency Variance   15,600
To isolate variances for the accounting period.

d. Fixed Manufacturing Overhead Efficiency Variance   15,600
    Variable Manufacturing Overhead Spending Variance   2,100
    Cost of Goods Sold   13,500
To write off variable manufacturing overhead variances to cost of goods sold.

Fixed Manufacturing Costs and Variances

a. Fixed Manufacturing Overhead Control   514,000
    Salaries Payable, Acc. Depreciation, various other accounts   514,000
  To record actual fixed manufacturing overhead costs incurred.

b. Work-in-Process Control   518,400
    Fixed Manufacturing Overhead Allocated   518,400
  To record fixed manufacturing overhead allocated.

c. Fixed Manufacturing Overhead Allocated   518,400
    Fixed Manufacturing Overhead Spending Variance   34,000
      Fixed Manufacturing Overhead Production-Volume Variance   38,400
      Fixed Manufacturing Overhead Control   514,000
  To isolate variances for the accounting period.

d. Variable Manufacturing Overhead Production-Volume Variance   38,400
    Fixed Manufacturing Overhead Spending Variance   34,000
  Cost of Goods Sold   4,400
To write off fixed manufacturing overhead variances to cost of goods sold.

3.   Planning and control of *variable* manufacturing overhead costs has both a long-run and a short-run focus. It involves Zircon planning to undertake only value-added overhead activities (a long-run view) and then managing the cost drivers of those activities in the most efficient way (a short-run view). Planning and control of *fixed* manufacturing overhead costs at Zircon have primarily a long-run focus. It involves undertaking only value-added fixed-overhead activities for a budgeted level of output. Zircon makes most of the key decisions that determine the level of fixed-overhead costs at the start of the accounting period.

8-22   (20–30 min.) **Straightforward 4-variance overhead analysis.**

1.   The budget for fixed manufacturing overhead is 4,000 units × 6 machine-hours × $15 machine-hours/unit = $360,000.

An overview of the 4-variance analysis is:

4-Variance Analysis	Spending Variance	Efficiency Variance	Production-Volume Variance
Variable Manufacturing Overhead	$17,800 U	$16,000 U	Never a Variance
Fixed Manufacturing Overhead	$13,000 U	Never a Variance	$36,000 F

Solution Exhibit 8-22 has details of these variances.

A detailed comparison of actual and flexible budgeted amounts is:

	Actual	Flexible Budget
Output units (auto parts)	4,400	4,400
Allocation base (machine-hours)	28,400	26,400[a]
Allocation base per output unit	6.45[b]	6.00
Variable MOH	$245,000	$211,200[c]
Variable MOH per hour	$8.63[d]	$8.00
Fixed MOH	$373,000	$360,000[e]
Fixed MOH per hour	$13.13[f]	–

[a] 4,400 units × 6.00 machine-hours/unit = 26,400 machine-hours
[b] 28,400 ÷ 4,400 = 6.45 machine-hours per unit
[c] 4,400 units × 6.00 machine-hours per unit × $8.00 per machine-hour = $211,200
[d] $245,000 ÷ 28,400 = $8.63
[e] 4,000 units × 6.00 machine-hours per unit × $15 per machine-hour = $360,000
[f] $373,000 ÷ 28,400 = $13.13

2. Variable Manufacturing Overhead Control 245,000
        Accounts Payable Control and other accounts 245,000

    Work-in-Process Control 211,200
        Variable Manufacturing Overhead Allocated 211,200

    Variable Manufacturing Overhead Allocated 211,200
    Variable Manufacturing Overhead Spending Variance 17,800
    Variable Manufacturing Overhead Efficiency Variance 16,000
        Variable Manufacturing Overhead Control 245,000

    Fixed Manufacturing Overhead Control 373,000
        Wages Payable Control, Accumulated Depreciation
            Control, etc. 373,000

    Work-in-Process Control 396,000
        Fixed Manufacturing Overhead Allocated 396,000

    Fixed Manufacturing Overhead Allocated 396,000
    Fixed Manufacturing Overhead Spending Variance 13,000
        Fixed Manufacturing Overhead Production-Volume Variance 36,000
        Fixed Manufacturing Overhead Control 373,000

3. The control of variable manufacturing overhead requires the identification of the cost drivers for such items as energy, supplies, and repairs. Control often entails monitoring nonfinancial measures that affect each cost item, one by one. Examples are kilowatt-hours used, quantities of lubricants used, and repair parts and hours used. The most convincing way to discover why overhead performance did not agree with a budget is to investigate possible causes, line item by line item.

Individual fixed manufacturing overhead items are not usually affected very much by day-to-day control. Instead, they are controlled periodically through planning decisions and budgeting procedures that may sometimes have horizons covering six months or a year (for example, management salaries) and sometimes covering many years (for example, long-term leases and depreciation on plant and equipment).

SOLUTION EXHIBIT 8-22

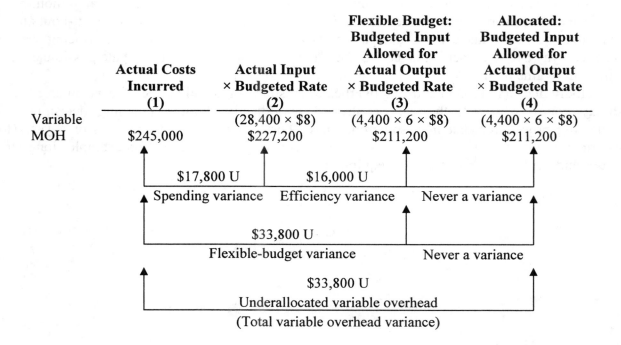

	Actual Costs Incurred (1)	Actual Input × Budgeted Rate (2)	Flexible Budget: Budgeted Input Allowed for Actual Output × Budgeted Rate (3)	Allocated: Budgeted Input Allowed for Actual Output × Budgeted Rate (4)
Variable MOH	$245,000	(28,400 × $8) $227,200	(4,400 × 6 × $8) $211,200	(4,400 × 6 × $8) $211,200

$17,800 U $16,000 U
Spending variance   Efficiency variance   Never a variance

$33,800 U
Flexible-budget variance   Never a variance

$33,800 U
Underallocated variable overhead
(Total variable overhead variance)

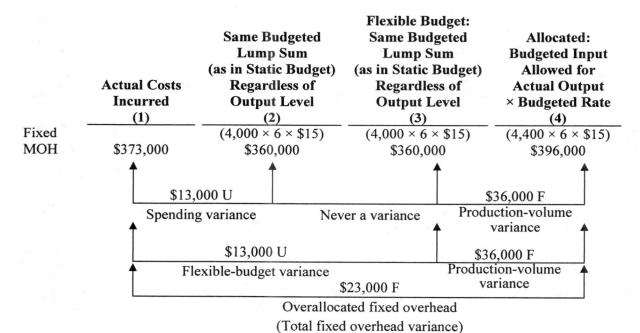

	Actual Costs Incurred (1)	Same Budgeted Lump Sum (as in Static Budget) Regardless of Output Level (2)	Flexible Budget: Same Budgeted Lump Sum (as in Static Budget) Regardless of Output Level (3)	Allocated: Budgeted Input Allowed for Actual Output × Budgeted Rate (4)
Fixed MOH	$373,000	(4,000 × 6 × $15) $360,000	(4,000 × 6 × $15) $360,000	(4,400 × 6 × $15) $396,000

$13,000 U $36,000 F
Spending variance   Never a variance   Production-volume variance

$13,000 U $36,000 F
Flexible-budget variance   Production-volume variance
$23,000 F
Overallocated fixed overhead
(Total fixed overhead variance)

8-24 (20–25 min.) **Overhead variances, service sector.**

1.

Meals on Wheels (May 2007)	Actual Results	Flexible Budget	Static Budget
Output units (number of deliveries)	8,800	8,800	10,000
Hours per delivery	0.65[a]	0.70	0.70
Hours of delivery time	5,720	6,160[b]	7,000[b]
Variable overhead costs per delivery hour	$1.80[c]	$1.50	$1.50
Variable overhead (VOH) costs	$10,296	$9,240[d]	$10,500[d]
Fixed overhead costs	$38,600	$35,000	$35,000
Fixed overhead cost per hour			$5.00[e]

[a] 5,720 hours ÷ 8,800 deliveries = 0.65 hours. per delivery
[b] hrs. per delivery × number of deliveries
[c] $10,296 VOH costs ÷ 5,720 delivery hours = $1.80 per delivery hour.
[d] Delivery hours. × VOH cost per delivery hour
[e] Static budget delivery hours = 10,000 units × 0.70 hours/unit = 7,000 hours;
    Fixed overhead rate = Fixed overhead costs ÷ Static budget delivery hours = $35,000 ÷ 7,000 hours = $5 per hour

VARIABLE OVERHEAD

Actual Costs Incurred	Actual Input Qty. × Budgeted Rate	Flexible Budget: Budgeted Input Qty. Allowed for Actual Output × Budgeted Rate
	5,720 hrs × $1.50 per hr.	6,160 hrs × $1.50 per hr.
$10,296	$8,580	$9,240

$1,716 U $660 F
Spending variance   Efficiency variance

2.

FIXED OVERHEAD

Actual Costs Incurred	Flexible Budget: Same Budgeted Lump Sum (as in Static Budget) Regardless of Output Level	Allocated: Budgeted Input Qty. Allowed for Actual Output × Budgeted Rate
		8,800 units × 0.70 hrs./unit × $5/hr.
		6,160 hrs. × $5/hr.
$38,600	$35,000	$30,800

$3,600 U $4,200 U
Spending variance   Production-volume variance

3.   The spending variances for variable and fixed overhead are both unfavorable. This means that MOW had increases over budget in either or both the cost of individual items (such as telephone calls and gasoline) in the overhead cost pools, or the usage of these individual items per unit of the allocation base (delivery time). The favorable efficiency variance for variable overhead costs results from more efficient use of the cost allocation base—each delivery takes 0.65 hours versus a budgeted 0.70 hours.

     MOW can best manage its fixed overhead costs by long-term planning of capacity rather than day-to-day decisions. This involves planning to undertake only value-added fixed-overhead activities and then determining the appropriate level for those activities. Most fixed overhead costs are committed well before they are incurred. In contrast, for variable overhead, a mix of long-run planning and daily monitoring of the use of individual items is required to manage costs efficiently. MOW should plan to undertake only value-added variable-overhead activities (a long-run focus) and then manage the cost drivers of those activities in the most efficient way (a short-run focus).

     There is no production-volume variance for variable overhead costs. The unfavorable production-volume variance for fixed overhead costs arises because MOW has unused fixed overhead resources that it may seek to reduce in the long run.

8-26 (30 min.) **Overhead variances, missing information.**

1.   In the columnar presentation of variable overhead variance analysis, all numbers shown in bold are calculated from the given information, in the order (a) – (e).

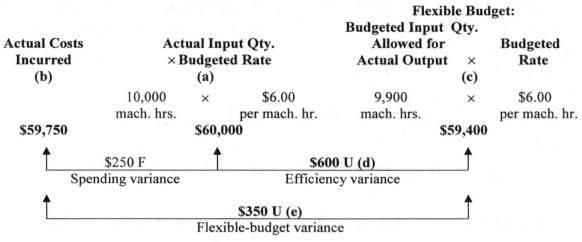

VARIABLE MANUFACTURING OVERHEAD

Actual Costs Incurred (b)	Actual Input Qty. × Budgeted Rate (a)	Flexible Budget: Budgeted Input Qty. Allowed for Actual Output (c)	Budgeted Rate
	10,000 mach. hrs. × $6.00 per mach. hr.	9,900 mach. hrs. ×	$6.00 per mach. hr.
$59,750	$60,000	$59,400	

$250 F — Spending variance

$600 U (d) — Efficiency variance

$350 U (e) — Flexible-budget variance

a.   10,000 machine-hours × $6 per machine-hour = $60,000

b.   Actual VMOH = $60,000 – $250F (VOH spending variance) = $59,750

c.   9,900 machine-hours × $6 per machine-hour = $59,400

d.   VOH efficiency variance = $60,000 – $59,400 = $600U

e.   VOH flexible budget variance = $600U – $250F = $350U

Allocated variable overhead will be the same as the flexible budget variable overhead of $59,400. The actual variable overhead cost is $59,750. Therefore, variable overhead is underallocated by $350.

2. In the columnar presentation of fixed overhead variance analysis, all numbers shown in bold are calculated from the given information, in the order (a) – (e).

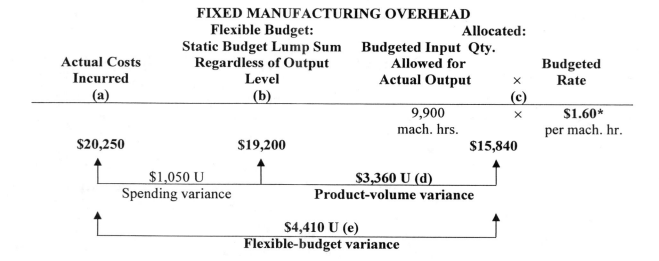

FIXED MANUFACTURING OVERHEAD

Actual Costs Incurred (a)	Flexible Budget: Static Budget Lump Sum Regardless of Output Level (b)	Allocated: Budgeted Input Qty. Allowed for Actual Output	×	Budgeted Rate (c)
		9,900 mach. hrs.	×	$1.60* per mach. hr.
$20,250	$19,200			$15,840

$1,050 U
Spending variance

$3,360 U (d)
Product-volume variance

$4,410 U (e)
Flexible-budget variance

a. Actual FOH costs = $80,000 total overhead costs – $59,750 VOH costs = $20,250

b. Static budget FOH lump sum = $20,250 – $1,050 spending variance = $19,200

c. *FOH allocation rate = $19,200 FOH static-budget lump sum ÷ 12,000 static-budget machine-hours
   = $1.60 per machine-hour
   Allocated FOH = 9,900 machine-hours × $1.60 per machine-hour = $15,840

d. PVV = $19,200 – $15,840 = $3,360U

e. FOH flexible budget variance = $1,050 + $3,360 = $4,410U

Allocated fixed overhead is $15,840. The actual fixed overhead cost is $20,250. Therefore, fixed overhead is underallocated by $4,410.

8-28 (40 min.)   **Flexible-budget variances, review of Chapters 7 and 8.**

1.

	Actual	Flexible Budget	Static Budget
No. of copies	320,000	320,000	300,000
Newsprint pages per copy	54[b]		50[a]
Number of pages of newsprint	17,280,000	16,000,000[c]	15,000,000
Cost per newsprint page	$ 0.013[e]		$ 0.012[d]
Cost of newsprint (direct materials)	$ 224,640	$ 192,000[f]	$ 180,000
VOH cost per newsprint page	$ 0.0037[h]		$ 0.0040[g]
Variable overhead	$ 63,936	$ 64,000[i]	$ 60,000
Fixed overhead	$ 97,000	$ 90,000	$ 90,000
FOH allocated per newsprint page			$ 0.0060[j]

[a]Budgeted newsprint pages per copy = 15,000,000 ÷ 300,000 = 50
[b]Actual newsprint pages per copy = 17,280,000 ÷ 320,000 = 54
[c]50 newsprint pages per copy × 320,000 copies = 16,000,000 newsprint pages
[d]Budgeted cost per newsprint page = $180,000 ÷ 15,000,000 = $0.012 per page
[e]Actual cost per newsprint page = $224,640 ÷ 17,280,000 = $0.013 per page
[f]Flexible budget cost of newsprint = $0.012 × 16,000,000 = $192,000
[g]Budgeted VOH per newsprint page = $60,000 ÷ 15,000,000 = $0.0040 per page
[h]Actual VOH per newsprint page = $63,936 ÷ 17,280,000 = $0.0037 per page
[i]Flexible budget VOH = $0.0040 × 16,000,000 = $64,000
[j]FOH allocated per page = $90,000 ÷ 15,000,000 = $0.0060 per page

	Actual	Price Variance	Actual Input Qty. × Budgeted Price	Efficiency Variance	Flexible Budget
Direct materials	224,640	$17,280 U	$207,360[a]	$15,360 U	$192,000
Variable overhead	$ 63,936	$ 5,184 F	$ 69,120[b]	$ 5,120 U	$ 64,000

	Actual	Spending Variance	Static/Flexible Budget Lump Sum	Production Volume Variance	Allocated
Fixed overhead	$ 97,000	$ 7,000 U	$ 90,000	$ 6,000 F	$ 96,000[c]

[a]17,280,000 pages × $0.012 DM per page = $207,360
[b]17,280,000 pages × $0.0040 VOH per page = $69,120
[c]16,000,000 pages × $0.0060 per page = $96,000

2.   The largest individual variance category is for direct materials—comprising a $17,280 U price variance (the actual cost per page of $0.013 exceeds the budgeted $0.012 per page) and a $15,360 U efficiency variance (the 1,280,000 (17,280,00 – 16,000,000) unusable pages × $0.012 budgeted cost).

      The variable overhead spending variance of $5,184 F is due to the actual variable overhead costs per newsprint page being less than budgeted ($0.0037 versus $0.0040).

      The unfavorable variable overhead efficiency variance of $5,120 U is due to 1,280,000 extra pages being used (the cost allocation base) over that budgeted for the actual level of output.

      The fixed overhead spending variance is due to actual costs being $7,000 above the budgeted $90,000. An analysis of the line items in this budget would help assist in determining the causes of this variance.

      The production-volume variance of $6,000 F arises because the denominator used to allocate the $90,000 of fixed indirect costs is 15,000,000 budgeted newsprint pages rather than the 16,000,000 actual newsprint pages which are used because actual output is 320,000 newspapers versus 300,000 budgeted.

8-30 (60 min.) **Journal entries (continuation of 8-29).**

1. Key information underlying the computation of variances is:

	Actual Results	Flexible Budget Amount	Static-Budget Amount
1. Output units (panels)	19,200	19,200	17,760
2. Machine-hours	36,480	38,400	35,520
3. Machine-hours per panel	1.90	2.00	2.00
4. Variable MOH costs	$1,532,160	$1,536,000	$1,420,800
5. Variable MOH costs per machine-hour (Row 4 ÷ Row 2)	$42.00	$40.00	$40.00
6. Variable MOH costs per unit (Row 4 ÷ Row 1)	$79.80	$80.00	$80.00
7. Fixed MOH costs	$7,004,160	$6,961,920	$6,961,920
8. Fixed MOH costs per machine-hour (Row 7 ÷ Row 2)	$192.00	$181.30	$196.00
9. Fixed MOH costs per unit (7 ÷ 1)	$364.80	$362.60	$392.00

Solution Exhibit 8-30 shows the computation of the variances.

Journal entries for variable MOH, year ended December 31, 2006:

Variable MOH Control	1,532,160	
Accounts Payable Control and Other Accounts		1,532,160
Work-in-Process Control	1,536,000	
Variable MOH Allocated		1,536,000
Variable MOH Allocated	1,536,000	
Variable MOH Spending Variance	72,960	
Variable MOH Control		1,532,160
Variable MOH Efficiency Variance		76,800

Journal entries for fixed MOH, year ended December 31, 2006:

Fixed MOH Control	7,004,160	
Wages Payable, Accumulated Depreciation, etc.		7,004,160
Work-in-Process Control	7,526,400	
Fixed MOH Allocated		7,526,400
Fixed MOH Allocated	7,526,400	
Fixed MOH Spending Variance	42,240	
Fixed MOH Control		7,004,160
Fixed MOH Production-Volume Variance		564,480

2. Adjustment of COGS

Variable MOH Efficiency Variance	76,800	
Fixed MOH Production-Volume Variance	564,480	
Variable MOH Spending Variance		72,960
Fixed MOH Spending Variance		42,240
Cost of Goods Sold		526,080

SOLUTION EXHIBIT 8-30

Variable Manufacturing Overhead

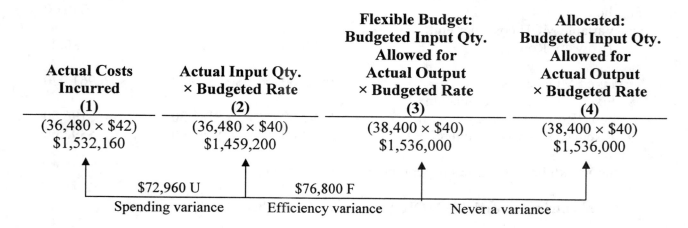

Fixed Manufacturing Overhead

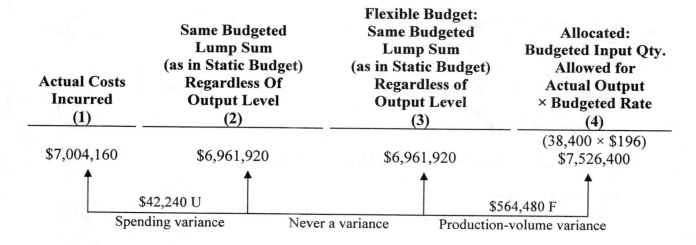

8-32 (30 min.) **4-variance analysis, find the unknowns.**

Known figures denoted by an *

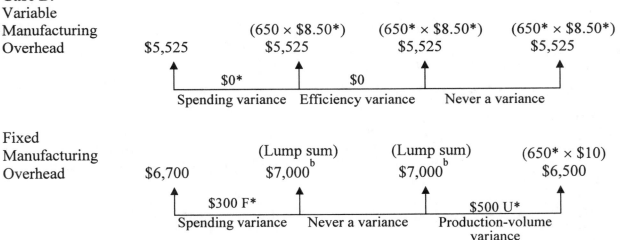

	Actual Costs Incurred	Actual Input Qty. × Budgeted Rate	Flexible Budget: Budgeted Input Qty. Allowed for Actual Output × Budgeted Rate	Allocated: Budgeted Input Qty. Allowed for Actual Output × Budgeted Rate
Case A: Variable Manufacturing Overhead	$7,000*	(530 × $15) $7,950	(500* × $15) $7,500*	(500* × $15) $7,500*

$950* F Spending variance $450 U Efficiency variance   Never a variance

| Fixed Manufacturing Overhead | $10,600* | (Lump sum) $10,000* | (Lump sum) $10,000* | (500 × $20^{a}) $10,000* |

$600 U Spending variance   Never a variance $0 Production-volume variance

Total budgeted manufacturing overhead = $7,500 + $10,000 = $17,500

| **Case B:** Variable Manufacturing Overhead | $5,525 | (650 × $8.50*) $5,525 | (650* × $8.50*) $5,525 | (650* × $8.50*) $5,525 |

$0* Spending variance $0 Efficiency variance   Never a variance

| Fixed Manufacturing Overhead | $6,700 | (Lump sum) $7,000^{b} | (Lump sum) $7,000^{b} | (650* × $10) $6,500 |

$300 F* Spending variance   Never a variance $500 U* Production-volume variance

Denominator level = Budgeted FMOH costs ÷ Budgeted FMOH rate = $7,000 ÷ $10 = 700 hours

Case C:

Variable
Manufacturing
Overhead

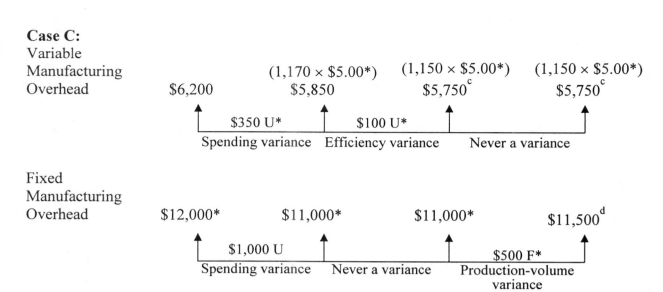

	$(1{,}170 \times \$5.00^*)$	$(1{,}150 \times \$5.00^*)$	$(1{,}150 \times \$5.00^*)$
\$6,200	\$5,850	\$5,750[c]	\$5,750[c]

       \$350 U*   \$100 U*

  Spending variance   Efficiency variance   Never a variance

Fixed
Manufacturing
Overhead

\$12,000*	\$11,000*	\$11,000*	\$11,500[d]

     \$1,000 U   \$500 F*

  Spending variance   Never a variance   Production-volume
                                           variance

Total budgeted manufacturing overhead = \$5,750 + \$11,000 = \$16,750

[a]Budgeted FMOH rate = Budgeted FMOH costs ÷ Denominator level = \$10,000 ÷ 500 = \$20

[b]
$$\text{Budgeted total overhead} = \text{Budgeted fixed manuf. overhead} + \text{Budgeted variable manuf. overhead}$$

$$\$12{,}525^* = \text{BFMOH} + (650 \times \$8.50)$$
$$\text{BFMOH} = \$7{,}000$$

[c] Budgeted hours allowed for actual output achieved must be derived from the output level variance before this figure can be derived, or, since the fixed manufacturing overhead rate is \$11,000 ÷ 1,100 = \$10, and the allocated amount is \$11,500, the budgeted hours allowed for the actual output achieved must be 1,150 (\$11,500 ÷ \$10).

[d] $1{,}150 \times (\$11{,}000^* \div 1{,}100^*) = \$11{,}500$

8-34 (20 min.) **Overhead analysis, sensitivity to denominator volume.**

1.

	Actual	Flexible Budget	Static Budget	
Production and sales in units	110,000	110,000	120,000	
Machine hours	30,000	33,000	36,000	
Fixed manuf. overhead	$440,000	$450,000	$ 450,000	
Variable manuf. overhead	$960,000	$990,000[a]	$1,080,000[b]	
Variable manuf. overhead rate = VMOH ÷ machine-hours	$ 32.00		$ 30.00	per machine-hour
Fixed Overhead Rate = FMOH ÷ machine-hours			$ 12.50	per machine-hour

[a]$30 per machine-hour × 33,000 machine-hours = $990,000
[b]$30 per machine-hour × 36,000 machine-hours = $1,080,000

Variable Manufacturing Overhead

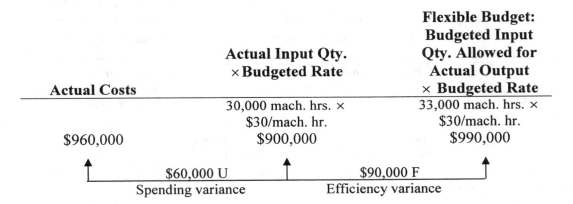

2.

Fixed Manufacturing Overhead

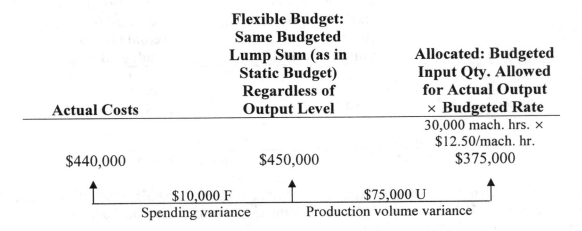

3.

	Actual	Flexible Budget	Static Budget	
Production and sales in units	110,000	110,000	150,000	
Machine hours	30,000	33,000	45,000	
Fixed manuf. overhead	$440,000	$450,000	$450,000	
Variable manuf. overhead	$960,000	$990,000	$1,350,000[a]	
Variable manuf. overhead rate =				
VMOH ÷ machine hours	$32.00		$30.00	per machine-hour
Fixed overhead rate =				
FMOH ÷ machine hours			$10.00	per machine-hour

[a] $30 per machine-hour × 45,000 machine-hours = $1,350,000

Variable Manufacturing Overhead

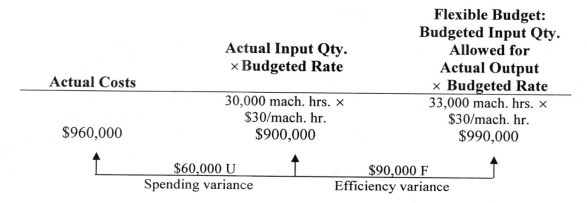

Fixed Manufacturing Overhead

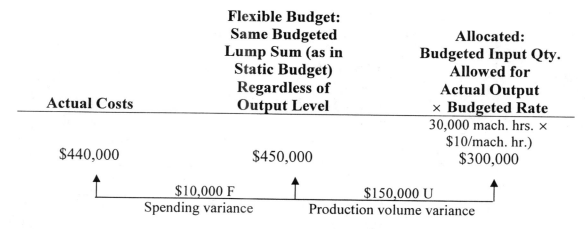

Note that with the change in the denominator volume, only the FMOH production-volume variance has changed. Variable manufacturing overhead is *variable* so the budgeted volume change has no effect on the VMOH variances.

4. If Armstrong writes off all variances to cost of goods sold, and if there are no inventories, then the change in the production volume variance between requirement 2 and requirement 3 will not affect the cost of goods sold or the operating income. After variances have been written off, COGS will include the actual fixed overhead costs of $440,000. In the requirement 2 setting, COGS will initially have the allocated $375,000 of fixed overhead, and at the end of the accounting period U will also be debited $75,000 for the production volume variance and credited $10,000 for the spending variance, resulting in a COGS of $440,000 (the actual FOH costs). In the requirement 3 setting, COGS will initially have the allocated $300,000 of fixed overhead, and at the end of the accounting period U will also be debited $150,000 for the production volume variance and credited $10,000 for the spending variance, resulting in a COGS of $440,000 (the actual FOH costs). The end result will be the same COGS in either situation. This is not the case if Armstrong has inventories as we will see in Chapter 9.

8-36 (40 min.) **Activity-based costing, variance analysis.**

1.

	Static-Budget Amounts	Actual Amounts
a. Units of TGC produced and sold	30,000	22,500
b. Batch size	250	225
c. Number of batches (a ÷ b)	120	100
d. Setup-hours per batch	5	5.25
e. Total setup-hours (c × d)	600	525
f. Variable overhead cost per setup-hour	$25	$24
g. Variable setup overhead costs (e × f)	$15,000	$12,600
h. Total fixed setup overhead costs	$18,000	$17,535
i. Fixed overhead cost per setup-hour (h ÷ e)	$30	$33.40

The flexible-budget is based on the budgeted number of setups for the actual output achieved:
22,500 units ÷ 250 units per batch= 90 batches

Computation of variable setup overhead cost variances follows:

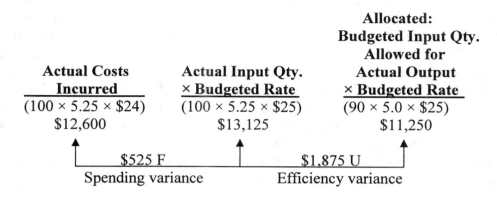

	Actual Costs Incurred	Actual Input Qty. × Budgeted Rate	Allocated: Budgeted Input Qty. Allowed for Actual Output × Budgeted Rate
	(100 × 5.25 × $24)	(100 × 5.25 × $25)	(90 × 5.0 × $25)
	$12,600	$13,125	$11,250

$525 F ← Spending variance → $1,875 U ← Efficiency variance

The favorable spending variance is due to the actual variable overhead cost per setup-hour declining from the budgeted $25 per hour to the actual rate of $24 per hour. The unfavorable efficiency variance is due to the actual output of 22,500 units (1) requiring more setups (100) than the budgeted amount (90), and (2) each setup taking longer time (5.25 hours) than the budgeted time (5.0 hours). The flexible-budget variance of $1,350 U reflects the larger unfavorable efficiency variance not being offset by the favorable spending variance.

2.   Computation of the fixed setup overhead cost variances follows:

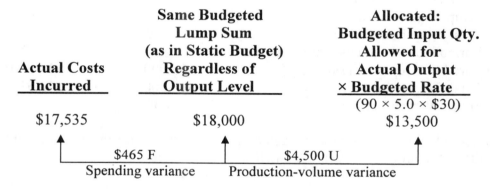

	Actual Costs Incurred	Same Budgeted Lump Sum (as in Static Budget) Regardless of Output Level	Allocated: Budgeted Input Qty. Allowed for Actual Output × Budgeted Rate
			(90 × 5.0 × $30)
	$17,535	$18,000	$13,500

$465 F ← Spending variance → $4,500 U ← Production-volume variance

The fixed setup overhead cost spending variance is $465 F because the amount of actual costs was lower than the budgeted amount of $18,000. The production-volume variance is $4,500 U because the actual units of TGC produced and sold require fewer budgeted setup-hours than the budgeted setup-hour capacity available. Toymaster would want to evaluate why actual units sold were much less than budgeted. Was it dues to a decline in market size, loss of market share, poor quality or increased competition?

8-38 (30 min.) **Comprehensive overhead variance analyses.**

	Actual	Flexible Budget	Static Budget	
Production volume (bottles)	450,000	450,000	420,000	
Bottling machine hours	3,000	3,000 [a]	2,800	
Variable overhead	$153,000	$150,000	$140,000	
Fixed overhead	$960,000	$980,000	$980,000	
Variable overhead rate =				
Variable overhead ÷ machine-hours	$ 51		$ 50	per machine-hour
Fixed overhead rate =				
Fixed overhead ÷ machine-hours			$ 350	per machine-hour

[a] (2,800 machine-hours ÷ 420,000 bottles) × 450,000 bottles = 3,000 machine-hours

1.

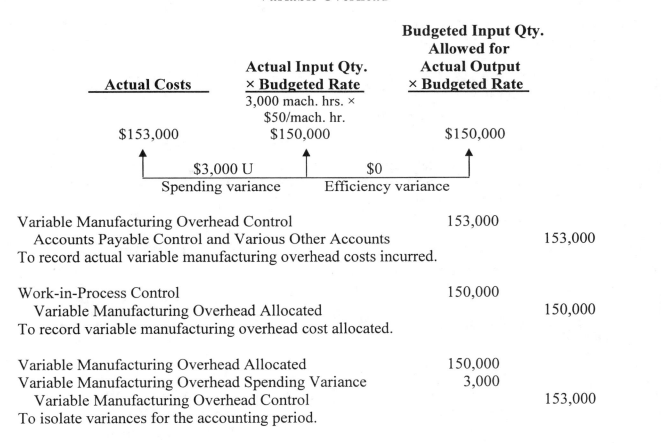

Variable Overhead

	Actual Costs	Actual Input Qty. × Budgeted Rate	Budgeted Input Qty. Allowed for Actual Output × Budgeted Rate
		3,000 mach. hrs. × $50/mach. hr.	
	$153,000	$150,000	$150,000

$3,000 U $0
Spending variance   Efficiency variance

Variable Manufacturing Overhead Control	153,000	
Accounts Payable Control and Various Other Accounts		153,000
To record actual variable manufacturing overhead costs incurred.		

Work-in-Process Control	150,000	
Variable Manufacturing Overhead Allocated		150,000
To record variable manufacturing overhead cost allocated.		

Variable Manufacturing Overhead Allocated	150,000	
Variable Manufacturing Overhead Spending Variance	3,000	
Variable Manufacturing Overhead Control		153,000
To isolate variances for the accounting period.		

2.

	Actual Costs (1)	Flexible Budget: Same Budgeted Lump Sum (as in Static Budget) Regardless of Output Level (2)	Allocated: Budgeted Input Qty. Allowed for Actual Output × Budgeted Rate (3)
			3,000 mach. hrs. × $350/mach. hr.
	$960,000	$980,000	$1,050,000

$20,000 F $70,000 F
Spending variance   Production volume variance

Fixed Manufacturing Overhead Control	960,000	
Salaries payable, Accumulated Depreciation, etc.		960,000
To record actual fixed overhead costs incurred.		
Work-in-Process Control	1,050,000	
Fixed Manufacturing Overhead Allocated		1,050,000
To record fixed manufacturing overhead cost allocated.		
Fixed Manufacturing Overhead Allocated	1,050,000	
Fixed Manufacturing Overhead Spending Variance		20,000
Fixed Manufacturing Overhead Production-Volume Variance		70,000
Fixed Manufacturing Overhead Control		960,000
To isolate variances for the accounting period.		

3.	Fixed Manufacturing Overhead Spending Variance	20,000	
	Variable Manufacturing Overhead Spending Variance		3,000
	Cost of Goods Sold		17,000

To write-off variable overhead variances and fixed overhead spending variance to Cost of Goods Sold

	Balances (1)	Balances as percentage of $4,800,000 (2)	Production-Volume Variance Allocated (3) = $70,000 × (2)
Work-in-Process Inventory	$ 900,000	18.75%	$13,125
Finished Good Inventory	$1,500,000	31.25%	21,875
Cost of Goods Sold	$2,400,000	50.00%	35,000
Total	$4,800,000		$70,000

Since the production-volume variance is a favorable variance, its prorated allocation to work-in-process inventory, finished goods inventory and cost of goods sold will result in a credit to each of those accounts.

Fixed Manufacturing Overhead Production-Volume Variance	70,000	
Work-in-Process Control		13,125
Finished Goods Control		21,875
Cost of Goods Sold		35,000

To write-off the production volume variance to WIP, FG, and COGS.

4.   If the plant manager's bonus is based on controlling cost of goods sold, and if fixed overhead production volume variance is written off to cost of goods sold, there is a potential for manipulation on the part of the manager. Being knowledgeable about the production process, she could be tempted to set the plant standards such that there is often a favorable production volume variance, which would ultimately reduce the period's cost of goods sold. The proration method is less susceptible to this problem because it spreads or blunts the benefit of a favorable production volume variance. The proration method would also reduce the negative effect of an unfavorable production volume variance on cost of goods sold (relative to the full write-off). In this sense, prorating may be better, given the bonus scheme—it makes manipulation less likely by reducing the upside of a favorable PVV and also reducing the downside of an unfavorable PVV.

8-40   (30–50 min.)   **Review of Chapters 7 and 8, 3-variance analysis.**

1.   Total standard production costs are based on 7,800 units of output.

Direct materials, 7,800 × $15.00	
7,800 × 3 lbs. × $5.00 (or 23,400 lbs. × $5.00)	$ 117,000
Direct manufacturing labor, 7,800 × $75.00	
7,800 × 5 hrs. × $15.00 (or 39,000 hrs. × $15.00)	585,000
Manufacturing overhead:	
Variable, 7,800 × $30.00 (or 39,000 hrs. × $6.00)	234,000
Fixed, 7,800 × $40.00 (or 39,000 hrs. × $8.00)	312,000
Total	$1,248,000

The following is for later use:
Fixed manufacturing overhead, a lump-sum budget $320,000[*]

$$^*\text{Fixed manufacturing overhead rate} = \frac{\text{Budgeted fixed manufacturing overhead}}{\text{Denominator level}}$$

$$\$8.00 = \frac{\text{Budget}}{40,000 \text{ hours}}$$

$$\text{Budget} = 40,000 \text{ hours} \times \$8.00 = \$320,000$$

2.   Solution Exhibit 8-40 presents a columnar presentation of the variances. An overview of the 3-variance analysis using the block format of the text is:

3-Variance Analysis	Spending Variance	Efficiency Variance	Production Volume Variance
Total Manufacturing Overhead	$39,400 U	$6,600 U	$8,000 U

SOLUTION EXHIBIT 8-40

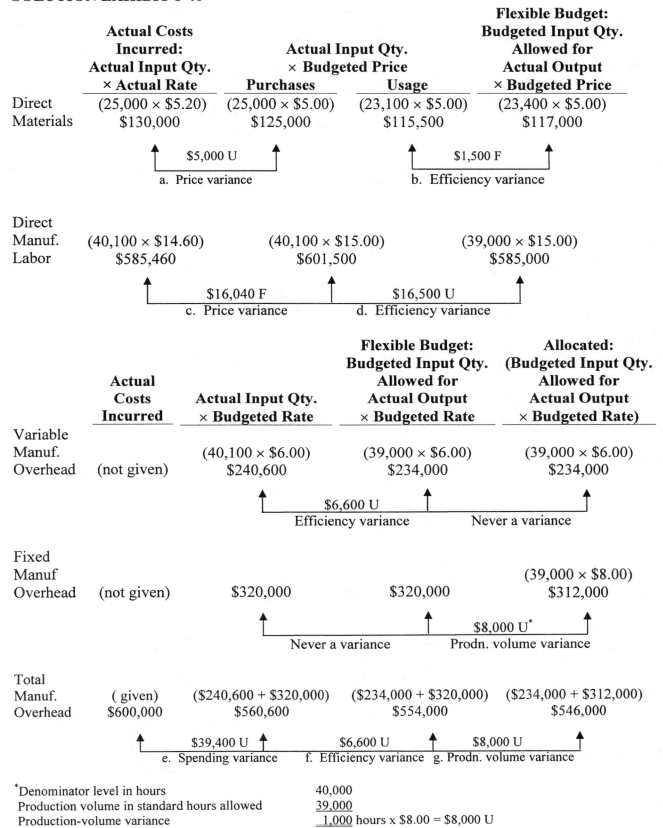

	Actual Costs Incurred: Actual Input Qty. × Actual Rate	Actual Input Qty. × Budgeted Price Purchases	Actual Input Qty. × Budgeted Price Usage	Flexible Budget: Budgeted Input Qty. Allowed for Actual Output × Budgeted Price
Direct Materials	(25,000 × $5.20) $130,000	(25,000 × $5.00) $125,000	(23,100 × $5.00) $115,500	(23,400 × $5.00) $117,000

↑ $5,000 U ↑
a. Price variance

↑ $1,500 F ↑
b. Efficiency variance

Direct Manuf. Labor	(40,100 × $14.60) $585,460	(40,100 × $15.00) $601,500		(39,000 × $15.00) $585,000

↑ $16,040 F ↑
c. Price variance

↑ $16,500 U ↑
d. Efficiency variance

	Actual Costs Incurred	Actual Input Qty. × Budgeted Rate	Flexible Budget: Budgeted Input Qty. Allowed for Actual Output × Budgeted Rate	Allocated: (Budgeted Input Qty. Allowed for Actual Output × Budgeted Rate)
Variable Manuf. Overhead	(not given)	(40,100 × $6.00) $240,600	(39,000 × $6.00) $234,000	(39,000 × $6.00) $234,000

↑ $6,600 U ↑
Efficiency variance

Never a variance

Fixed Manuf Overhead	(not given)	$320,000	$320,000	(39,000 × $8.00) $312,000

↑ Never a variance ↑

↑ $8,000 U* ↑
Prodn. volume variance

Total Manuf. Overhead	(given) $600,000	($240,600 + $320,000) $560,600	($234,000 + $320,000) $554,000	($234,000 + $312,000) $546,000

↑ $39,400 U ↑
e. Spending variance

↑ $6,600 U ↑
f. Efficiency variance

↑ $8,000 U ↑
g. Prodn. volume variance

*Denominator level in hours   40,000
Production volume in standard hours allowed   39,000
Production-volume variance   1,000 hours x $8.00 = $8,000 U

CHAPTER 9
INVENTORY COSTING AND CAPACITY ANALYSIS

9-2   The term direct costing is a misnomer for variable costing for two reasons:
a. Variable costing does not include all direct costs as inventoriable costs. Only variable direct manufacturing costs are included. Any fixed direct manufacturing costs, and any direct nonmanufacturing costs (either variable or fixed), are excluded from inventoriable costs.
b. Variable costing includes as inventoriable costs not only direct manufacturing costs but also some indirect costs (variable indirect manufacturing costs).

9-4   The main issue between variable costing and absorption costing is the proper timing of the release of fixed manufacturing costs as costs of the period:
a. at the time of incurrence, or
b. at the time the finished units to which the fixed overhead relates are sold.
Variable costing uses (a) and absorption costing uses (b).

9-6   Variable costing does not view fixed costs as unimportant or irrelevant, but it maintains that the distinction between behaviors of different costs is crucial for certain decisions. The planning and management of fixed costs is critical, irrespective of what inventory costing method is used.

9-8   (a) The factors that affect the breakeven point under variable costing are:
1. Fixed (manufacturing and operating) costs.
2. Contribution margin per unit.

(b) The factors that affect the breakeven point under absorption costing are:
1. Fixed (manufacturing and operating) costs.
2. Contribution margin per unit.
3. Production level in units in excess of breakeven sales in units.
4. Denominator level chosen to set the fixed manufacturing cost rate.

9-10   Approaches used to reduce the negative aspects associated with using absorption costing include:
a. Change the accounting system:
- Adopt either variable or throughput costing, both of which reduce the incentives of managers to produce for inventory.
- Adopt an inventory holding charge for managers who tie up funds in inventory.
b. Extend the time period used to evaluate performance. By evaluating performance over a longer time period (say, 3 to 5 years), the incentive to take short-run actions that reduce long-term income is lessened.
c. Include nonfinancial as well as financial variables in the measures used to evaluate performance.

9-12   The *downward demand spiral* is the continuing reduction in demand for a company's product that occurs when the prices of competitors' products are not met and (as demand drops further), higher and higher unit costs result in more and more reluctance to meet competitors' prices. Pricing decisions need to consider competitors and customers as well as costs.

9-14 For tax reporting in the U.S., the IRS requires companies to use the practical capacity concept. At year-end, proration of any variances between inventories and cost of goods sold is required (unless the variance is immaterial in amount).

9-16 (30 min.) **Variable and absorption costing, explaining operating-income differences.**

1. Key inputs for income statement computations are

	April	May
Beginning inventory	0	150
Production	500	400
Goods available for sale	500	550
Units sold	350	520
Ending inventory	150	30

The budgeted fixed cost per unit and budgeted total manufacturing cost per unit under absorption costing are

		April	May
(a)	Budgeted fixed manufacturing costs	$2,000,000	$2,000,000
(b)	Budgeted production	500	500
(c)=(a)÷(b)	Budgeted fixed manufacturing cost per unit	$4,000	$4,000
(d)	Budgeted variable manufacturing cost per unit	$10,000	$10,000
(e)=(c)+(d)	Budgeted total manufacturing cost per unit	$14,000	$14,000

(a) Variable costing

	April 2006		May 2006	
Revenues[a]		$8,400,000		$12,480,000
Variable costs				
Beginning inventory	$ 0		$1,500,000	
Variable manufacturing costs[b]	5,000,000		4,000,000	
Cost of goods available for sale	5,000,000		5,500,000	
Deduct ending inventory[c]	1,500,000		300,000	
Variable cost of goods sold	3,500,000		5,200,000	
Variable operating costs[d]	1,050,000		1,560,000	
Total variable costs		4,550,000		6,760,000
Contribution margin		3,850,000		5,720,000
Fixed costs				
Fixed manufacturing costs	2,000,000		2,000,000	
Fixed operating costs	600,000		600,000	
Total fixed costs		2,600,000		2,600,000
Operating income		$1,250,000		$3,120,000

[a] $24,000 × 350; $24,000 × 520
[b] $10,000 × 500; $10,000 × 400
[c] $10,000 × 150; $10,000 × 30
[d] $3,000 × 350; $3,000 × 520

(b)   Absorption costing

	April 2006		May 2006	
Revenues[a]		$8,400,000		$12,480,000
Cost of goods sold				
Beginning inventory	$ 0		$2,100,000	
Variable manufacturing costs[b]	5,000,000		4,000,000	
Allocated fixed manufacturing costs[c]	2,000,000		1,600,000	
Cost of goods available for sale	7,000,000		7,700,000	
Deduct ending inventory[d]	2,100,000		420,000	
Adjustment for prod.-vol. variance[e]	0		400,000 U	
Cost of goods sold		4,900,000		7,680,000
Gross margin		3,500,000		4,800,000
Operating costs				
Variable operating costs[f]	1,050,000		1,560,000	
Fixed operating costs	600,000		600,000	
Total operating costs		1,650,000		2,160,000
Operating income		$1,850,000		$ 2,640,000

[a] $24,000 × 350; $24,000 × 520
[b] $10,000 × 500; $10,000 × 400
[c] $4,000 × 500; $4,000 × 400
[d] $14,000 × 150; $14,000 × 30
[e] $2,000,000 – $2,000,000; $2,000,000 – $1,600,000
[f] $3,000 × 350; $3,000 × 520

2. $\left(\begin{array}{c}\text{Absorption-costing}\\\text{operating income}\end{array}\right) - \left(\begin{array}{c}\text{Variable-costing}\\\text{operating income}\end{array}\right) = \left(\begin{array}{c}\text{Fixed manufacturing}\\\text{costs in}\\\text{ending inventory}\end{array}\right) - \left(\begin{array}{c}\text{Fixed manufacturing}\\\text{costs in}\\\text{beginning inventory}\end{array}\right)$

April:

$$\$1,850,000 - \$1,250,000 = (\$4,000 \times 150) - (\$0)$$
$$\$600,000 = \$600,000$$

May:

$$\$2,640,000 - \$3,120,000 = (\$4,000 \times 30) - (\$4,000 \times 150)$$
$$-\$480,000 = \$120,000 - \$600,000$$
$$-\$480,000 = -\$480,000$$

The difference between absorption and variable costing is due solely to moving fixed manufacturing costs into inventories as inventories increase (as in April) and out of inventories as they decrease (as in May).

9-18 (40 min.) **Variable and absorption costing, explaining operating-income differences.**

1.   Key inputs for income statement computations are:

	January	February	March
Beginning inventory	0	300	300
Production	1,000	800	1,250
Goods available for sale	1,000	1,100	1,550
Units sold	700	800	1,500
Ending inventory	300	300	50

The budgeted fixed manufacturing cost per unit and budgeted total manufacturing cost per unit under absorption costing are:

		January	February	March
(a)	Budgeted fixed manufacturing costs	$400,000	$400,000	$400,000
(b)	Budgeted production	1,000	1,000	1,000
(c)=(a)÷(b)	Budgeted fixed manufacturing cost per unit	$400	$400	$400
(d)	Budgeted variable manufacturing cost per unit	$900	$900	$900
(e)=(c)+(d)	Budgeted total manufacturing cost per unit	$1,300	$1,300	$1,300

(a)   Variable Costing

	January 2007		February 2007		March 2007	
Revenues[a]		$1,750,000		$2,000,000		$3,750,000
Variable costs						
Beginning inventory[b]	$ 0		$270,000		$ 270,000	
Variable manufacturing costs[c]	900,000		720,000		1,125,000	
Cost of goods available for sale	900,000		990,000		1,395,000	
Ending inventory[d]	270,000		270,000		45,000	
Variable cost of goods sold	630,000		720,000		1,350,000	
Variable operating costs[e]	420,000		480,000		900,000	
Total variable costs		1,050,000		1,200,000		2,250,000
Contribution margin		700,000		800,000		1,500,000
Fixed costs						
Fixed manufacturing costs	400,000		400,000		400,000	
Fixed operating costs	140,000		140,000		140,000	
Total fixed costs		540,000		540,000		540,000
Operating income		$ 160,000		$ 260,000		$ 960,000

[a] $2,500 × 700; $2,500 × 800; $2,500 × 1,500
[b] $? × 0; $900 × 300; $900 × 300
[c] $900 × 1,000; $900 × 800; $900 × 1,250
[d] $900 × 300; $900 × 300; $900 × 50
[e] $600 × 700; $600 × 800; $600 × 1,500

9-5

(b) Absorption Costing

	January 2007		February 2007		March 2007	
Revenues[a]		$1,750,000		$2,000,000		$3,750,000
Cost of goods sold						
Beginning inventory[b]	$ 0		$ 390,000		$ 390,000	
Variable manufacturing costs[c]	900,000		720,000		1,125,000	
Allocated fixed manufacturing costs[d]	400,000		320,000		500,000	
Cost of goods available for sale	1,300,000		1,430,000		2,015,000	
Deduct ending inventory[e]	390,000		390,000		65,000	
Adjustment for prod. vol. var.[f]	0		80,000 U		100,000 F	
Cost of goods sold		910,000		1,120,000		1,850,000
Gross margin		840,000		880,000		1,900,000
Operating costs						
Variable operating costs[g]	420,000		480,000		900,000	
Fixed operating costs	140,000		140,000		140,000	
Total operating costs		560,000		620,000		1,040,000
Operating income		$ 280,000		$ 260,000		$ 860,000

[a] $2,500 × 700; $2,500 × 800; $2,500 × 1,500
[b] $?× 0; $1,300 × 300; $1,300 × 300
[c] $900 × 1,000; $900 × 800; $900 × 1,250
[d] $400 × 1,000; $400 × 800; $400 × 1,250
[e] $1,300 × 300; $1,300 × 300; $1,300 × 50
[f] $400,000 − $400,000; $400,000 − $320,000; $400,000 − $500,000
[g] $600 × 700; $600 × 800; $600 × 1,500

2.

$$\begin{pmatrix} \text{Absorption-costing} \\ \text{operating income} \end{pmatrix} - \begin{pmatrix} \text{Variable costing} \\ \text{operating income} \end{pmatrix} = \begin{pmatrix} \text{Fixed manufacturing} \\ \text{costs in} \\ \text{ending inventory} \end{pmatrix} - \begin{pmatrix} \text{Fixed manufacturing} \\ \text{costs in} \\ \text{beginning inventory} \end{pmatrix}$$

January:

$$\$280,000 - \$160,000 = (\$400 \times 300) - \$0$$
$$\$120,000 = \$120,000$$

February:

$$\$260,000 - \$260,000 = (\$400 \times 300) - (\$400 \times 300)$$
$$\$0 = \$0$$

March:

$$\$860,000 - \$960,000 = (\$400 \times 50) - (\$400 \times 300)$$
$$-\$100,000 = -\$100,000$$

The difference between absorption and variable costing is due solely to moving fixed manufacturing costs into inventories as inventories increase (as in January) and out of inventories as they decrease (as in March).

9-20 (40 min)   **Variable versus absorption costing.**

1.

Income Statement for the Zwatch Company, Variable Costing
for the Year Ended December 31, 2007

Revenues: $22 × 345,400		$7,598,800
Variable costs		
Beginning inventory: $5.10 × 85,000	$ 433,500	
Variable manufacturing costs: $5.10 × 294,900	1,503,990	
Cost of goods available for sale	1,937,490	
Deduct ending inventory: $5.10 × 34,500	175,950	
Variable cost of goods sold	1,761,540	
Variable operating costs: $1.10 × 345,400	379,940	
Total variable costs (at standard costs)	2,141,480	
Adjustment for variances	0	
Total variable costs		2,141,480
Contribution margin		5,457,320
Fixed costs		
Fixed manufacturing overhead costs	1,440,000	
Fixed operating costs	1,080,000	
Total fixed costs		2,520,000
Operating income		$2,937,320

Absorption Costing Data

Fixed manufacturing overhead allocation rate =
  Fixed manufacturing overhead/Denominator level machine-hours = $1,440,000 ÷ 6,000
                                                    = $240 per machine-hour

Fixed manufacturing overhead allocation rate per unit =
  Fixed manufacturing overhead allocation rate/standard production rate = $240 ÷ 50
                                                    = $4.80 per unit

**Income Statement for the Zwatch Company, Absorption Costing
for the Year Ended December 31, 2007**

Revenues: $22 × 345,400		$7,598,800
Cost of goods sold		
Beginning inventory ($5.10 + $4.80) × 85,000	$ 841,500	
Variable manuf. costs: $5.10 × 294,900	1,503,990	
Allocated fixed manuf. costs: $4.80 × 294,900	1,415,520	
Cost of goods available for sale	$3,761,010	
Deduct ending inventory: ($5.10 + $4.80) × 34,500	(341,550)	
Adjust for manuf. variances ($4.80 × 5,100)[a]	24,480	
Cost of goods sold		3,443,940
Gross margin		4,154,860
Operating costs		
Variable operating costs: $1.10 × 345,400	$ 379,940	
Fixed operating costs	1,080,000	
Total operating costs		1,459,940
Operating income		$2,694,920

[a] Production volume variance $= [(6{,}000 \text{ hours} \times 50) - 294{,}900] \times \$4.80$
$= (300{,}000 - 294{,}900) \times \$4.80$
$= \$24{,}480$

2. Zwatch's operating margins as a percentage of revenues are

Under variable costing:

Revenues	$7,598,800
Operating income	2,937,320
Operating income as percentage of revenues	38.7%

Under absorption costing:

Revenues	$7,598,800
Operating income	2,694,920
Operating income as percentage of revenues	35.5%

3. Operating income using variable costing is about 9% higher than operating income calculated using absorption costing.

Variable costing operating income – Absorption costing operating income =
$$\$2{,}937{,}320 - \$2{,}694{,}920 = \$242{,}400$$

Fixed manufacturing costs in beginning inventory under absorption costing –
Fixed manufacturing costs in ending inventory under absorption costing =
$$(\$4.80 \times 85{,}000) - (\$4.80 \times 34{,}500) = \$242{,}400$$

4. The factors the CFO should consider include
    (a) Effect on managerial behavior.
    (b) Effect on external users of financial statements.

I would recommend absorption costing because it considers all the manufacturing resources (whether variable or fixed) used to produce units of output. Absorption costing has many critics. However, the dysfunctional aspects associated with absorption costing can be reduced by
- Careful budgeting and inventory planning.
- Adding a capital charge to reduce the incentives to build up inventory.
- Monitoring nonfinancial performance measures.

9-22 (40 min) Absorption versus variable costing.

1. The variable manufacturing cost per package of Mimic is $55 + $45 + $120 = $220.

2007 Variable-costing based Operating Income Statement

Revenues (44,800 pkgs. × $1,200 per pkg.)		$53,760,000
Variable costs		
Beginning inventory	$ 0	
Variable manufacturing costs (50,000 pkgs. × $220 per pkg.)	11,000,000	
Cost of goods available for sale	11,000,000	
Deduct: Ending inventory (5,200[a] pkgs. × $220 per pkg.)	1,144,000	
Variable cost of goods sold	9,856,000	
Variable marketing costs (44,800 pkgs. × $75 per pkg.)	3,360,000	
Total variable costs		13,216,000
Contribution margin		$40,544,000
Fixed costs		
Fixed manufacturing costs	$ 7,358,400	
Fixed R&D	4,905,600	
Fixed marketing	15,622,400	
Total fixed costs		27,886,400
Operating income		$12,657,600

[a] Beginning Inventory 0 + Production 50,000 – Sales 44,800 = Ending Inventory 5,200 packages

2.

2007 Absorption-costing based Operating Income Statement

Revenues (44,800 pkgs. × $1,200 per pkg.)		$53,760,000
Cost of goods sold		
Beginning inventory	$ 0	
Variable manufacturing costs (50,000 pkgs. × $220 per pkg.)	11,000,000	
Allocated fixed manufacturing costs (50,000 pkgs. × $165 per pkg.)	8,250,000	
Cost of goods available for sale	19,250,000	
Deduct ending inventory (5,200 pkgs. × ($220 + $165) per pkg.)	2,002,000	
Deduct favorable production volume variance	891,600[a]	
Cost of goods sold		16,356,400
Gross margin		$37,403,600
Operating costs		
Variable marketing costs (44,800 pkgs. × $75 per pkg.)	$ 3,360,000	
Fixed R&D	4,905,600	
Fixed marketing	15,622,400	
Total operating costs		23,888,000
Operating income		$13,515,600

[a] PVV = Allocated $8,250,000 ($165 × 50,000) – Actual $7,358,400 = $891,600

3.   2007 operating income under absorption costing is greater than the operating income under variable costing because in 2007 inventories increased by 5,200 packages, and under absorption costing fixed overhead remained in the ending inventory, and resulted in a lower cost of goods sold (relative to variable costing). As shown below, the difference in the two operating incomes is exactly the same as the difference in the fixed manufacturing costs included in ending vs. beginning inventory (under absorption costing).

Operating income under absorption costing	$13,515,600
Operating income under variable costing	$12,657,600
Difference in operating income under absorption vs. variable costing	$ 858,000

Under absorption costing:

Fixed mfg. costs in ending inventory (5,200 pkgs. × $165 per pkg.)	$ 858,000
Fixed mfg. costs in beginning inventory (0 pkgs. × $165 per pkg.)	$ 0
Change in fixed mfg. costs between ending and beginning inventory	$ 858,000

4.   Relative to the obvious alternative of using contribution margin (from variable costing), the absorption-costing based gross margin has some pros and cons as a performance measure for Mimic's plant manager. It takes into account both variable costs and fixed costs—costs that the plant manager should be able to control in the long-run—and therefore it is a more complete measure than contribution margin which ignores fixed costs (and may cause the manager to pay less attention to fixed costs). The downside of using absorption-costing-based gross margin is the plant manager's temptation to use inventory levels to control the gross margin—in particular, to shore up a sagging gross margin by building up inventories. This can be offset by specifying, or limiting, the inventory build-up that can occur, charging the plant manager a carrying cost for holding inventory, and using nonfinancial performance measures such as limiting the ratio of ending to beginning inventory.

9-24 (40 min.) **Variable and absorption costing, sales, and operating-income changes.**

1. Headsmart's annual fixed manufacturing costs are $1,200,000. It allocates $24 of fixed manufacturing costs to each unit produced. Therefore, it must be using $1,200,000÷$24 = 50,000 units (annually) as the denominator level to allocate fixed manufacturing costs to the units produced.

We can see from Headsmart's income statements that it disposes off any production volume variance against cost of goods sold. In 2007, 60,000 units were produced instead of the budgeted 50,000 units. This resulted in a favorable production volume variance of $240,000 F ((60,000 – 50,000) units × $24 per unit), which, when written off against cost of goods sold, increased gross margin by that amount.

2.   2.   The breakeven calculation, same for each year, is shown below:

Calculation of breakeven volume	2006	2007	2008
Selling price ($2,100,000÷50,000; $2,100,000÷50,000; $2,520,000÷60,000)	$42	$42	$42
Variable cost per unit (all manufacturing)	14	14	14
Contribution margin per unit	$28	$28	$28
Total fixed costs			
(fixed mfg. costs + fixed selling & admin. costs)	$1,400,000	$1,400,000	$1,400,000
Breakeven quantity =			
Total fixed costs ÷ contribution margin per unit	50,000	50,000	50,000

3.

Variable Costing

	2006	2007	2008
Sales (units)	50,000	50,000	60,000
Revenues	$2,100,000	$2,100,000	$2,520,000
Variable cost of goods sold			
Beginning inventory $14 × 0; 0; 10,000	0	0	140,000
Variable manuf. costs $14 × 50,000; 60,000; 50,000	700,000	840,000	700,000
Deduct ending inventory $14 × 0; 10,000; 0	0	(140,000)	0
Variable cost of goods sold	700,000	700,000	840,000
Contribution margin	$1,400,000	$1,400,000	$1,680,000
Fixed manufacturing costs	$1,200,000	$1,200,000	$1,200,000
Fixed selling and administrative expenses	200,000	200,000	200,000
Operating income	$ 0	$ 0	$ 280,000

Explaining variable costing operating income

Contribution margin			
($28 contribution margin per unit × sales units)	$1,400,000	$1,400,000	$1,680,000
Total fixed costs	1,400,000	1,400,000	1,400,000
Operating income	$ 0	$ 0	$ 280,000

4.

Reconciliation of absorption/variable costing operating incomes

operating incomes	2006	2007	2008
(1) Absorption costing operating income	$0	$240,000	$ 40,000
(2) Variable costing operating income	0	0	280,000
(3) Difference (ACOI – VCOI)	$0	$240,000	-$240,000
(4) Fixed mfg. costs in ending inventory under absorption costing (ending inventory in units × $24 per unit)	0	240,000	0
(5) Fixed mfg. costs in beginning inventory under absorption costing (beginning inventory in units × $24 per unit)	0	0	240,000
(6) Difference = (4) – (5)	$0	$240,000	-$240,000

In the table above, row (3) shows the difference between the operating income under absorption costing and the operating income under variable costing, for each of the three years. In 2006, the difference is $0; in 2007, absorption costing income is greater by $240,000; and in 2008, it is less by $240,000. Row (6) above shows the difference between the fixed costs in ending inventory and the fixed costs in beginning inventory under absorption costing, which is $0 in 2006, $240,000 in 2007 and -$240,000 in 2008. Row (3) and row (6) explain and reconcile the operating income differences between absorption costing and variable costing.

Stuart Weil is surprised at the non-zero, positive net income (reported under absorption costing) in 2007, when sales were at the 'breakeven volume' of 50,000; further, he is concerned about the drop in operating income in 2008, when, in fact, sales increased to 60,000 units. In 2007, starting with zero inventories, 60,000 units were produced, 50,000 were sold, i.e., at the end of the year, 10,000 units remained in inventory. These 10,000 units had each absorbed $24 of fixed costs (total of $240,000), which would remain as assets on Headsmart's balance sheet until they were sold. Cost of goods sold, representing only the costs of the 50,000 units sold in 2007, was accordingly reduced by $240,000, the production volume variance, resulting in a positive operating income even though sales were at breakeven levels. The following year, in 2008, production was 50,000 units, sales were 60,000 units i.e., all of the fixed costs that were included in 2007 ending inventory, flowed through COGS in 2008. Contribution margin in 2008 was $1,680,000 (60,000 units × $28), but, in absorption costing, COGS also contains the allocated fixed manufacturing costs of the units sold, which were $1,440,000 (60,000 units × $24), resulting in an operating income of $40,000 = 1,680,000 – $1,440,000 – $200,000 (fixed sales and admin.) Hence the drop in operating income under absorption costing, even though sales were greater than the computed breakeven volume: inventory levels decreased sufficiently in 2008 to cause 2008's operating income to be lower than 2007 operating income.

Note that beginning and ending with zero inventories during the 2006–2008 period, under both costing methods, Headsmart's total operating income was $280,000.

9-26 (25 min.) **Denominator-level problem.**

1.   Budgeted fixed manufacturing overhead costs rates:

Denominator Level Capacity Concept	Budgeted Fixed Manufacturing Overhead per Period	Budgeted Capacity Level	Budgeted Fixed Manufacturing Overhead Cost Rate
Theoretical	$ 3,800,000	2,880	$ 1,319.44
Practical	3,800,000	1,800	2,111.11
Normal	3,800,000	1,000	3,800.00
Master-budget	3,800,000	1,200	3,166.67

The rates are different because of varying denominator-level concepts. Theoretical and practical capacity levels are driven by supply-side concepts, i.e., "how much can I produce?" Normal and master-budget capacity levels are driven by demand-side concepts, i.e., "how much can I sell?" (or "how much should I produce?")

2.   The variances that arise from use of the theoretical or practical level concepts will signal that there is a divergence between the supply of capacity and the demand for capacity. This is useful input to managers. As a general rule, however, it is important not to place undue reliance on the production volume variance as a measure of the economic costs of unused capacity.

3.   Under a cost-based pricing system, the choice of a master-budget level denominator will lead to high prices when demand is low (more fixed costs allocated to the individual product level), further eroding demand; conversely, it will lead to low prices when demand is high, forgoing profits. This has been referred to as the downward demand spiral—the continuing reduction in demand that occurs when the prices of competitors are not met and demand drops, resulting in even higher unit costs and even more reluctance to meet the prices of competitors. The positive aspect of the master-budget denominator level is that it indicates the price at which all costs per unit would be recovered to enable the company to make a profit. Master-budget denominator level is also a good benchmark against which to evaluate performance.

9-28 (15–20 min.) **Capacity usage, cost behavior, service firm.**

1.   Calculations based on practical capacity

Practical capacity	100,000	bills
Total variable costs	$ 75,000	
Total fixed costs	$200,000	
Budgeted variable cost per bill (Total variable costs ÷ practical capacity)	$ 0.75	
Budgeted fixed cost per bill (Total fixed costs ÷ capacity)	$ 2.00	
Budgeted full cost per bill	$ 2.75	

2.

Practical capacity	100,000	bills
Capacity used in 2007	80,000	bills
Unused capacity in units	20,000	bills
Cost of unused capacity (Unused capacity × $2 budgeted fixed cost per unit)	$40,000	

None of the cost of unused capacity is attributable to variable costs. Variable costs, by definition, vary with, or adjust to, the used capacity.

3.   Calculations based on new denominator level of 80,000 bills

Denominator level	80,000
Total variable costs	$ 75,000
Total fixed costs	$200,000
Budgeted variable cost per bill	
(Total variable costs ÷ practical capacity)	$ 0.75
Budgeted fixed cost per bill	
(Total fixed costs ÷ new capacity)	$ 2.50
Budgeted full cost per bill	$ 3.25

Note that the budgeted variable cost per bill is still $0.75 because the variable cost of $75,000 was budgeted based on the practical capacity level of $100,000 bills.

4.   A&S Security pays $3 per bill processed. It was a profitable customer at the practical capacity of 100,000 units (payment per bill is greater than the full cost of $2.75 per bill), but it is not a profitable customer at the 80,000 units denominator capacity (full cost is now $3.25 per bill). But, A&S work is 40% of the business. Losing it would mean a downward spiral. Possible actions (medium-to-long term) are as follows:
- first conduct studies to ensure that 80,000 bills is the correct practical capacity for the company
- pare down fixed costs (if 4 employees can do the job for fixed costs of $160,000, then for a denominator capacity of 80,000 bills, the fixed cost per bill will once again be $2.00)
- study the competition—if their prices are lower, how are they doing it?
- discuss with A&S—gradually raise prices
- raise prices and offer a value-added proposition to A&S which is relatively "costless" to Finn & Sawyer (usually hard to do this).

9-30 (40 min.) **Variable costing versus absorption costing.**

1. Absorption Costing:

Mavis Company Income Statement
For the Year Ended December 31, 2007

Revenues (540,000 × $5.00)		$2,700,000
Cost of goods sold:		
Beginning inventory (30,000 × $3.70[a])	$ 111,000	
Variable manufacturing costs (550,000 × $3.00)	1,650,000	
Allocated fixed manufacturing costs (550,000 × $0.70)	385,000	
Cost of goods available for sale	2,146,000	
Deduct ending inventory (40,000 × $3.70)	(148,000)	
Deduct adjustment for prod.-vol. variance (50,000[b] × $0.70)	(35,000)	
Cost of goods sold		1,963,000
Gross margin		667,000
Operating costs:		
Variable operating costs (540,000 × $1)	540,000	
Fixed operating costs	120,000	
Total operating costs		660,000
Operating income		$ 7,000

[a] $3.00 + ($7.00 ÷ 10) = $3.00 + $0.70 = $3.70

[b] [(10 × 60,000) − 550,000)] = 50,000 units

2. Variable Costing:

Mavis Company Income Statement
For the Year Ended December 31, 2007

Revenues		$2,700,000
Variable cost of goods sold:		
Beginning inventory (30,000 × $3.00)	$ 90,000	
Variable manufacturing costs		
(550,000 × $3.00)	1,650,000	
Cost of goods available for sale	1,740,000	
Deduct ending inventory (40,000 × $3.00)	(120,000)	
Variable cost of goods sold		1,620,000
Variable operating costs		540,000
Contribution margin		540,000
Fixed costs:		
Fixed manufacturing overhead costs	420,000	
Fixed operating costs	120,000	
Total fixed costs		540,000
Operating income		$ 0

3. The difference in operating income between the two costing methods is:

$$\begin{pmatrix} \text{Absorption-} \\ \text{costing} \\ \text{operating} \\ \text{income} \end{pmatrix} - \begin{pmatrix} \text{Variable-} \\ \text{costing} \\ \text{operating} \\ \text{income} \end{pmatrix} = \begin{pmatrix} \text{Fixed} \\ \text{manuf. costs} \\ \text{in ending} \\ \text{inventory} \end{pmatrix} - \begin{pmatrix} \text{Fixed} \\ \text{manuf. costs} \\ \text{in beginning} \\ \text{inventory} \end{pmatrix}$$

$$\$7,000 - \$0 = [(40,000 \times \$0.70) - (30,000 \times \$0.70)]$$
$$\$7,000 = \$28,000 - \$21,000$$
$$\$7,000 = \$7,000$$

The absorption-costing operating income exceeds the variable costing figure by $7,000 because of the increase of $7,000 during 2007 of the amount of fixed manufacturing costs in ending inventory vis-a-vis beginning inventory.

4.

Total fixed manufacturing costs

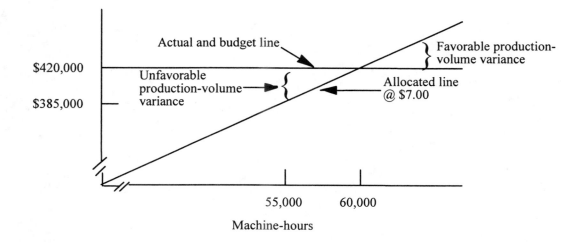

Machine-hours

5.   Absorption costing is more likely to lead to buildups of inventory than does variable costing. Absorption costing enables managers to increase reported operating income by building up inventory which reduces the amount of fixed manufacturing overhead included in the current period's cost of goods sold.

  Ways to reduce this incentive include
  (a) Careful budgeting and inventory planning.
  (b) Change the accounting system to variable costing or throughput costing.
  (c) Incorporate a carrying charge for carrying inventory.
  (d) Use a longer time period to evaluate performance than a quarter or a year.
  (e) Include nonfinancial as well as financial measures when evaluating management performance.

9-32 (40 min.) **Variable costing and absorption costing, the All-Fixed Company.**

This problem always generates active classroom discussion.

1.   The treatment of fixed manufacturing overhead in absorption costing is affected primarily by what denominator level is selected as a base for allocating fixed manufacturing costs to units produced. In this case, is 10,000 tons per year, 20,000 tons, or some other denominator level the most appropriate base?

  We usually place the following possibilities on the board or overhead projector and then ask the students to indicate by vote how many used one denominator level versus another. Incidentally, discussion tends to move more clearly if variable-costing income statements are discussed first, because there is little disagreement as to computations under variable costing.

a.   Variable-Costing Income Statement:

		2006	2007	Together
Revenues (and contribution margin)		$300,000	$300,000	$600,000
Fixed costs:				
Manufacturing costs	$280,000			
Operating costs	40,000	320,000	320,000	640,000
Operating income		$ (20,000)	$ (20,000)	$ (40,000)

b.   Absorption-Costing Income Statement:

The ambiguity about the 10,000- or 20,000-unit denominator level is intentional. IF YOU WISH, THE AMBIGUITY MAY BE AVOIDED BY GIVING THE STUDENTS A SPECIFIC DENOMINATOR LEVEL IN ADVANCE.

Alternative 1. Use 20,000 units as a denominator; fixed manufacturing overhead per unit is $280,000 ÷ 20,000 = $14.

	2006	2007	Together
Revenues	$300,000	$ 300,000	$600,000
Cost of goods sold			
Beginning inventory	0	140,000*	0
Allocated fixed manufacturing costs at $14	280,000	—	280,000
Deduct ending inventory	(140,000)	—	—
Adjustment for production-volume variance	0	280,000	280,000
Cost of goods sold	140,000	420,000	560,000
Gross margin	160,000	(120,000)	40,000
Operating costs	40,000	40,000	80,000
Operating income	$120,000	$(160,000)	$(40,000)

*Inventory carried forward from 2006 and sold in 2007.

Alternative 2. Use 10,000 units as a denominator; fixed manufacturing overhead per unit is $280,000 ÷10,000 = $28.

	2006	2007	Together
Revenues	$300,000	$300,000	$600,000
Cost of goods sold			
Beginning inventory	0	280,000*	0
Allocated fixed manufacturing costs at $28	560,000	—	560,000
Deduct ending inventory	(280,000)	—	—
Adjustment for production-volume variance	(280,000)	280,000	0
Cost of goods sold	0	560,000	560,000
Gross margin	300,000	(260,000)	40,000
Operating costs	40,000	40,000	80,000
Operating income	$260,000	$(300,000)	$ (40,000)

*Inventory carried forward from 2006 and sold in 2007.

Note that operating income under variable costing follows sales and is not affected by inventory changes.

Note also that students will understand the variable-costing presentation much more easily than the alternatives presented under absorption costing.

2. $$\text{Breakeven point under variable costing} = \frac{\text{Fixed costs}}{\text{Contribution margin per ton}} = \frac{\$320{,}000}{\$30}$$

$$= 10{,}667 \text{ (rounded) tons per year or } 21{,}334 \text{ for two years.}$$

If the company could sell 667 more tons per year at $30 each, it could get the extra $20,000 contribution margin needed to break even.

Most students will say that the breakeven point is 10,667 tons per year under both absorption costing and variable costing. The logical question to ask a student who answers 10,667 tons for variable costing is: "What operating income do you show for 2006 under absorption costing?" If a student answers $120,000 (alternative 1 above), or $260,000 (alternative 2 above), ask: "But you say your breakeven point is 10,667 tons. How can you show an operating income on only 10,000 tons sold during 2006?"

The answer to the above dilemma lies in the fact that operating income is affected by both sales and production under absorption costing.

Given that sales would be 10,000 tons in 2006, solve for the production level that will provide a breakeven level of zero operating income. Using the formula in the chapter, sales of 10,000 units, and a fixed manufacturing overhead rate of $14 (based on $280,000 ÷ 20,000 units denominator level = $14):

Let P = Production level

$$\text{Breakeven sales in units} = \frac{\left(\begin{array}{c}\text{Total fixed}\\ \text{costs}\end{array}\right) + \left(\begin{array}{c}\text{Target}\\ \text{operating}\\ \text{income}\end{array}\right) + \left[\left(\begin{array}{c}\text{Fixed manuf.}\\ \text{overhead}\\ \text{rate}\end{array}\right) \times \left(\begin{array}{c}\text{Breakeven}\\ \text{sales in}\\ \text{units}\end{array} - \begin{array}{c}\text{Units}\\ \text{produced}\end{array}\right)\right]}{\text{Unit contribution margin}}$$

$$10{,}000 \text{ tons} = \frac{\$320{,}000 + \$0 + \$14(10{,}000 - P)}{\$30}$$

$$\begin{aligned}\$300{,}000 &= \$320{,}000 + \$140{,}000 - \$14P\\ \$14P &= \$160{,}000\\ P &= 11{,}429 \text{ units (rounded)}\end{aligned}$$

Proof:

Gross margin, 10,000 × ($30 – $14)		$160,000
Production-volume variance, (20,000 – 11,429) × $14	$119,994	
Marketing and administrative costs	40,000	159,994
Operating income (due to rounding)		$ 6

Given that production would be 20,000 tons in 2006, solve for the breakeven unit sales level. Using the formula in the chapter and a fixed manufacturing overhead rate of $14 (based on a denominator level of 20,000 units):

Let N = Breakeven sales in units

$$N = \frac{\left(\begin{array}{c}\text{Total fixed}\\ \text{costs}\end{array}\right) + \left(\begin{array}{c}\text{Target}\\ \text{operating}\\ \text{income}\end{array}\right) + \left[\left(\begin{array}{c}\text{Fixed manuf.}\\ \text{overhead}\\ \text{rate}\end{array}\right) \times \left(N - \begin{array}{c}\text{Units}\\ \text{produced}\end{array}\right)\right]}{\text{Unit contribution margin}}$$

$$N = \frac{\$320,000 + \$0 + \$14(N - 20,000)}{\$30}$$

$30N = \$320,000 + \$14N - \$280,000$

$16N = \$40,000$

$N = 2,500$ units

Proof:

Gross margin, 2,500 × ($30 – $14)		$40,000
Production-volume variance	$ 0	
Marketing and administrative costs	40,000	40,000
Operating income		$ 0

We find it helpful to put the following comparisons on the board:

Variable costing breakeven   = f(sales)
                              = 10,667 tons

Absorption costing breakeven = f(sales and production)
                              = f(10,000 and 11,429)
                              = f(2,500 and 20,000)

3.   Absorption costing inventory cost: Either $140,000 or $280,000 at the end of 2006 and zero at the end of 2007.

        Variable costing: Zero at all times. This is a major criticism of variable costing and focuses on the issue of the definition of an asset.

4.   Operating income is affected by both production and sales under absorption costing. Hence, most managers would prefer absorption costing because their performance in any given reporting period, at least in the short run, is influenced by how much production is scheduled near the end of a period.

9-34 (25–30 min.) **Alternative denominator-level capacity concepts, effect on operating income.**

1.

Denominator-Level Capacity Concept	Budgeted Fixed Manuf. Overhead per Period (1)	Days of Production per Period (2)	Hours of Production per Day (3)	Barrels per Hour (4)	Budgeted Denominator Level (Barrels) (5) = (2) × (3) × (4)	Budgeted Fixed Manufacturing Overhead Rate per Barrel (6) = (1) ÷ (5)
Theoretical capacity	$42,000,000	365	24	600	5,256,000	$ 7.99
Practical capacity	42,000,000	350	20	500	3,500,000	12.00
Normal capacity utilization	42,000,000	350	20	400	2,800,000	15.00
Master-budget utilization						
(a) January-June 2006	21,000,000	175	20	320	1,120,000	18.75
(b) July-December 2006	21,000,000	175	20	480	1,680,000	12.50

The differences arise for several reasons:

a. The theoretical and practical capacity concepts emphasize supply factors, while normal capacity utilization and master-budget utilization emphasize demand factors.

b. The two separate six-month rates for the master-budget utilization concept differ because of seasonal differences in budgeted production.

2. Using column (6) from above,

	Per Barrel				
Denominator-Level Capacity Concept	Budgeted Fixed Mfg. Overhead Rate per Barrel (6)	Budgeted Variable Mfg. Cost Rate (7)	Budgeted Total Mfg Cost Rate (8) = (6) + (7)	Fixed Mfg. Overhead Costs Allocated (9) = 2,600,000 × (6)	Fixed Mfg. Overhead Variance (10) = $40,632,000 − (9)
Theoretical capacity	$7.99	$46.30[a]	$54.29	$20,774,000	$19,858,000 U
Practical capacity	12.00	46.30	58.30	31,200,000	9,432,000 U
Normal capacity utilization	15.00	46.30	61.30	39,000,000	1,632,000 U

[a] $120,380,000 ÷ 2,600,000 barrels

Absorption-costing Income Statement

	Theoretical capacity	Practical capacity	Normal capacity utilization
Revenues (2,400,000 bbls. × $68 per bbl.)	$163,200,000	$163,200,000	$163,200,000
Cost of goods sold			
Beginning inventory	$0	$0	$0
Variable mfg. costs	120,380,000	120,380,000	120,380,000
Fixed mfg. overhead costs allocated			
(2,600,000 units × $7.99; $12.00; $15.00 per unit)	20,774,000	31,200,000	39,000,000
Cost of goods available for sale	141,154,000	151,580,000	159,380,000
Deduct ending inventory			
(200,000 units × $54.29; $58.30; $61.30 per unit)	(10,858,000)	(11,660,000)	(12,260,000)
Adjustment for variances (add: all unfavorable)	19,858,000	9,432,000	1,632,000
Cost of goods sold	$150,154,000	$149,352,000	$148,752,000
Gross margin	$13,046,000	$13,848,000	$14,448,000
Other costs	0	0	0
Operating income	$13,046,000	$13,848,000	$14,448,000

9-36 (25 min.) **Denominator-level choices, changes in inventory levels, effect on operating income.**

1.

	Theoretical Capacity	Practical Capacity	Utilization Capacity
Denominator level in units	360,000	300,000	240,000
Budgeted fixed manuf. costs	$3,600,000	$3,600,000	$3,600,000
Budgeted fixed manuf. cost allocated per unit	$ 10.00	$ 12.00	$ 15.00
Production in units	260,000	260,000	260,000
Allocated fixed manuf. costs (production in units × budgeted fixed manuf. cost allocated per unit)	$2,600,000	$3,120,000	$3,900,000
Production volume variance (Budgeted fixed manuf. costs – allocated fixed manuf. costs)[a]	$1,000,000 U	$ 480,000 U	$ 300,000 F

[a]PVV is unfavorable if budgeted fixed manuf. costs are greater than allocated fixed costs

2.

	Theoretical Capacity	Practical Capacity	Normal Utilization Capacity
Units sold	280,000	280,000	280,000
Budgeted fixed mfg. cost allocated per unit	$10	$12	$15
Budgeted var. mfg. cost per unit	$3	$3	$3
Budgeted cost per unit of inventory or production	$13	$15	$18

ABSORPTION-COSTING BASED INCOME STATEMENTS

	Theoretical Capacity	Practical Capacity	Normal Utilization Capacity
Revenues ($3 selling price per unit × units sold)	$8,400,000	$8,400,000	$8,400,000
Cost of goods sold			
Beginning inventory (25,000 units × budgeted cost per unit of inventory)	325,000	375,000	450,000
Variable manufacturing costs (260,000 units × $3 per unit)	780,000	780,000	780,000
Allocated fixed manufacturing overhead (260,000 units × budgeted fixed mfg. cost allocated per unit)	2,600,000	3,120,000	3,900,000
Cost of goods available for sale	3,705,000	4,275,000	5,130,000
Deduct ending inventory (5,000[b] units × budgeted cost per unit of inventory)	(65,000)	(75,000)	(90,000)
Adjustment for production-volume variance	1,000,000	480,000	(300,000)
Total cost of goods sold	4,640,000	4,680,000	4,740,000
Gross margin	3,760,000	3,720,000	3,660,000
Operating costs	1,000,000	1,000,000	1,000,000
Operating income	$2,760,000	$2,720,000	$2,660,000

[b]Ending inventory = Beginning inventory + production – sales = 25,000 + 260,000 – 280,000 = 5,000 units

3.   Accel's 2007 beginning inventory was 25,000 units; its ending inventory was 5,000 units. So, during 2007, there was a drop of 20,000 units in inventory levels (matching the 20,000 more units sold than produced). The smaller the denominator level, the larger is the budgeted fixed cost allocated to each unit of production, and, when those units are sold (all the current production is sold, and then some), the larger is the cost of each unit sold, and the smaller is the operating income. Normal utilization capacity is the smallest capacity of the three, hence in this year, when production was less than sales, the absorption-costing based operating income is the smallest when normal capacity utilization is used as the denominator level.

4.

Reconciliation

Theoretical Capacity Operating Income – Practical Capacity Operating Income		$40,000
Decrease in inventory level during 2007	20,000	
Fixed mfg cost allocated per unit under practical capacity – fixed mfg. cost allocated per unit under theoretical capacity ($12 – $10)	$2	
Additional allocated fixed cost included in COGS under practical capacity = 20,000 units × $2 per unit =		$40,000

More fixed manufacturing costs are included in inventory under practical capacity, so, when inventory level decreases (as it did in 2007), more fixed manufacturing costs are included in COGS under practical capacity than under theoretical capacity, resulting in a lower operating income.

9-38 (20 min.) **Downward demand spiral.**

1. and 2.

	Original	Competitive Situation
Practical capacity (units)	5,000	5,000
Budgeted capacity (units)	5,000	4,000
Variable manufacturing cost per unit	$100	$100
Fixed manufacturing costs	$1,500,000	$1,500,000
Markup percentage	100%	100%
Manufacturing cost per unit		
Variable	$100	$100
Fixed (fixed mfg costs ÷ budgeted capacity)		
($1,500,000 ÷ 5,000; $1,500,000 ÷ 4,000)	300	375
Full manufacturing cost per unit	$400	$475
Selling Price (200% of full manuf. cost per unit)	$800	$950

3.   We can see that when the budgeted production is used as the denominator level and this level changes with anticipated demand, then the full manufacturing cost per unit and therefore the selling price can be quite sensitive to the denominator level. In this case, the denominator level has fallen by 20% [(5,000 − 4,000) ÷ 5,000] and the allocated fixed cost has increased by 25% [($375 − $300) ÷ 300], resulting in an 18.75% [($950 − $800) ÷ $800] increase in selling price. If MetaTech's market is becoming more competitive because of foreign entrants, raising the selling price could further drive away customers, lower the budgeted capacity and raise the fixed cost per unit, that is, lead to a downward spiral. If MetaTech's production plant was built for a practical capacity of 5,000 units, a denominator level of 5,000 units should be used, and the cost of excess capacity should not be charged to the units produced and sold. This will focus managerial attention on the unused capacity. If the competitive trends continue, MetaTech will need to cut back its installed capacity to stay competitive.

4.   Suppose MetaTech sells x units each year. Its total cost to manufacture the x units would be $100x + $1,500,000. Its total cost to purchase x units would be $400x + $300,000. Therefore, Metatech should manufacture in-house, if $100x + $1,500,000 < $400x + $300,000; i.e., if $x >$ 4,000 units. In-house, the cost structure is a low variable cost, high fixed cost structure, and only worth pursuing for high volumes. The source-outside cost structure is a high variable cost, low fixed cost structure, and only worth pursuing for small volumes. Currently, demand is exactly at 4,000 units. MetaTech should conduct some research to forecast future demand patterns. If it seems likely that demand is going to fall below 4,000, it may be better to shut down its production capacity and outsource all of its needed units. This may also allow the management to examine and pursue other business options, as its current business gets increasingly competitive.

9-40 (30 min.) **Cost allocation, downward demand spiral.**

SOLUTION EXHIBIT 9-40

	2007 Master Budget (1)	Practical Capacity (2)	2008 Master Budget (3)
Budgeted fixed costs	$3,832,500	$3,832,500	$3,832,500
Denominator level	2,555,000	3,650,000	2,190,000
Budgeted fixed cost per meal			
Budgeted fixed costs ÷ Denominator level			
($3,832,500 ÷ 2,555,000; $3,832,500 ÷ 3,650,000;			
$3,832,500 ÷ 2,190,000)	$ 1.50	$ 1.05	$ 1.75
Budgeted variable cost per meal	$ 3.80	$ 3.80	$ 3.80
Total budgeted cost per meal	$ 5.30	$ 4.85	$ 5.55

1.   The 2007 budgeted fixed costs are $3,832,500. MedChef budgets for 2,555,000 meals in 2007, and this is used as the denominator level to calculate the fixed cost per meal. $3,832,500 ÷ 2,555,000 = $1.50 fixed cost per meal. (see column (1) in Solution Exhibit 9-40).

2.   In 2008, 3 hospitals have dropped out of the purchasing group and the master budget is 2,190,000 meals. If this is used as the denominator level, fixed cost per meal = $3,832,500 ÷ 2,190,000 = $1.75 per meal, and the total budgeted cost per meal would be $5.55 (see column (3) in Solution Exhibit 9-40). If the hospitals have already been complaining about quality and cost and are allowed to purchase from outside, they will not accept this higher price. More hospitals may begin to purchase meals from outside the system, leading to a downward demand spiral, possibly putting MedChef out of business.

3.   The basic problem is that MedChef has excess capacity and the associated excess fixed costs. If Jenkins uses the practical capacity of 3,650,000 meals as the denominator level, the fixed cost per meal will be $1.05 (see column (2) in Solution Exhibit 9-40), and the total budgeted cost per meal would be $4.85, probably a more acceptable price to the customers (it may even draw back the three hospitals that have chosen to buy outside). This denominator level will also isolate the cost of unused capacity and not allocate it to the meals produced. To make the $4.85 price per meal profitable in the long run, Jenkins will have to find ways to either use the extra capacity or reduce MedChef's practical capacity and the related fixed costs.

9-42 (60 min.) **Absorption, variable, and throughput costing.**

1.

(a)

$$\text{Fixed manufacturing overhead cost per unit} = \frac{\$7,500,000}{3,000 \text{ vehicles} \times 20 \text{ standard hours}}$$

$$= \frac{\$7,500,000}{60,000}$$

$$= \$125 \text{ per standard assembly hour or } \$2,500 \text{ per vehicle}$$

(b)

Direct materials per unit	$ 6,000
Direct manufacturing labor per unit	1,800
Variable manufacturing overhead per unit	2,000
Fixed manufacturing overhead per unit	2,500
Total manufacturing cost per unit	$12,300

2. Amounts in thousands.

	Absorption Costing		
	January	**February**	**March**
Revenues ($16,000 × 2,000; 2,900; 3200)	$32,000	$46,400	$51,200
Cost of goods sold			
Beginning inventory	$ 0	$14,760	$ 8,610
Variable manufacturing costs ($9.8 × 3,200; 2,400; 3,800)	31,360	23,520	37,240
Allocated fixed manufacturing costs ($2.5 × 3,200; 2,400; 3,800)	8,000	6,000	9,500
Cost of goods available for sale	39,360	44,280	55,350
Deduct ending inventory ($12.3 × 1,200; 700; 1,300)	(14,760)	(8,610)	(15,990)
Adjustment for production-volume variance[a]	(500) F	1,500 U	(2,000) F
Cost of goods sold	24,100	37,170	37,360
Gross margin	7,900	9,230	13,840
Marketing costs	0	0	0
Operating income	$ 7,900	$ 9,230	$13,840
Inventory Details (Units)			
Beginning inventory	0	1,200	700
Production	3,200	2,400	3,800
Goods available for sale	3,200	3,600	4,500
Sales	2,000	2,900	3,200
Ending inventory	1,200	700	1,300
Inventory Details ($12.30 per unit)			
Beginning inventory	$ 0	$14,760	$ 8,610
Ending inventory	$14,760	$ 8,610	$15,990

Computation of Bonus	**January**	**February**	**March**
Operating income	$7,900,000	$9,230,000	$13,840,000
× 0.5%	$ 39,500	$46,150	$ 69,200

[a]Production–volume variance = (Denominator level – Production) × Budgeted rate
January: (3,000 – 3,200) × $2,500 per vehicle = $500,000 F
February: (3,000 – 2,400) × $2,500 per vehicle = $1,500,000 U
March: (3,000 – 3,800) × $2,500 per vehicle = $2,000,000 F

3.   Amounts in thousands.

	Variable Costing		
	January	February	March
Revenues	$32,000	$46,400	$51,200
Variable cost of goods sold			
Beginning inventory	0	11,760	6,860
Variable manuf. costs ($9.80 × 3,200; 2,400, 3,800)	31,360	23,520	37,240
Cost of goods available for sale	31,360	35,280	44,100
Deduct ending inventory ($9.80 ×1,200; 700, 1,300)	(11,760)	(6,860)	(12,740)
Variable cost of goods sold	19,600	28,420	31,360
Variable marketing costs	0	0	0
Total variable costs	19,600	28,420	31,360
Contribution margin	12,400	17,980	19,840
Fixed costs			
Fixed manuf. overhead costs	7,500	7,500	7,500
Fixed marketing costs	0	0	0
Total fixed costs	7,500	7,500	7,500
Operating income	$ 4,900	$10,480	$12,340
Inventory details ($9.80 per unit)			
Beginning inventory (units)	0	1,200	700
Ending inventory (units)	1,200	700	1,300
Beginning inventory	$0	$11,760	$ 6,860
Ending inventory	$11,760	$ 6,860	$12,740

Computation of Bonus	January	February	March
Operating income	$4,900,000	$10,480,000	$12,340,000
Bonus (Operating income × 0.5%)	$ 24,500	$ 52,400	$ 61,700

4.

	January	February	March	Total
Absorption-Costing Bonus	$39,500	$46,150	$69,200	$154,850
Variable-Costing Bonus	24,500	52,400	61,700	138,600
Difference	$15,000	$ (6,250)	$ 7,500	$16,250

The difference between absorption and variable costing arises because of differences in production and sales:

	January	February	March	Total
Production	3,200	2,400	3,800	9,400
Sales	2,000	2,900	3,200	8,100
Increase (decrease) in inventory	1,200	(500)	600	1,300

With absorption costing, by building for inventory, Hart can capitalize $2,500 of fixed manufacturing overhead cost per unit. This will provide a bonus payment of $12.50 (0.5% × $2,500) per unit. Operating income under absorption costing will exceed that under variable costing when production is greater than sales. Over the three-month period, the inventory buildup is 1,300 units, giving a difference of $16,250 ($12.50 × 1,300) in bonus payments.

5.   Amounts in thousands

	Throughput Costing		
	January	February	March
Revenues	$32,000	$46,400	$51,200
Direct material cost of goods sold			
Beginning inventory ($6 × 0;1,200; 700)	0	7,200	4,200
Direct materials ($6 × 3,200; 2,400; 3,800)	19,200	14,400	22,800
Cost of goods available for sale	19,200	21,600	27,000
Deduct ending inventory ($6 × 1,200; 700; 1,300)	(7,200)	(4,200)	(7,800)
Total direct material cost of goods sold	12,000	17,400	19,200
Throughput contribution	20,000	29,000	32,000
Other costs			
Manufacturing[a]	19,660	16,620	21,940
Marketing	0	0	0
Total other costs	19,660	16,620	21,940
Operating income	$ 340	$12,380	$10,060

[a]($3,800 × 3,200) + $7,500,000
($3,800 × 2,400) + $7,500,000
($3,800 × 3,800) + $7,500,000

Computation of Bonus	January	February	March
Operating income	$340,000	$12,380,000	$10,060,000
Bonus (Operating income × 0.5%)	$ 1,700	$ 61,900	$ 50,300

A summary of the bonuses paid is:

	January	February	March	Total
Absorption Costing	$39,500	$46,150	$69,200	$154,850
Variable Costing	24,500	52,400	61,700	138,600
Throughput Costing	1,700	61,900	50,300	113,900

6.   Alternative approaches include:
  (a) Careful budgeting and inventory planning,
  (b) Use an alternative income computation approach to absorption costing (such as variable costing or throughput costing),
  (c) Use a financial charge for inventory buildup,
  (d) Change the compensation package to have a longer-term focus using either an external variable (e.g., stock options) or an internal variable (e.g., five-year average income), and
  (e) Adopt non-financial performance targets, e.g., attaining but not exceeding present inventory levels.

CHAPTER 10
DETERMINING HOW COSTS BEHAVE

10-2   Three alternative linear cost functions are
1.   Variable cost function—a cost function in which total costs change in proportion to the changes in the level of activity in the relevant range.
2.   Fixed cost function—a cost function in which total costs do not change with changes in the level of activity in the relevant range.
3.   Mixed cost function—a cost function that has both variable and fixed elements. Total costs change but not in proportion to the changes in the level of activity in the relevant range.

10-4   No. High correlation merely indicates that the two variables move together in the data examined. It is essential also to consider economic plausibility before making inferences about cause and effect. Without any economic plausibility for a relationship, it is less likely that a high level of correlation observed in one set of data will be similarly found in other sets of data.

10-6   The conference method estimates cost functions on the basis of analysis and opinions about costs and their drivers gathered from various departments of a company (purchasing, process engineering, manufacturing, employee relations, etc.). Advantages of the conference method include
1.   The speed with which cost estimates can be developed.
2.   The pooling of knowledge from experts across functional areas.
3.   The improved credibility of the cost function to all personnel.

10-8   The six steps are
1.   Choose the dependent variable (the variable to be predicted, which is some type of cost).
2.   Identify the independent variable or cost driver.
3.   Collect data on the dependent variable and the cost driver.
4.   Plot the data.
5.   Estimate the cost function.
6.   Evaluate the cost driver of the estimated cost function.
Step 3 typically is the most difficult for a cost analyst.

10-10   Three criteria important when choosing among alternative cost functions are
1.   Economic plausibility.
2.   Goodness of fit.
3.   Slope of the regression line.

10-12   Frequently encountered problems when collecting cost data on variables included in a cost function are
1.   The time period used to measure the dependent variable is not properly matched with the time period used to measure the cost driver(s).
2.   Fixed costs are allocated as if they are variable.
3.   Data are either not available for all observations or are not uniformly reliable.
4.   Extreme values of observations occur.

5.   A homogeneous relationship between the individual cost items in the dependent variable cost pool and the cost driver(s) does not exist.

6.   The relationship between the cost and the cost driver is not stationary.

7.   Inflation has occurred in a dependent variable, a cost driver, or both.

10-14 No. A cost driver is any factor whose change causes a change in the total cost of a related cost object. A cause-and-effect relationship underlies selection of a cost driver. Some users of regression analysis include numerous independent variables in a regression model in an attempt to maximize goodness of fit, irrespective of the economic plausibility of the independent variables included. Some of the independent variables included may not be cost drivers.

10-16 (10 min.) **Estimating a cost function.**

1.   Slope coefficient $= \dfrac{\text{Difference in costs}}{\text{Difference in machine-hours}}$

$$= \frac{\$3,900 - \$3,000}{7,000 - 4,000}$$

$$= \frac{\$900}{3,000} = \$0.30 \text{ per machine-hour}$$

Constant = Total cost – (Slope coefficient × Quantity of cost driver)

$$= \$3,900 - (\$0.30 \times 7,000) = \$1,800$$

$$= \$3,000 - (\$0.30 \times 4,000) = \$1,800$$

The cost function based on the two observations is
Maintenance costs $= \$1,800 + \$0.30 \times$ Machine-hours

2.   The cost function in requirement 1 is an estimate of how costs behave within the relevant range, not at cost levels outside the relevant range. If there are no months with zero machine-hours represented in the maintenance account, data in that account cannot be used to estimate the fixed costs at the zero machine-hours level. Rather, the constant component of the cost function provides the best available starting point for a straight line that approximates how a cost behaves within the relevant range.

10-18 (20 min.)   **Various cost-behavior patterns.**

1.	K
2.	B
3.	G
4.	J	Note that A is incorrect because, although the cost per pound eventually equals a constant at $9.20, the total dollars of cost increases linearly from that point onward.
5.	I	The total costs will be the same regardless of the volume level.
6.	L
7.	F	This is a classic step-cost function.
8.	K
9.	C

10-20 (15 min.) **Account analysis method.**

1. Variable costs:

Car wash labor	$240,000
Soap, cloth, and supplies	32,000
Water	28,000
Electric power to move conveyor belt	72,000
Total variable costs	$372,000

Fixed costs:

Depreciation	$ 64,000
Salaries	46,000
Total fixed costs	$110,000

Some costs are classified as variable because the *total* costs in these categories change in proportion to the number of cars washed in Lorenzo's operation. Some costs are classified as fixed because the *total* costs in these categories do not vary with the number of cars washed. If the conveyor belt moves regardless of the number of cars on it, the electricity costs to power the conveyor belt would be a fixed cost.

2.   Variable costs per car = $\dfrac{\$372,000}{80,000}$ = $4.65 per car

   Total costs estimated for 90,000 cars = $110,000 + ($4.65 × 90,000) = $528,500

10-22 (15–20 min.) **Estimating a cost function, high-low method.**

1.   The key point to note is that the problem provides high-low values of X (annual round trips made by a helicopter) and $Y \div X$ (the operating cost per round trip). We first need to calculate the annual operating cost Y (as in column (3) below), and then use those values to estimate the function using the high-low method.

	Cost Driver: Annual Round-Trips (X) (1)	Operating Cost per Round-Trip (2)	Annual Operating Cost (Y) (3) = (1) × (2)
Highest observation of cost driver	2,000	$250	$500,000
Lowest observation of cost driver	1,000	$300	$300,000
Difference	1,000		$200,000

Slope coefficient = $200,000 \div 1,000 = $200 per round-trip
Constant = $500,000 – ($200 × 2,000) = $100,000

The estimated relationship is $Y = $100,000 + $200\,X$; where Y is the annual operating cost of a helicopter and X represents the number of round trips it makes annually.

2.   The constant a (estimated as $100,000) represents the fixed costs of operating a helicopter, irrespective of the number of round trips it makes. This would include items such as insurance, registration, depreciation on the aircraft, and any fixed component of pilot and crew salaries. The coefficient b (estimated as $200 per round-trip) represents the variable cost of each round trip—costs that are incurred only when a helicopter actually flies a round trip. The coefficient b may include costs such as landing fees, fuel, refreshments, baggage handling, and any regulatory fees paid on a per-flight basis.

3.   If each helicopter is, on average, expected to make 1,200 round trips a year, we can use the estimated relationship to calculate the expected annual operating cost per helicopter:

$Y = $100,000 + $200\,X$
$X = 1,200$
$Y = $340,000$

With 10 helicopters in its fleet, Reisen's estimated operating budget is 10 × $340,000 = $3,400,000.

10-24 (30–40 min.) **Linear cost approximation.**

1.   Slope coefficient (b) $= \dfrac{\text{Difference in cost}}{\text{Difference in labor-hours}}$

$$= \frac{\$529,000 - \$400,000}{7,000 - 4,000} = \$43.00$$

Constant (a) $= \$529,000 - (\$43.00 \times 7,000)$
$ = \$228,000$

Cost function $= \$228,000 + \$43.00 \times \text{professional labor-hours}$

The linear cost function is plotted in Solution Exhibit 10-24.

No, the constant component of the cost function does not represent the fixed overhead cost of the Memphis Group. The relevant range of professional labor-hours is from 3,000 to 8,000. The constant component provides the best available starting point for a straight line that approximates how a cost behaves within the 3,000 to 8,000 relevant range.

2.   A comparison at various levels of professional labor-hours follows. The linear cost function is based on the formula of $228,000 per month plus $43.00 per professional labor-hour.

Total overhead cost behavior:

	Month 1	Month 2	Month 3	Month 4	Month 5	Month 6
Professional labor-hours	3,000	4,000	5,000	6,000	7,000	8,000
Actual total overhead costs	$340,000	$400,000	$435,000	$477,000	$529,000	$587,000
Linear approximation	357,000	400,000	443,000	486,000	529,000	572,000
Actual minus linear approximation	$(17,000)	$ 0	$ (8,000)	$ (9,000)	$ 0	$ 15,000

The data are shown in Solution Exhibit 10-24. The linear cost function overstates costs by $8,000 at the 5,000-hour level and understates costs by $15,000 at the 8,000-hour level.

3.

	Based on Actual	Based on Linear Cost Function
Contribution before deducting incremental overhead	$38,000	$38,000
Incremental overhead	35,000	43,000
Contribution after incremental overhead	$ 3,000	$ (5,000)

The total contribution margin actually forgone is $3,000.

SOLUTION EXHIBIT 10-24
Linear Cost Function Plot of Professional Labor-Hours
on Total Overhead Costs for Memphis Consulting Group

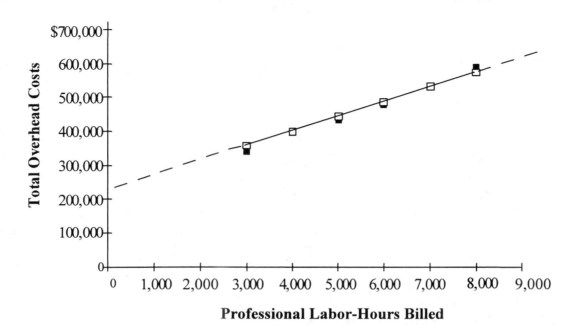

10-26 (25 min.) **Regression analysis, service company.**

1.   Solution Exhibit 10-26 plots the relationship between labor-hours and overhead costs and shows the regression line.

$$y = \$48,271 + \$3.93\ X$$

Economic plausibility. Labor-hours appears to be an economically plausible driver of overhead costs for a catering company. Overhead costs such as scheduling, hiring and training of workers, and managing the workforce are largely incurred to support labor.

Goodness of fit The vertical differences between actual and predicted costs are extremely small, indicating a very good fit. The good fit indicates a strong relationship between the labor-hour cost driver and overhead costs.

Slope of regression line. The regression line has a reasonably steep slope from left to right. Given the small scatter of the observations around the line, the positive slope indicates that, on average, overhead costs increase as labor-hours increase.

2.   The regression analysis indicates that, within the relevant range of 2,500 to 7,500 labor-hours, the variable cost per person for a cocktail party equals:

Food and beverages	$15.00
Labor (0.5 hrs. × $10 per hour)	5.00
Variable overhead (0.5 hrs × $3.93 per labor-hour)	1.97
Total variable cost per person	$21.97

3.   To earn a positive contribution margin, the minimum bid for a 200-person cocktail party would be any amount greater than $4,394. This amount is calculated by multiplying the variable cost per person of $21.97 by the 200 people. At a price above the variable costs of $4,394, Bob Jones will be earning a contribution margin toward coverage of his fixed costs.

     Of course, Bob Jones will consider other factors in developing his bid including (a) an analysis of the competition—vigorous competition will limit Jones's ability to obtain a higher price (b) a determination of whether or not his bid will set a precedent for lower prices—overall, the prices Bob Jones charges should generate enough contribution to cover fixed costs and earn a reasonable profit, and (c) a judgment of how representative past historical data (used in the regression analysis) is about future costs.

SOLUTION EXHIBIT 10-26
Regression Line of Labor-Hours on Overhead Costs for Bob Jones's Catering Company

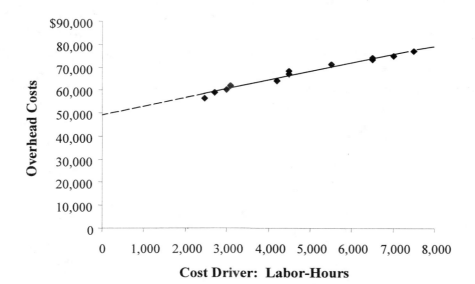

10-28 (20 min.) **Learning curve, cumulative average-time learning model.**

The direct manufacturing labor-hours (DMLH) required to produce the first 2, 4, and 8 units given the assumption of a cumulative average-time learning curve of 90%, is as follows:

90% Learning Curve

Cumulative Number of Units (X) (1)	Cumulative Average Time per Unit (y): Labor Hours (2)		Cumulative Total Time: Labor-Hours (3) = (1) ×(2)
1	3,000		3,000
2	2,700	= (3,000 × 0.90)	5,400
3	2,539		7,616
4	2,430	= (2,700 × 0.90)	9,720
5	2,349		11,745
6	2,285		13,710
7	2,232		15,624
8	2,187	= (2,430 × 0.90)	17,496

Alternatively, to compute the values in column (2) we could use the formula

$$y = aX^b$$

where $a = 3,000$, $X = 2$, 4, or 8, and $b = -0.152004$, which gives

when $X = 2$, $y = 3,000 \times 2^{-0.152004} = 2,700$

when $X = 4$, $y = 3,000 \times 4^{-0.152004} = 2,430$

when $X = 8$, $y = 3,000 \times 8^{-0.152004} = 2,187$

	Variable Costs of Producing		
	2 Units	4 Units	8 Units
Direct materials $80,000 × 2; 4; 8	$160,000	$320,000	$ 640,000
Direct manufacturing labor			
$25 × 5,400; 9,720; 17,496	135,000	243,000	437,400
Variable manufacturing overhead			
$15 × 5,400; 9,720; 17,496	81,000	145,800	262,440
Total variable costs	$376,000	$708,800	$1,339,840

10-30 (25 min.) **High-low method.**

1.

	Machine-Hours	Maintenance Costs
Highest observation of cost driver	125,000	$250,000
Lowest observation of cost driver	85,000	170,000
Difference	40,000	$ 80,000

Maintenance costs $= a + b \times$ Machine-hours

Slope coefficient $(b) = \dfrac{\$80,000}{40,000} = \$2$ per machine-hour

Constant (a) $= \$250,000 - (\$2 \times 125,000)$

$= \$250,000 - \$250,000 = \$0$

or   Constant (a) $= \$170,000 - (\$2 \times 85,000)$

$= \$170,000 - \$170,000 = \$0$

Maintenance costs $= \$2 \times$ Machine-hours

2.
SOLUTION EXHIBIT 10-30
Plot and High-Low Line of Machine-Hours on Maintenance Costs

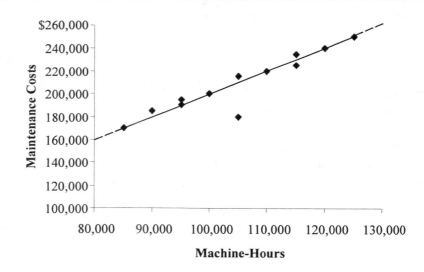

Solution Exhibit 10-30 presents the high-low line.

Economic plausibility. The cost function shows a positive economically plausible relationship between machine-hours and maintenance costs. There is a clear-cut engineering relationship of higher machine-hours and maintenance costs.

Goodness of fit. The high-low line appears to "fit" the data well. The vertical differences between the actual and predicted costs appear to be quite small.

Slope of high-low line. The slope of the line appears to be reasonably steep indicating that, on average, maintenance costs in a quarter vary with machine-hours used.

3.   Using the cost function estimated in 1, predicted maintenance costs would be $2 × 90,000 = $180,000.

     Howard should budget $180,000 in quarter 13 because the relationship between machine-hours and maintenance costs in Solution 10-30 is economically plausible, has an excellent goodness of fit, and indicates that an increase in machine-hours in a quarter causes maintenance costs to increase in the quarter.

10-32 (30–40 min.)   **High-low method, regression analysis.**

1.   Solution Exhibit 10-32 presents the plots of advertising costs on revenues.

SOLUTION EXHIBIT 10-32
Plot and Regression Line of Advertising Costs on Revenues

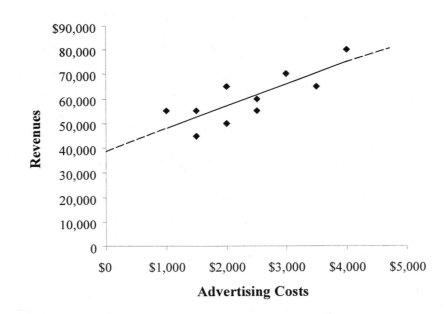

2.   Solution Exhibit 10-32 also shows the regression line of advertising costs on revenues. We evaluate the estimated regression equation using the criteria of economic plausibility, goodness of fit, and slope of the regression line.

Economic plausibility. Advertising costs appears to be a plausible cost driver of revenues. Restaurants frequently use newspaper advertising to promote their restaurants and increase their patronage.

Goodness of fit. The vertical differences between actual and predicted revenues appears to be reasonably small. This indicates that advertising costs are related to restaurant revenues.

Slope of regression line. The slope of the regression line appears to be relatively steep. Given the small scatter of the observations around the line, the steep slope indicates that, on average, restaurant revenues increase with newspaper advertising.

3.   The high-low method would estimate the cost function as follows:

	Advertising Costs	**Revenues**
Highest observation of cost driver	$4,000	$80,000
Lowest observation of cost driver	1,000	55,000
Difference	$3,000	$25,000

$$\text{Revenues} = a + (b \times \text{advertising costs})$$

$$\text{Slope coefficient } (b) = \frac{\$25,000}{\$3,000} = 8.333$$

$$\text{Constant } (a) = \$80,000 - (\$4,000 \times 8.333)$$

$$= \$80,000 - \$33,332 = \$46,668$$

$$\text{or} \quad \text{Constant } (a) = \$55,000 - (\$1,000 \times 8.333)$$

$$= \$55,000 - \$8,333 = \$46,667$$

$$\text{Revenues} = \$46,667 + (8.333 \times \text{Advertising costs})$$

4.   The increase in revenues for each $1,000 spent on advertising within the relevant range is

a. Using the regression equation, $8.723 \times \$1,000 = \$8,723$
b. Using the high-low equation, $8.333 \times \$1,000 = \$8,333$

The high-low equation does fairly well in estimating the relationship between advertising costs and revenues. However, Martinez should use the regression equation because it uses information from all observations. The high-low method, on the other hand, relies only on the observations that have the highest and lowest values of the cost driver and these observations are generally not representative of all the data.

10-34 (15-20min.)   **Interpreting regression results, matching time periods.**

1.   The regression of 2 years of Brickman's monthly data yields the following estimated relationships:

Maintenance costs = $21,000 – ($2.20 per machine-hour × Number of machine-hours);
Sales revenue = $310,000 – ($1.80 × advertising expenditure)

Sascha Green is commenting about some surprising and economically-implausible regression results. In the first regression, the coefficient on machine-hours has a negative sign. This implies that the greater the number of machine-hours (i.e., the longer the machines are run), the smaller will be the maintenance costs; specifically, it suggests that each extra machine hour reduces maintenance costs by $2.20. Similarly, the second regression, with its negative coefficient on advertising expenditure, implies that each extra dollar spent on advertising will actually *reduce* sales revenue by $1.80! Clearly, these estimated relationships are not economically plausible.

2.   The problem statement tells us that Brickman has four peak sales periods, each lasting two months and it schedules maintenance in the intervening months, when production volume is low. To correctly understand the relationship between machine-hours and maintenance costs, Brickman should estimate the regression equation of maintenance costs on lagged (i.e., previous months') machine-hours. The greater the machine use in one month, the greater is the expected maintenance costs in later months.

3.   The negative coefficient on advertising expenditure in the second regression can likely be explained by (1) the fact that advertising during a particular period increases sales revenues in subsequent periods (2) the possibility that Brickman may be increasing advertising outlays during periods of declining sales in an attempt to clear out its end-of-season merchandise. Brickman should therefore estimate the relationship between advertising costs in a particular period and sales in future periods. In fact, Brickman's marketing and sales staff may be able to provide a good sense of what the time lag should be—how long before advertising has an effect on sales.

10-36 (20–30 min.) **Cost estimation, incremental unit-time learning model.**

1. Cost to produce the 2nd through the 8th boats:

Direct materials, 7 × $100,000	$700,000
Direct manufacturing labor, 49,358* × $30	1,480,740
Variable manufacturing overhead, 49,358 × $20	987,160
Other manufacturing overhead, 25% of DML costs	370,185
Total costs	$3,538,085

*The direct labor hours to produce the second through the eighth boats can be calculated via a table format, given the assumption of an incremental unit-time learning curve of 85%:

85% Learning Curve

Cumulative Number of Units (X) (1)	Individual Unit Time for Xth Unit (y^*): Labor Hours (2)		Cumulative Total Time: Labor-Hours (3)
1	10,000		10,000
2	8,500	= (10,000 ×0.85)	18,500
3	7,729		26,229
4	7,225	= (8,500 ×0.85)	33,454
5	6,857		40,311
6	6,570		46,881
7	6,337		53,217
8	6,141	= (7,225 ×0.85)	59,358

*Calculated as $y = pX^q$ where $p = 10,000$, $q = -0.234465$, and $X = 1, 2, 3, ...8$.

The direct manufacturing labor-hours to produce the second through the eighth boat is 59,358 – 10,000 = 49,358 hours.

2.   Difference in total costs to manufacture the second through the eighth boat under the incremental unit-time learning model and the cumulative average-time learning model is $3,538,085 (calculated in requirement 1 of this problem) – $2,949,975 (from requirement 1 of Problem 10-35) = $588,110, i.e., the total costs are higher for the incremental unit-time model.

The incremental unit-time learning curve has a slower rate of decline in the time required to produce successive units than does the cumulative average-time learning curve (see Problem 10-35, requirement 1). Assuming the same 85% factor is used for both curves:

Cumulative Number of Units	Estimated Cumulative Direct Manufacturing Labor-Hours	
	Cumulative Average-Time Learning Model	Incremental Unit-Time Learning Model
1	10,000	10,000
2	17,000	18,500
4	28,900	33,454
8	49,130	59,358

The reason is that, in the incremental unit-time learning model, as the number of units double, only the last unit produced has a cost of 85% of the initial cost. In the cumulative average-time learning model, doubling the number of units causes the average cost of *all* the additional units produced (not just the last unit) to be 85% of the initial cost.

Nautilus should examine its own internal records on past jobs and seek information from engineers, plant managers, and workers when deciding which learning curve better describes the behavior of direct manufacturing labor-hours on the production of the PT109 boats.

10-38 (30 min.) **Evaluating multiple regression models, nonprofit (continuation of 10-37) (chapter appendix).**

1. Given the results of the simple regressions, Schonberg should ask Day to run a multiple regression model with number of minicourses and number of campers as independent variables. It is economically plausible that both the number of minicourses and the number of campers affect the course overhead costs, and the multiple regression model may well provide Schonberg with an understanding of how these two factors affect costs. Also, to the extent that the two independent variables are modestly correlated, the simple regressions would yield biased values for the coefficients. A multiple regression would provide a better estimate of cost per minicourse and the cost per camper.

2. Yes, Schonberg should use the multiple regression model to predict course overhead instead of the two simple regression models. As indicated in the table below, the multiple-regression model is as good as or better than the simple regression models on all relevant criteria.

Criterion	Cost Function 1: Number of Mini-courses as Independent Variable
Economic plausibility	A positive relationship between course overhead costs and each of the independent variables (number of minicourses and number of campers) is economically plausible.
Goodness of fit	$R^2 = 0.81$ Excellent goodness of fit; better than any one of the simple regressions by itself.
Significance of independent variable	The t-values of 3.54 for the coefficient on number of mini-courses and 2.06 on the number of campers indicates that each is statistically significant (its magnitude is greater than 0).
Specification analysis of estimation assumptions	Assuming linearity, constant variance and normality of residuals; reasonable independence of residuals is indicated (Durbin-Watson statistic = 1.91); however, we must be cautious when drawing inferences from only 12 observations.
Multicollinearity	The coefficient of correlation between the two independent variables is 0.59. This is high enough to justify running a multiple regression (as opposed to using two simple regressions), but not so high as to cause overly large standard errors. Note that even if the standard errors have been inflated due to multicollinearity, each coefficient is still statistically significant.

3.　　The multiple regression reveals that the incremental cost of each additional course offered is about $607—or, at the very least, we can say that it is several hundred dollars per course. This information could be used to price the courses, or to price the camp experience, if the courses are included. It could also be used to set and justify a minimum-registration requirement for each course (which, if not met, would cause the course offering to be canceled). With the number of minicourses up to 52 in the current year, there are probably a number of minicourses that are not very popular; they could be taken off the menu and a significant amount of money (approximately $607) saved with each discontinued course.

　　Each additional camper causes a $6.36 increase in costs. Even if he doesn't use the exact coefficient, this regression tells Schonberg that each extra camper seems to cause a small increase in costs. Assuming that the cost structure at Fallen Leaf Summer Camp is such that each additional camper is sufficiently profitable, clearly Schonberg should focus on limiting the number of courses offered. A further investigation of the components of the course overhead costs may provide additional insights.

10-40 (30–40 min.)　**Purchasing Department cost drivers, multiple regression analysis (continuation of 10-39) (chapter appendix).**

The problem reports the exact t-values from the computer runs of the data. Because the coefficients and standard errors given in the problem are rounded to three decimal places, dividing the coefficient by the standard error may yield slightly different t-values.

1.　　Regression 4 is a well-specified regression model:

Economic plausibility: Both independent variables are plausible and are supported by the findings of the Couture Fabrics study.

Goodness of fit: The r^2 of 0.63 indicates an excellent goodness of fit.

Significance of independent variables: The t-value on # of POs is 2.14 while the t-value on # of Ss is 2.00. These t-values are either significant or border on significance.

Specification analysis: Results are available to examine the independence of residuals assumption. The Durbin-Watson statistic of 1.90 indicates that the assumption of independence is not rejected.

　　Regression 4 is consistent with the findings in Problem 10-39 that both the number of purchase orders and the number of suppliers are drivers of purchasing department costs. Regressions 2, 3, and 4 all satisfy the four criteria outlined in the text. Regression 4 has the best goodness of fit (0.63 for Regression 4 compared to 0.42 and 0.39 for Regressions 2 and 3, respectively). Most importantly, it is economically plausible that both the number of purchase orders and the number of suppliers drive purchasing department costs. We would recommend that Lee use Regression 4 over Regressions 2 and 3.

2.   Regression 5 adds an additional independent variable (MP$) to the two independent variables in Regression 4. This additional variable (MP$) has a t-value of –0.07, implying its slope coefficient is insignificantly different from zero. The r^2 in Regression 5 (0.63) is the same as that in Regression 4 (0.63), implying the addition of this third independent variable adds close to zero explanatory power. In summary, Regression 5 adds very little to Regression 4. We would recommend that Lee use Regression 4 over Regression 5.

3.   Budgeted purchasing department costs for the Baltimore store next year are

$$\$485,384 + (\$123.22 \times 3,900) + (\$2,952 \times 110) = \$1,290,662$$

4.   Multicollinearity is a frequently encountered problem in cost accounting; it does not arise in simple regression because there is only one independent variable in a simple regression. One consequence of multicollinearity is an increase in the standard errors of the coefficients of the individual variables. This frequently shows up in reduced t-values for the independent variables in the multiple regression relative to their t-values in the simple regression:

Variables	t-value in Multiple Regression	t-value from Simple Regressions in Problem 10-39
Regression 4:		
# of POs	2.14	2.43
# of Ss	2.00	2.28
Regression 5:		
# of POs	1.95	2.43
# of Ss	1.84	2.28
MP$	–0.07	0.84

The decline in the t-values in the multiple regressions is consistent with some (but not very high) collinearity among the independent variables. Pairwise correlations between the independent variables are:

	Correlation
# of POs ÷ # of Ss	0.29
# of POs ÷ MP$	0.27
# of Ss ÷ MP$	0.34

There is no evidence of difficulties due to multicollinearity in Regressions 4 and 5.

5.   Decisions in which the regression results in Problems 10-39 and 10-40 could be useful are

Cost management decisions: Fashion Flair could restructure relationships with the suppliers so that fewer separate purchase orders are made. Alternatively, it may aggressively reduce the number of existing suppliers.

Purchasing policy decisions: Fashion Flair could set up an internal charge system for individual retail departments within each store. Separate charges to each department could be made for each purchase order and each new supplier added to the existing ones. These internal charges would signal to each department ways in which their own decisions affect the total costs of Fashion Flair.

Accounting system design decisions: Fashion Flair may want to discontinue allocating purchasing department costs on the basis of the dollar value of merchandise purchased. Allocation bases better capturing cause-and-effect relations at Fashion Flair are the number of purchase orders and the number of suppliers.

CHAPTER 11
DECISION MAKING AND RELEVANT INFORMATION

11-2 Relevant costs are expected future costs that differ among the alternative courses of action being considered. Historical costs are irrelevant because they are past costs and, therefore, cannot differ among alternative future courses of action.

11-4 Quantitative factors are outcomes that are measured in numerical terms. Some quantitative factors are financial—that is, they can be easily expressed in monetary terms. Direct materials is an example of a quantitative financial factor. Qualitative factors are outcomes that are difficult to measure accurately in numerical terms. An example is employee morale.

11-6 No. Some variable costs may not differ among the alternatives under consideration and, hence, will be irrelevant. Some fixed costs may differ among the alternatives and, hence, will be relevant.

11-8 Opportunity cost is the contribution to income that is forgone (rejected) by not using a limited resource in its next-best alternative use.

11-10 No. Managers should aim to get the highest contribution margin per unit of the constraining (that is, scarce, limiting, or critical) factor. The constraining factor is what restricts or limits the production or sale of a given product (for example, availability of machine-hours).

11-12 Cost written off as depreciation is irrelevant when it pertains to a past cost such as equipment already purchased. But the purchase cost of new equipment to be acquired in the future that will then be written off as depreciation is often relevant.

11-14 The three steps in solving a linear programming problem are
  (i)   Determine the objective function.
  (ii) Specify the constraints.
  (iii) Compute the optimal solution.

11-16 (20 min.)   **Disposal of assets.**

1.   This is an unfortunate situation, yet the $80,000 costs are irrelevant regarding the decision to remachine or scrap. The only relevant factors are the future revenues and future costs. By ignoring the accumulated costs and deciding on the basis of expected future costs, operating income will be maximized (or losses minimized). The difference in favor of remachining is $3,000:

	(a) Remachine	(b) Scrap
Future revenues	$35,000	$2,000
Deduct future costs	30,000	–
Operating income	$ 5,000	$2,000

Difference in favor of remachining ⬆ $3,000 ⬆

2.   This, too, is an unfortunate situation. But the $100,000 original cost is irrelevant to this decision. The difference in relevant costs in favor of rebuilding is $7,000 as follows:

	(a) Replace	(b) Rebuild
New truck	$102,000	–
Deduct current disposal price of existing truck	10,000	–
Rebuild existing truck	–	$85,000
	$ 92,000	$85,000

Difference in favor of rebuilding ⬆ $7,000 ⬆

Note, here, that the current disposal price of $10,000 is relevant, but the original cost (or book value, if the truck were not brand new) is irrelevant.

11-18 (15 min.)   **Multiple choice.**

1. (b)   Special order price per unit $6.00
            Variable manufacturing cost per unit   4.50
            Contribution margin per unit $1.50

    Effect on operating income   = $1.50 × 20,000 units
                                   = $30,000 increase

2. (b) Costs of purchases, 20,000 units × $60 $1,200,000
        Total relevant costs of making:
            Variable manufacturing costs, $64 – $16 $48
            Fixed costs eliminated   9
            Costs saved by not making $57
            Multiply by 20,000 units, so total
                costs saved are $57 × 20,000   1,140,000
        Extra costs of purchasing outside   60,000
        Minimum overall savings for Reno   25,000
        Necessary relevant costs that would have
            to be saved in manufacturing Part No. 575 $ 85,000

11-20 (30 min.)   Make versus buy, activity-based costing.

1.   The expected manufacturing cost per unit of CMCBs in 2007 is as follows:

	Total Manufacturing Costs of CMCB (1)	Manufacturing Cost per Unit (2) = (1) ÷ 10,000
Direct materials, $170 × 10,000	$1,700,000	$170
Direct manufacturing labor, $45 × 10,000	450,000	45
Variable batch manufacturing costs, $1,500 × 80	120,000	12
Fixed manufacturing costs		
Avoidable fixed manufacturing costs	320,000	32
Unavoidable fixed manufacturing costs	800,000	80
Total manufacturing costs	$3,390,000	$339

2.   The following table identifies the incremental costs in 2007 if Svenson (a) made CMCBs and (b) purchased CMCBs from Minton.

	Total Incremental Costs		Per-Unit Incremental Costs	
Incremental Items	Make	Buy	Make	Buy
Cost of purchasing CMCBs from Minton		$ 3,000,000		$300
Direct materials	$1,700,000		$170	
Direct manufacturing labor	450,000		45	
Variable batch manufacturing costs	120,000		12	
Avoidable fixed manufacturing costs	320,000		32	
Total incremental costs	$2,590,000	$3,000,000	$259	$300
Difference in favor of making		$410,000		$41

Note that the opportunity cost of using capacity to make CMCBs is zero since Svenson would keep this capacity idle if it purchases CMCBs from Minton.

Svenson should continue to manufacture the CMCBs internally since the incremental costs to manufacture are $259 per unit compared to the $300 per unit that Minton has quoted. Note that the unavoidable fixed manufacturing costs of $800,000 ($80 per unit) will continue to be incurred whether Svenson makes or buys CMCBs. These are not incremental costs under either the make or the buy alternative and hence, are irrelevant.

3.   Svenson should continue to make CMCBs. The simplest way to analyze this problem is to recognize that Svenson would prefer to keep any excess capacity idle rather than use it to make CB3s. Why? Because expected incremental future revenues from CB3s, $2,000,000, are *less* than expected incremental future costs, $2,150,000. If Svenson keeps its capacity idle, we know from requirement 2 that it should make CMCBs rather than buy them.

An important point to note is that, because Svenson forgoes no contribution by not being able to make and sell CB3s, the opportunity cost of using its facilities to make CMCBs is zero. It is, therefore, not forgoing any profits by using the capacity to manufacture CMCBs. If it does not manufacture CMCBs, rather than lose money on CB3s, Svenson will keep capacity idle.

A longer and more detailed approach is to use the total alternatives or opportunity cost analyses shown in Exhibit 11-7 of the chapter.

Relevant Items	Choices for Svenson		
	Make CMCBs and Do Not Make CB3s	Buy CMCBs and Do Not Make CB3s	Buy CMCBs and Make CB3s
TOTAL-ALTERNATIVES APPROACH TO MAKE-OR-BUY DECISIONS			
Total incremental costs of making/buying CMCBs (from requirement 2)	$2,590,000	$3,000,000	$3,000,000
Excess of future costs over future revenues from CB3s	0	0	150,000
Total relevant costs	$2,590,000	$3,000,000	$3,150,000

Svenson will minimize manufacturing costs by making CMCBs.

Relevant Items	Make CMCBs and Do Not Make CB3s	Buy CMCBs and Do Not Make CB3s	Buy CMCBs and Make CB3s
OPPORTUNITY-COST APPROACH TO MAKE-OR-BUY DECISIONS			
Total incremental costs of making/buying CMCBs (from requirement 2)	$2,590,000	$3,000,000	$3,000,000
Opportunity cost: profit contribution forgone because capacity will not be used to make CB3s	0*	0*	0
Total relevant costs	$2,590,000	$3,000,000	$3,000,000

*Opportunity cost is 0 because Svenson does not give up anything by not making CB3s. Svenson is best off leaving the capacity idle (rather than manufacturing and selling CB3s).

11-22 (20–25 min.)   **Relevant costs, contribution margin, product emphasis.**

1.

	Cola	Lemonade	Punch	Natural Orange Juice
Selling price	$18.00	$19.20	$26.40	$38.40
Deduct variable cost per case	13.50	15.20	20.10	30.20
Contribution margin per case	$ 4.50	$ 4.00	$ 6.30	$ 8.20

2.   The argument fails to recognize that shelf space is the constraining factor. There are only 12 feet of front shelf space to be devoted to drinks. Sexton should aim to get the highest daily contribution margin per foot of front shelf space:

	Cola	Lemonade	Punch	Natural Orange Juice
Contribution margin per case	$ 4.50	$ 4.00	$ 6.30	$ 8.20
Sales (number of cases) per foot of shelf space per day	× 25	× 24	× 4	× 5
Daily contribution per foot of front shelf space	$112.50	$96.00	$25.20	$41.00

3.   The allocation that maximizes the daily contribution from soft drink sales is:

	Feet of Shelf Space	Daily Contribution per Foot of Front Shelf Space	Total Contribution Margin per Day
Cola	6	$112.50	$ 675.00
Lemonade	4	96.00	384.00
Natural Orange Juice	1	41.00	41.00
Punch	1	25.20	25.20
			$1,125.20

The maximum of six feet of front shelf space will be devoted to Cola because it has the highest contribution margin per unit of the constraining factor. Four feet of front shelf space will be devoted to Lemonade, which has the second highest contribution margin per unit of the constraining factor. No more shelf space can be devoted to Lemonade since each of the remaining two products, Natural Orange Juice and Punch (that have the second lowest and lowest contribution margins per unit of the constraining factor) must each be given at least one foot of front shelf space.

11-24 (20 min.) **Which base to close, relevant-cost analysis, opportunity costs.**

The future outlay operating costs will be $400 million regardless of which base is closed, given the additional $100 million in costs at Everett if Alameda is closed. Further, one of the bases will permanently remain open while the other will be shut down. The only relevant revenue and cost comparisons are

    a. $500 million from sale of the Alameda base. Note that the historical cost of building the Alameda base ($100 million) is irrelevant. Note also that future increases in the value of the land at the Alameda base is also irrelevant. One of the bases must be kept open, so if it is decided to keep the Alameda base open, the Defense Department will not be able to sell this land at a future date.

    b. $60 million in savings in fixed income note if the Everett base is closed. Again, the historical cost of building the Everett base ($150 million) is irrelevant.

    The relevant costs and benefits analysis favors closing the Alameda base despite the objections raised by the California delegation in Congress. The net benefit equals $440 ($500 – $60) million.

11-26 (20 min.) **Choosing customers.**

If Broadway accepts the additional business from Kelly, it would take an additional 500 machine-hours. If Broadway accepts all of Kelly's and Taylor's business for February, it would require 2,500 machine-hours (1,500 hours for Taylor and 1,000 hours for Kelly). Broadway has only 2,000 hours of machine capacity. It must, therefore, choose how much of the Taylor or Kelly business to accept.

    To maximize operating income, Broadway should maximize contribution margin per unit of the constrained resource. (Fixed costs will remain unchanged at $100,000 regardless of the business Broadway chooses to accept in February, and is, therefore, irrelevant.) The contribution margin per unit of the constrained resource for each customer in January is:

	Taylor Corporation	Kelly Corporation
Contribution margin per machine-hour	$\dfrac{\$78,000}{1,500} = \$52$	$\dfrac{\$32,000}{500} = \$64$

    Since the $80,000 of additional Kelly business in February is identical to jobs done in January, it will also have a contribution margin of $64 per machine-hour, which is greater than the contribution margin of $52 per machine-hour from Taylor. To maximize operating income, Broadway should first allocate all the capacity needed to take the Kelly Corporation business (1,000 machine-hours) and then allocate the remaining 1,000 (2,000 – 1,000) machine-hours to Taylor.

	Taylor Corporation	Kelly Corporation	Total
Contribution margin per machine-hour	$52	$64	
Machine-hours to be worked	× 1,000	× 1,000	
Contribution margin	$52,000	$64,000	$116,000
Fixed costs			100,000
Operating income			$ 16,000

11-28 (30 min.) **Equipment upgrade versus replacement.**

1.   Based on the analysis in the table below, TechMech will be better off by $180,000 over three years if it replaces the current equipment.

| | Over 3 years | | Difference |
Comparing Relevant Costs of Upgrade and Replace Alternatives	Upgrade (1)	Replace (2)	in favor of Replace (3) = (1) − (2)
Cash operating costs			
$140; $80 per desk × 6,000 desks per yr. × 3 yrs.	$2,520,000	$1,440,000	$1,080,000
Current disposal price		(600,000)	600,000
One time capital costs, written off periodically as depreciation	2,700,000	4,200,000	(1,500,000)
Total relevant costs	$5,220,000	$5,040,000	$ 180,000

Note that the book value of the current machine ($900,000) would either be written off as depreciation over three years under the upgrade option, or, all at once in the current year under the replace option. Its net effect would be the same in both alternatives: to increase costs by $900,000 over three years, hence it is irrelevant in this analysis.

2.   Suppose the capital expenditure to replace the equipment is $X. From requirement 1, column (2), substituting for the one-time capital cost of replacement, the relevant cost of replacing is $1,440,000 − $600,000 + $X. From column (1), the relevant cost of upgrading is $5,220,000. We want to find X such that
        $1,440,000 − $600,000 + $X < $5,220,000 (i.e., TechMech will favor replacing)
Solving the above inequality gives us X < $5,220,000 − $840,000 = $4,380,000.

TechMech would prefer to replace, rather than upgrade, if the replacement cost of the new equipment does not exceed $4,380,000. Note that this result can also be obtained by taking the original replacement cost of $4,200,000 and adding to it the $180,000 difference in favor of replacement calculated in requirement 1.

3.   Suppose the units produced and sold over 3 years equal y. Using data from requirement 1, column (1), the relevant cost of upgrade would be $140y + $2,700,000, and from column (2), the relevant cost of replacing the equipment would be $80y − $600,000 + $4,200,000. TechMech would want to upgrade if

$$\$140y + \$2,700,000 < \$80y - \$600,000 + \$4,200,000$$
$$\$60y < \$900,000$$
$$y < \$900,000 \div \$60 = 15,000 \text{ units}$$

or upgrade when y < 15,000 units (or 5,000 per year for 3 years) and replace when y > 15,000 units over 3 years.
        When production and sales volume is low (less than 5,000 per year), the higher operating costs under the upgrade option are more than offset by the savings in capital costs from upgrading. When production and sales volume is high, the higher capital costs of replacement are more than offset by the savings in operating costs in the replace option.

4.   Operating income for the first year under the upgrade and replace alternatives are shown below:

	Year 1	
	Upgrade **(1)**	**Replace** **(2)**
Revenues (6,000 × $500)	$3,000,000	$3,000,000
Cash operating costs		
$140; $80 per desk × 6,000 desks per year	840,000	480,000
Depreciation ($900,000[a] + $2,700,000) ÷ 3; $4,200,000 ÷ 3	1,200,000	1,400,000
Loss on disposal of old equipment (0; $900,000 – $600,000)	0	300,000
Total costs	2,040,000	2,180,000
Operating Income	$ 960,000	$ 820,000

[a]The book value of the current production equipment is $1,500,000 × 3 ÷ 5 = $900,000; it has a remaining useful life of 3 years.

First-year operating income is higher by $140,000 under the upgrade alternative, and Dan Doria, with his one-year horizon and operating income-based bonus, will choose the upgrade alternative, even though, as seen in requirement 1, the replace alternative is better in the long run for TechMech. This exercise illustrates the possible conflict between the decision model and the performance evaluation model.

11-30 (30 min.) **Contribution approach, relevant costs.**

1.

Average one-way fare per passenger	$ 500
Commission at 8% of $500	(40)
Net cash to Air Frisco per ticket	$ 460
Average number of passengers per flight	× 200
Revenues per flight ($460 × 200)	$ 92,000
Food and beverage cost per flight ($20 × 200)	4,000
Total contribution margin from passengers per flight	$ 88,000

2.

If fare is	$ 480.00
Commission at 8% of $480	(38.40)
Net cash per ticket	441.60
Food and beverage cost per ticket	20.00
Contribution margin per passenger	$ 421.60
Total contribution margin from passengers per flight ($421.60 × 212)	$89,379.20

All other costs are irrelevant.

On the basis of quantitative factors alone, Air Frisco should decrease its fare to $480 because reducing the fare gives Air Frisco a higher contribution margin from passengers ($89,379.20 versus $88,000).

3.   In evaluating whether Air Frisco should charter its plane to Travel International, we compare the charter alternative to the solution in requirement 2 because requirement 2 is preferred to requirement 1.

Under requirement 2, contribution from passengers	$89,379.20
Deduct fuel costs	14,000.00
Total contribution per flight	$75,379.20

Air Frisco gets $74,500 per flight from chartering the plane to Travel International. On the basis of quantitative financial factors, Air Frisco is better off not chartering the plane and, instead, lowering its own fares.

Other qualitative factors that Air Frisco should consider in coming to a decision are
   a. The lower risk from chartering its plane relative to the uncertainties regarding the number of passengers it might get on its scheduled flights.
   b. The stability of the relationship between Air Frisco and Travel International. If this is not a long-term arrangement, Air Frisco may lose current market share and not benefit from sustained charter revenues.

11-32 (20 min.) **Opportunity costs.**

1.   The opportunity cost to Wolverine of producing the 2,000 units of Orangebo is the contribution margin lost on the 2,000 units of Rosebo that would have to be forgone, as computed below:

Selling price		$20
Variable costs per unit:		
Direct materials	$2	
Direct manufacturing labor	3	
Variable manufacturing overhead	2	
Variable marketing costs	4	11
Contribution margin per unit		$ 9
Contribution margin for 2,000 units		$ 18,000

The opportunity cost is $18,000. Opportunity cost is the maximum contribution to operating income that is forgone (rejected) by not using a limited resource in its next-best alternative use.

2.   Contribution margin from manufacturing 2,000 units of Orangebo and purchasing 2,000 units of Rosebo from Buckeye is $16,000, as follows:

	Manufacture Orangebo	Purchase Rosebo	Total
Selling price	$15	$20	
Variable costs per unit:			
Purchase costs	–	14	
Direct materials	2		
Direct manufacturing labor	3		
Variable manufacturing costs	2		
Variable marketing overhead	2	4	
Variable costs per unit	9	18	
Contribution margin per unit	$ 6	$ 2	
Contribution margin from selling 2,000 units of Orangebo and 2,000 units of Rosebo	$12,000	$4,000	$16,000

As calculated in requirement 1, Wolverine's contribution margin from continuing to manufacture 2,000 units of Rosebo is $18,000. Accepting the Miami Company and Buckeye offer will cost Wolverine $2,000 ($16,000 – $18,000). Hence, Wolverine should refuse the Miami Company and Buckeye Corporation's offers.

3.   The minimum price would be $9, the sum of the incremental costs as computed in requirement 2. This follows because, if Wolverine has surplus capacity, the opportunity cost = $0. For the short-run decision of whether to accept Orangebo's offer, fixed costs of Wolverine are irrelevant. Only the incremental costs need to be covered for it to be worthwhile for Wolverine to accept the Orangebo offer.

11-34 (35–40 min.)   **Dropping a product line, selling more units.**

1.   The incremental revenue losses and incremental savings in cost by discontinuing the Tables product line follows:

	Difference: Incremental (Loss in Revenues) and Savings in Costs from Dropping Tables Line
Revenues	$(500,000)
Direct materials and direct manufacturing labor	300,000
Depreciation on equipment	0
Marketing and distribution	70,000
General administration	0
Corporate office costs	0
Total costs	370,000
Operating income (loss)	$(130,000)

Dropping the Tables product line results in revenue losses of $500,000 and cost savings of $370,000. Hence, Grossman Corporation's operating income will be $130,000 lower if it drops the Tables line.

Note that, by dropping the Tables product line, Home Furnishings will save none of the depreciation on equipment, general administration costs, and corporate office costs, but it will save variable manufacturing costs and all marketing and distribution costs on the Tables product line.

2.   Grossman's will generate incremental operating income of $128,000 from selling 4,000 additional tables and, hence, should try to increase table sales. The calculations follow:

	Incremental Revenues (Costs) and Operating Income
Revenues	$500,000
Direct materials and direct manufacturing labor	(300,000)
Cost of equipment written off as depreciation	(42,000)*
Marketing and distribution costs	(30,000)†
General administration costs	0**
Corporate office costs	0**
Operating income	$128,000

*Note that the additional costs of equipment are relevant future costs for the "selling more tables decision" because they represent incremental future costs that differ between the alternatives of selling and not selling additional tables.

†Current marketing and distribution costs which varies with number of shipments = $70,000 – $40,000 = $30,000. As the sales of tables double, the number of shipments will double, resulting in incremental marketing and distribution costs of (2 × $30,000) – $30,000 = $30,000.

**General administration and corporate office costs will be unaffected if Grossman decides to sell more tables. Hence, these costs are irrelevant for the decision.

3. Solution Exhibit 11-34, Column 1, presents the relevant loss of revenues and the relevant savings in costs from closing the Northern Division. As the calculations show, Grossman's operating income would decrease by $140,000 if it shut down the Northern Division (loss in revenues of $1,500,000 versus savings in costs of $1,360,000).

Grossman will save variable manufacturing costs, marketing and distribution costs, and division general administration costs by closing the Northern Division but equipment-related depreciation and corporate office allocations are irrelevant to the decision. Equipment-related costs are irrelevant because they are past costs (and the equipment has zero disposal price). Corporate office costs are irrelevant because Grossman will not save any actual corporate office costs by closing the Northern Division. The corporate office costs that used to be allocated to the Northern Division will be allocated to other divisions.

4.   Solution Exhibit 11-34, Column 2, presents the relevant revenues and relevant costs of opening the Southern Division (a division whose revenues and costs are expected to be identical to the revenues and costs of the Northern Division). Grossman should open the Southern Division because it would increase operating income by $40,000 (increase in relevant revenues of $1,500,000 and increase in relevant costs of $1,460,000). The relevant costs include direct materials, direct manufacturing labor, marketing and distribution, equipment, and division general administration costs but not corporate office costs. Note, in particular, that the cost of equipment written off as depreciation is relevant because it is an expected future cost that Grossman will incur only if it opens the Southern Division. Corporate office costs are irrelevant because actual corporate office costs will not change if Grossman opens the Southern Division. The current corporate staff will be able to oversee the Southern Division's operations. Grossman will allocate some corporate office costs to the Southern Division but this allocation represents corporate office costs that are already currently being allocated to some other division. Because actual total corporate office costs do not change, they are irrelevant to the division.

SOLUTION EXHIBIT 11-34
Relevant-Revenue and Relevant-Cost Analysis for Closing Northern Division and Opening Southern Division

	(Loss in Revenues) and Savings in Costs from Closing Northern Division (1)	Incremental Revenues and (Incremental Costs) from Opening Southern Division (2)
Revenues	$(1,500,000)	$1,500,000
Variable direct materials and direct manufacturing labor costs	825,000	(825,000)
Equipment cost written off as depreciation	0	(100,000)
Marketing and distribution costs	205,000	(205,000)
Division general administration costs	330,000	(330,000)
Corporate office costs	0	0
Total costs	1,360,000	(1,460,000)
Effect on operating income (loss)	$ (140,000)	$ 40,000

11-36 (30 min.) **Make versus buy, activity-based costing, opportunity costs.**

1.   Relevant costs under buy alternative:
        Purchases, 10,000 × $8.20 $82,000

        Relevant costs under make alternative:
        Direct materials $40,000
        Direct manufacturing labor   20,000
        Variable manufacturing overhead   15,000
        Inspection, setup, materials handling   2,000
        Machine rent   3,000
            Total relevant costs under make alternative $80,000

The allocated fixed plant administration, taxes, and insurance will not change if Ace makes or buys the chains. Hence, these costs are irrelevant to the make-or-buy decision. The analysis indicates that Ace should make and not buy the chains from the outside supplier.

2.   Relevant costs under the make alternative:

Relevant costs (as computed in requirement 1)	$80,000

Relevant costs under the buy alternative:

Costs of purchases (10,000 × $8.20)	$82,000
Additional fixed costs	16,000
Additional contribution margin from using the space where the chains were made to upgrade the bicycles by adding mud flaps and reflector bars, 10,000 × ($20 – $18)	(20,000)
Total relevant costs under the buy alternative	$78,000

Ace should now buy the chains from an outside vendor and use its own capacity to upgrade its own bicycles.

3.   In this requirement, the decision on mud flaps and reflectors is irrelevant to the analysis.

Cost of manufacturing chains:

Variable costs, ($4 + $2 + $1.50 = $7.50) × 6,200	$46,500
Batch costs, $200/batch[a] × 8 batches	1,600
Machine rent	3,000
	$51,100

Cost of buying chains, $8.20 × 6,200	$50,840

[a]$2,000 ÷ 10 batches

In this case, Ace should buy the chains from the outside vendor.

11-38 (15 min.) **Make or buy (continuation of 11-37).**

The maximum price Class Company should be willing to pay is $3.9417 per unit.

Expected unit production and sales of new product must be half of the old product (1/2 × 240,000 = 120,000) because the fixed manufacturing overhead rate for the new product is twice that of the fixed manufacturing overhead rate for the old product.

| | | Proposed | | |
| | | Make New | Old | |
	Present	Product	Product	Total
Revenues	$1,440,000	$1,080,000	$1,440,000	$2,520,000
Variable (or purchase) costs:				
Manufacturing	720,000	600,000	946,000*	1,546,000
Marketing and other	360,000	240,000	288,000	528,000
Total variable costs	1,080,000	840,000	1,234,000	2,074,000
Contribution margin	360,000	240,000	206,000	446,000
Fixed costs:				
Manufacturing	120,000	120,000		120,000
Marketing and other	216,000	60,000	216,000	276,000
Total fixed costs	336,000	180,000	216,000	396,000
Operating income	$ 24,000	$ 60,000	$ (10,000)	$ 50,000

*This is an example of opportunity costs, whereby subcontracting at a price well above the $3.50 current manufacturing (absorption) cost is still desirable because the old product will be displaced in manufacturing by a new product that is more profitable.

Because the new product promises an operating income of $60,000 (ignoring the irrelevant problem of how fixed marketing costs should be reallocated between products), the old product can sustain up to a $10,000 loss and still help accomplish management's overall objectives. Maximum costs that can be incurred on the old product are $1,440,000 plus the $10,000 loss, or $1,450,000. Maximum purchase cost: $1,450,000 − ($288,000 + $216,000) = $946,000. Maximum purchase cost per unit: $946,000 ÷ 240,000 units = $3.9417 per unit.

Alternative Computation

Operating income is $9.00 − $8.50 = $0.50 per unit		
for 120,000 new units		$60,000
Target operating income		50,000
Maximum loss allowed on old product		$10,000
Maximum loss per unit allowed on old product,		
$10,000 ÷ 240,000 =		$0.0417
Selling price of old product		$6.0000
Allowance for loss		0.0417
Total costs allowed per unit		6.0417
Continuing costs for old product other than purchase cost:		
Fixed manufacturing costs—all transferred to new product	$ —	
Variable marketing costs	1.20	
Fixed marketing costs	0.90	2.1000
Maximum purchase cost per unit		$3.9417

11-40 (30–40 min.)   **Optimal product mix.**

1.   Let D represent the batches of Della's Delight made and sold.
        Let B represent the batches of Bonny's Bourbon made and sold.
        The contribution margin per batch of Della's Delight is $300.
        The contribution margin per batch of Bonny's Bourbon is $250.

        The LP formulation for the decision is:

        Maximize $300D + $250 B
        Subject to   30D + 15B   ≤ 660 (Mixing Department constraint)
                      15B   ≤ 270 (Filling Department constraint)
                      10D + 15B   ≤ 300 (Baking Department constraint)

2.   Solution Exhibit 11-40 presents a graphical summary of the relationships. The optimal
corner is the point (18, 8) i.e., 18 batches of Della's Delights and 8 of Bonny's Bourbons.

SOLUTION EXHIBIT 11-40
Graphic Solution to Find Optimal Mix, Della Simpson, Inc.

Della Simpson Production Model

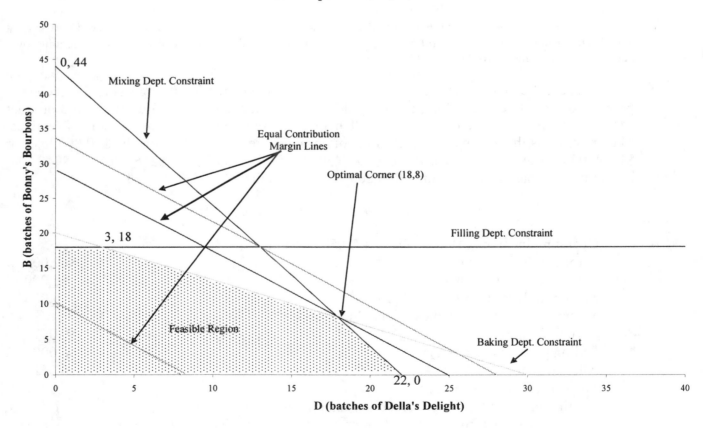

We next calculate the optimal production mix using the trial-and-error method.

The corner point where the Mixing Dept. and Baking Dept. constraints intersect can be calculated as (18, 8) by solving:

$$30D + 15B = 660 \text{ (1) Mixing Dept. constraint}$$
$$10D + 15B = 300 \text{ (2) Baking Dept. constraint}$$

Subtracting (2) from (1), we have
$$20D = 360$$
$$\text{or } D = 18$$

Substituting in (2)
$$(10 \times 18) + 15B = 300$$
$$\text{that is, } \quad 15B = 300 - 180 = 120$$
$$\text{or } \quad B = 8$$

The corner point where the Filling and Baking Department constraints intersect can be calculated as (3,18) by substituting B = 18 (Filling Department constraint) into the Baking Department constraint:

$$10D + (15 \times 18) = 300$$
$$10D = 300 - 270 = 30$$
$$D = 3$$

The feasible region, defined by 5 corner points, is shaded in Solution Exhibit 11-40. We next use the trial-and-error method to check the contribution margins at each of the five corner points of the area of feasible solutions.

Trial	Corner (D,B)	Total Contribution Margin
1	(0,0)	($300 × 0) + ($250 × 0) = $0 .
2	(22,0)	($300 × 22) + ($250 × 0) = $6,600
3	(18,8)	($300 × 18) + ($250 × 8) = $7,400
4	(3,18)	($300 × 3) + ($250 × 18) = $5,400
5	(0,18)	($300 × 0) + ($250 × 18) = $4,500

The optimal solution that maximizes contribution margin and operating income is 18 batches of Della's Delights and 8 batches of Bonny's Bourbons.

11-42 (40 min.) **Optimal product mix** (CMA, adapted).

1.

Machine hours per pair of skates = Variable machine operating cost per pair skates ÷ $16 per mach. hr. = $24 ÷ $16   1.50

Machine hours per pair of bindings = Variable machine operating cost per pair of bindings ÷ $16 per machine hour = $8 ÷ $16   0.50

Full machine hour capacity = Machine hours for 5,000 pairs of skates = 5,000 × 1.50   7,500

Machine hours used for 12,000 pairs of bindings = 12,000 × 0.50   6,000

Percentage capacity used if only 12,000 pairs of bindings are produced = 6,000 ÷ 7,500   80%

Cost of manufacturing capacity = Fixed manufacturing overhead costs $30,000

Cost of unused capacity if only 12,000 pairs of bindings are produced = 20% of $30,000 $ 6,000

2.

Variable and fixed manufacturing overhead cost per skate (when at full capacity of 5,000 units) $ 18

Total variable and fixed manufacturing overhead costs = 5,000 × $18 $90,000

Total fixed manufacturing overhead costs (full capacity) $30,000

Total variable manufacturing overhead costs (for 5,000 pairs of skates or 7,500 machine hours) = $90,000 – $30,000 $60,000

Variable manufacturing overhead cost per machine hour = $60,000 ÷ 7,500 machine hours $ 8.00

3.

	Manufactured Skates	Manufactured Snowboard Bindings	Purchased Skates
Selling price	$98	$60	$98
Variable costs per unit			
Purchase cost	—	—	75
Direct material	20	20	—
Variable machine operating cost ($16 per machine hour)	24	8	—
Variable manufacturing overhead (1.5 mach. hrs.; 0.5 mach. hrs.; × $8 VMOH per mach. hr.)	12	4	—
Variable marketing and administrative cost	9	8	4
Total variable cost per unit	65	40	79
Contribution margin per unit	$33	$20	$19
Contribution margin per machine hour (Contribution margin per unit ÷ machine hours per unit = $33 ÷ 1.5; $20 ÷ 0.5)	$22	$40	

4.   In order to maximize OmniSport, Inc.'s profitability, OmniSport should manufacture 12,000 snowboard bindings (the maximum that it can sell; this uses up 80% of manufacturing capacity), manufacture 1,000 pairs of skates (uses up the remaining 20% of manufacturing capacity), and purchase the total offered 6,000 pairs of skates from Colcott, Inc. This combination of manufactured and purchased goods maximizes the contribution margin per available machine-hour, which is the limiting resource.

Because snowboard bindings have a higher contribution margin per machine-hour than in-line skates, OmniSport should manufacture the maximum number of snowboard bindings. Because the contribution margin per manufactured pair of in-line skates is higher than the contribution margin from a purchased pair of in-line skates, total contribution margin will be maximized by using the remaining manufacturing capacity to produce in-line skates and then purchasing the remaining required skates. The calculations for the optimal combination follow:

	Purchased In-line Skates 6,000		Manufactured In-line Skates 1,000		Manufactured Snowboard Bindings 12,000		Total
	Per Unit	Total	Per Unit	Total	Per Unit	Total	
Selling price	$98	$588,000	$98	$98,000	$60	$720,000	$1,406,000
Variable costs							
Direct materials	75	450,000	20	20,000	20	240,000	710,000
Machine operating costs	–	–	24	24,000	8	96,000	120,000
Manufacturing overhead costs	–	–	12	12,000	4	48,000	60,000
Markt. & admn. costs	4	24,000	9	9,000	8	96,000	129,000
Variable costs	79	474,000	65	65,000	40	480,000	1,019,000
Contribution margin	19	114,000	33	33,000	20	240,000	387,000
Fixed costs							
Manufacturing overhead							30,000
Marketing & administrative costs							60,000
Fixed costs							90,000
Operating income							$ 297,000
Machine-hours per unit	–		1.5		0.5		
Contribution per machine-hour	–		$22.0		$40.0		

CHAPTER 12
PRICING DECISIONS AND COST MANAGEMENT

12-2 Not necessarily. For a one-time-only special order, the relevant costs are only those costs that will change as a result of accepting the order. In this case, full product costs will rarely be relevant. It is more likely that full product costs will be relevant costs for long-run pricing decisions.

12-4 Activity-based costing helps managers in pricing decisions in two ways.
1. It gives managers more accurate product-cost information for making pricing decisions.
2. It helps managers to manage costs during value engineering by identifying the cost impact of eliminating, reducing, or changing various activities.

12-6 A target cost per unit is the estimated long-run cost per unit of a product (or service) that, when sold at the target price, enables the company to achieve the targeted operating income per unit.

12-8 A value-added cost is a cost that customers perceive as adding value, or utility, to a product or service. Examples are costs of materials, direct labor, tools, and machinery. A nonvalue-added cost is a cost that customers do not perceive as adding value, or utility, to a product or service. Examples of nonvalue-added costs are costs of rework, scrap, expediting, and breakdown maintenance.

12-10 Cost-plus pricing is a pricing approach in which managers add a markup to cost in order to determine price.

12-12 Two examples where the difference in the costs of two products or services is much smaller than the differences in their prices follow:
1. The difference in prices charged for a telephone call, hotel room, or car rental during busy versus slack periods is often much greater than the difference in costs to provide these services.
2. The difference in costs for an airplane seat sold to a passenger traveling on business or a passenger traveling for pleasure is roughly the same. However, airline companies routinely charge business travelers—those who are likely to start and complete their travel during the same week excluding the weekend—a much higher price than pleasure travelers who generally stay at their destinations over at least one weekend.

12-14 Three benefits of using a product life-cycle reporting format are:
1. The full set of revenues and costs associated with each product becomes more visible.
2. Differences among products in the percentage of total costs committed at early stages in the life cycle are highlighted.
3. Interrelationships among business function cost categories are highlighted.

12-16 (20–30 min.)   **Relevant-cost approach to pricing decisions, special order.**

1.

Relevant revenues, $3.80 × 1,000		$3,800
Relevant costs		
Direct materials, $1.50 × 1,000	$1,500	
Direct manufacturing labor, $0.80 × 1,000	800	
Variable manufacturing overhead, $0.70 × 1,000	700	
Variable selling costs, 0.05 × $3,800	190	
Total relevant costs		3,190
Increase in operating income		$ 610

This calculation assumes that:
- a. The monthly fixed manufacturing overhead of $150,000 and $65,000 of monthly fixed marketing costs will be unchanged by acceptance of the 1,000 unit order.
- b. The price charged and the volumes sold to other customers are not affected by the special order.

Chapter 12 uses the phrase "one-time-only special order" to describe this special case.

2.   The president's reasoning is defective on at least two counts:
- a. The inclusion of irrelevant costs—assuming the monthly fixed manufacturing overhead of $150,000 will be unchanged; it is irrelevant to the decision.
- b. The exclusion of relevant costs—variable selling costs (5% of the selling price) are excluded.

3.   Key issues are:
- a. Will the existing customer base demand price reductions? If this 1,000-tape order is not independent of other sales, cutting the price from $5.00 to $3.80 can have a large negative effect on total revenues.
- b. Is the 1,000-tape order a one-time-only order, or is there the possibility of sales in subsequent months? The fact that the customer is not in Dill Company's "normal marketing channels" does not necessarily mean it is a one-time-only order. Indeed, the sale could well open a new marketing channel. Dill Company should be reluctant to consider only short-run variable costs for pricing long-run business.

12-18 (15-20 min.)   **Short-run pricing, capacity constraints.**

1. Per kilogram of hard cheese:

Milk (10 liters × $1.50 per liter)	$15
Direct manufacturing labor	5
Variable manufacturing overhead	3
Fixed manufacturing cost allocated	6
Total manufacturing cost	$29

If Vermont Hills can get all the Holstein milk it needs, and has sufficient production capacity, then, the minimum price per kilo it should charge for the hard cheese is the variable cost per kilo = $15+5+3 = $23 per kilo.

2.   If milk is in short supply, then each kilo of hard cheese displaces 2.5 kilos of soft cheese (10 liters of milk per kilo of hard cheese versus 4 liters of milk per kilo of soft cheese). Then, for the hard cheese, the minimum price Vermont should charge is the variable cost per kilo of hard cheese plus the contribution margin from 2.5 kilos of soft cheese, or,

$$\$23 + (2.5 \times \$8 \text{ per kilo}) = \$43 \text{ per kilo}$$

That is, if milk is in short supply, Vermont should not agree to produce any hard cheese unless the buyer is willing to pay at least $43 per kilo.

12-20 (25–30 min.)   **Target operating income, value-added costs, service company.**

1.   The classification of total costs in 2007 into value-added, nonvalue-added, or in the gray area in between follows:

	Value Added (1)	Gray Area (2)	Nonvalue-added (3)	Total (4) = (1)+(2)+(3)
Doing calculations and preparing drawings 75% × $400,000	$300,000			$300,000
Checking calculations and drawings 4% × $400,000		$16,000		16,000
Correcting errors found in drawings 7% × $400,000			$28,000	28,000
Making changes in response to client requests 6% × $400,000	24,000			24,000
Correcting errors to meet government building code, 8% × $400,000			32,000	32,000
Total professional labor costs	324,000	16,000	60,000	400,000
Administrative and support costs at 40% ($160,000 ÷ $400,000) of professional labor costs	129,600	6,400	24,000	160,000
Travel	18,000		—	18,000
Total	$471,600	$22,400	$84,000	$578,000

Doing calculations and responding to client requests for changes are value-added costs because customers perceive these costs as necessary for the service of preparing architectural drawings. Costs incurred on correcting errors in drawings and making changes because they were inconsistent with building codes are nonvalue-added costs. Customers do not perceive these costs as necessary and would be unwilling to pay for them. Carasco should seek to eliminate these costs by making sure that all associates are well-informed regarding building code requirements and by training associates to improve the quality of their drawings. Checking calculations and drawings is in the gray area (some, but not all, checking may be needed). There is room for disagreement on these classifications. For example, checking calculations may be regarded as value added.

2.   Reduction in professional labor-hours by

a. Correcting errors in drawings (7% × 8,000)	560 hours
b. Correcting errors to conform to building code (8% × 8,000)	640 hours
Total	1,200 hours
Cost savings in professional labor costs (1,200 hours × $50)	$ 60,000
Cost savings in variable administrative and support costs (40% × $60,000)	24,000
Total cost savings	$ 84,000
Current operating income in 2007	$102,000
Add cost savings from eliminating errors	84,000
Operating income in 2007 if errors eliminated	$186,000

3.   Currently 85% × 8,000 hours = 6,800 hours are billed to clients generating revenues of $680,000. The remaining 15% of professional labor-hours (15% × 8,000 = 1,200 hours) is lost in making corrections. Carasco bills clients at the rate of $680,000 ÷ 6,800 = $100 per professional labor-hour. If the 1,200 professional labor-hours currently not being billed to clients were billed to clients, Carasco's revenues would increase by 1,200 hours × $100 = $120,000 from $680,000 to $800,000.

Costs remain unchanged	
Professional labor costs	$400,000
Administrative and support (40% × $400,000)	160,000
Travel	18,000
Total costs	$578,000
Carasco's operating income would be	
Revenues	$800,000
Total costs	578,000
Operating income	$222,000

12-22 (20 min.) **Target costs, effect of product-design changes on product costs.**

1. and 2. Manufacturing costs of HJ6 in 2006 and 2007 are as follows:

	2006		2007	
	Total	**Per Unit**	**Total**	**Per Unit**
	(1)	**(2) =** **(1) ÷ 3,500**	**(3)**	**(4) =** **(3) ÷ 4,000**
Direct materials, $1,200 × 3,500; $1,100 × 4,000	$4,200,000	$1,200	$4,400,000	$1,100
Batch-level costs, $8,000 × 70; $7,500 × 80	560,000	160	600,000	150
Manuf. operations costs, $55 × 21,000; $50 × 22,000	1,155,000	330	1,100,000	275
Engineering change costs, $12,000 × 14; $10,000 × 10	168,000	48	100,000	25
Total	$6,083,000	$1,738	$6,200,000	$1,550

3. $$\frac{\text{Target manufacturing cost}}{\text{per unit of HJ6 in 2007}} = \frac{\text{Manufacturing cost}}{\text{per unit in 2006}} \times 90\%$$

$$= \$1,738 \times 0.90 = \$1,564.20$$

Actual manufacturing cost per unit of HJ6 in 2007 was $1,550. Hence, Medical Instruments did achieve its target manufacturing cost per unit of $1,564.20

4.   To reduce the manufacturing cost per unit in 2007, Medical Instruments reduced the cost per unit in each of the four cost categories—direct materials costs, batch-level costs, manufacturing operations costs, and engineering change costs. It also reduced machine-hours and number of engineering changes made—the quantities of the cost drivers. In 2006, Medical Instruments used 6 machine-hours per unit of HJ6 (21,000 machine-hours ÷3,500 units). In 2007, Medical Instruments used 5.5 machine-hours per unit of HJ6 (22,000 machine-hours ÷ 4,000 units). Medical Instruments reduced engineering changes from 14 in 2006 to 10 in 2007. Medical Instruments achieved these gains through value engineering activities that retained only those product features that customers wanted while eliminating nonvalue-added activities and costs.

12-24 (20–25 min.) **Cost-plus, target pricing, working backwards.**

1.	Investment	$2,400,000
	Return on investment	20%
	Operating income (20% × $2,400,000)	$480,000
	Operating income per unit of RF17 ($480,000 ÷ 20,000)	$24
	Full cost per unit of RF17	$300
	Selling price ($300 + $24)	$324
	Markup percentage on full cost ($24 ÷ $300)	8%

With a 50% markup on variable costs,
Selling price of RF17 = Variable cost per unit of RF17 × 1.50, so:

$$\text{Variable costs per unit of RF17} = \frac{\text{Selling price of RF17}}{1.50} = \frac{\$324}{1.50} = \$216$$

2.	Fixed costs per unit = $300 – $216 =	$84
	Total fixed costs = $84 per unit × 20,000 units =	$1,680,000
	At a price of $38, sales = 20,000 units × 0.90	18,000
	Revenues ($348 × 18,000)	$6,264,000
	Variable costs ($216 × 18,000)	3,888,000
	Contribution margin ($132 × 18,000)	2,376,000
	Fixed costs	1,680,000
	Operating income	$ 696,000

If Waterbuy increases the selling price of RF17 to $348, its operating income will be $696,000. This would be more than the $480,000 operating income Waterbury earns by selling 20,000 units at a price of $324, so, if its forecast is accurate, and based on financial considerations alone, Waterbury should increase the selling price to $348.

3.

Target investment in 2008		$2,100,000
Target return on investment		20%
Target operating income in 2008, 20% × $2,100,000		$420,000
Anticipated revenues in 2008, $315 × 20,000		$6,300,000
Less target operating income in 2008		420,000
Target full costs in 2008		$5,880,000
Less: total target fixed costs		1,680,000
Total target variable costs in 2008		$4,200,000

Target variable cost per unit in 2008, $4,200,000 ÷ 20,000 = $210

12-26 (15 min.) Considerations other than cost in pricing.

1.   Most of the costs of running a hotel are fixed relative to the number of guests in the hotel. The variable costs of each guest are a relatively minor part of the total costs and relate mainly to linen services and perhaps a small portion of utilities. In particular, the incremental costs of a weekend guest are no different from the incremental costs of a weekday guest, and they are small, in any case.

2.   Business travelers predominantly stay on a Sunday through Thursday basis. They usually return home after their business is conducted during weekdays. They are price insensitive because they must conduct their business during weekdays and their travel costs are reimbursed to them by their companies. Hotels earn higher operating income by charging business travelers higher prices because higher prices have little effect on business travelers' demand for hotel stays.

In contrast, leisure travelers who are paying for their own hotel rooms are more sensitive to the hotel room rates. They may make their travel plans in a way that enables them to take advantage of lower weekend room rates. This may be done either by "mini" vacations taken during the weekends only, or extending their stay over the weekend because of lower rates. Charging lowers rates stimulates demand among leisure travelers and increases contribution margin and operating income.

The hotels also tend to be less busy during weekends when business activity is low. Therefore, during "off-peak" periods, hotels often reduce their room rates to attract customers. Even at reduced rates, hotels can cover their variable costs and generate contribution margin. Since fixed costs do not increase, any increase in contribution margin contributes to higher profits.

3.   The hotels located in Anaheim and San Francisco's Fisherman's Wharf cater primarily to people who are traveling for pleasure and to visit tourist attractions. Therefore, the occupancy rate in those hotels does not go down during weekends. For this reason, the hotels can charge the same rate both during weekdays and weekends.

12-28 (25–30 min.)   **Target rate of return on investment, activity-based costing.**

1.

Operating Income Statement, April 2006	
Revenues (12,000 disks × $22 per disk)	$264,000
Materials (12,000 disks × $15 per disk)	180,000
Gross margin	84,000
Ordering (40 vendors × $250 per vendor)	10,000
Cataloging (20 new titles × $100 per title)	2,000
Delivery and support (400 deliveries × $15 per delivery)	6,000
Billing and collection (300 customers × $50 per customer)	15,000
Operating Income	$ 51,000
Rate of return on investment ($51,000 ÷ $300,000)	17.00%

2.   The table below shows that if the selling price of game disks falls to $18 and the cost of each disk falls to $12, monthly gross margin falls to $72,000 (from $84,000 in April), and this results in a return on investment of 13%, which is below EA's target rate of return on investment of 15%. EA will have to cut costs to earn its target rate of return on investment.

Operating Income Statement, May 2006	
Revenues (12,000 disks × $18 per disk)	$216,000
Materials (12,000 disks × $12 per disk)	144,000
Gross margin	72,000
Ordering (40 vendors × $250 per vendor)	10,000
Cataloging (20 new titles × $100 per title)	2,000
Delivery and support (400 deliveries × $15 per delivery)	6,000
Billing and collection (300 customers × $50 per customer)	15,000
Operating Income	$ 39,000
Rate of return on investment ($39,000 ÷ $300,000)	13.00%

3.   After EA's workforce has implemented process improvements, its monthly support costs are $31,500, as shown below.

Monthly support costs after process improvements, May 2006	
Ordering (30 vendors × $200 per vendor)	$6,000
Cataloging (15 new titles × $100 per title)	1,500
Delivery and support (450 deliveries × $20 per delivery)	9,000
Billing and collection (300 customers × $50 per customer)	15,000
Total monthly support costs	$31,500

EA now earns $6 ($18 – $12) gross margin per disk. Suppose it needs to sell X game disks to earn at least its 15% target rate of return on investment of $300,000. Then X needs to be such that:

$$\$6\,X - \$31,500 \;\geq\; \$300,000 \times 15\% = \$45,000$$
$$\$6\,X \;\geq\; \$76,500$$
$$X \;\geq\; 76,500 \div 6 = 12,750 \text{ game disks}$$

i.e., EA must now sell at least 12,750 game disks per month to earn its target rate of return on investment of 15%.

12-30 (40–45 min.)   **Target prices, target costs, value engineering, cost incurrence, locked-in cost, activity-based costing.**

1.

	Old CE100	Cost Change	New CE100
Direct materials costs	$182,000	$2.20 × 7,000 = $15,400 less	$166,600
Direct manufacturing labor costs	28,000	$0.50 × 7,000 = $3,500 less	24,500
Machining costs	31,500	Unchanged because capacity same	31,500
Testing costs	35,000	(20% × 2.5 × 7,000) $2 = $7,000	28,000
Rework costs	14,000	(See Note 1)	5,600
Ordering costs	3,360	(See Note 2)	2,100
Engineering costs	21,140	Unchanged because capacity same	21,140
Total manufacturing costs	$315,000		$279,440

Note 1:
10% of old CE100s are reworked. That is, 700 (10% of 7,000) CE100s made are reworked. Rework costs = $20 per unit reworked × 700 = $14,000. If rework falls to 4% of New CE100s manufactured, 280 (4% of 7,000) New CE100s manufactured will require rework. Rework costs = $20 per unit × 280 = $5,600.

Note 2 :
Ordering costs for New CE100 = 2 orders/month × 50 components × $21/order
$$= \$2,100$$

Unit manufacturing costs of New CE100 = $279,440 ÷ 7,000 = $39.92

2.   Total manufacturing cost reductions based on new design   = $315,000 – $279,440
                                                                                                                       = $35,560

Reduction in unit manufacturing costs based on new design   = $35,560 ÷ 7,000
                                                                                                          = $5.08 per unit.

The reduction in unit manufacturing costs based on the new design can also be calculated as

Unit cost of old design, $45 ($315,000 ÷ 7,000 units) – Unit cost of new design, $39.92 = $5.08

Therefore, the target cost reduction of $6 per unit is not achieved by the redesign.

3.   Changes in design have a considerably larger impact on costs per unit relative to improvements in manufacturing efficiency ($5.08 versus $1.50). One explanation is that many costs are locked in once the design of the radio-cassette is completed. Improvements in manufacturing efficiency cannot reduce many of these costs. Design choices can influence many direct and overhead cost categories, for example, by reducing direct materials requirements, by reducing defects requiring rework, and by designing in fewer components that translate into fewer orders placed and lower ordering costs.

12-32 (20 min.) **Cost-plus, time and materials.**

1.   The different markup rates used by Mazzoli for direct materials and direct labor may represent the approximate overheads (plus a profit margin) associated with each: for example, direct materials would incur ordering and handling overhead, and direct labor would incur overheads such as benefits, insurance, etc., and these may be approximately 50% and 100% of costs. These markups could also be driven by industry practice and competitive factors.

2.   As shown in the table below, Bariess will tell White that she will have to pay $270 get the clutch plate repaired and $390 to get it replaced.

COST	Labor	Materials	Total cost
Repair option (3.5 hrs. × $30 per hr.; $40)	$105	$40	$145
Replace option(1.5 hrs. × $30 per hr.; $200)	45	200	245
PRICE (100% markup on labor cost; 50% markup on materials)	**Labor**	**Materials**	**Total Price**
Repair option ($105 × 2; $40 × 1.5)	$210	$60	$270
Replace option ($45 × 2; $200 × 1.5)	90	300	390

3.   If the repair and replace options are equally safe and effective, White will choose to get the clutch plate repaired for $270 (rather than spend $390 on a replacement plate).

4.   Mazzoli Brothers will earn a greater contribution toward overhead in the replace option ($145 = $390 − $245) than in the repair option ($125 = $270 − $145). If we assume that Mazzoli Brothers earns a constant profit margin on each job, it will earn a larger profit by replacing the clutch plate on Johanna White's car for $390 than by repairing it for $270. Therefore, Bariess will recommend the replace option to White, which is not the one she would prefer. Recognizing this conflict, Bariess may even present only the replace option to Johanna White, or suggest that the repair option will result in a less-than-safe car. Of course, he runs the risk of White walking away and thinking of other options (at which point, he could present the repair option as a compromise). The problem is that Bariess has superior information about the repairs needed but his incentives may cause him to not reveal his information an instead use it to his advantage. It is only the seller's desire to build a reputation, to have a long-term relationship with the customer, and to have the customer recommend the seller to other potential buyers of the service that encourages an honest discussion of the options.

12-34 (60 min.) **Cost-plus and market-based pricing.**

1. Single pool:

$$= \frac{\$1,262,460}{106,000 \text{ hours}}$$

$$= \$11.91 \text{ per hour}$$

Hourly billing rate = $11.91 per hour × 1.45
= $17.27 per billing hour

2. See Solution Exhibit 12-34.

SOLUTION EXHIBIT 12-34

	HTT	ATT	SST	ACT	AQT	Total
Test pool labor (.3, .2, .2, .1, .2)	$126,000	$ 84,000	$ 84,000	$ 42,000	$ 84,000	$ 420,000
Supervision (.40, .15, .15, .15, .15)	28,800	10,800	10,800	10,800	10,800	72,000
Equip. depreciation	48,230	22,000	39,230	32,000	37,000	178,460
Heat (.50, .05, .05, .30, .10)	85,000	8,500	8,500	51,000	17,000	170,000
Electricity (.30, .10, .10, .40, .10)	37,200	12,400	12,400	49,600	12,400	124,000
Water (.00, .00, .20, .20, .60)	0	0	14,800	14,800	44,400	74,000
Set-up (.20, .15, .30, .15, .20)	11,600	8,700	17,400	8,700	11,600	58,000
Indirect materials (.15, .15, .30, .20, .20)	15,600	15,600	31,200	20,800	20,800	104,000
Operating supplies (.10, .10, .25, .20, .35)	6,200	6,200	15,500	12,400	21,700	62,000
Total costs	$358,630	$168,200	$233,830	$242,100	$259,700	$1,262,460
Total test-hours	29,680	12,720	27,560	22,260	13,780	
Hourly test-cost	$12.08	$13.22	$8.48	$10.88	$18.85	
Hourly billing rate (hourly test-cost × 1.45)	$17.52	$19.17	$12.30	$15.78	$27.33	

3.   The new costing method will have the following effects on the pricing structure for each of the five test types given the competitors' hourly billing rates.

	HTT	ATT	SST	ACT	AQT
New hourly billing rate (hourly test-cost × 1.45)	$17.52	$19.17	$12.30	$15.78	$27.33
Competitor rate	$17.50	$19.00	$15.50	$16.00	$20.00
New rate over/(under) market	$ .02	$ .17	$(3.20)	$ (.22)	$ 7.33
Percent over/(under) market	0.1%	0.9%	(20.6)%	(1.4)%	36.7%
Common pool rate	$17.27	$17.27	$17.27	$17.27	$17.27
New rate over/(under) old rate	$0.25	$1.90	$(4.97)	$(1.49)	$10.06
Percent over/(under) old rate	1.4%	11.0%	(28.8)%	(8.6)%	58.3%

- Best Test will now be pricing all its lab tests more competitively in the market.

- For Heat Testing (HTT), there is minimal variance between the common pool rate, the new separate rate, and the competitors' rates. The HTT rate could either be left at the old rate, or nominally raised to the competitors' rates or new pool rate without much impact, depending upon how Best Test wanted to position the test compared to the competition.

- For Air Turbulence Testing (ATT), the new separate computed billing rate is significantly different than the common pool rate as well as close to the competitors' rates. The same is true of Arctic Condition Testing (ACT). In both cases, Best Test would probably want to adjust billing rates (raise ATT rate and lower ACT rate) to the newly computed rates or competitors' rates to better reflect resources consumed by the tests.

- For Stress Testing (SST), the newly computed rate is dramatically less than both the common pool rate and the competitors' rates. Best Test would want to significantly reduce the price to at least meet the competitors' price or reduce it further to the newly computed price, depending upon how aggressively it wanted to market this test.

- For Aquatic Testing (AQT), the newly computed rate is significantly higher than both the common pool rate and the competitors' rates. Best Test would want to raise the billing rate at least to the competitors' rates to recover its cost plus some contribution towards administrative costs. Its current common billing rate of $17.27 is below the $18.85 cost to perform the AQT test.

- Because the newly computed billing prices for both SST and AQT are significantly different than competitors' prices, the cost assumptions should be further analyzed to verify accuracy and identify opportunities.

4. In general, at least three other internal or external determinants of pricing structure include the

- number and nature of competitors for additional tests and their quality and timeliness of service.
- company's overall capacity and its ability to react to volume and mix changes for tests if the demand changes due to the new pricing structure.
- number of potential customers, overall demand for the tests, and price elasticity of demand for the tests.
- strategic focus, such as desire to gain or defend market share, long-term support for entry into or exit from a market, or stage in the test's product life cycle (introduction, growth, mature, or dying).

12-36 (30 min.) **Airline pricing, considerations other than cost in pricing.**

1. If the fare is $500,
    a. Air Americo would expect to have 200 business and 100 pleasure travelers.
    b. Variable costs per passenger would be $80.
    c. Contribution margin per passenger = $500 – $80 = $420.

    If the fare is $2,000,
    a. Air Americo would expect to have 190 business and 20 pleasure travelers.
    b. Variable costs per passenger would be $180.
    c. Contribution margin per passenger = $2,000 – $180 = $1,820.

    Contribution margin from business travelers at prices of $500 and $2,000, respectively, follow:

At a price of $500: $420 × 200 passengers	= $ 84,000
At a price of $2,000: $1,820 × 190 passengers	= $345,800

    Air Americo would maximize contribution margin and operating income by charging business travelers a fare of $2,000.

    Contribution margin from pleasure travelers at prices of $500 and $2,000, respectively, follow:

At a price of $500: $420 × 100 passengers	= $42,000
At a price of $2,000: $1,820 × 20 passengers	= $36,400

    Air Americo would maximize contribution margin and operating income by charging pleasure travelers a fare of $500. Air Americo would maximize contribution margin and operating income by a price differentiation strategy, where business travelers are charged $2,000 and pleasure travelers $500.
    In deciding between the alternative prices, all other costs such as fuel costs, allocated annual lease costs, allocated ground services costs, and allocated flight crew salaries are irrelevant. Why? Because these costs will not change whatever price Air Americo chooses to charge.

2. The elasticity of demand of the two classes of passengers drives the different demands of the travelers. Business travelers are relatively price insensitive because they must get to their destination during the week (exclusive of weekends) and their fares are paid by their companies. A 300% increase in fares from $500 to $2,000 will deter only 5% of the business passengers from flying with Air Americo.

In contrast, a similar fare increase will lead to an 80% drop in pleasure travelers who are paying for their own travels, unlike business travelers, and who may have alternative vacation plans they could pursue instead.

3. Since business travelers often want to return within the same week, while pleasure travelers often stay over weekends, a requirement that a Saturday night stay is needed to qualify for the $500 discount fare would discriminate between the passenger categories. This price discrimination is legal because airlines are service companies rather than manufacturing companies and because these practices do not, nor are they intended to, destroy competition.

12-38 (40 min.) **Target prices, target costs, value engineering.**

1.

| | | | | | | TX-40-1 50,000 output units | |
| | | | | | | | |
Cost Category (1)	Cost Driver (2)	Details of Cost Driver Quantities (3)			(4)	Total Quantity of Cost Driver (5)	Cost per Unit of Cost Driver (6)
Direct materials	Number of kits	1	kit per output unit	50,000	output units	50,000[a]	$ 17
Direct manufacturing labor (DML)	DML hours	0.25	DML hours per output unit	50,000	output units	12,500[b]	$ 24
Direct machining (fixed)	Machine-hours					50,000	$ 3
Setup	Setup-hours	12	setup-hours per batch	100	batches	1,200[c]	$ 25
Testing	Testing-hours	2.5	testing-hours per output unit	50,000	output units	125,000[d]	$ 2
Engineering	Engineering-hours					1,700	$100

[a] 1 kit per output unit × 50,000 output units
[b] 0.25 DMLH per output unit × 50,000 output units
[c] 12 setup hours per batch × 100 batches
[d] 2.5 testing-hours per output unit × 50,000 output units

Costs of TX-40-1

Cost Category	
Direct materials (50,000 kits × $17 per kit)	$ 850,000
Direct manufacturing labor (12,500 DMLH × $24 per DMLH)	300,000
Direct machining (fixed) (50,000 mach. hrs. × $3 per mach. hr.)	150,000
Setup (1,200 setup hrs. × $25 per setup hr.)	30,000
Testing (125,000 testing hrs. × $2 per testing hr.)	250,000
Engineering (1,700 engg. hrs. × $100 per engg. hr.)	170,000
Total	$1,750,000
Full cost per unit = $1,750,000 ÷ 50,000 =	$35.00

2. Mark-up on full product cost per unit of TX-40-1 $= \dfrac{\text{Selling price} - \text{Full product cost}}{\text{Full product cost}}$

$$= \frac{\$40.60 - \$35}{\$35} = \frac{\$5.60}{\$35} = 16\%$$

3. The target price for TX-40-2 is $34.80.
Suppose the target cost per unit of TX-40-2 is $X

Then $X (1.16) = $34.80

That is $X $= \dfrac{\$34.80}{1.16} =$ $30

Avery's target cost per unit of TX-40-2 is $30.

4.

TX-40-2
50,000 output units

Cost Category	Cost Driver	Details of Cost Driver Quantities				Total Quantity of Cost Driver	Cost per Unit of Cost Driver
(1)	(2)	(7)		(8)		(9)	(10)
Direct Materials	Number of kits	1	kit per output unit	50,000	output units	50,000[a]	$ 14
Direct manufacturing labor (DML)	DML hours	0.25	DML hours per output unit	50,000	output units	12,500[b]	$ 21
Direct machining (fixed)	Machine-hours					50,000	$ 3
Setup	Setup-hours	6	setup-hours per batch	100	batches	600[c]	$ 25
Testing	Testing-hours	2	testing-hours per output unit	50,000	output units	100,000[d]	$ 2
Engineering	Engineering-hours					1,700	$100

[a] 1 kit per output unit × 50,000 output units
[b] 0.25 DMLH per output unit × 50,000 output units
[c] 6 set-up hours per batch × 100 batches
[d] 2 testing-hours per output unit × 50,000 output units

Costs of TX-40-2

Cost Category	
Direct materials (50,000 kits × $14 per kit)	$ 700,000
Direct manufacturing labor (12,500 DMLH × $21 per DMLH)	262,500
Direct machining (fixed) (50,000 mach. hrs. × $3 per mach. hr.)	150,000
Setup (600 setup hrs. × $25 per setup hr.)	15,000
Testing (100,000 testing hrs. × $2 per testing hr.)	200,000
Engineering (1,700 engg. hrs. × $100 per engg. hr.)	170,000
Total	$1,497,500
Full cost per unit = $1,497,500 ÷ 50,000 =	$ 29.95

The TX-40-2 design will reduce the manufacturing costs per unit of TX-40-2 to $29.95, which is just less than the target cost of $30. Therefore, TX-40-2 will achieve the targeted cost reductions.

5.   The price of TX-40-2 using a 16% mark-up (on full product costs of $29.95) = $29.95 × 1.16 = $34.74.

CHAPTER 13
STRATEGY, BALANCED SCORECARD, AND
STRATEGIC PROFITABILITY ANALYSIS

13-2 The five key forces to consider in industry analysis are: (a) competitors, (b) potential entrants into the market, (c) equivalent products, (d) bargaining power of customers, and (e) bargaining power of input suppliers.

13-4 The four key perspectives in the balanced scorecard are: (1) Financial perspective—this perspective evaluates the profitability of the strategy, (2) Customer perspective—this perspective identifies the targeted customer and market segments and measures the company's success in these segments, (3) Internal business process perspective—this perspective focuses on internal operations that further both the customer perspective by creating value for customers and the financial perspective by increasing shareholder value, and (4) Learning and growth perspective—this perspective identifies the capabilities the organization must excel at to achieve superior internal processes that create value for customers and shareholders.

13-6 A good balanced scorecard design has several features:
1. It tells the story of a company's strategy by articulating a sequence of cause-and-effect relationships.
2. It helps to communicate the strategy to all members of the organization by translating the strategy into a coherent and linked set of understandable and measurable operational targets.
3. It places strong emphasis on financial objectives and measures in for-profit companies. Nonfinancial measures are regarded as part of a program to achieve future financial performance.
4. It limits the number of measures to only those that are critical to the implementation of strategy.
5. It highlights suboptimal tradeoffs that managers may make when they fail to consider operational and financial measures together.

13-8 Three key components in doing a strategic analysis of operating income are:
1. The growth component which measures the change in operating income attributable solely to the change in quantity of output sold from one year to the next.
2. The price-recovery component which measures the change in operating income attributable solely to changes in the prices of inputs and outputs from one year to the next.
3. The productivity component which measures the change in costs attributable to a change in the quantity and mix of inputs used in the current year relative to the quantity and mix of inputs that would have been used in the previous year to produce current year output.

13-10 Engineered costs result from a cause-and-effect relationship between the cost driver, output, and the (direct or indirect) resources used to produce that output. Discretionary costs arise from periodic (usually annual) decisions regarding the maximum amount to be incurred. There is no measurable cause-and-effect relationship between output and resources used.

13-12 Downsizing (also called rightsizing) is an integrated approach configuring processes, products, and people to match costs to the activities that need to be performed for operating effectively and efficiently in the present and future. Downsizing is an attempt to eliminate unused capacity.

13-14 Total factor productivity is the quantity of output produced divided by the costs of all inputs used, where the inputs are costed on the basis of current period prices.

13-16 (15 min.) **Balanced scorecard.**

1. La Quinta's 2007 strategy is a cost leadership strategy. La Quinta plans to grow by producing high-quality boxes at a low cost delivered to customers in a timely manner. La Quinta's boxes are not differentiated, and there are many other manufacturers who produce similar boxes. To succeed, La Quinta must achieve lower costs relative to competitors through productivity and efficiency improvements.

2. Measures that we would expect to see on a La Quinta's balanced scorecard for 2007 are

Financial Perspective
(1) Operating income from productivity gain, (2) operating income from growth, (3) cost reductions in key areas.
   These measures evaluate whether La Quinta has successfully reduced costs and generated growth through cost leadership.

Customer Perspective
(1) Market share, (2) new customers, (3) customer satisfaction index, (4) customer retention, (5) time taken to fulfill customer orders.
   The logic is that improvements in these customer measures are leading indicators of whether La Quinta's cost leadership strategy is succeeding with its customers and helping it to achieve superior financial performance.

Internal Business Process Perspective
(1) Yield, (2) productivity, (3) order delivery time, (4) on-time delivery.
   Improvements in these measures are key drivers of achieving cost leadership and are expected to lead to more satisfied customers and in turn to superior financial performance

Learning and Growth Perspective
(1) Percentage of employees trained in process and quality management, (2) employee satisfaction, (3) number of major process improvements.
   Improvements in these measures aim to improve La Quinta's ability to achieve cost leadership and have a cause-and-effect relationship with improvements in internal business processes, which in turn lead to customer satisfaction and financial performance.

13-18 (20 min.) **Strategy, balanced scorecard, merchandising operation.**

1.   Oceano & Sons follows a product differentiation strategy. Oceano's designs are "trendsetting," its T-shirts are distinctive, and it aims to make its T-shirts a "must have" for each and every teenager. These are all clear signs of a product differentiation strategy, and, to succeed, Oceano must continue to innovate and be able to charge a premium price for its product.

2.   Possible key elements of Oceano's balance scorecard, given its product differentiation strategy:

Financial Perspective

(1) Increase in operating income from charging higher margins, (2) price premium earned on products.

These measures will indicate whether Oceano has been able to charge premium prices and achieve operating income increases through product differentiation.

Customer Perspective

(1) Market share in distinctive, name-brand T-shirts, (2) customer satisfaction, (3) new customers, (4) number of mentions of Oceano's T-shirts in the leading fashion magazines

Oceano's strategy should result in improvements in these customer measures that help evaluate whether Oceano's product differentiation strategy is succeeding with its customers. These measures are, in turn, leading indicators of superior financial performance.

Internal Business Process Perspective

(1)   Quality of silk-screening (number of colors, use of glitter, durability of the design), (2) frequency of new designs, (3) time between concept and delivery of design

Improvements in these measures are expected to result in more distinctive and trendsetting designs delivered to its customers and in turn, superior financial performance.

Learning and Growth Perspective

(1) Ability to attract and retain talented designers (2) improvements in silk-screening processes, (3) continuous education and skill levels of marketing and sales staff, (4) employee satisfaction.

Improvements in these measures are expected to improve Oceano's capabilities to produce distinctive designs that have a cause-and-effect relationship with improvements in internal business processes, which in turn lead to customer satisfaction and financial performance.

13-20 (20 min.) **Analysis of growth, price-recovery, and productivity components (continuation of 13-19).**

Effect of the industry-market-size factor on operating income

Of the 48,700-unit (246,700 – 198,000) increase in sales between 2006 and 2007, 19,800 (10% × 198,000) units are due to growth in market size, and 28,900 units are due to an increase in market share.

The change in Oceano's operating income from the industry-market size factor rather than from specific strategic actions is:

$725,580 (the growth component in Exercise 13-19) × $\dfrac{19,800}{48,700}$ \$295,000 F

Effect of product differentiation on operating income

The change in operating income due to:

Increase in the selling price (revenue effect of price recovery)	$246,700 F
Increase in price of inputs (cost effect of price recovery)	308,788 F

Growth in market share due to product differentiation

$725,580 (the growth component in Exercise 13-19) × $\dfrac{28,900}{48,700}$ 430,580 F

Change in operating income due to product differentiation	$986,068 F

Effect of cost leadership on operating income

The change in operating income from cost leadership is:

Productivity component	$70,632 F

The change in operating income between 2006 and 2007 can be summarized as follows:

Change due to industry-market-size	$ 295,000 F
Change due to product differentiation	986,068 F
Change due to cost leadership	70,632 F
Change in operating income	$1,351,700 F

Oceano has been very successful in implementing its product differentiation strategy. Nearly 73% ($986,068 ÷ $1,351,700) of the increase in operating income during 2007 was due to product differentiation, i.e., the distinctiveness of its T-shirts. It was able to raise prices of its products despite a decline in the cost of the T-shirts purchased. Oceano's operating income increase in 2007 was also helped by a growth in the overall market and a small productivity improvement, which it did not pass on to its customers in the form of lower prices.

13-22 (15 min.)   **Strategy, balanced scorecard.**

1.   Meredith Corporation follows a product differentiation strategy in 2006. Meredith's D4H machine is distinct from its competitors and generally regarded as superior to competitors' products. To succeed, Meredith must continue to differentiate its product and charge a premium price.

2.   Balanced Scorecard measures for 2006 follow:

Financial Perspective

(1) Increase in operating income from charging higher margins, (2) price premium earned on products.

These measures indicate whether Meredith has been able to charge premium prices and achieve operating income increases through product differentiation.

Customer Perspective

(1) Market share in high-end special-purpose textile machines, (2) customer satisfaction, (3) new customers.

Meredith's strategy should result in improvements in these customer measures that help evaluate whether Meredith's product differentiation strategy is succeeding with its customers. These measures are leading indicators of superior financial performance.

Internal Business Process Perspective

(1) Manufacturing quality, (2) new product features added, (3) order delivery time.

Improvements in these measures are expected to result in more distinctive products delivered to its customers and in turn superior financial performance.

Learning and Growth Perspective

(1) Development time for designing new machines, (2) improvements in manufacturing processes, (3) employee education and skill levels, (4) employee satisfaction.

Improvements in these measures are likely to improve Meredith's capabilities to produce distinctive products that have a cause-and-effect relationship with improvements in internal business processes, which in turn lead to customer satisfaction and financial performance.

13-24 (20 min.) Analysis of growth, price-recovery, and productivity components (continuation of 13-23).

Effect of the industry-market-size factor on operating income

If the 10-unit increase in sales from 200 to 210 units, 3% or 6 (3% × 200) units are due to growth in market size, and 4 (10 − 6) units are due to an increase in market share.
The change in Meredith's operating income from the industry-market size factor rather than from specific strategic actions is:

$280,000 (the growth component in Exercise 13-23) × $\dfrac{6}{10}$ $168,000 F

Effect of product differentiation on operating income

The change in operating income due to:

Increase in the selling price of D4H (revenue effect of price recovery)	$420,000 F
Increase in price of inputs (cost effect of price recovery)	184,500 U

Growth in market share due to product differentiation

$280,000 (the growth component in Exercise 13-23) × $\dfrac{4}{10}$ 112,000 F

Change in operating income due to product differentiation $347,500 F

Effect of cost leadership on operating income

The change in operating income from cost leadership is:

Productivity component	$ 92,000 F

The change in operating income between 2005 and 2006 can be summarized as follows:

Change due to industry-market-size	$168,000 F
Change due to product differentiation	347,500 F
Change due to cost leadership	92,000 F
Change in operating income	$607,500 F

Meredith has been successful in implementing its product differentiation strategy. More than 57% ($347,500 ÷ $607,500) of the increase in operating income during 2006 was due to product differentiation, i.e., the distinctiveness of its machines. It was able to raise the prices of its machines faster than the costs of its inputs and still grow market share. Meredith's operating income increase in 2006 was also helped by a growth in the overall market and some productivity improvements.

13-26 (15 min.)   Strategy, balanced scorecard, service company.

1.   Snyder Corporation's strategy in 2006 is cost leadership. Snyder's consulting services for implementing sales management software is not distinct from its competitors. The market for these services is very competitive. To succeed, Snyder must deliver quality service at low cost. Improving productivity while maintaining quality is key.

2.   Balanced Scorecard measures for 2006 follow:

Financial Perspective
(1) Increase operating income from productivity gains and growth, (2) revenues per employee, (3) cost reductions in key areas, for example, software implementation and overhead costs.
      These measures indicate whether Snyder has been able to reduce costs and achieve operating income increases through cost leadership.

Customer Perspective
(1) Market share, (2) new customers, (3) customer responsiveness, (4) customer satisfaction.
      Snyder's strategy should result in improvements in these customer measures that help evaluate whether Snyder's cost leadership strategy is succeeding with its customers. These measures are leading indicators of superior financial performance.

Internal Business Process Perspective
(1)   Time to complete customer jobs, (2) time lost due to errors, (3) quality of job (Is system running smoothly after job is completed?)
      Improvements in these measures are key drivers of achieving cost leadership and are expected to lead to more satisfied customers, lower costs, and superior financial performance.

Learning and Growth Perspective
(1)   Time required to analyze and design implementation steps, (2) time taken to perform key steps implementing the software, (3) skill levels of employees, (4) hours of employee training, (5) employee satisfaction and motivation.
      Improvements in these measures are likely to improve Snyder's ability to achieve cost leadership and have a cause-and-effect relationship with improvements in internal business processes, customer satisfaction, and financial performance.

13-28 (25 min.)   **Analysis of growth, price-recovery, and productivity components (continuation of 13-27).**

Effect of industry-market-size factor on operating income
Of the 10-unit increase in sales from 60 to 70 units, 5% or 3 units (5% × 60) are due to growth in market size, and 7 (10 – 3) units are due to an increase in market share.

The change in Snyder's operating income from the industry market-size factor rather than from specific strategic actions is:

$200,000 (the growth component in Exercise 13-27) × $\frac{3}{10}$ $60,000 F

Effect of product differentiation on operating income
Of the $2,000 decrease in selling price, 1% or $500 (1% × $50,000) is due to a general decline in prices, and the remaining decrease of $1,500 ($2,000 – $500) is due to a strategic decision by Snyder's management to implement its cost leadership strategy of lowering prices to stimulate demand.

The change in operating income due to a decline in selling price (other than the strategic reduction in price included in the cost leadership component) $500 × 70 units	$ 35,000 U
Increase in prices of inputs (cost effect of price recovery)	129,000 U
Change in operating income due to product differentiation	$164,000 U

Effect of cost leadership on operating income

Productivity component	$189,000 F
Effect of strategic decision to reduce selling price, $1,500 × 70	105,000 U
Growth in market share due to productivity improvement and strategic decision to reduce selling price	
$200,000 (the growth component in Exercise 13-27) × $\frac{7}{10}$	140,000 F
Change in operating income due to cost leadership	$224,000 F

The change in operating income between 2005 and 2006 can then be summarized as

Change due to industry-market-size	$ 60,000 F
Change due to product differentiation	164,000 U
Change due to cost leadership	224,000 F
Change in operating income	$120,000 F

Snyder has been very successful in implementing its cost leadership strategy. Due to a lack of product differentiation, Snyder was unable to pass along increases in labor costs by increasing the selling price—in fact, the selling price declined by $2,000 per work unit. However, Snyder was able to take advantage of its productivity gains to reduce price, gain market share, and increase operating income.

13-30 (20–30 min.) **Balanced scorecard.**

Perspectives	Strategic Objectives	Performance Measures
• Financial	• Increase shareholder value	• Earnings per share • Net income • Return on assets • Return on sales • Return on equity • Product cost per unit • Customer cost per unit
	• Increase profit generated by each salesperson	• Profit per salesperson
• Customer	• Acquire new customers • Retain customers • Develop profitable customers	• Number of new customers • Percentage of customers retained • Customer profitability
• Internal Business Processs	• Improve manufacturing quality • Introduce new products	• Percentage of defective product units
	• Minimize invoice error rate • On-time delivery by suppliers	• Percentage of error-free invoices • Percentage of on-time deliveries by suppliers
	• Increase proprietary products	• Number of patents
• Learning and Growth	• Increase information system capabilities • Enhance employee skills	• Percentage of processes with real-time feedback • Employee turnover rate • Average job-related training hours per employee

13-32 (30 min.) **Balanced scorecard.**

1.   The market for color laser printers is competitive. Lee's strategy is to produce and sell high quality laser printers at a low cost. The key to achieving higher quality is reducing defects in its manufacturing operations. The key to managing costs is dealing with the high fixed costs of Lee's automated manufacturing facility. To reduce costs per unit, Lee would have to either produce more units or eliminate excess capacity.

The scorecard correctly measures and evaluates Lee's broad strategy of growth through productivity gains and cost leadership. There are some deficiencies, of course, that subsequent assignment questions will consider.

It appears from the scorecard that Lee was not successful in implementing its strategy in 2006. Although it achieved targeted performance in the learning and growth and internal business process perspectives, it significantly missed its targets in the customer and financial perspectives. Lee has not had the success it targeted in the market and has not been able to reduce fixed costs.

2.   Lee's scorecard does not provide any explanation of why the target market share was not met in 2006. Was it due to poor quality? Higher prices? Poor post-sales service? Inadequate supply of products? Poor distribution? Aggressive competitors? The scorecard is not helpful for understanding the reasons underlying the poor market share.

Lee may want to include some measures in the customer perspective (and internal business process perspective) that get at these issues. These measures would then serve as leading indicators (based on cause-and-effect relationships) for lower market share. For example, Lee should measure customer satisfaction with its printers on various dimensions of product features, quality, price, service, and availability. It should measure how well its printers match up against other color laser printers on the market. This is critical information for Lee to successfully implement its strategy.

3.   Lee should include a measure of employee satisfaction to the learning and growth perspective and a measure of new product development to the internal business process perspective. The focus of its current scorecard measures is on processes and not on people and innovation.

    Lee considers training and empowering workers as important for implementing its high-quality, low-cost strategy. Therefore employee training and employee satisfaction should appear in the learning and growth perspective of the scorecard. Lee can then evaluate if improving employee-related measures results in improved internal-business process measures, market share and financial performance.

    Adding new product development measures to internal business processes is also important. As Lee reduces defects, Lee's costs will not automatically decrease because many of Lee's costs are fixed. Instead, Lee will have more capacity available to it. The key question is how Lee will obtain value from this capacity. One important way is to use the capacity to produce and sell new models of its products. Of course if this strategy is to work, Lee must develop new products at the same time that it is improving quality. Hence, the scorecard should contain some measure to monitor progress in new product development. Improving quality without developing and selling new products (or downsizing) will result in weak financial performance.

4.   Improving quality and significantly downsizing to eliminate unused capacity is difficult. Recall that the key to improving quality at Lee Corporation is training and empowering workers. As quality improvements occur, capacity will be freed up, but because costs are fixed, quality improvements will not automatically lead to lower costs. To reduce costs, Lee's management must take actions such as selling equipment and laying off employees. But how can management lay off the very employees whose hard work and skills led to improved quality? If it did lay off employees now, will the remaining employees ever work hard to improve quality in the future? For these reasons, Lee's management should first focus on using the newly available capacity to sell more product. If it cannot do so and must downsize, management should try to downsize in a way that would not hurt employee morale, such as through retirements and voluntary severance.

13-34 (25 min.) **Analysis of growth, price-recovery, and productivity components**.

1.   Winchester follows a product differentiation strategy in 2007. Winchester's ball bearings are regarded as superior to its competitors. Winchester's strategy is to charge a premium price for its ball bearings.

2.   The growth component is favorable because Winchester sold more units in 2007 compared to 2006. The price-recovery component is favorable because output prices increased faster than the input prices between 2006 and 2007. The productivity component is favorable because Winchester used fewer inputs to produce year 2007 output relative to what it would have used in 2006 (calculated using 2007 prices).

3.

Effect of the industry-market-size factor		$ 750,000 F
Effect of product differentiation		
Price recovery component	$400,000 F	
Change in market share ($300,000 – $750,000)	450,000 U	
Net effect of product differentiation		50,000 U
Effect of cost leadership (productivity component)		350,000 F
Change in operating income		$1,050,000 F

The analysis of the growth, price-recovery, and productivity components indicates that the $1,050,000 increase in operating income between 2006 and 2007 is due to growth in the market and to productivity gains. Winchester's strategy is product differentiation, and the product differentiation component is $50,000 unfavorable. Winchester was unable to pass along increases in input prices to customers, while maintaining and increasing its market share. Its sales did not keep up with the growth in market size. As a result, the gain in operating income in 2007 is not consistent with the product differentiation strategy described in requirement 1.

13-36 (20 min.) **Partial productivity measurement.**

1. Berkshire Corporation's partial productivity ratios in 2008 are as follows:

$$\text{Direct materials partial productivity} = \frac{\text{Quantity of output produced in 2008}}{\text{Kilograms of direct materials used in 2008}} = \frac{550,000}{630,000} = 0.87 \text{ units per kg.}$$

$$\text{Direct manuf. labor partial productivity} = \frac{\text{Quantity of output produced in 2008}}{\text{Direct manuf. labor-hours used in 2008}} = \frac{550,000}{10,100} = 54.46 \text{ units per labor-hour}$$

$$\text{Manufacturing overhead partial productivity} = \frac{\text{Quantity of output produced in 2008}}{\text{Units of manuf. capacity in 2008}} = \frac{550,000}{582,000} = 0.95 \text{ units per unit of capacity}$$

To compare partial productivities in 2008 with partial productivities in 2007, we first calculate the inputs that would have been used in 2007 to produce year 2008's 550,000 units of output assuming the year 2007 relationship between inputs and outputs.

Direct materials $\quad = \quad 450,000 \text{ kg (2007)} \times \dfrac{550,000 \text{ output units in 2008}}{400,000 \text{ output units in 2007}}$

$\qquad\qquad\qquad = \quad 450,000 \times 1.375 = 618,750 \text{ kg.}$

Direct manuf. labor $\quad = \quad 7,500 \text{ hours (2007)} \times \dfrac{550,000 \text{ output units in 2008}}{400,000 \text{ output units in 2007}}$

$\qquad\qquad\qquad = \quad 7,500 \times 1.375 = 10,312.5 \text{ labor-hours}$

Manufacturing capacity $\quad = \quad$ 600,000 units of capacity, because manufacturing capacity is fixed, and adequate capacity existed in 2007 to produce year 2008 output.

Partial productivity calculations for 2007 based on year 2008 output (to make the partial productivities comparable across the two years):

$$\text{Direct materials partial productivity} = \frac{\text{Quantity of output produced in 2008}}{\substack{\text{Kilograms of direct materials that would} \\ \text{have been used in 2007 to produce} \\ \text{year 2008 output}}} = \frac{550,000}{618,750} = 0.89 \text{ units per kg}$$

$$\text{Direct manufac. labor partial productivity} = \frac{\text{Quantity of output produced in 2008}}{\substack{\text{Direct manuf. labor-hours that would} \\ \text{have been used in 2007 to produce} \\ \text{year 2008 output}}} = \frac{550,000}{10,312.5} = 53.33 \text{ units per labor-hour}$$

$$\text{Manufacturing overhead partial productivity} = \frac{\text{Quantity of output produced in 2008}}{\substack{\text{Units of manuf. capacity that would} \\ \text{have been used in 2007 to produce} \\ \text{year 2008 output}}} = \frac{550,000}{600,000} = 0.92 \text{ units per unit of capacity}$$

The calculations indicate that Berkshire improved the partial productivity of direct manufacturing labor and manufacturing overhead between 2007 and 2008 via efficiency improvements and by reducing unused manufacturing capacity. The partial productivity of direct materials declined from 2007 to 2008.

2.   The partial productivities of some inputs (direct manufacturing labor and manufacturing overhead) rose between 2007 and 2008, while that of direct materials declined. Therefore, we cannot determine whether total factor productivity increased or decreased overall between 2007 and 2008. Partial productivities cannot tell us how much total factor productivity changed, because partial productivity measures cannot be aggregated over different inputs.

3.   Berkshire Corporation management can use the partial productivity measures to set targets for the next year. Partial productivity measures can easily be compared over multiple periods. For example, they may specify bonus payments if partial productivity of direct manufacturing labor increases to 60 units of output per direct manufacturing labor-hour and if partial productivity of direct materials improves to 0.98 units of output per kilogram of direct materials. A major advantage of partial productivity measures is that they focus on a single input; hence, they are simple to calculate and easy to understand at the operations level. Managers and operators can also examine these numbers to understand the reasons underlying productivity changes from one period to the next—better training of workers, lower absenteeism, lower labor turnover, better incentives, or improved methods. Management can then implement and sustain these factors in the future.

13-38 (25 min.) **Balanced scorecard, ethics.**

1. Yes, the Household Products Division (HPD) should include measures of employee satisfaction and customer satisfaction even if these measures are subjective. For a maker of kitchen dishwashers, employee and customer satisfaction are leading indicators of future financial performance. There is a cause-and-effect linkage between these measures and future financial performance. If HPD's strategy is correct and if the scorecard has been properly designed, employee and customer satisfaction information is very important in evaluating the implementation of HPD's strategy.

HPD should use employee and customer satisfaction measures even though these measures are subjective. One of the pitfalls to avoid when implementing a balanced scorecard is not to use only objective measures in the scorecard. Of course, HPD should guard against imprecision and potential for manipulation. Patricia Conley appears to be aware of this. She has tried to understand the reasons for the poor scores and has been able to relate these scores to other objective evidence such as employee dissatisfaction with the new work rules and customer unhappiness with missed delivery dates.

2. Incorrect reporting of employee and customer satisfaction ratings to make divisions performance look good is unethical. In assessing the situation, the specific "Standards of Ethical Conduct for Management Accountants" (described in Exhibit 1-7) that the management account should consider are listed below.

Competence
Clear reports using relevant and reliable information should be prepared. Preparing reports on the basis of incorrect employee and customer satisfaction ratings to make the division's performance look better than it is violates competence standards. It is unethical for Conley to change the employee and customer satisfaction ratings to make the division's performance look good.

Integrity
The management accountant has a responsibility to avoid actual or apparent conflicts of interest and advise all appropriate parties of any potential conflict. Conley may be tempted to report better employee and customer satisfaction ratings to please Emburey. This action, however, violates the responsibility for integrity. The Standards of Ethical Conduct require the management accountant to communicate favorable as well as unfavorable information.

Objectivity
The management accountant's standards of ethical conduct require that information should be fairly and objectively communicated and that all relevant information should be disclosed. From a management accountant's standpoint, modifying employee and customer satisfaction ratings to make division performance look good would violate the standard of objectivity.

Conley should indicate to Emburey that the employee and customer satisfaction ratings are, indeed, appropriate. If Emburey still insists on reporting better employee and customer satisfaction numbers, Conley should raise the matter with one of Emburey's superiors. If, after taking all these steps, there is continued pressure to overstate employee and customer satisfaction ratings, Conley should consider resigning from the company and not engage in unethical behavior.

CHAPTER 14
COST ALLOCATION, CUSTOMER-PROFITABILITY ANALYSIS, AND SALES-VARIANCE ANALYSIS

14-2 Exhibit 14-1 outlines four purposes for allocating costs:
1.   To provide information for economic decisions.
2.   To motivate managers and other employees.
3.   To justify costs or compute reimbursement amounts.
4.   To measure income and assets.

14-4 Disagree. In general, companies have three choices regarding the allocation of corporate costs to divisions: allocate all corporate costs, allocate some corporate costs (those "controllable" by the divisions), and allocate none of the corporate costs. Which one of these is appropriate depends on several factors: the composition of corporate costs, the purpose of the costing exercise, and the time horizon, to name a few. For example, one can easily justify allocating all corporate costs when they are closely related to the running of the divisions and when the purpose of costing is, say, pricing products or motivating managers to consume corporate resources judiciously.

14-6 Customer profitability analysis highlights to managers how individual customers differentially contribute to total profitability. It helps managers to see whether customers who contribute sizably to total profitability are receiving a comparable level of attention from the organization.

14-8 No. A customer-profitability profile highlights differences in current period's profitability across customers. Dropping customers should be the last resort. An unprofitable customer in one period may be highly profitable in subsequent future periods. Moreover, costs assigned to individual customers need not be purely variable with respect to short-run elimination of sales to those customers. Thus, when customers are dropped, costs assigned to those customers may not disappear in the short run.

14-10 Using the levels approach introduced in Chapter 7, the sales-volume variance is a Level 2 variance. By sequencing through Level 3 (sales-mix and sales-quantity variances) and then Level 4 (market-size and market-share variances), managers can gain insight into the causes of a specific sales-volume variance caused by changes in the mix and quantity of the products sold as well as changes in market size and market share.

14-12 A favorable sales-quantity variance arises because the actual units of all products sold exceed the budgeted units of all products sold.

14-14 Some companies believe that reliable information on total market size is not available and therefore they choose not to compute market-size and market-share variances.

14-16 (15-20 min.) **Cost allocation in hospitals, alternative allocation criteria.**

1. Direct costs   = $2.40
    Indirect costs ($11.52 – $2.40) = $9.12

    Overhead rate $= \dfrac{\$9.12}{\$2.40} = 380\%$

2. The answers here are less than clear-cut in some cases.

Overhead Cost Item	Allocation Criteria
Processing of paperwork for purchase	Cause and effect
Supplies room management fee	Benefits received
Operating-room and patient-room handling costs	Cause and effect
Administrative hospital costs	Benefits received
University teaching-related costs	Ability to bear
Malpractice insurance costs	Ability to bear or benefits received
Cost of treating uninsured patients	Ability to bear
Profit component	None. This is not a cost.

3.   Assuming that Meltzer's insurance company is responsible for paying the $4,800 bill, Meltzer probably can only express outrage at the amount of the bill. The point of this question is to note that even if Meltzer objects strongly to one or more overhead items, it is his insurance company that likely has the greater incentive to challenge the bill. Individual patients have very little power in the medical arena. In contrast, insurance companies have considerable power and may decide that certain costs are not reimbursable—for example, the costs of treating uninsured patients.

14-18 (30 min.) **Cost allocation to divisions.**

1.

	Hotel	Restaurant	Casino	Rembrandt
Revenue	$16,425,000	$5,256,000	$12,340,000	$34,021,000
Direct costs	9,819,260	3,749,172	4,248,768	17,817,200
Segment margin	$ 6,605,740	$1,506,828	$ 8,091,232	16,203,800
Fixed overhead costs				14,550,000
Income before taxes				$ 1,653,800
Segment margin %	40.22%	28.67%	65.57%	

2.

	Hotel	Restaurant	Casino	Rembrandt
Direct costs	$9,819,260	$3,749,172	$4,248,768	$17,817,200
Direct cost %	55.11%	21.04%	23.85%	100.00%
Square footage	80,000	16,000	64,000	160,000
Square footage %	50.00%	10.00%	40.00%	100.00%
Number of employees	200	50	250	500
Number of employees %	40.00%	10.00%	50.00%	100.00%

A: Cost allocation based on direct costs:

	Hotel	Restaurant	Casino	Rembrandt
Revenue	$16,425,000	$ 5,256,000	$12,340,000	$34,021,000
Direct costs	9,819,260	3,749,172	4,248,768	17,817,200
Segment margin	6,605,740	1,506,828	8,091,232	16,203,800
Allocated fixed overhead costs	8,018,505	3,061,320	3,470,175	14,550,000
Segment pre-tax income	$ (1,412,765)	$ (1,554,492)	$ 4,621,057	$ 1,653,800
Segment pre-tax income %	-8.60%	-29.58%	37.45%	

B: Cost allocation based on floor space:

	Hotel	Restaurant	Casino	Rembrandt
Allocated fixed overhead costs	$7,275,000	$1,455,000	$5,820,000	$14,550,000
Segment pre-tax income	$ (669,260)	$ 51,828	$2,271,232	$ 1,653,800
Segment pre-tax income %	-4.07%	0.99%	18.41%	

C: Cost allocation based on number of employees

	Hotel	Restaurant	Casino	Rembrandt
Allocated fixed overhead costs	$5,820,000	$1,455,000	$7,275,000	$14,550,000
Segment pre-tax income	$ 785,740	$ 51,828	$ 816,232	$ 1,653,800
Segment pre-tax income %	4.78%	0.99%	6.61%	

3.   Requirement 2 shows the dramatic effect of choice of cost allocation base on segment pre-tax income percentages:

Allocation Base	Pre-tax Income Percentage		
	Hotel	Restaurant	Casino
Direct costs	-8.60%	-29.58%	37.45%
Floor space	-4.07	0.99	18.41
Number of employees	4.78	0.99	6.61

The decision context should guide (a) whether costs should be allocated, and (b) the preferred cost allocation base. Decisions about, say, performance measurement, may be made on a combination of financial and nonfinancial measures. It may well be that Rembrandt may prefer to exclude allocated costs from the financial measures to reduce areas of dispute.

Where cost allocation is required, the cause-and-effect and benefits-received criteria are recommended in Chapter 14. The $14,550,000 is a fixed overhead cost. This means that on a short-run basis, the cause-and-effect criterion is not appropriate but Rembrandt could attempt to identify the cost drivers for these costs in the long run when these costs are likely to be more variable. Rembrandt should look at how the $14,550,000 cost benefits the three divisions. This will help guide the choice of an allocation base in the short run.

4.   The analysis in requirement 2 should not guide the decision on whether to shut down any of the divisions. The overhead costs are fixed costs in the short run. It is not clear how these costs would be affected in the long run if Rembrandt shut down one of the divisions. Also, each division is not independent of the other two. A decision to shut down, say, the restaurant, likely would negatively affect the attendance at the casino and possibly the hotel. Rembrandt should examine the future revenue and future cost implications of different resource investments in the three divisions. This is a future-oriented exercise, whereas the analysis in requirement 2 is an analysis of past costs.

14-20 (30 min.) **Customer profitability, customer cost hierarchy.**

1.

| | All amounts in thousands of U.S. dollars | | | |
| | Wholesale | | Retail | |
	North America Wholesaler	South America Wholesaler	Big Sam Stereo	World Market
Revenues at list prices	$420,000	$580,000	$130,000	$100,000
Price discounts	30,000	40,000	7,000	500
Revenues (at actual prices)	390,000	540,000	123,000	99,500
Cost of goods sold	325,000	455,000	118,000	90,000
Gross margin	65,000	85,000	5,000	9,500
Customer-level operating costs				
Delivery	450	650	200	125
Order processing	800	1,000	200	130
Sales visit	5,600	5,500	2,300	1,350
Total cust.-level optg.costs	6,850	7,150	2,700	1,605
Customer-level operating income	$ 58,150	$ 77,850	$ 2,300	$ 7,895

2.

Customer Distribution Channels
(all amounts in $000s)

| | Total (all customers) | Wholesale Customers | | | Retail Customers | | |
| | | Total Wholesale | North America Wholesaler | South America Wholesaler | Total Retail | Big Sam Stereo | World Market |
	(1) = (2) + (5)	(2) = (3) + (4)	(3)	(4)	(5) = (6) + (7)	(6)	(7)
Revenues (at actual prices)	$1,152,500	$930,000	$390,000	$540,000	$222,500	$123,000	$99,500
Customer-level costs	1,006,305	794,000	331,850[a]	462,150[a]	212,305	120,700[a]	91,605[a]
Customer-level operating income	146,195	136,000	$58,150	$77,850	10,195	$2,300	$7,895
Distribution-channel costs	43,000	35,000			8,000		
Distribution-channel-level oper. income	103,195	101,000			2,195		
Corporate-sustaining costs	60,000						
Operating income	43,195						

[a]Cost of goods sold + Total customer-level operating costs from Requirement 1

3.   If corporate costs are allocated to the channels, the retail channel will show an operating loss of $9,805,000 ($2,195,000 − $12,000,000), and the wholesale channel will show an operating profit of only $53,000,000 ($101,000,000 − $48,000,000). The overall operating profit, of course, is still $43,195,000, as in requirement 2. There is, however, no cause-and-effect or benefits-received relationship between corporate costs and any allocation base, i.e., the allocation of $48,000,000 to the wholesale channel and of $12,000,000 to the retail channel is arbitrary and not useful for decision-making. Therefore, the management of Ramish Electronics should not base any performance evaluations or investment/disinvestment decisions based on these channel-level operating income numbers. They may want to take corporate costs into account, however, when making pricing decisions.

14-6

14-22 (20–25 min.) **Customer profitability, distribution.**

1.   The activity-based costing for each customer is:

	Charleston Pharmacy	Chapel Hill Pharmacy
1. Order processing, $40 × 12; $40 × 10	$ 480	$ 400
2. Line-item ordering, $3 × (12 × 10;10 × 18)	360	540
3. Store deliveries, $50 × 6; $50 ×10	300	500
4. Carton deliveries, $1 × (6 × 24; 10 × 20)	144	200
5. Shelf-stocking, $16 × (6 × 0; 10 × 0.5)	0	80
Operating costs	$1,284	$1,720

The operating income of each customer is:

	Charleston Pharmacy	Chapel Hill Pharmacy
Revenues, $2,400 × 6; $1,800 × 10	$14,400	$18,000
Cost of goods sold, $2,100 × 6; $1,650 × 10	12,600	16,500
Gross margin	1,800	1,500
Operating costs	1,284	1,720
Operating income	$ 516	$ (220)

Chapel Hill Pharmacy has a lower gross margin percentage than Charleston (8.33% vs. 12.50%) and consumes more resources to obtain this lower margin.

2.   Ways Figure Four could use this information include:

a.   Pay increased attention to the top 20% of the customers. This could entail asking them for ways to improve service. Alternatively, you may want to highlight to your own personnel the importance of these customers; e.g., it could entail stressing to delivery people the importance of never missing delivery dates for these customers.

b.   Work out ways internally at Figure Four to reduce the rate per cost driver; e.g., reduce the cost per order by having better order placement linkages with customers. This cost reduction by Figure Four will improve the profitability of all customers.

c.   Work with customers so that their behavior reduces the total "system-wide" costs. At a minimum, this approach could entail having customers make fewer orders and fewer line items. This latter point is controversial with students; the rationale is that a reduction in the number of line items (diversity of products) carried by Ma and Pa stores may reduce the diversity of products Figure Four carries.

There are several options here:

- Simple verbal persuasion by showing customers cost drivers at Figure Four.
- Explicitly pricing out activities like cartons delivered and shelf-stocking so that customers pay for the costs they cause.
- Restricting options available to certain customers, e.g., customers with low revenues could be restricted to one free delivery per week.

An even more extreme example is working with customers so that deliveries are easier to make and shelf-stocking can be done faster.

d.   Offer salespeople bonuses based on the operating income of each customer rather than the gross margin of each customer.

Some students will argue that the bottom 40% of the customers should be dropped. This action should be only a last resort after all other avenues have been explored. Moreover, an unprofitable customer today may well be a profitable customer tomorrow, and it is myopic to focus on only a 1-month customer-profitability analysis to classify a customer as unprofitable.

14-24 (30 min.) **Variance analysis, working backward**.

1. and 2. Solution Exhibit 14-24 presents the sales-volume, sales-quantity, and sales-mix variances for the Plain and Chic wine glasses and in total for Jinwa Corporation in June 2006. The steps to fill in the numbers in Solution Exhibit 14-24 follow:

Step 1

Consider the static budget column (Column 3):

Static budget total contribution margin	$5,600
Budgeted units of all glasses to be sold	2,000
Budgeted contribution margin per unit of Plain	$2
Budgeted contribution margin per unit of Chic	$6

Suppose that the budgeted sales-mix percentage of Plain is y. Then the budgeted sales-mix percentage of Chic is $(1 - y)$. Therefore,

$$
\begin{aligned}
(2{,}000y \times \$2) + (2{,}000 \times (1 - y) \times \$6) &= \$5{,}600 \\
\$4000y + \$12{,}000 - \$12{,}000y &= \$5{,}600 \\
\$8{,}000y &= \$6{,}400 \\
y &= 0.8 \text{ or } 80\% \\
1 - y &= 20\%
\end{aligned}
$$

Jinwa's budgeted sales mix is 80% of Plain and 20% of Chic. We can then fill in all the numbers in Column 3.

Step 2

Next, consider Column 2 of Solution Exhibit 14-24.

The total of Column 2 in Panel C is $4,200 (the static budget total contribution margin of $5,600 – the total sales-quantity variance of $1,400 U which was given in the problem).

We need to find the actual units sold of all glasses, which we denote by q. From Column 2, we know that

$$
\begin{aligned}
(q \times 0.8 \times \$2) + (q \times 0.2 \times \$6) &= \$4{,}200 \\
\$1.6q + \$1.2q &= \$4{,}200 \\
\$2.8q &= \$4{,}200 \\
q &= 1{,}500 \text{ units}
\end{aligned}
$$

So, the total quantity of all glasses sold is 1,500 units. This computation allows us to fill in all the numbers in Column 2.

Step 3
Next, consider Column 1 of Solution Exhibit 14-24. We know actual units sold of all glasses (1,500 units), the actual sales-mix percentage (given in the problem information as Plain, 60%; Chic, 40%), and the budgeted unit contribution margin of each product (Plain, $2; Chic, $6). We can therefore determine all the numbers in Column 1.

Solution Exhibit 14-24 displays the following sales-quantity, sales-mix, and sales-volume variances:

Sales-Volume Variance

Plain	$1,400 U
Chic	1,200 F
All Glasses	$ 200 U

Sales-Mix Variances		Sales-Quantity Variances	
Plain	$ 600 U	Plain	$ 800 U
Chic	1,800 F	Chic	600 U
All Glasses	$1,200 F	All Glasses	$1,400 U

3.   Jinwa Corporation shows an unfavorable sales-quantity variance because it sold fewer wine glasses in total than was budgeted. This unfavorable sales-quantity variance is partially offset by a favorable sales-mix variance because the actual mix of wine glasses sold has shifted in favor of the higher contribution margin Chic wine glasses. The problem illustrates how failure to achieve the budgeted market penetration can have negative effects on operating income.

SOLUTION EXHIBIT 14-24
Columnar Presentation of Sales-Volume, Sales-Quantity and Sales-Mix Variances
for Jinwa Corporation

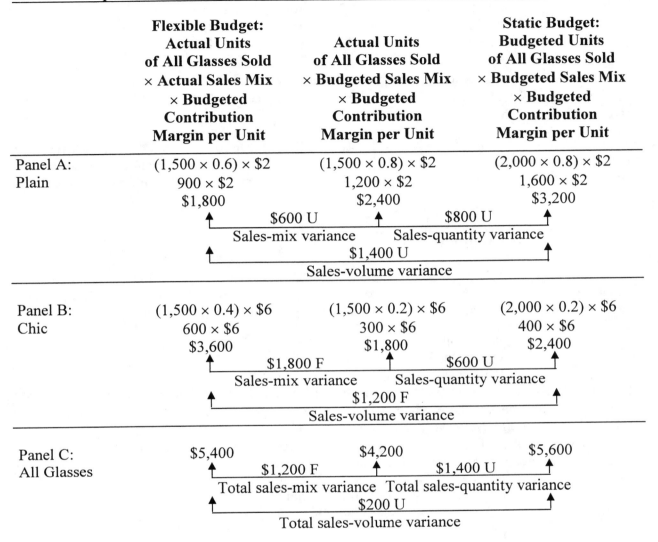

	Flexible Budget: **Actual Units** **of All Glasses Sold** **× Actual Sales Mix** **× Budgeted** **Contribution** **Margin per Unit**	**Actual Units** **of All Glasses Sold** **× Budgeted Sales Mix** **× Budgeted** **Contribution** **Margin per Unit**	**Static Budget:** **Budgeted Units** **of All Glasses Sold** **× Budgeted Sales Mix** **× Budgeted** **Contribution** **Margin per Unit**
Panel A: Plain	(1,500 × 0.6) × $2 900 × $2 $1,800	(1,500 × 0.8) × $2 1,200 × $2 $2,400	(2,000 × 0.8) × $2 1,600 × $2 $3,200
	↑——— $600 U ———↑ Sales-mix variance	↑——— $800 U ———↑ Sales-quantity variance	
	↑———————— $1,400 U ————————↑ Sales-volume variance		
Panel B: Chic	(1,500 × 0.4) × $6 600 × $6 $3,600	(1,500 × 0.2) × $6 300 × $6 $1,800	(2,000 × 0.2) × $6 400 × $6 $2,400
	↑——— $1,800 F ———↑ Sales-mix variance	↑——— $600 U ———↑ Sales-quantity variance	
	↑———————— $1,200 F ————————↑ Sales-volume variance		
Panel C: All Glasses	$5,400	$4,200	$5,600
	↑——— $1,200 F ———↑ Total sales-mix variance	↑——— $1,400 U ———↑ Total sales-quantity variance	
	↑———————— $200 U ————————↑ Total sales-volume variance		

F = favorable effect on operating income; U = unfavorable effect on operating income.

14-26 (20 min.) **Market-share and market-size variances (continuation of 14-25).**

	Actual	Budgeted
Western region	24 million	25 million
Soda King	3 million	2.5 million
Market share	12.5%	10%

Average budgeted contribution margin per unit = $2.108 ($5,270,000 ÷ 2,500,000)

Solution Exhibit 14-26 presents the sales-quantity variance, market-size variance, and market-share variance for 2006.

$$
\begin{array}{l}
\text{Market-share} \\
\text{variance}
\end{array}
=
\begin{array}{l}
\text{Actual} \\
\text{market size} \\
\text{in units}
\end{array}
\times
\left[
\begin{array}{l}
\text{Actual} \\
\text{market} \\
\text{share}
\end{array}
-
\begin{array}{l}
\text{Budgeted} \\
\text{market} \\
\text{share}
\end{array}
\right]
\times
\begin{array}{l}
\text{Budgeted contribution} \\
\text{margin per composite} \\
\text{unit for budgeted mix}
\end{array}
$$

$$= 24,000,000 \times (0.125 - 0.10) \times \$2.108$$
$$= 24,000,000 \times .025 \times \$2.108$$
$$= \$1,264,800 \text{ F}$$

$$
\begin{array}{l}
\text{Market-size} \\
\text{variance}
\end{array}
=
\left[
\begin{array}{l}
\text{Actual} \\
\text{market size} \\
\text{in units}
\end{array}
-
\begin{array}{l}
\text{Budgeted} \\
\text{market size} \\
\text{in units}
\end{array}
\right]
\times
\begin{array}{l}
\text{Budgeted} \\
\text{market} \\
\text{share}
\end{array}
\times
\begin{array}{l}
\text{Budgeted contribution} \\
\text{margin per composite} \\
\text{unit for budgeted mix}
\end{array}
$$

$$= (24,000,000 - 25,000,000) \times 0.10 \times \$2.108$$
$$= -1,000,000 \times 0.10 \times \$2.108$$
$$= 210,800 \text{ U}$$

The market share variance is favorable because the actual 12.5% market share was higher than the budgeted 10% market share. The market size variance is unfavorable because the market size decreased 4% [(25,000,000 − 24,000,000) ÷ 25,000,000].

While the overall total market size declined (from 25 million to 24 million), the increase in market share meant a favorable sales-quantity variance.

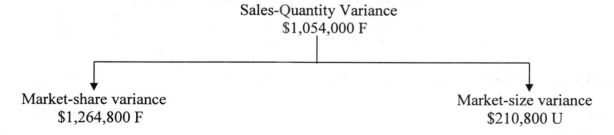

Sales-Quantity Variance
$1,054,000 F

Market-share variance
$1,264,800 F

Market-size variance
$210,800 U

SOLUTION EXHIBIT 14-26
Market-Share and Market-Size Variance Analysis of Soda King for 2006

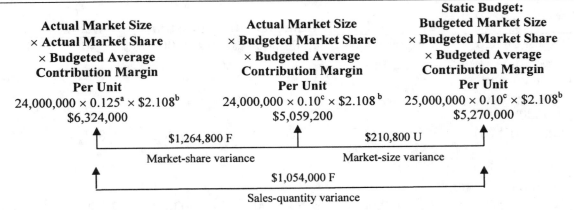

Actual Market Size × Actual Market Share × Budgeted Average Contribution Margin Per Unit $24,000,000 \times 0.125^a \times \$2.108^b$ $\$6,324,000$	Actual Market Size × Budgeted Market Share × Budgeted Average Contribution Margin Per Unit $24,000,000 \times 0.10^c \times \$2.108^b$ $\$5,059,200$	Static Budget: Budgeted Market Size × Budgeted Market Share × Budgeted Average Contribution Margin Per Unit $25,000,000 \times 0.10^c \times \$2.108^b$ $\$5,270,000$
	$\$1,264,800$ F	$\$210,800$ U
	Market-share variance	Market-size variance
	$\$1,054,000$ F	
	Sales-quantity variance	

F = favorable effect on operating income; U = unfavorable effect on operating income

[a]Actual market share: 3,000,000 units ÷ 24,000,000 units = 0.125, or 12.5%

[b]Budgeted average contribution margin per unit $5,270,000 ÷ 2,500,000 units = $2.108 per unit

[c]Budgeted market share: 2,500,000 units ÷ 25,000,000 units = 0.10, or 10%

14-28 (25–30 min.)   **Allocation of central corporate costs to divisions.**

	Total	Multimedia	Broadcasting	Print Media	Book Publishing
Interest on debt	$ 10,000,000	$ 3,500,000	$ 6,500,000	$ -0-	$ -0-
Human resource management (1,000: 3,000: 2,500: 1,500)	150,000,000	18,750,000	56,250,000	46,875,000	28,125,000
Corporate administration (150: 400: 250: 200)	50,000,000	7,500,000	20,000,000	12,500,000	10,000,000
Research and development (40%, 30%, 0%, 30%)	100,000,000	40,000,000	30,000,000	-0-	30,000,000
Advertising (1,400: 4,500: 2,500: 1,600)	200,000,000	28,000,000	90,000,000	50,000,000	32,000,000
Total	$510,000,000	$ 97,750,000	$202,750,000	$109,375,000	$100,125,000

14-30 (40 min.) **Customer profitability, distribution.**

1.

	Customer				
	P	**Q**	**R**	**S**	**T**
Revenues at list prices[a]	$29,952	$126,000	$875,520	$457,920	$56,160
Discount[b]	0	2,100	72,960	15,264	5,616
Revenues (at actual prices)	29,952	123,900	802,560	442,656	50,544
Cost of goods sold[c]	24,960	105,000	729,600	381,600	46,800
Gross margin	4,992	18,900	72,960	61,056	3,744
Customer-level operating costs					
Order taking[d]	1,500	2,500	3,000	2,500	3,000
Customer visits[e]	160	240	480	160	240
Delivery vehicles[f]	280	240	360	640	1,600
Product handling[g]	1,040	4,375	30,400	15,900	1,950
Expedited runs[h]	0	0	0	0	300
Total	2,980	7,355	34,240	19,200	7,090
Customer-level operating income	$ 2,012	$ 11,545	$ 38,720	$ 41,856	$ (3,346)

[a] $14.40 × 2,080; 8,750; 60,800; 31,800; 3,900

[b] ($14.40 – $14.40) × 50,000; ($14.40 – $14.16) × 8,750; ($14.40 – $13.20) × 60,800; ($14.40 – $13.92) × 31,800; ($14.40 – $12.96) × 3,900

[c] $12 × 2,080; 8,750; 60,800, 31,800; 3,900

[d] $100 × 15; 25; 30; 25; 30

[e] $80 × 2; 3; 6; 2; 3

[f] $2 × (10 × 14); (30 × 4); (60 × 3); (40 × 8); (20 × 40)

[g] $0.50 × 2,080; 8,750; 60,800; 31,800; 3,900

[h] $300 × 0; 0; 0; 0; 1

Customer S is the most profitable customer, despite having only 52% (31,800 ÷ 60,800) of the unit volume of Customer R. A major explanation is that Customer R receives a $1.20 discount per case while Customer S receives only a $0.48 discount per case.

Customer T is unprofitable, while the smaller customer P is profitable. Customer T receives a $1.44 discount per case, makes more frequent orders, requires more customer visits, and requires more delivery miles than Customer P.

2.   Separate reporting of both the list selling price and the actual selling price enables Spring Distribution to examine which customers receive different discounts and how salespeople may differ in the discounts they grant. There is a size pattern in the discounts across the five customers, except for Customer T, larger volume customers get larger discounts:

Sales Volume	Discount per case
R (60,800 cases)	$1.20
S (31,800 cases)	$0.48
Q (8,750 cases)	$0.24
T (3,900 cases)	$1.44
P (2,080 cases)	$0.00

The reasons for the $1.44 discount for T should be explored.

3.   Dropping customers should be the last resort taken by Spring Distribution. Factors to consider include:

a.   What is the expected future profitability of each customer? Are the currently unprofitable (T) or low-profit (P) customers likely to be highly profitable in the future?

b.   Are there externalities from having some customers, even if they are unprofitable in the short run? For example, some customers have a marquee-value that is "in effect" advertising that benefits the business.

c.   What costs are avoidable if one or more customers are dropped?

d.   Can the relationship with the "problem" customers be restructured so that there is a "win-win" situation? For example, could Customer T get by with fewer deliveries per month?

14-32 (60 min.) **Variance analysis, sales-mix and sales-quantity variances.**

1. Actual Contribution Margins

Product	Actual Selling Price	Actual Variable Cost per Unit	Actual Contribution Margin per Unit	Actual Sales Volume in Units	Actual Contribution Dollars	Actual Contribution Percent
Palm Pro	$349	$178	$171	11,000	$ 1,881,000	16%
Palm CE	285	92	193	44,000	8,492,000	71%
PalmKid	102	73	29	55,000	1,595,000	13%
				110,000	$11,968,000	100%

The actual average contribution margin per unit is $108.80 ($11,968,000 ÷ 110,000 units).

Budgeted Contribution Margins

Product	Budgeted Selling Price	Budgeted Variable Cost per Unit	Budgeted Contribution Margin per Unit	Budgeted Sales Volume in Units	Budgeted Contribution Dollars	Budgeted Contribution Percent
Palm Pro	$379	$182	$197	12,500	$ 2,462,500	19%
Palm CE	269	98	171	37,500	6,412,500	49%
Palm Kid	149	65	84	50,000	4,200,000	32%
				100,000	$13,075,000	100%

The budgeted average contribution margin per unit is $130.75 ($13,075,000 ÷ 100,000 units).

2. Actual Sales Mix

Product	Actual Sales Volume in Units	Actual Sales Mix
Palm Pro	11,000	10.0% (11,000 ÷ 110,000)
Palm CE	44,000	40.0% (44,000 ÷ 110,000)
Palm Kid	55,000	50.0% (55,000 ÷ 110,000)
	110,000	100.0%

Budgeted Sales Mix

Product	Budgeted Sales Volume in Units	Budgeted Sales Mix
Palm Pro	12,500	12.5% (12,500 ÷ 100,000)
Palm CE	37,500	37.5% (37,500 ÷ 100,000)
Palm Kid	50,000	50.0% (50,000 ÷ 100,000)
	100,000	100.0%

3. Sales-volume variance:

$$= \begin{pmatrix} \text{Actual} & & \text{Budgeted} \\ \text{quantity of} & - & \text{quantity of} \\ \text{units sold} & & \text{units sold} \end{pmatrix} \times \begin{array}{c} \text{Budgeted} \\ \text{contribution margin} \\ \text{per unit} \end{array}$$

PalmPro	(11,000	–	12,500)	×	$197	$ 295,500 U
PalmCE	(44,000	–	37,500)	×	$171	1,111,500 F
PalmKid	(55,000	–	50,000)	×	$ 84	420,000 F
Total sales-volume variance						$1,236,000 F

Sales-mix variance:

$$= \begin{array}{c} \text{Actual units} \\ \text{of all} \\ \text{products sold} \end{array} \times \begin{pmatrix} \text{Actual} & & \text{Budgeted} \\ \text{sales mix} & - & \text{sales mix} \\ \text{percentage} & & \text{percentage} \end{pmatrix} \times \begin{array}{c} \text{Budgeted} \\ \text{contrib. margin} \\ \text{per unit} \end{array}$$

PalmPro	=	110,000	×	(0.10	–	0.125)	×	$197	$541,750 U
PalmCE	=	110,000	×	(0.40	–	0.375)	×	$171	470,250 F
PalmKid	=	110,000	×	(0.50	–	0.50)	×	$ 84	0 F
Total sales-mix variance									$ 71,500 U

Sales-quantity variance:

$$= \begin{pmatrix} \text{Actual units} & & \text{Budgeted units} \\ \text{of all} & - & \text{of all} \\ \text{products sold} & & \text{products sold} \end{pmatrix} \times \begin{array}{c} \text{Budgeted} \\ \text{sales mix} \\ \text{percentage} \end{array} \times \begin{array}{c} \text{Budgeted} \\ \text{contrib. margin} \\ \text{per unit} \end{array}$$

PalmPro	(110,000	–	100,000)	×	0.125	×	$197	$ 246,250 F
PalmCE	(110,000	–	100,000)	×	0.375	×	$171	641,250 F
PalmKid	(110,000	–	100,000)	×	0.50	×	$ 84	420,000 F
Total sales-quantity variance								$1,307,500 F

Solution Exhibit 14-32 presents the sales-volume variance, the sales-mix variance, and the sales-quantity variance for Palm Pro, Palm CE, and PalmKid and in total for the third quarter 2007.

SOLUTION EXHIBIT 14-32

Sales-Mix and Sales-Quantity Variance Analysis of Aussie Infonautics for the Third Quarter 2007.

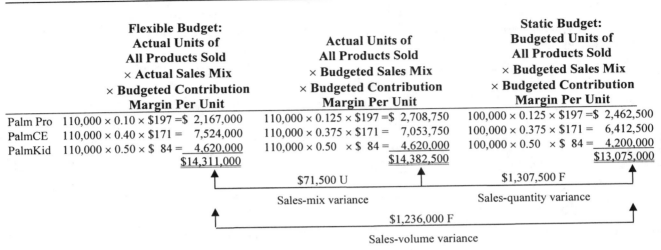

	Flexible Budget: Actual Units of All Products Sold × Actual Sales Mix × Budgeted Contribution Margin Per Unit	Actual Units of All Products Sold × Budgeted Sales Mix × Budgeted Contribution Margin Per Unit	Static Budget: Budgeted Units of All Products Sold × Budgeted Sales Mix × Budgeted Contribution Margin Per Unit
Palm Pro	110,000 × 0.10 × $197 =$ 2,167,000	110,000 × 0.125 × $197 =$ 2,708,750	100,000 × 0.125 × $197 =$ 2,462,500
PalmCE	110,000 × 0.40 × $171 = 7,524,000	110,000 × 0.375 × $171 = 7,053,750	100,000 × 0.375 × $171 = 6,412,500
PalmKid	110,000 × 0.50 × $ 84 = 4,620,000	110,000 × 0.50 × $ 84 = 4,620,000	100,000 × 0.50 × $ 84 = 4,200,000
	$14,311,000	$14,382,500	$13,075,000

$71,500 U — Sales-mix variance

$1,307,500 F — Sales-quantity variance

$1,236,000 F — Sales-volume variance

F = favorable effect on operating income; U= unfavorable effect on operating income

4.   The following factors help us understand the differences between actual and budgeted amounts:

- The difference in actual versus budgeted contribution margins was $1,107,000 unfavorable ($11,968,000 – $13,075,000). However, the contribution margin from the PalmCE exceeded budget by $2,079,500 ($8,492,000 – $6,412,500) while the contributions from the PalmPro and the PalmKid were lower than expected and offset this gain. This is attributable to lower unit sales in the case of PalmPro and lower contribution margins in the case of PalmKid.
- In percentage terms, the PalmCE accounted for 71% of actual contribution margin versus a planned 49% contribution margin. However, the PalmPro accounted for 16% versus planned 19% and the PalmKid accounted for only 13% versus a planned 32%.
- In unit terms (rather than in contribution terms), the PalmKid accounted for 50% of the sales mix as planned. However, the PalmPro accounted for only 10% versus a budgeted 12.5% and the PalmCE accounted for 40% versus a planned 37.5%.
- Variance analysis for the PalmPro shows an unfavorable sales-mix variance outweighing a favorable sales-quantity variance and producing an unfavorable sales-volume variance. The drop in sales-mix share was far larger than the gain from an overall greater quantity sold.
- The PalmCE gained both from an increase in share of the sales mix as well as from the increase in the overall number of units sold.
- The PalmKid maintained sales-mix share at 50%—as a result, the sales-mix variance is zero. However, PalmKid sales gained from the overall increase in units sold.

- Overall, there was a favorable total sales-volume variance. However, the large drop in PalmKid's contribution margin per unit combined with a decrease in the actual number of PalmPro units sold as well as a drop in the actual contribution margin per unit below budget, led to the total contribution margin being much lower than budgeted.

Other factors could be discussed here—for example, it seems that the PalmKid did not achieve much success with a three digit price point—selling price was budgeted at $149 but dropped to $102. At the same time, variable costs increased. This could have been due to a marketing push that did not succeed.

14-34 (40 min.) Variance analysis, multiple products.

1, 2, and 3. Solution Exhibit 14-34 presents the sales-volume, sales-quantity, and sales-mix variances for each type of cookie and in total for Debbie's Delight, Inc., in August 2006.

The sales-volume variances can also be computed as

$$\text{Sales-volume variance} = \left(\begin{array}{c}\text{Actual quantity} \\ \text{of pounds sold}\end{array} - \begin{array}{c}\text{Budgeted quantity} \\ \text{of pounds sold}\end{array}\right) \times \begin{array}{c}\text{Budgeted contribution} \\ \text{margin per pound}\end{array}$$

The sales-volume variances are

Chocolate chip	=	$(57,600 - 45,000) \times \$2.00$	=	$25,200 F
Oatmeal raisin	=	$(18,000 - 25,000) \times \$2.30$	=	16,100 U
Coconut	=	$(9,600 - 10,000) \times \$2.60$	=	1,040 U
White chocolate	=	$(13,200 - 5,000) \times \$3.00$	=	24,600 F
Macadamia nut	=	$(21,600 - 15,000) \times \$3.10$	=	20,460 F
All cookies				$53,120 F

The sales-quantity variance can also be computed as

$$\text{Sales-volume variance} = \left(\begin{array}{c}\text{Actual pounds} \\ \text{of all cookies} \\ \text{sold}\end{array} - \begin{array}{c}\text{Budgeted pounds} \\ \text{of all cookies} \\ \text{sold}\end{array}\right) \times \begin{array}{c}\text{Budgeted} \\ \text{sales-mix} \\ \text{percentage}\end{array} \times \begin{array}{c}\text{Budgeted} \\ \text{contribution} \\ \text{margin per pound}\end{array}$$

The sales-quantity variances are

Chocolate chip	=	$(120,000 - 100,000) \times 0.45 \times \$2.00$	=	$18,000 F
Oatmeal raisin	=	$(120,000 - 100,000) \times 0.25 \times \$2.30$	=	11,500 F
Coconut	=	$(120,000 - 100,000) \times 0.10 \times \$2.60$	=	5,200 F
White chocolate	=	$(120,000 - 100,000) \times 0.05 \times \$3.00$	=	3,000 F
Macadamia nut	=	$(120,000 - 100,000) \times 0.15 \times \$3.10$	=	9,300 F
All cookies				$47,000 F

The sales-mix variance can also be computed as:

$$\text{Sales-quantity variance} = \left(\begin{array}{c}\text{Actual sales-} \\ \text{mix percentage}\end{array} - \begin{array}{c}\text{Budgeted sales-} \\ \text{mix percentage}\end{array}\right) \times \begin{array}{c}\text{Actual pounds} \\ \text{of all cookies} \\ \text{sold}\end{array} \times \begin{array}{c}\text{Budgeted} \\ \text{contribution} \\ \text{margin per pound}\end{array}$$

The sales-mix variances are:

Chocolate chip	=	$(0.48 - 0.45) \times 120,000 \times \$2.00$	=	$ 7,200 F
Oatmeal raisin	=	$(0.15 - 0.25) \times 120,000 \times \$2.30$	=	27,600 U
Coconut	=	$(0.08 - 0.10) \times 120,000 \times \$2.60$	=	6,240 U
White chocolate	=	$(0.11 - 0.05) \times 120,000 \times \$3.00$	=	21,600 F
Macadamia nut	=	$(0.18 - 0.15) \times 120,000 \times \$3.10$	=	11,160 F
All cookies				$ 6,120 F

A summary of the variances is:

Sales-Volume Variance

Chocolate chip	$25,200 F
Oatmeal raisin	16,100 U
Coconut	1,040 U
White chocolate	24,600 F
Macadamia nut	20,460 F
All cookies	$53,120 F

Sales-Mix Variance

Chocolate chip	$ 7,200 F
Oatmeal raisin	27,600 U
Coconut	6,240 U
White chocolate	21,600 F
Macadamia nut	11,160 F
All cookies	$ 6,120 F

Sales-Quantity Variance

Chocolate chip	$18,000 F
Oatmeal raisin	11,500 F
Coconut	5,200 F
White chocolate	3,000 F
Macadamia nut	9,300 F
All cookies	$47,000 F

4.   Debbie's Delight shows a favorable sales-quantity variance because it sold more cookies in total than was budgeted. Together with the higher quantities, Debbie's also sold more of the high-contribution margin white chocolate and macadamia nut cookies relative to the budgeted mix—as a result, Debbie's also showed a favorable total sales-mix variance.

SOLUTION EXHIBIT 14-34
Columnar Presentation of Sales-Volume, Sales-Quantity, and Sales-Mix Variances
for Debbie's Delight, Inc.

	Flexible Budget: Actual Pounds of All Cookies Sold × Actual Sales Mix × Budgeted Contribution Margin per Pound (1)	Actual Pounds of All Cookies Sold × Budgeted Sales Mix × Budgeted Contribution Margin per Pound (2)	Static Budget: Budgeted Pounds of All Cookies Sold × Budgeted Sales Mix × Budgeted Contribution Margin per Pound (3)
Panel A: Chocolate Chip	$(120{,}000 \times 0.48^a) \times \$2$ $57{,}600 \times \$2$ $\$115{,}200$	$(120{,}000 \times 0.45^b) \times \$2$ $54{,}000 \times \$2$ $\$108{,}000$	$(100{,}000 \times 0.45^b) \times \$2$ $45{,}000 \times \$2$ $\$90{,}000$

$\$7{,}200$ F Sales-mix variance $\$18{,}000$ F Sales-quantity variance

$\$25{,}200$ F Sales-volume variance

Panel B: Oatmeal Raisin	$(120{,}000 \times 0.15^c) \times \$2.30$ $18{,}000 \times \$2.30$ $\$41{,}400$	$(120{,}000 \times 0.25^d) \times \$2.30$ $30{,}000 \times \$2.30$ $\$69{,}000$	$(100{,}000 \times 0.25^d) \times \$2.30$ $25{,}000 \times \$2.30$ $\$57{,}500$

$\$27{,}600$ U Sales-mix variance $\$11{,}500$ F Sales-quantity variance

$\$16{,}100$ U Sales-volume variance

Panel C: Coconut	$(120{,}000 \times 0.08^e) \times \$2.60$ $9{,}600 \times \$2.60$ $\$24{,}960$	$(120{,}000 \times 0.10^f) \times \$2.60$ $12{,}000 \times \$2.60$ $\$31{,}200$	$(100{,}000 \times 0.10^f) \times \$2.60$ $10{,}000 \times \$2.60$ $\$26{,}000$

$\$6{,}240$ U Sales-mix variance $\$5{,}200$ F Sales-quantity variance

$\$1{,}040$ U Sales-volume variance

F = favorable effect on operating income; U = unfavorable effect on operating income.

Actual Sales Mix:

[a]Chocolate Chip = 57,600 ÷ 120,000 = 48%
[c]Oatmeal Raisin = 18,000 ÷ 120,000 = 15%
[e]Coconut = 9,600 ÷ 120,000 = 8%

Budgeted Sales Mix:

[b]Chocolate Chip = 45,000 ÷ 100,000 = 45%
[d]Oatmeal Raisin = 25,000 ÷ 100,000 = 25%
[f]Coconut = 10,000 ÷ 100,000 = 10%

SOLUTION EXHIBIT 14-34 (Cont'd.)
Columnar Presentation of Sales-Volume, Sales-Quantity, and Sales-Mix Variances for Debbie's Delight, Inc.

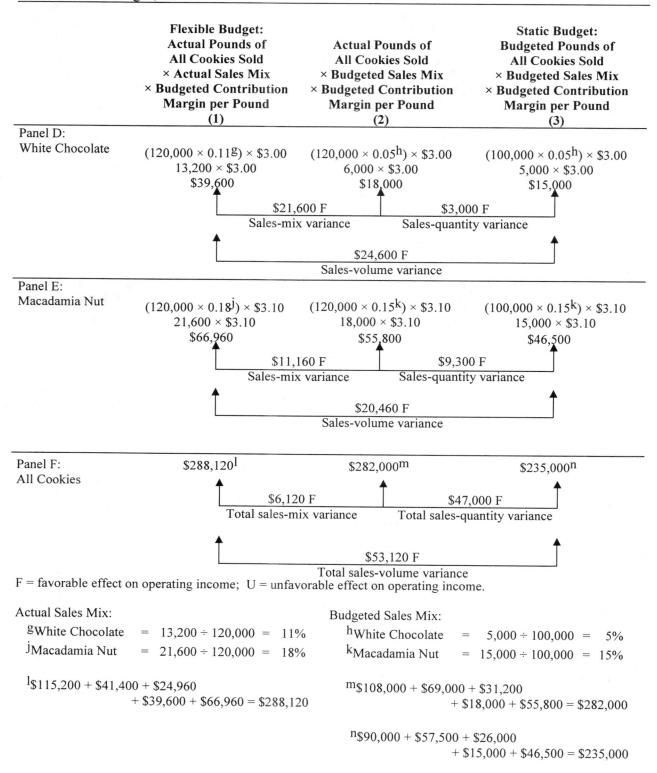

	Flexible Budget: Actual Pounds of All Cookies Sold × Actual Sales Mix × Budgeted Contribution Margin per Pound (1)	Actual Pounds of All Cookies Sold × Budgeted Sales Mix × Budgeted Contribution Margin per Pound (2)	Static Budget: Budgeted Pounds of All Cookies Sold × Budgeted Sales Mix × Budgeted Contribution Margin per Pound (3)

Panel D: White Chocolate

$(120,000 \times 0.11^g) \times \$3.00$ $(120,000 \times 0.05^h) \times \$3.00$ $(100,000 \times 0.05^h) \times \$3.00$
$13,200 \times \$3.00$ $6,000 \times \$3.00$ $5,000 \times \$3.00$
$39,600 $18,000 $15,000

$21,600 F Sales-mix variance $3,000 F Sales-quantity variance

$24,600 F Sales-volume variance

Panel E: Macadamia Nut

$(120,000 \times 0.18^j) \times \$3.10$ $(120,000 \times 0.15^k) \times \$3.10$ $(100,000 \times 0.15^k) \times \$3.10$
$21,600 \times \$3.10$ $18,000 \times \$3.10$ $15,000 \times \$3.10$
$66,960 $55,800 $46,500

$11,160 F Sales-mix variance $9,300 F Sales-quantity variance

$20,460 F Sales-volume variance

Panel F: All Cookies

$288,120^l $282,000^m $235,000^n

$6,120 F Total sales-mix variance $47,000 F Total sales-quantity variance

$53,120 F Total sales-volume variance

F = favorable effect on operating income; U = unfavorable effect on operating income.

Actual Sales Mix:

  ^{g}White Chocolate = $13,200 \div 120,000$ = 11%
  ^{j}Macadamia Nut = $21,600 \div 120,000$ = 18%

Budgeted Sales Mix:

  ^{h}White Chocolate = $5,000 \div 100,000$ = 5%
  ^{k}Macadamia Nut = $15,000 \div 100,000$ = 15%

^{l}\$115,200 + \$41,400 + \$24,960
    + \$39,600 + \$66,960 = \$288,120

^{m}\$108,000 + \$69,000 + \$31,200
    + \$18,000 + \$55,800 = \$282,000

^{n}\$90,000 + \$57,500 + \$26,000
    + \$15,000 + \$46,500 = \$235,000

14-36 (20–25 min.) **Direct materials efficiency, mix, and yield variances.**

1 & 2. Actual total quantity of all inputs used and actual input mix percentages for each input are as follows:

Chemical	Actual Quantity	Actual Mix Percentage		
Protex	16,200	$16,200 \div 54,000$	=	30%
Benz	37,800	$37,800 \div 54,000$	=	70%
Total	54,000			100%

Budgeted total quantity of all inputs allowed and budgeted input mix percentages for each input are as follows:

Chemical	Budgeted Quantity	Budgeted Mix Percentage		
Protex	20,800	$20,800 \div 52,000$	=	40%
Benz	31,200	$31,200 \div 52,000$	=	60%
Total	52,000			100%

Solution Exhibit 14-36 presents the total direct materials efficiency, yield, and mix variances for August 2007.

Total direct materials efficiency variance can also be computed as:

$$\begin{array}{c}\text{Direct materials} \\ \text{efficiency variance} \\ \text{for each input}\end{array} = \left(\begin{array}{c}\text{Actual input} \\ \text{quantity}\end{array} - \begin{array}{c}\text{Budgeted input quantity} \\ \text{allowed for actual output}\end{array}\right) \times \begin{array}{c}\text{Budgeted} \\ \text{price}\end{array}$$

Protex	= $(16,200 - 20,800) \times \$0.40$ =	1,840 F
Benz	= $(37,800 - 31,200) \times \$0.25$ =	1,650 U
Total direct materials efficiency variance		$ 190 F

The total direct materials yield variance can also be computed as the sum of the direct materials yield variances for each input:

$$\begin{array}{c}\text{Direct materials} \\ \text{yield variance} \\ \text{for each input}\end{array} = \left(\begin{array}{c}\text{Actual total} \\ \text{quantity of all} \\ \text{direct materials} \\ \text{inputs used}\end{array} - \begin{array}{c}\text{Budgeted total quantity} \\ \text{of all direct materials} \\ \text{inputs allowed for} \\ \text{actual output}\end{array}\right) \times \begin{array}{c}\text{Budgeted} \\ \text{direct materials} \\ \text{input mix} \\ \text{percentage}\end{array} \times \begin{array}{c}\text{Budgeted} \\ \text{price of} \\ \text{direct materials} \\ \text{inputs}\end{array}$$

Protex	= $(54,000 - 52,000) \times 0.40 \times \$0.40$ = $2,000 \times 0.40 \times \$0.40$ =		320 U
Benz	= $(54,000 - 52,000) \times 0.60 \times \$0.25$ = $2,000 \times 0.60 \times \$0.25$ =		300 U
Total direct materials yield variance			$620 U

The total direct materials mix variance can also be computed as the sum of the direct materials mix variances for each input:

$$
\begin{pmatrix} \text{Direct} \\ \text{materials} \\ \text{mix variance} \\ \text{for each input} \end{pmatrix} = \begin{pmatrix} \text{Actual} \\ \text{direct materials} \\ \text{input mix} \\ \text{percentage} \end{pmatrix} - \begin{pmatrix} \text{Budgeted} \\ \text{direct materials} \\ \text{input mix} \\ \text{percentage} \end{pmatrix} \times \begin{pmatrix} \text{Actual total} \\ \text{quantity of all} \\ \text{direct materials} \\ \text{inputs used} \end{pmatrix} \times \begin{pmatrix} \text{Budgeted} \\ \text{price of} \\ \text{direct materials} \\ \text{inputs} \end{pmatrix}
$$

Protex = (0.30 – 0.40) × 54,000 × \$0.40 = – 0.10 × 54,000 × \$0.40 = 2,160 F
Benz   = (0.70 – 0.60) × 54,000 × \$0.25 =   0.10 × 54,000 × \$0.25 = 1,350 U

Total direct materials mix variance \$ 810 F

3.   Energex Company used a larger total quantity of direct materials inputs than budgeted, and so it showed an unfavorable yield variance. The mix variance was favorable because the actual mix contained more of the cheaper input, Benz, and less of the more costly input, Protex, than the budgeted mix. The favorable mix variance offset all of the unfavorable yield variance—the overall efficiency variance was favorable. Energex Company must also consider the effect on output quality of using the cheaper mix, and the potential consequences for future revenues.

SOLUTION EXHIBIT 14-36
Columnar Presentation of Direct Materials Efficiency, Yield and Mix Variances
for Energex Company for August 2007

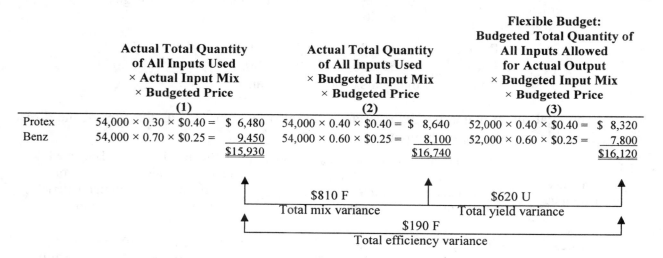

	Actual Total Quantity of All Inputs Used × Actual Input Mix × Budgeted Price (1)	Actual Total Quantity of All Inputs Used × Budgeted Input Mix × Budgeted Price (2)	Flexible Budget: Budgeted Total Quantity of All Inputs Allowed for Actual Output × Budgeted Input Mix × Budgeted Price (3)
Protex	54,000 × 0.30 × \$0.40 = \$ 6,480	54,000 × 0.40 × \$0.40 = \$ 8,640	52,000 × 0.40 × \$0.40 = \$ 8,320
Benz	54,000 × 0.70 × \$0.25 = 9,450	54,000 × 0.60 × \$0.25 = 8,100	52,000 × 0.60 × \$0.25 = 7,800
	\$15,930	\$16,740	\$16,120

\$810 F
Total mix variance

\$620 U
Total yield variance

\$190 F
Total efficiency variance

F = favorable effect on operating income; U = unfavorable effect on operating income

14-38 (15–20 min.) **Customer profitability, responsibility for environmental clean-up, ethics.**

1. Customer-profitability analysis examines how individual customers differ in their profitability. The revenues and costs of each customer can be estimated with varying degrees of accuracy. Revenues of IF typically would be known at the time of sale. Many costs also would be known, e.g., the cost of materials used to manufacture the fluids sold to each customer. A major area of uncertainty is future costs associated with obligations arising from the sale. There are several issues here:

a. Uncertainty as to the existence and extent of legal liability. Each customer has primary responsibility to dispose of its own toxic waste. However, under some U.S. laws (such as the "Superfund" laws), suppliers to a company may be partially liable for disposal of toxic material. Papandopolis needs to determine the extent of IF's liability. It would be necessary to seek legal guidance on this issue.

b. Uncertainty as to when the liability will occur. The further in the future, the lower the amount of the liability (assuming discounting for the time-value of money.)

c. Uncertainty as to the amount of the liability, given that the liability exists and the date of the liability can be identified. Papandopolis faces major difficulties here—see the answer to requirement 2.

Many companies argue that uncertainties related to (a), (b), and (c) make the inclusion of "hard-dollar estimates meaningless." However, at a minimum, a contingent liability should be recognized and included in the internal customer-profitability reports.

2. Papandopolis' controller may believe that if estimates of future possible legal exposure are sufficiently uncertain, then they should not be recorded. His concern about "smoking guns" may have a very genuine basis—that is, if litigation arises, third parties may misrepresent Papandopolis' concerns to the detriment of IF. Any written comments that she makes may surface 5 or 10 years later and be interpreted as "widespread knowledge" within IF that they have responsibility for large amounts of environmental clean-up.

Given this background, Papandopolis still has the responsibility to prepare a report in an objective and competent way. Moreover, she has visited 10 customer sites and has details as to their toxic-waste handling procedures. If Acme goes bankrupt and they have no liability insurance, one of the "deep pockets" available to meet toxic waste handling costs is likely to be IF. At a minimum, she should report the likely bankruptcy and the existence of IF's contingent liability for toxic-waste clean-up in her report. Whether she quantifies this contingent liability is a more difficult question. Papandopolis has limited information available to make a meaningful quantification. She is not an employee of Acme Metal and has no information about Acme's liability insurance. Moreover, she does not know what other parties (such as other suppliers) are also jointly liable to pay Acme's clean-up costs.

The appropriate course appears to highlight the contingent liability but to not attempt to quantify it.

CHAPTER 15
ALLOCATION OF SUPPORT-DEPARTMENT COSTS, COMMON COSTS, AND REVENUES

15-2 The dual-rate method provides information to division managers about cost behavior. Knowing how fixed costs and variable costs behave differently is useful in decision making.

15-4 Examples of bases used to allocate support department cost pools to operating departments include the number of employees, square feet of space, number of hours, and machine-hours.

15-6 Disagree. Allocating costs on "the basis of estimated long-run use by user department managers" means department managers can lower their cost allocations by deliberately underestimating their long-run use (assuming all other managers do not similarly underestimate their usage).

15-8 The reciprocal method is theoretically the most defensible method because it fully recognizes the mutual services provided among all departments, irrespective of whether those departments are operating or support departments.

15-10 All contracts with U.S. government agencies must comply with cost accounting standards issued by the Cost Accounting Standards Board (CASB).

15-12 Companies increasingly are selling packages of products or services for a single price. Revenue allocation is required when managers in charge of developing or marketing individual products in a bundle are evaluated using product-specific revenues.

15-14 Managers typically will argue that their individual product is the prime reason why consumers buy a bundle of products. Evidence on this argument could come from the sales of the products when sold as individual products. Other pieces of evidence include surveys of users of each product and surveys of people who purchase the bundle of products.

15-16 (20 min.)   **Single-rate versus dual-rate methods, support department.**

Bases available (kilowatt hours):

	Rockford	Peoria	Hammond	Kankakee	Total
Practical capacity	10,000	20,000	12,000	8,000	50,000
Expected monthly usage	8,000	9,000	7,000	6,000	30,000

1a. Single-rate method based on practical capacity:

Total costs in pool	=	$6,000 + $9,000	= $15,000
Practical capacity	=	50,000 kilowatt hours	
Allocation rate	=	$15,000 ÷ 50,000	= $0.30 per hour of capacity

	Rockford	Peoria	Hammond	Kankakee	Total
Practical capacity in hours	10,000	20,000	12,000	8,000	50,000
Costs allocated at $0.30 per hour	$3,000	$6,000	$3,600	$2,400	$15,000

1b. Single-rate method based on expected monthly usage:

Total costs in pool	= $6,000 + $9,000	= $15,000
Expected usage	= 30,000 kilowatt hours	
Allocation rate	= $15,000 ÷ 30,000	= $0.50 per hour of expected usage

	Rockford	Peoria	Hammond	Kankakee	Total
Expected monthly usage in hours	8,000	9,000	7,000	6,000	30,000
Costs allocated at $0.50 per hour	$4,000	$4,500	$3,500	$3,000	$15,000

2. Variable-Cost Pool:

Total costs in pool	=	$6,000
Expected usage	=	30,000 kilowatt hours
Allocation rate	=	$6,000 ÷ 30,000 = $0.20 per hour of expected usage

Fixed-Cost Pool:

Total costs in pool	=	$9,000
Practical capacity	=	50,000 kilowatt hours
Allocation rate	=	$9,000 ÷ 50,000 = $0.18 per hour of capacity

	Rockford	Peoria	Hammond	Kankakee	Total
Variable-cost pool					
$0.20 × 8,000; 9,000; 7,000, 6,000	$1,600	$1,800	$1,400	$1,200	$ 6,000
Fixed-cost pool					
$0.18 × 10,000; 20,000; 12,000, 8,000	1,800	3,600	2,160	1,440	9,000
Total	$3,400	$5,400	$3,560	$2,640	$15,000

The dual-rate method permits a more refined allocation of the power department costs; it permits the use of different allocation bases for different cost pools. The fixed costs result from decisions most likely associated with the practical capacity level. The variable costs result from decisions most likely associated with monthly usage.

15-18 (20 min.) **Dual-rate method, budgeted versus actual costs, and practical capacity vs. actual quantities (continuation of 15-17).**

1. Charges with dual rate method.

   Variable indirect cost rate = $1,500 per trip

   Fixed indirect cost rate = $\dfrac{\$200,000 \text{ budgeted costs}}{250 \text{ round trips budgeted}}$

   = $800 per trip

   Juices Division
Variable indirect costs, $1,500 × 150	$225,000
Fixed indirect costs, $800 × 150	120,000
	$345,000

   Preserves Division
Variable indirect costs, $1,500 × 75	$112,500
Fixed indirect costs, $800 × 100	80,000
	$192,500

2. The dual rate changes how the fixed indirect cost component is treated. By using budgeted trips made, the Juices Division is unaffected by changes from its own budgeted usage or that of other divisions.

15-20 (50 min.) **Support-department cost allocation, reciprocal method (continuation of 15-19).**

1a.

	Support Departments		Operating Departments	
	AS	IS	Govt.	Corp.
Costs	$600,000	$2,400,000		
Alloc. of AS costs				
(0.25, 0.40, 0.35)	(861,538)	215,385	$ 344,615	$ 301,538
Alloc. of IS costs				
(0.10, 0.30, 0.60)	261,538	(2,615,385)	784,616	1,569,231
	$ 0	$ 0	$1,129,231	$1,870,769

Reciprocal Method Computation

$$AS = \$600,000 + 0.10\ IS$$
$$IS = \$2,400,000 + 0.25\,AS$$
$$IS = \$2,400,000 + 0.25\,(\$600,000 + 0.10\ IS)$$
$$= \$2,400,000 + \$150,000 + 0.025\ IS$$
$$0.975\ IS = \$2,550,000$$
$$IS = \$2,550,000 \div 0.975$$
$$= \$2,615,385$$
$$AS = \$600,000 + 0.10\,(\$2,615,385)$$
$$= \$600,000 + \$261,538$$
$$= \$861,538$$

1b.

| | Support Departments | | Operating Departments | |
	AS	IS	Govt.	Corp.
Costs	$600,000	$2,400,000		
1st Allocation of AS				
(0.25, 0.40, 0.35)	(600,000)	150,000	$ 240,000	$ 210,000
		2,550,000		
1st Allocation of IS				
(0.10, 0.30, 0.60)	255,000	(2,550,000)	765,000	1,530,000
2nd Allocation of AS				
(0.25, 0.40, 0.35)	(255,000)	63,750	102,000	89,250
2nd Allocation of IS				
(0.10, 0.30, 0.60)	6,375	(63,750)	19,125	38,250
3rd Allocation of AS				
(0.25, 0.40, 0.35)	(6,375)	1,594	2,550	2,231
3rd Allocation of IS				
(0.10, 0.30, 0.60)	160	(1,594)	478	956
4th Allocation of AS				
(0.25, 0.40, 0.35)	(160)	40	64	56
4th Allocation of IS				
(0.10, 0.30, 0.60)	4	(40)	12	24
5th Allocation of AS				
(0.25, 0.40, 0.35)	(4)	1	2	1
5th Allocation of IS				
(0.10, 0.30, 0.60)	0	(1)	0	1
Total allocation	$ 0	$ 0	$1,129,231	$1,870,769

2.

		Govt. Consulting	Corp. Consulting
a.	Direct	$1,120,000	$1,880,000
b.	Step-Down (AS first)	1,090,000	1,910,000
c.	Step-Down (IS first)	1,168,000	1,832,080
d.	Reciprocal (linear equations)	1,129,231	1,870,769
e.	Reciprocal (repeated iterations)	1,129,231	1,870,769

The four methods differ in the level of support department cost allocation across support departments. The level of reciprocal service by support departments is material. Administrative Services supplies 25% of its services to Information Systems. Information Systems supplies 10% of its services to Administrative Services. The Information Department has a budget of $2,400,000 that is 400% higher than Administrative Services.

The reciprocal method recognizes all the interactions and is thus the most accurate. It is especially clear from looking at the repeated iterations calculations.

15-22 (30 min.) **Reciprocal cost allocation (continuation of 15-21).**

1.   The reciprocal allocation method explicitly includes the mutual services provided among all support departments. Interdepartmental relationships are fully incorporated into the support department cost allocations.

2.

$$HR = \$72,700 + .08333IS$$
$$IS = \$234,400 + .23077HR$$
$$HR = \$72,700 + [.08333(\$234,400 + .23077HR)]$$
$$= \$72,700 + [\$19,532.55 + 0.01923HR]$$
$$0.98077HR = \$92,232.55$$
$$HR = \$92,232.55 \div 0.98077$$
$$= \$94,041$$
$$IS = \$234,400 + (0.23077 \times \$94,041)$$
$$= \$256,102$$

	Support Depts.		Operating Depts.		
	HR	**Info. Systems**	**Corporate**	**Consumer**	**Total**
Costs Incurred	$72,700	$234,400	$ 998,270	$489,860	$1,795,230
Alloc. of HR costs (21/91, 42/91, 28/91)	(94,041)	21,702	43,404	28,935	
Alloc. of Info. Syst. costs (320/3,840, 1,920/3,840, 1,600/3,840)	21,341	(256,102)	128,051	106,710	
	$ 0	$ 0	$1,169,725	$625,505	$1,795,230

Solution Exhibit 15-22 presents the reciprocal method using repeated iterations.

SOLUTION EXHIBIT 15-22
Reciprocal Method of Allocating Support Department Costs for September 2007 at E-books Using Repeated Iterations

	Support Departments		Operating Departments		
	Human Resources	**Information Systems**	**Corporate Sales**	**Consumer Sales**	**Total**
Budgeted manufacturing overhead costs before any interdepartmental cost allocation	$72,700	$234,400	$ 998,270	$489,860	$1,795,230
1st Allocation of HR (21/91, 42/91, 28/91)[a]	(72,700)	16,777 251,177	33,554	22,369	
1st Allocation of Information Systems (320/3,840, 1,920/3,840, 1,600/3,840)[b]	20,931	(251,177)	125,589	104,657	
2nd Allocation of HR (21/91, 42/91, 28/91)[a]	(20,931)	4,830	9,661	6,440	
2nd Allocation of Information Systems (320/3,840, 1,920/3,840, 1,600/3,840)[b]	402	(4,830)	2,415	2,013	
3rd Allocation of HR (21/91, 42/91, 28/91)[a]	(402)	93	185	124	
3rd Allocation of Information Systems (320/3,840, 1,920/3,840, 1,600/3,840)[b]	8	(93)	46	39	
4th Allocation of HR (21/91, 42/91, 28/91)[a]	(8)	2	4	2	
4th Allocation of Information Systems: (320/3,840, 1,920/3,840, 1,600/3,840)[b]	0	(2)	1	1	
Total budgeted manufacturing overhead of operating departments	$ 0	$ 0	$1,169,725	$625,505	$1,795,230

Total accounts allocated and reallocated (the numbers in parentheses in first two columns)
HR $72,700 + $20,931 + $402 + $8 = $94,041
Information Systems $251,177 + $4,830 + $93 + $2 = $256,102

[a]Base is (21 + 42 + 28) or 91 employees
[b]Base is (320 + 1,920 + 1,600) or 3,840 minutes

3.   The reciprocal method is more accurate than the direct and step-down methods when there are reciprocal relationships among support departments.

A summary of the alternatives is:

	Corporate Sales	Consumer Sales
Direct method	$1,169,745	$625,485
Step-down method (HR first)	1,168,830	626,400
Reciprocal method	1,169,725	625,505

The reciprocal method is the preferred method, although for September 2007 the numbers do not appear materially different across the alternatives.

15-24 (20 min.) Allocation of common costs.

1.   Alternative approaches for the allocation of the $1,800 airfare include the following:

   a. The stand-alone cost allocation method. This method would allocate the air fare on the basis of each employer's percentage of the total of the individual stand-alone costs.

   Baltimore employer $\dfrac{\$1,400}{(\$1,400+\$1,100)} \times \$1,800 = \$1,008$

   Chicago employer $\dfrac{\$1,100}{(\$1,400+\$1,100)} \times \$1,800 = \underline{\quad 792\quad}$

   $\qquad\qquad\qquad\qquad\qquad\qquad\qquad\qquad\qquad\quad$ $\underline{\underline{\$1,800}}$

   Advocates of this method often emphasize an equity or fairness rationale.

   b. The incremental cost allocation method. This requires the choice of a primary party and an incremental party.

   If the Baltimore employer is the primary party, the allocation would be:

Baltimore employer	$1,400
Chicago employer	400
	$1,800

One rationale is that Ernst was planning to make the Baltimore trip, and the Chicago stop was added subsequently. Some students have suggested allocating as much as possible to the Baltimore employer since Ernst was not joining them.

If the Chicago employer is the primary party, the allocation would be:

Chicago employer	$1,100
Baltimore employer	700
	$1,800

One rationale is that the Chicago employer is the successful recruiter and presumably receives more benefits from the recruiting expenditures.

   c. Ernst could calculate the Shapley value that considers each employer in turn as the primary party: The Baltimore employer is allocated $1,400 as the primary party and $700 as the incremental party for an average of ($1,400 + $700) ÷ 2 = $1,050. The Chicago employer is allocated $1,100 as the primary party and $400 as the incremental party for an average of ($1,100 + 400) ÷ 2 = $750. The Shapley value approach would allocate $1,050 to the Baltimore employer and $750 to the Chicago employer.

2.   I would recommend Ernst use the Shapley value. It is fairer than the incremental method because it avoids considering one party as the primary party and allocating more of the common costs to that party. It also avoids disputes about who is the primary party. It allocates costs in a manner that is close to the costs allocated under the stand-alone method but takes a more comprehensive view of the common cost allocation problem by considering primary and incremental users, which the stand-alone method ignores.

The Shapley value (or the stand-alone cost allocation methods) would be the preferred methods if Ernst was to send the travel expenses to the Baltimore and Chicago employers before deciding which job offer to take. Other factors such as whether to charge the Chicago employer more because Ernst is joining the Chicago company or the Baltimore employer more because Ernst is not joining the Baltimore company can be considered if Ernst sends in his travel expenses after making her job decision. However, each company would not want to be considered as the primary party and so is likely to object to these arguments.

3.   A simple approach is to split the $60 equally between the two employers. The limousine costs at the Sacramento end are not a function of distance traveled on the plane.

An alternative approach is to add the $60 to the $1,800 and repeat requirement 1:

a. Stand-alone cost allocation method.

Baltimore employer $\dfrac{\$1,460}{(\$1,460+\$1,160)} \times \$1,860 = \$1,036$

Chicago employer $\dfrac{\$1,160}{(\$1,460+\$1,160)} \times \$1,860 = \$\ 824$

b. Incremental cost allocation method.

With Baltimore employer as the primary party:
Baltimore employer	$1,460
Chicago employer	400
	$1,860

With Chicago employer as the primary party:
Chicago employer	$1,160
Baltimore employer	700
	$1,860

c. Shapley value.
Baltimore employer: ($1,460 + $700) ÷ 2 = $1,080
Chicago employer: ($400 + $1,160) ÷ 2 = $780

As discussed in requirement 2, the Shapley value or the stand-alone cost allocation method would probably be the preferred approaches.

Note: If any students in the class have faced this situation, ask them how they handled it.

15-26 (20 min.) **Units sold, revenue allocation (continuation of 15-25).**

1.   Since L'Amour's sales are three times more likely to be driven by Monaco, the weighted Shapley method would weight the allocation made to Monaco when it is the primary product by three times as much as it would weight the allocation made to Monaco when it is the secondary product. This would result in an allocation of $75 of the selling price of L'Amour to Monaco and $105 of the selling price to Innocence, as shown below.

> Monaco: ($ 80 × 3 + $ 60 × 1) ÷ (3 + 1) = $300 ÷ 4 = $ 75
> Innocence: ($120 × 1 + $100 × 3) ÷ (3 + 1) = $420 ÷ 4 =   105
> Total: $180

Note that if we take the $20 difference between the two allocations to Monaco when it is primary and when it is secondary ($80 vs. $60), the weighted Shapley method essentially assigns $15 or ¾ of that difference to Monaco (at the cost of allocation to Innocence), to reflect the fact that Monaco is three times more important to L'Amour's sales than is Innocence.

2.   The advantage of the weighted Shapley value is that is uses all the available information about the demand for the individual products in allocating revenue. It does not just use the fact that one product is more important than the other (reflected in the ranks), but takes into account by how much a product is less or more important than others. For this reason, it is probably more palatable to "secondary product" division managers than the incremental method, and also more acceptable to the "primary product" division manager than the unweighted Shapley value.

15-28 (15 min.) **Single-rate versus dual-rate methods.**

1.   Single-rate method; budgeted rate based on practical capacity; allocation based on actual usage.

Budgeted fixed cost rate = $\dfrac{\$1,000,000}{200,000}$ = $ 5.00 per kilowatt-hour

Budgeted variable cost rate   = $12.50 per kilowatt-hour
Single fixed and variable cost rate = $17.50 per kilowatt-hour

Allocation to:

Durham $17.50 × 85,000 = $1,487,500
Charlotte $17.50 × 40,000 = $ 700,000
Raleigh $17.50 × 35,000 = $ 612,500

2.   Single-rate method; budgeted rated based on budgeted usage; allocation based on actual usage.

Budgeted fixed cost rate = $\dfrac{\$1,000,000}{160,000}$ = $ 6.25 per kilowatt-hour

Budgeted variable cost rate   = $12.50 per kilowatt-hour
Single fixed and variable cost rate = $18.75 per kilowatt-hour

Allocation to:

Durham $18.75 × 85,000 = $1,593,750
Charlotte $18.75 × 40,000 = $ 750,000
Raleigh $18.75 × 35,000 = $ 656,250

3.   Dual-rate method, budgeted fixed-cost rate based on practical capacity; fixed costs allocated on practical capacity; variable-cost rate based on budgeted usage; variable costs allocated on actual usage.

Budgeted fixed cost rate: $\dfrac{\$1,000,000}{200,000}$ = $5 per kilowatt-hour

Budgeted variable cost rate: $12.50 per kilowatt-hour

Allocation to Durham:
Fixed costs $5 × 100,000 $ 500,000
Variable costs $12.50 × 85,000   1,062,500
Total $1,562,500

Allocation to Charlotte:
Fixed costs $5 × 60,000 $ 300,000
Variable costs $12.50 × 40,000   500,000
Total $ 800,000

Allocation to Raleigh:
Fixed costs $5 × 40,000 $ 200,000
Variable costs $12.50 × 35,000   437,500
Total $ 637,500

4.   Dual-rate method, budgeted fixed-cost rate based on budgeted usage; fixed costs allocated on budgeted usage; variable-cost rate based on budgeted usage; variable costs allocated on actual usage.

$$\text{Budgeted fixed cost rate: } \frac{\$1,000,000}{160,000} = \$6.25 \text{ per kilowatt-hour}$$

Budgeted variable cost rate: $12.50 per kilowatt-hour

Allocation to Durham:
Fixed costs $6.25 × 80,000	$ 500,000
Variable costs $12.50 × 85,000	1,062,500
Total	$1,562,500

Allocation to Charlotte:
Fixed costs $6.25 × 50,000	$ 312,500
Variable costs $12.50 × 40,000	500,000
Total	$ 812,500

Allocation to Raleigh:
Fixed costs $6.25 × 30,000	$ 187,500
Variable costs $12.50 × 35,000	437,500
Total	$ 625,000

5.

Factory	Requirement 1 Total	Requirement 2 Total	Requirement 3 Fixed	Variable	Total	Requirement 4 Fixed	Variable	Total
Durham	$1,487,500	$1,593,750	$ 500,000	$1,062,500	$1,562,500	$ 500,000	$1,062,500	$1,562,500
Charlotte	700,000	750,000	300,000	500,000	800,000	312,500	500,000	812,500
Raleigh	612,500	656,250	200,000	437,500	637,500	187,500	437,500	625,000
Total	$2,800,000	$3,000,000	$1,000,000	$2,000,000	$3,000,000	$1,000,000	$2,000,000	$3,000,000

In the case of Carolina Company in 2006, we see that budgeted usage and actual usage both totaled 160,000 KWH. This explains why in requirement 2 all of the budgeted costs (total of $3,000,000) are allocated. The method in requirement 1 highlights the available excess capacity. The allocations of requirements 3 and 4 are not significantly different. These dual-rate allocations are preferred to the single-rate allocations in requirements 1 and 2 because fixed costs and variable costs are allocated differently.

15-30 (30 min.)   **Cost allocation, actual versus budgeted usage.**

1.   Problems with the monthly allocation report include:

    a. The single-rate method used does not distinguish between fixed versus variable costs.

    b. Actual costs and actual quantities are used. This results in managers not knowing cost rates until year-end.

    c. Monthly time periods are used to determine cost rates. The use of a monthly time period can result in highly variable cost rates depending on seasonality, days in a month, demand surges, and so on.

2. Budgeted variable cost (based on normal usage):

$$\frac{\$7,500,000}{100,000,000} = \$0.075 \text{ per kWh}$$

Monthly Allocation Report
November 2006

Allocations of Variable Costs (based on budgeted rate × actual usage)[*]

      To Department A: 60,000,000 × $0.075 $4,500,00

      To Department B: 20,000,000 × $0.075

                                                <u>1,500,000</u>
                                              <u>$6,000,00</u>

[*]There will be $1,500,000 of unallocated variable costs for November 2006.

Allocation of fixed costs (Based on budgeted usage × budgeted amount)

      To Department A: 60% × $30,000,000 $18,000,000
      To Department B: 40% × $30,000,000   <u> 12,000,000</u>
      Total   <u>$30,000,000</u>

Or alternatively,

$$\text{Budgeted fixed cost rate} = \frac{\text{Budgeted fixed costs}}{\text{Budgeted kWh}} = \frac{\$30,000,000}{60,000,000 + 40,000,000}$$

$$= \$0.30 \text{ per kWh}$$

Allocation of fixed costs (based on budgeted usage)
To Department A: $0.30 × 60,000,000 kWh = $18,000,000
To Department B: $0.30 × 40,000,000 kWh = 12,000,000
Total $30,000,000

Department A allocation of costs
Variable costs	$ 4,500,000
Fixed costs	18,000,000
Total	$22,500,000

Department B allocation of costs
Variable costs	$ 1,500,000
Fixed costs	12,000,000
Total	$13,500,000

3.   Under Lamb's allocation report, the production manager has both risk-exposure and uncertainty concerns:

Risk-exposure—Changes in the demand for energy by Department A affect the costs Lamb will report for Department B. Increases in demand by A will reduce B's cost per kWh and vice versa. Department B's production manager may seek to curtail production in periods when Departments A's production declines. This could create an ever-diminishing cycle of production. Alternatively, Department B may subcontract outside to avoid a higher energy rate, even if it is not in Bulldog's best interest to subcontract.

Uncertainty—When actual costs are used, managers cannot plan costs with certainty. Managers typically have less ability to bear uncertainty than do companies. The result is that managers may reject alternatives that are good risks from Bulldog's perspective but not attractive risks for themselves.

15-32 (40–60 min.) **Support-department cost allocations; single-department cost pools; direct, step-down, and reciprocal methods.**

All the following computations are in dollars.

1.

Direct method:

	To X	To Y
A	250/400 × $100,000 = $62,500	150/400 × $100,000 = $37,500
B	100/500 × $ 40,000 = __8,000__	400/500 × $40,000 = __32,000__
Total	$70,500	$69,500

Step-down method, allocating A first:

	A	B	X	Y
Costs to be allocated	$100,000	$40,000	—	—
Allocate A: (100; 250; 150 ÷ 500)	(100,000)	20,000	$50,000	$30,000
Allocate B: (100; 400 ÷ 500)	—	(60,000)	12,000	48,000
Total	$ 0	$ 0	$62,000	$78,000

Step-down method, allocating B first:

	A	B	X	Y
Costs to be allocated	$100,000	$ 40,000	—	—
Allocate B: (500; 100; 400 ÷ 1,000)	20,000	(40,000)	$ 4,000	$16,000
Allocate A: (250/400, 150/400)	(120,000)	—	75,000	45,000
Total	$ 0	$ 0	$79,000	$61,000

Note that these methods produce significantly different results, so the choice of method may frequently make a difference in the budgeted department overhead rates.

Reciprocal method:

Stage 1: Let   A =   total costs of materials-handling department
                 B =   total costs of power-generating department
       (1)   A = $100,000 + 0.5B
       (2)   B = $ 40,000 + 0.2A

Stage 2: Substituting in (1):

	A	=	$100,000 + 0.5($40,000 + 0.2A)
	A	=	$100,000 + $20,000 + 0.1A
	0.9A	=	$120,000
	A	=	$133,333

Substituting in (2):

	B	=	$40,000 + 0.2($133,333)
	B	=	$66,666

Stage 3:

	A	B	X	Y
Original amounts	$100,000	$40,000	—	—
Allocation of A	(133,333)	26,666(20%)	$66,667(50%)	$40,000(30%)
Allocation of B	33,333(50%)	(66,666)	6,667(10%)	26,666(40%)
Totals accounted for	$ 0	$ 0	$73,334	$66,666

SOLUTION EXHIBIT 15-32
Reciprocal Method of Allocating Support Department Costs for Manes Company Using Repeated Iterations.

	Support Departments		Operating Departments	
	A	B	X	Y
Budgeted manufacturing overhead costs before any interdepartmental cost allocations	$100,000	$40,000		
1st Allocation of Dept. A: (2/10, 5/10, 3/10)[a]	(100,000)	20,000 / 60,000	$50,000	$30,000
1st Allocation of Dept. B (5/10, 1/10, 4/10)[b]	30,000	(60,000)	6,000	24,000
2nd Allocation of Dept. A (2/10, 5/10, 3/10)[a]	(30,000)	6,000	15,000	9,000
2nd Allocation of Dept B: (5/10, 1/10, 4/10)[b]	3,000	(6,000)	600	2,400
3rd Allocation of Dept A: (2/10, 5/10, 3/10)[a]	(3,000)	600	1,500	900
3rd Allocation of Dept. B: (5/10, 1/10, 4/10)[b]	300	(600)	60	240
4th Allocation of Dept. A (2/10, 5/10, 3/10)[a]	(300)	60	150	90
4th Allocation of Dept. B (5/10, 1/10, 4/10)[b]	30	(60)	6	24
5th Allocation of Dept A (2/10, 5/10, 3/10)	(30)	6	15	9
5th Allocation of Dept B (5/10, 1/10, 4/10)	3	(6)	1	2
6th Allocation of Dept A (2/10, 5/10, 3/10)	(3)	0	2	1
Total budgeted manufacturing overhead of operating departments	$ 0	$ 0	$73,334	$66,666

Total accounts allocated and reallocated (the numbers in parentheses in first two columns)
Dept A; Materials Handling: $100,000 + $30,000 + $3,000 + $300 + $30 + $3 = $133,333
Dept B; Power Generation: $60,000 + $6,000 + $600 + $60 + $6 = $66,666

[a]Base is (100 + 250 +150) or 500 labor-hours; 100 ÷ 500 = 2/10, 250 ÷ 500 = 5/10, 150 ÷ 500 = 3/10.
[b]Base is (500 + 100 + 400) or 1,000 kWh ; 500 ÷ 1,000 = 5/10, 100 ÷ 1,000 = 1/10, 400 ÷ 1,000 = 4/10.

Comparison of methods:

Method of Allocation	X	Y
Direct method	$70,500	$69,500
Step-down: A first	62,000	78,000
Step-down: B first	79,000	61,000
Reciprocal method	73,334	66,666

Note that *in this case* the direct method produces answers that are the closest to the "correct" answers (that is, those from the reciprocal method), step-down allocating B first is next, and step-down allocating A first is least accurate.

2.   At first glance, it appears that the cost of power is $40 per unit plus the material handling costs. If so, Manes would be better off by purchasing from the power company. However, the decision should be influenced by the effects of the interdependencies and the fixed costs. Note that the power needs would be less (students frequently miss this) if they were purchased from the outside:

	Outside Power Units Needed
X	100
Y	400
A (500 units minus 20% of 500 units, because there is no need to service the nonexistent power department)	400
Total units	900

Total costs, 900 × $40 = $36,000

In contrast, the total costs that would be saved by not producing the power inside would depend on the effects of the decision on various costs:

	Avoidable Costs of 1,000 Units of Power Produced Inside
Variable indirect labor and indirect material costs	$10,000
Supervision in power department	10,000
Materials handling, 20% of $70,000*	14,000
Probable minimum cost savings	$34,000
Possible additional savings:	
a. Can any supervision in materials handling be saved because of overseeing less volume? Minimum savings is probably zero; the maximum is probably 20% of $10,000 or $2,000.	?
b. Is any depreciation a truly variable, wear-and-tear type of cost?	?
Total savings by not producing 1,000 units of power	$34,000 + ?

* Materials handling costs are higher because the power department uses 20% of materials handling. Therefore, materials-handling costs will decrease by 20%.

In the short run (at least until a capital investment in equipment is necessary), the data suggest continuing to produce internally because the costs eliminated would probably be less than the comparable purchase costs.

15-34 (20–25 min.)**Revenue allocation, bundled products.**

1.a.   The stand-alone revenues (using unit selling prices) of the three components of the $700 package are:

$$
\begin{array}{lll}
\text{Lodging} & \$320 \times 2 = \$\ 640 \\
\text{Recreation} & \$150 \times 2 = \ \ \ 300 \\
\text{Food} & \$\ 80 \times 2 = \ \underline{\ \ \ 160} \\
& \underline{\$1{,}100}
\end{array}
$$

Lodging $\dfrac{\$640}{\$1{,}100} \times \$700 \ = \ 0.582 \times \$700 = \$407$

Recreation $\dfrac{\$300}{\$1{,}100} \times \$700 \ = \ 0.273 \times \$700 = \$191$

Food $\dfrac{\$160}{\$1{,}100} \times \$700 \ = \ 0.145 \times \$700 = \$102$

b.

Product	Revenue Allocated		Cumulative Revenue Allocated
Recreation	$300		$300
Lodging	400	($700 – $300)	$700
Food	$\underline{\quad 0}$		$700
	$\underline{\$700}$		

2. The pros of the stand-alone-revenue-allocation method include the following:
    a. Each item in the bundle receives a positive weight, which means the resulting allocations are more likely to be accepted by all parties than a method allocating zero revenues to one or more products.

    b. It uses market-based evidence (unit selling prices) to decide the revenue allocations—unit prices are one indicator of benefits received .

    c. It is simple to implement.

    The cons of the stand-alone revenue-allocation method include:
    a. It ignores the relative importance of the individual components in attracting consumers to purchase the bundle.

    b. It ignores the opportunity cost of the individual components in the bundle. The golf course operates at 100% capacity. Getaway participants must reserve a golf booking one week in advance, or else they are not guaranteed playing time. A getaway participant who does not use the golf option may not displace anyone. Thus, under the stand-alone method, the golf course may be paid twice—once from the non-getaway person who does play and second from an allocation of the $700 package amount for the getaway person who does not play (either did not want to play or wanted to play but made a booking too late, or failed to show).

    c. The weight can be artificially inflated by individual product managers setting "high" list unit prices and then being willing to frequently discount these prices. The use of *actual* unit prices or actual revenues per product in the stand-alone formula will reduce this problem.

    d. The weights may change frequently if unit prices are constantly changing. This is not so much a criticism as a reflection that the marketplace may be highly competitive.

    The pros of the incremental method include:
    a. It has the potential to reflect that some products in the bundle are more highly valued than others. Not all products in the bundle have a similar "write-down" from unit list prices. Ensuring this "potential pro" becomes an "actual pro" requires that the choice of the primary product be guided by reliable evidence on consumer preferences. This is not an easy task.

    b. Once the sequence is chosen, it is straightforward to implement.

    The cons of the incremental method include:
    a. Obtaining the rankings can be highly contentious and place managers in a "no-win" acrimonious debate. The revenue allocations can be highly sensitive to the chosen rankings.

    b. Some products will have zero revenues assigned to them. Consider the Food division. It would incur the costs for the two dinners but receive no revenue.

15-36 (30–40 min.) **Overhead-allocation disputes, ethics.**

1.   This problem, which is based on an actual case, shows how overhead cost allocation can affect contract pricing. This is how the Navy would claim a refund of $689,658:

The overhead cost would be allocated differently:

Previous overhead allocation rate $= \dfrac{\$30}{\$50 + \$100} = \$0.20$ per DL$

Revised overhead allocation rate $= \dfrac{\$30}{\$45 + \$100} = \$0.2068965$ per DL$

	Navy Costs	Commercial Costs
Original cost assignment:		
Direct materials	$ —	$ —
Direct labor	45,000,000	100,000,000
SE group	5,000,000	—
Allocated overhead (20% × DL$)	10,000,000[a]	20,000,000[b]
Total	$60,000,000	$120,000,000
Revised cost assignment:		
Direct materials	$ —	$ —
Direct labor	45,000,000	100,000,000
SE group	5,000,000	—
Allocated overhead	9,310,343[c]	20,689,650[d]
Total	$59,310,343	$120,689,650

[a]20% × ($45,000,000 direct labor + $5,000,000 SE group classified as direct labor) = $10,000,000
[b]20% × $100,000,000 = $20,000,000
[c]20.68965% × $45,000,000 = $9,310,343
[d]20.68965% × $100,000,000 = $20,689,650

The Navy's claim would be:

Remove the original overhead allocation of $50 million × 0.20	$10,000,000
This means that the overhead pool, which has been totally allocated to products, is now underallocated by $10 million. This overhead must be reallocated in proportion to the "corrected" direct labor in nuclear work and commercial work. In short, if the overhead allocation base shrinks from $150 to $145 million, the overhead rate increases from 20% to 20.68965%. The revised allocation is $45 million × 0.2068965.	9,310,343
	$ 689,657

2a. Revised overhead allocation rate $= \dfrac{\$26}{\$45 + \$100} = 17.93103\%$

	Navy Costs	Commercial Costs
Revised cost assignment:		
Direct materials	$ –	$ –
Direct labor	45,000,000	100,000,000
SE group	5,000,000	–
Commercial purchasing		4,000,000
Allocated overhead (17.93103% × DL$)	8,068,964	17,931,030
	$58,068,964	$121,931,030

Given that the original Navy cost was $60,000,000, and the revised cost is $58,068,964, the Navy would claim a total refund of $1,931,036. The additional refund is $1,241,379 (which is $59,310,343 – $58,068,964).

2b. Although both discoveries (the $5 million of the SE group cost that is not a direct labor costs and the $4 million in general yard overhead for commercial customers) will increase the costs allocated to commercial customers and will hurt Marden's ability to meet cost targets this year, she should not wait for the government auditors to "discover" the second issue. She should discuss this with her managers, explain how the situation arose, pro-actively reveal both issues and issue the appropriate refund to the US Navy. Hopefully, her managers will appreciate her honesty and understand that such unexpected things can occur despite the best planning and her commercial customers will be willing to bear the extra costs as well.

Even if her superiors are not understanding, Marden should adhere to the standards of integrity and objectivity prescribed for management accountants and reveal the mistakes made, being prepared to suffer the consequences.

CHAPTER 16
COST ALLOCATION: JOINT PRODUCTS AND BYPRODUCTS

16-2 A *joint cost* is a cost of a production process that yields multiple products simultaneously. A s*eparable cost* is a cost incurred beyond the splitoff point that is assignable to each of the specific products identified at the splitoff point.

16-4 A *product* is any output that has a positive sales value (or an output that enables a company to avoid incurring costs). In some joint-cost settings, outputs can occur that do not have a positive sales value. The offshore processing of hydrocarbons yields water that is recycled back into the ocean as well as yielding oil and gas. The processing of mineral ore to yield gold and silver also yields dirt as an output, which is recycled back into the ground.

16-6 The joint production process yields individual products that are either sold this period or held as inventory to be sold in subsequent periods. Hence, the joint costs need to be allocated between total production rather than just those sold this period.

16-8 Both methods use market selling-price data in allocating joint costs, but they differ in which sales-price data they use. The *sales value at splitoff method* allocates joint costs to joint products on the basis of the relative total sales value at the splitoff point of the total production of these products during the accounting period. The *net realizable value method* allocates joint costs to joint products on the basis of the relative net realizable value (the final sales value minus the separable costs of production and marketing) of the total production of the joint products during the accounting period.

16-10 The NRV method can be simplified by assuming (a) a standard set of post-splitoff point processing steps, and (b) a standard set of selling prices. The use of (a) and (b) achieves the same benefits that the use of standard costs does in costing systems.

16-12 No. Any method used to allocate joint costs to individual products that is applicable to the problem of joint product-cost allocation should not be used for management decisions regarding whether a product should be sold or processed further. When a product is an inherent result of a joint process, the decision to process further should not be influenced by either the size of the total joint costs or by the portion of the joint costs assigned to particular products. Joint costs are irrelevant for these decisions. The only relevant items for these decisions are the incremental revenue and the incremental costs beyond the splitoff point.

16-14 Two methods to account for byproducts are:
   a. Production method—recognizes byproducts in the financial statements at the time production is completed.
   b. Sales method—delays recognition of byproducts until the time of sale.

16-16 (20-30 min.) **Joint-cost allocation, insurance settlement.**

1. (a) Sales value at splitoff-point method.

	Pounds of Product	Wholesale Selling Price per Pound	Sales Value at Splitoff	Weighting: Sales Value at Splitoff	Joint Costs Allocated	Allocated Costs per Pound
Breasts	100	$1.10	$110	0.675	$ 67.50	0.6750
Wings	20	0.40	8	0.049	4.90	0.2450
Thighs	40	0.70	28	0.172	17.20	0.4300
Bones	80	0.20	16	0.098	9.80	0.1225
Feathers	10	0.10	1	0.006	0.60	0.0600
	250		$163	1.000	$100.00	

Costs of Destroyed Product

Breasts: $0.6750 per pound × 20 pounds = $13.50

Wings: $0.2450 per pound × 10 pounds = 2.45

$15.95

b. Physical measures method.

	Pounds of Product	Weighting: Physical Measures	Joint Costs Allocated	Allocated Costs per Pound
Breasts	100	0.400	$ 40.00	$0.400
Wings	20	0.080	8.00	0.400
Thighs	40	0.160	16.00	0.400
Bones	80	0.320	32.00	0.400
Feathers	10	0.040	4.00	0.400
	250	1.000	$100.00	

Costs of Destroyed Product

Breast: $0.40 per pound × 20 pounds = $ 8

Wings: $0.40 per pound × 10 pounds = 4

$12

Note: Although not required, it is useful to highlight the individual product profitability figures:

		Sales Value at Splitoff Method		Physical Measures Method	
Product	Sales Value	Joint Costs Allocated	Gross Income	Joint Costs Allocated	Gross Income
Breasts	$110	$67.50	$42.50	$40.00	$70.00
Wings	8	4.90	3.10	8.00	0.00
Thighs	28	17.20	10.80	16.00	12.00
Bones	16	9.80	6.20	32.00	(16.00)
Feathers	1	0.60	0.40	4.00	(3.00)

2.   The sales-value at splitoff method captures the benefits-received criterion of cost allocation and is the preferred method. The costs of processing a chicken are allocated to products in proportion to the ability to contribute revenue. Chicken Little's decision to process chicken is heavily influenced by the revenues from breasts and thighs. The bones provide relatively few benefits to Chicken Little despite their high physical volume.

The physical measures method shows profits on breasts and thighs and losses on bones and feathers. Given that Chicken Little has to jointly process all the chicken products, it is non-intuitive to single out individual products that are being processed simultaneously as making losses while the overall operations make a profit. Chicken Little is processing chicken mainly for breasts and thighs and not for wings, bones, and feathers, while the physical measure method allocates a disproportionate amount of costs to wings, bones and feathers.

16-18 (10 min.)   **Net realizable value method.**

A diagram of the situation is in Solution Exhibit 16-18 (all numbers are in thousands).

	Cooking Oil	**Soap Oil**	**Total**
Final sales value of total production,			
$1,000 \times \$50$; $500 \times \$25$	$50,000	$12,500	$62,500
Deduct separable costs	30,000	7,500	37,500
Net realizable value at splitoff point	$20,000	$ 5,000	$25,000
Weighting, $20,000; $5,000 ÷ $25,000	0.8	0.2	
Joint costs allocated, 0.8; 0.2 × $24,000	$19,200	$ 4,800	$24,000

SOLUTION EXHIBIT 16-18 (all numbers are in thousands)

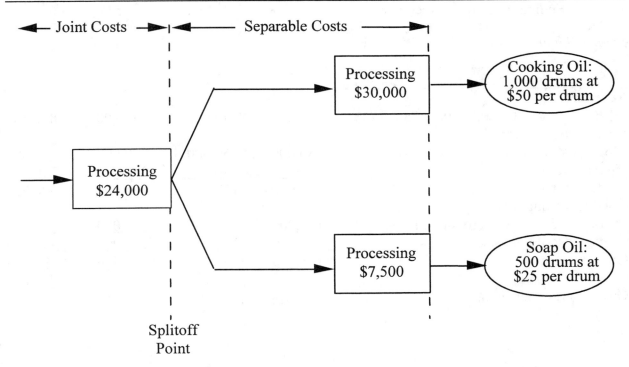

16-20 (40 min.) **Alternative methods of joint-cost allocation, ending inventories.**

Total production for the year was:

	Sold	Ending Inventories	Total Production
X	120	180	300
Y	340	60	400
Z	475	25	500

A diagram of the situation is in Solution Exhibit 16-20.

1.   a. Net realizable value (NRV) method:

	X	Y	Z	Total
Final sales value of total production,				
300 × $1,500; 400 × $1,000; 500 × $700	$450,000	$400,000	$350,000	$1,200,000
Deduct separable costs	—	—	200,000	200,000
Net realizable value at splitoff point	$450,000	$400,000	$150,000	$1,000,000
Weighting, $450; $400; $150 ÷ $1,000	0.45	0.40	0.15	
Joint costs allocated,				
0.45, 0.40, 0.15 × $400,000	$180,000	$160,000	$ 60,000	$ 400,000

Ending Inventory Percentages:

	X	Y	Z
Ending inventory	180	60	25
Total production	300	400	500
Ending inventory percentage	60%	15%	5%

Income Statement

	X	Y	Z	Total
Revenues,				
120 × $1,500; 340 × $1,000; 475 × $700	$180,000	$340,000	$332,500	$852,500
Cost of goods sold:				
Joint costs allocated	180,000	160,000	60,000	400,000
Separable costs	—	—	200,000	200,000
Production costs	180,000	160,000	260,000	600,000
Deduct ending inventory,				
60%; 15%; 5% of production costs	108,000	24,000	13,000	145,000
Cost of goods sold	72,000	136,000	247,000	455,000
Gross margin	$108,000	$204,000	$ 85,500	$397,500
Gross-margin percentage	60%	60%	25.71%	

b.   Constant gross-margin percentage NRV method:

Step 1:

Final sales value of prodn., (300 × $1,500) + (400 × $1,000) + (500 × $700)	$1,200,000
Deduct joint and separable costs, $400,000 + $200,000	600,000
Gross margin	$ 600,000
Gross-margin percentage, $600,000 ÷ $1,200,000	50%

Step 2:

	X	Y	Z	Total
Final sales value of total production,				
300 × $1,500; 400 × $1,000; 500 × $700	$450,000	$400,000	$350,000	$1,200,000
Deduct gross margin, using overall				
gross-margin percentage of sales, 50%	225,000	200,000	175,000	600,000
Total production costs	225,000	200,000	175,000	600,000
Step 3: Deduct separable costs			200,000	200,000
Joint costs allocated	$225,000	$200,000	$(25,000)	$ 400,000

The negative joint-cost allocation to Product Z illustrates one "unusual" feature of the constant gross-margin percentage NRV method: some products may receive negative cost allocations so that all individual products have the same gross-margin percentage.

Income Statement

	X	Y	Z	Total
Revenues, 120 × $1,500;				
340 × $1,000; 475 × $700	$180,000	$340,000	$332,500	$852,500
Cost of goods sold:				
Joint costs allocated	225,000	200,000	(25,000)	400,000
Separable costs	-	-	200,000	200,000
Production costs	225,000	200,000	175,000	600,000
Deduct ending inventory,				
60%; 15%; 5% of production costs	135,000	30,000	8,750	173,750
Cost of goods sold	90,000	170,000	166,250	426,250
Gross margin	$ 90,000	$170,000	$166,250	$426,250
Gross-margin percentage	50%	50%	50%	50%

Summary

	X	Y	Z	Total
a. NRV method:				
Inventories on balance sheet	$108,000	$ 24,000	$ 13,000	$145,000
Cost of goods sold on income statement	72,000	136,000	247,000	455,000
				$600,000
b. Constant gross-margin percentage NRV method				
Inventories on balance sheet	$135,000	$ 30,000	$ 8,750	$173,750
Cost of goods sold on income statement	90,000	170,000	166,250	426,250
				$600,000

2. Gross-margin percentages:

	X	Y	Z
NRV method	60%	60%	25.71%
Constant gross-margin percentage NRV	50%	50%	50.00%

SOLUTION EXHIBIT 16-20

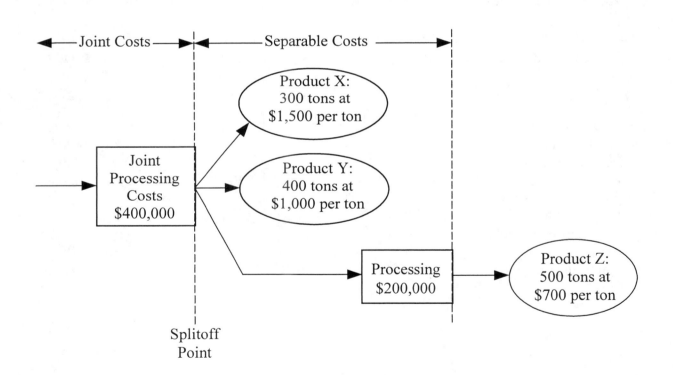

16-22 (30 min.) **Joint-cost allocation, sales value, physical measure, NRV methods.**

1a.

PANEL A: Allocation of Joint Costs using Sales Value at Splitoff	Ricito	Pancito	Total
Sales value of total production at splitoff point (25,000 tons × $10 per ton; 50,000 × $15 per ton)	$250,000	$750,000	$1,000,000
Weighting ($250,000; $750,000 ÷ $1,000,000)	0.25	0.75	
Joint costs allocated (0.25; 0.75 × $600,000)	$150,000	$450,000	$600,000

PANEL B: Product-Line Income Statement for June 2006	Ricito	Pancito	Total
Revenues (25,000 tons × $10 per ton; 50,000 × $15 per ton)	$250,000	$750,000	$1,000,000
Joint costs allocated (from Panel A)	150,000	450,000	600,000
Gross margin	$100,000	$300,000	$ 400,000
Gross margin percentage	40%	40%	40%

1b.

PANEL A: Allocation of Joint Costs using Physical Measure Method	Ricito	Pancito	Total
Physical measure of total production (tons)	25,000	50,000	75,000
Weighting (25,000 tons; 50,000 tons ÷ 75,000 tons)	33%	67%	
Joint costs allocated (0.33; 0.67 × $600,000)	$200,000	$400,000	$600,000

PANEL B: Product-Line Income Statement for June 2006	Ricito	Pancito	Total
Revenues (25,000 tons × $10 per ton; 50,000 × $15 per ton)	$250,000	$750,000	$1,000,000
Joint costs allocated (from Panel A)	200,000	400,000	600,000
Gross margin	$50,000	$350,000	$ 400,000
Gross margin percentage	20%	47%	40%

1c.

PANEL A: Allocation of Joint Costs using Net Realizable Value	Rilaf	Pilaf	Total
Final sales value of total production during accounting period (30,000 tons × $18 per ton; 60,000 tons × $25 per ton)	$540,000	$1,500,000	$2,040,000
Deduct separable costs	120,000	420,000	540,000
Net realizable value at splitoff point	$420,000	$1,080,000	$1,500,000
Weighting ($420,000; $1,080,000 ÷ $1,500,000)	28%	72%	
Joint costs allocated (0.28; 0.72 × $600,000)	$168,000	$432,000	$600,000

PANEL B: Product-Line Income Statement for June 2006	Rilaf	Pilaf	Total
Revenues (30,000 tons × $18 per ton; 60,000 tons × $25 per ton)	$540,000	$1,500,000	$2,040,000
Joint costs allocated (from Panel A)	168,000	432,000	600,000
Separable costs	120,000	420,000	540,000
Gross margin	$252,000	$ 648,000	$ 900,000
Gross margin percentage	46.7%	43.2%	44.1%

2.　　Shel Brown probably performed the analysis shown below to arrive at the net loss of $5,571 from marketing the sludge:

PANEL A: Allocation of Joint Costs using

Sales Value at Splitoff	Ricito	Pancito	Sludge	Total
Sales value of total production at splitoff point (25,000 tons × $10 per ton; 50,000 × $15 per ton; 10,000 × $5 per ton)	$250,000	$750,000	$50,000	$1,050,000
Weighting ($250,000; $750,000; $50,000 ÷ $1,050,000)	23.8095%	71.4286%	4.7619%	100%
Joint costs allocated (0.238095; 0.714286; 0.047619 × $600,000)	$142,857	$428,571	$28,571	$600,000

PANEL B: Product-Line Income Statement

for June 2006	Ricito	Pancito	Sludge	Total
Revenues (25,000 tons ×$10 per ton; 50,000 × $15 per ton; 10,000 ×$5 per ton)	$250,000	$750,000	$50,000	$1,050,000
Joint costs allocated (from Panel A)	142,857	428,572	28,571	600,000
Gross margin	$107,143	$321,428	$21,429	$ 450,000
Deduct marketing costs			27,000	27,000
Operating income			($5,571)	$ 423,000

In this (misleading) analysis, the $600,000 of joint costs are re-allocated between Ricito, Pancito and the sludge. Irrespective of the method of allocation, this analysis is wrong. Joint costs are always irrelevant in a process-further decision. Only incremental costs and revenues past the splitoff point are relevant. In this case, the correct analysis is much simpler: the incremental revenues from selling the sludge are $50,000, and the incremental costs are the marketing costs of $27,000. So, Armstrong Foods should sell the sludge—this will increase its operating income by $23,000 ($50,000 – $27,000).

16-24 (30 min.) **Accounting for a main product and a byproduct.**

	Production Method	Sales Method
1. Revenues		
Main product	$160,000[a]	$160,000
Byproduct	—	2,800[d]
Total revenues	160,000	162,800
Cost of goods sold		
Total manufacturing costs	120,000	120,000
Deduct byproduct revenue	4,000[b]	0
Net manufacturing costs	116,000	120,000
Deduct main product inventory	23,200[c]	24,000[e]
Cost of goods sold	92,800	96,000
Gross margin	$ 67,200	$ 66,800

[a] $8,000 \times \$20.00$
[b] $2,000 \times \$2.00$
[c] $\left(\dfrac{2,000}{10,000} \times \$116,000\right) = \$23,200$

[d] $1,400 \times \$2.00$
[e] $\left(\dfrac{2,000}{10,000} \times \$120,000\right) = \$24,000$

	Production Method	Sales Method
2. Rainbow Dew	$23,200	$24,000
Resi-Dew	1,200[a]	0

[a] Ending inventory shown at unrealized selling price.
BI + Production – Sales = EI
0 + 2,000 – 1,400 = 600 gallons
Ending inventory = 600 gallons × $2 per gallon = $1,200

16-26 (40 min.) Alternative methods of joint-cost allocation, product-mix decision.

1.   Joint costs = $300,000

a.   **Sales value at splitoff method**

		Select	White	Knotty	Total
1.	Sales value of total prodn. at splitoff (30,000 × $8, 50,000 × $4, 20,000 × $3)	$240,000	$200,000	$60,000	$500,000
2.	Weighting (240/500, 200/500, 60/500)	0.48	0.40	0.12	
3.	Joint costs allocated (0.48, 0.40, 0.12 × $300,000)	$144,000	$120,000	$36,000	$300,000
4.	Total cost computation				
	Joint costs	$144,000	$120,000	$36,000	$300,000
	Separable processing costs	60,000	90,000	15,000	165,000
	Total costs	$204,000	$210,000	$51,000	$465,000
	Total board feet	25,000	40,000	15,000	
	Total cost per board foot	$8.16	$5.25	$3.40	

b.   **Physical-measures method**

		Select	White	Knotty	Total
1.	Physical measure of total production (board feet)	30,000	50,000	20,000	100,000
2.	Weighting (30/100, 50/100, 20/100)	0.30	0.50	0.20	
3.	Joint costs allocated (0.30, 0.50, 0.20 × $300,000)	$90,000	$150,000	$60,000	$300,000
4.	Total cost computation				
	Joint costs	$90,000	$150,000	$60,000	$300,000
	Separable processing	60,000	90,000	15,000	165,000
	Total costs	$150,000	$240,000	$75,000	$465,000
	Total board feet	25,000	40,000	15,000	
	Total cost per board foot	$6.00	$6.00	$5.00	

16-10

c. **Net realizable value method**

		Select	White	Knotty	Total
1.	Final sales value of total production (25,000 × $16, 40,000 × $9, 15,000 × $7)	$400,000	$360,000	$105,000	$865,000
2.	Deduct separable costs	60,000	90,000	15,000	165,000
3.	NRV at splitoff	$340,000	$270,000	$90,000	$700,000
4.	Weighting (340 ÷ 700, 270 ÷ 700, 90 ÷ 700)	0.4857	0.3857	0.1286	
5.	Joint costs allocated (0.4857, 0.3857, 0.1286 × $300,000)	$145,710	$115,710	$38,580	$300,000
	Total cost computation				
	Joint costs	$145,710	$115,710	$38,580	$300,000
	Separable processing	60,000	90,000	15,000	165,000
	Total costs	$205,710	$205,710	$53,580	$465,000
	Total units	25,000	40,000	15,000	
	Unit cost	$8.23	$5.14	$3.57	

2. **Ending Inventory Values**

		Select	White	Knotty	Total
a.	Sales value at splitoff method ($8.16 × 1,000, $5.25 × 2,000, $3.40 × 500)	$8,160	$10,500	$1,700	$20,360
b.	Physical measures method ($6.00 × 1,000, $6.00 × 2,000, $5.00 × 500)	6,000	12,000	2,500	20,500
c.	NRV method ($8.23 × 1,000, $5.14 × 2,000, $3.57 × 500)	8,230	10,280	1,785	20,295

3. **Raw to Select Oak**

Incremental revenues: $400,000 – $240,000	$160,000
Deduct incremental processing costs	60,000
Increase in operating income	$100,000

Raw to White Oak

Incremental revenues: $360,000 – $200,000	$160,000
Deduct incremental processing costs	90,000
Increase in operating income	$ 70,000

Raw to Knotty Oak

Incremental revenues: $105,000 – $60,000	$ 45,000
Deduct incremental processing costs	15,000
Increase in operating income	$ 30,000

Since the processing of each raw-oak product into finished-product form increases operating income, Pacific Lumber is indeed maximizing operating income by processing all products fully.

16-28 (40–60 min.) **Comparison of alternative joint-cost allocation methods, further-processing decision, chocolate products.**

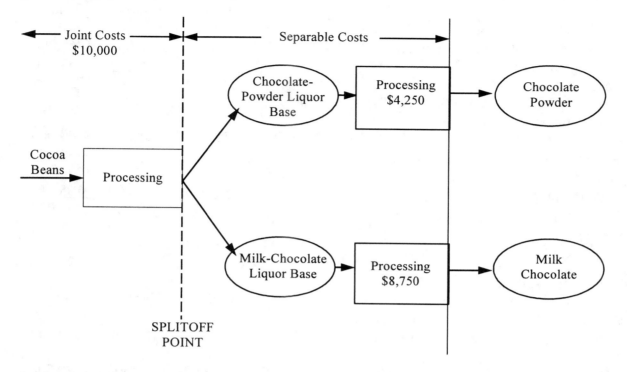

1a.   Sales value at splitoff method:

	Chocolate-Powder Liquor Base	Milk-Chocolate Liquor Base	Total
Sales value of total production at splitoff, 200 × $21; 300[b] × $26	$4,200	$7,800	$12,000
Weighting, $4,200; $7,800 ÷ $12,000	0.35	0.65	
Joint costs allocated, 0.35; 0.65 × $10,000	$3,500	$6,500	$10,000

1b.

Physical-measure method:

Physical measure of total production (5,000 ÷ 500) × 20; 30	200 gallons	300 gallons	500 gallons
Weighting, 200; 300 ÷ 500	0.40	0.60	
Joint costs allocated, 0.40; 0.60 × $10,000	$4,000	$6,000	$10,000

1c.   Net realizable value method:

	Chocolate-Powder Liquor Base	Milk-Chocolate Liquor Base	Total
Final sales value of total production, 2,000 × $4; 3,400 × $5	$8,000	$17,000	$25,000
Deduct separable costs	4,250	8,750	13,000
Net realizable value at splitoff point	$3,750	$ 8,250	$12,000
Weighting, $3,750; $8,250 ÷ $12,000	0.3125	0.6875	
Joint costs allocated, 0.3125; 0.6875 × $10,000	$3,125	$6,875	$10,000

d.   Constant gross-margin percentage NRV method:

Step 1:

Final sales value of total production, (2,000 × $4) + (3,400 × $5)	$25,000
Deduct joint and separable costs, ($10,000 + $4,250 + $8,750)	23,000
Gross margin	$ 2,000
Gross-margin percentage ($2,000 ÷ $25,000)	8%

Step 2:

	Chocolate-Powder Liquor Base	Milk-Chocolate Liquor Base	Total
Final sales value of total production (2,000 × $4); (3,400 × $5)	$8,000	$17,000	$25,000
Deduct gross margin, using overall gross-margin percentage of sales (8%)	640	1,360	2,000
Total production costs	7,360	15,640	23,000

Step 3:

	Chocolate-Powder Liquor Base	Milk-Chocolate Liquor Base	Total
Deduct separable costs	4,250	8,750	13,000
Joint costs allocated	$3,110	$ 6,890	$10,000

2.		Chocolate-Powder Liquor Base	Milk-Chocolate Liquor Base	Total
a.	Revenues	$8,000	$17,000	$25,000
	Joint costs	3,500	6,500	10,000
	Separable costs	4,250	8,750	13,000
	Total cost of goods sold	7,750	15,250	23,000
	Gross margin	$ 250	$ 1,750	$ 2,000
	Gross-margin percentage	3.125%	10.294%	8%
b.	Revenues	$8,000	$17,000	$25,000
	Joint costs	4,000	6,000	10,000
	Separable costs	4,250	8,750	13,000
	Total cost of goods sold	8,250	14,750	23,000
	Gross margin	$ (250)	$ 2,250	$ 2,000
	Gross-margin percentage	(3.125)%	13.235%	8%
c.	Revenues	$8,000	$17,000	$25,000
	Joint costs	3,125	6,875	10,000
	Separable costs	4,250	8,750	13,000
	Total cost of goods sold	7,375	15,625	23,000
	Gross margin	$ 625	$ 1,375	$ 2,000
	Gross-margin percentage	7.812%	8.088%	8%
d.	Revenues	$8,000	$17,000	$25,000
	Joint costs	3,110	6,890	10,000
	Separable costs	4,250	8,750	13,000
	Total cost of goods sold	7,360	15,640	23,000
	Gross margin	$ 640	$ 1,360	$ 2,000
	Gross-margin percentage	8%	8%	8%

3.   Further processing of chocolate-powder liquor base into chocolate powder:

Incremental revenue, $8,000 – $4,200	$ 3,800
Incremental costs	4,250
Incremental operating income from further processing	$ (450)

Further processing of milk-chocolate liquor base into milk chocolate:

Incremental revenue, $17,000 – $7,800	$ 9,200
Incremental costs	8,750
Incremental operating income from further processing	$ 450

Roundtree Chocolates could increase operating income by $450 (to $2,450) if chocolate-powder liquor base is sold at the split off point and if milk-chocolate liquor base is further processed into milk chocolate.

16-30 (25 min.) **Joint-cost allocation, relevant costs.**

1. The "four-day progressive product trimming" ignores the fundamental point that the $300 cost to buy the pig is a joint cost. A pig is purchased as a whole. The butcher's challenge is to maximize the total revenues minus incremental costs (assumed zero) from the sale of all products.

At each stage, the decision made ignores the general rule that product emphasis decisions should consider relevant revenues and relevant costs. Allocated joint costs are not relevant. For example, the Day 1 decision to drop bacon ignores the fact that the $300 joint cost has been paid to acquire the whole pig. The $414 of revenues are relevant inflows. This same position also holds for the Day 2 to Day 4 decisions.

2. The revenue amounts are the figures to use in the sales value at splitoff method:

Product	Sales Value of Total Prodn.	Weighting	Joint Costs Allocated
Pork chops	$120	0.2899	$ 86.97
Ham	150	0.3623	108.69
Bacon	144	0.3478	104.34
	$414	1.0000	$300.00

3. No. The decision to sell or not sell individual products should consider relevant revenues and relevant costs. In the butcher's context, the relevant costs would be the additional time and other incidentals to take each pig part and make it a salable product. The relevant revenues would be the difference between the selling price at the consumer level for the pig parts and what the butcher may receive for the whole pig.

16-32 (30 min.) **NRV method, byproducts.**

1.a. For the month of November 2006, Purity Corporation's output was:
- apple slices   89,100 lbs.
- applesauce   81,000 lbs.
- apple juice   67,500 lbs.
- animal feed   27,000 lbs.

These amounts were calculated as follows:

Product	Input	Proportion	Total Pounds	Pounds Lost	Net Pounds
Slices	270,000 lbs.	0.33	89,100	–	89,100
Sauce	270,000	0.30	81,000	–	81,000
Juice	270,000	0.27	72,900	5,400	67,500[a]
Feed	270,000	0.10	27,000	–	27,000
		1.00	270,000	5,400	264,600

[a]Net pounds: =   72,900 – (0.08 × net pounds)
1.08 × net pounds   =   72,900
Net pounds   =   72,900 ÷ 1.08 = 67,500

b. The net realizable value for each of the three main products is calculated below:

Product	Net Pounds	Price per Pound	Sales Value of Total Production	Separable Costs	Net Realizable Value at Splitoff
Slices	89,100	$1.60	$ 142,560	$22,560	$ 120,000
Sauce	81,000	1.10	89,100	17,100	72,000
Juice	67,500	0.80	54,000	6,000	48,000
			$285,660	$45,660	$240,000

c. and d.

The net realizable value of the byproduct is deducted from the production costs prior to allocation to the joint products, as presented below:

Allocation of Preparation Department Costs to Joint Products and Byproducts

Net realizable value
(NRV) of byproduct

$$
\begin{aligned}
&= \text{Byproduct revenue} - \text{Separable costs} \\
&= \$0.20 \, (27,000 \text{ lbs}) - \$1,400 \\
&= \$5,400 - \$1,400 \\
&= \$4,000
\end{aligned}
$$

Costs to be allocated

$$
\begin{aligned}
&= \text{Joint costs} - \text{NRV of byproduct} \\
&= \$120,000 - \$4,000 \\
&= \$116,000
\end{aligned}
$$

Product	Sales Value of Total Production	Separable Costs	Joint Costs Allocated[a]	Gross Margin
Slices	$ 142,560	$22,560	$58,000	$62,000
Sauce	89,100	17,100	34,800	37,200
Juice	54,000	6,000	23,200	24,800
	$285,660	$45,660	$116,000	$124,000

[a]Allocated using NRV of the three joint products from requirement 1b:

Slices	($120,000 ÷ $240,000) × $116,000 =	$58,000
Sauce	($72,000 ÷ $240,000) × $116,000 =	34,800
Juice	($48,000 ÷ $240,000) × $116,000 =	23,200

2.   The gross-margin dollar information by main product is determined by the arbitrary allocation of joint production costs. As a result, these cost figures and the resulting gross-margin information are of little significance for planning and control purposes. The allocation is made only for purposes of inventory costing and income determination.

16-34 (20 min.) **Byproduct, disposal costs, ethics.**

1.   The comparative analysis prepared by the management accountant is flawed. In the process further alternative, he or she has erroneously included the $250,000 allocated joint costs. Allocated joint costs are irrelevant because they are not incremental costs of the alternative being considered. If the joint costs allocated are taken out, it becomes clear that financially it would be to the advantage of the company to further process the TXT45 as it would actually *increase* the operating income by $150,000 [$600,000 − ($400,000 + $50,000)]. Furthermore, the dumping alternative does not consider potential future costs that may arise from environmental liabilities.

2.   It appears that there would be no legal ramifications if the company decided to dump TXT45 into the ocean. The country either may have no laws against such dumping, or even if they exist, they are not enforced in accordance with the government policy. A more important consideration, however, is the ethical implications. To knowingly dump a hazardous material into the ocean would certainly result in water pollution. This is an unacceptable action from a societal standpoint. *It is important to remember that an act that does not violate any laws is not necessarily an ethical act.* Ethical considerations go beyond legal considerations. In different parts of the world, legal systems are imperfect and not comprehensive. It is the responsibility of top management to take a broader, societal view when making decisions. In other words, a business should take its social responsibility seriously, by making it an integral part of the decision-making process. In the long run it is in the best interest of all stakeholders as well as the business itself.

CHAPTER 17
PROCESS COSTING

17-2   Process costing systems separate costs into cost categories according to the timing of when costs are introduced into the process. Often, only two cost classifications, direct materials and conversion costs, are necessary. Direct materials are frequently added at one point in time, often the start or the end of the process, and all conversion costs are added at about the same time, but in a pattern different from direct materials costs.

17-4   The accuracy of the estimates of completion depends on the care and skill of the estimator and the nature of the process. Semiconductor chips may differ substantially in the finishing necessary to obtain a final product. The amount of work necessary to finish a product may not always be easy to ascertain in advance.

17-6   Three inventory methods associated with process costing are:
- Weighted average.
- First-in, first-out.
- Standard costing.

17-8   FIFO computations are distinctive because they assign the cost of the previous accounting period's equivalent units in beginning work-in-process inventory to the first units completed and transferred out of the process and assigns the cost of equivalent units worked on during the current period first to complete beginning inventory, next to start and complete new units, and finally to units in ending work-in-process inventory. In contrast, the weighted-average method costs units completed and transferred out and in ending work in process at the same average cost.

17-10   A major advantage of FIFO is that managers can judge the performance in the current period independently from the performance in the preceding period.

17-12   Standard-cost procedures are particularly appropriate to process-costing systems where there are various combinations of materials and operations used to make a wide variety of similar products as in the textiles, paints, and ceramics industries. Standard-cost procedures also avoid the intricacies involved in detailed tracking with weighted-average or FIFO methods when there are frequent price variations over time.

17-14   No. Transferred-in costs or previous department costs are costs incurred in a previous department that have been charged to a subsequent department. These costs may be costs incurred in that previous department during this accounting period or a preceding accounting period.

17-16 (25 min.) **Equivalent units, zero beginning inventory.**

1. Direct materials cost per unit ($720,000 ÷ 10,000) $ 72
    Conversion cost per unit ($760,000 ÷ 10,000)   76
    Assembly Department cost per unit $148

2a. Solution Exhibit 17-16A calculates the equivalent units of direct materials and conversion costs in the Assembly Department of International Electronics in February 2007.
    Solution Exhibit 17-16B computes equivalent unit costs.

2b. Direct materials cost per unit $ 72
    Conversion cost per unit   80
    Assembly Department cost per unit $152

3. The difference in the Assembly Department cost per unit calculated in requirements 1 and 2 arises because the costs incurred in January and February are the same but fewer equivalent units of work are done in February relative to January. In January, all 10,000 units introduced are fully completed resulting in 10,000 equivalent units of work done with respect to direct materials and conversion costs. In February, of the 10,000 units introduced, 10,000 equivalent units of work is done with respect to direct materials but only 9,500 equivalent units of work is done with respect to conversion costs. The Assembly Department cost per unit is, therefore, higher.

SOLUTION EXHIBIT 17-16A

Steps 1 and 2: Summarize Output in Physical Units and Compute Output in Equivalent Units; Assembly Department of International Electronics for February 2007.

| | (Step 1) | (Step 2) Equivalent Units | |
Flow of Production	Physical Units	Direct Materials	Conversion Costs
Work in process, beginning (given)	0		
Started during current period (given)	10,000		
To account for	10,000		
Completed and transferred out during current period	9,000	9,000	9,000
Work in process, ending* (given)	1,000		
1,000 × 100%; 1,000 × 50%		1,000	500
Accounted for	10,000		
Work done in current period only		10,000	9,500

*Degree of completion in this department: direct materials, 100%; conversion costs, 50%.

SOLUTION EXHIBIT 17-16B
Compute Equivalent Unit Costs,
Assembly Department of International Electronics for February 2007.

	Total Production Costs	Direct Materials	Conversion Costs
(Step 3) Costs added during February	$1,480,000	$720,000	$760,000
Divide by equivalent units of work done in current period (Solution Exhibit 17-l6A)		÷ 10,000	÷ 9,500
Cost per equivalent unit		$ 72	$ 80

17-18 (25 min.) **Zero beginning inventory, materials introduced in middle of process.**

1. Solution Exhibit 17-18A shows equivalent units of work done in the current period of Chemical P, 50,000; Chemical Q, 35,000; Conversion costs, 45,000.

2. Solution Exhibit 17-18B calculates cost per equivalent unit of work done in the current period for Chemical P, Chemical Q, and Conversion costs, summarizes the total Mixing Department costs for July 2007, and assigns these costs to units completed (and transferred out) and to units in ending work in process.

SOLUTION EXHIBIT 17-18A

Steps 1 and 2: Summarize Output in Physical Units and Compute Output in Equivalent Units; Mixing Department of Vaasa Chemicals for July 2007.

| | (Step 1) | (Step 2) Equivalent Units | | |
| | | | | |
Flow of Production	**Physical Units**	**Chemical P**	**Chemical Q**	**Conversion Costs**
Work in process, beginning (given)	0			
Started during current period (given)	50,000			
To account for	50,000			
Completed and transferred out during current period	35,000	35,000	35,000	35,000
Work in process, ending* (given)	15,000			
15,000 × 100%; 15,000 × 0%;				
15,000 × 66 2/3%		15,000	0	10,000
Accounted for	50,000			
Work done in current period only		50,000	35,000	45,000

*Degree of completion in this department: Chemical P, 100%; Chemical Q, 0%; conversion costs, 66 2/3%.

SOLUTION EXHIBIT 17-18B

Steps 3, 4, and 5: Compute Cost per Equivalent Unit, Summarize Total Costs to Account For, and Assign Total Costs to Units Completed and to Units in Ending Work in Process; Mixing Department of Vaasa Chemicals for July 2007.

	Total Production Costs	Chemical P	Chemical Q	Conversion Costs
(Step 3) Costs added during July	$455,000	$250,000	$70,000	$135,000
Divide by equivalent units of work done in current period (Solution Exhibit 17-18A)		÷ 50,000	÷35,000	÷ 45,000
Cost per equivalent unit		$ 5	$ 2	$ 3
(Step 4) Total costs to account for	$455,000			
(Step 5) Assignment of costs:				
Completed and transferred out (35,000 units)	$350,000	(35,000* × $5) +	(35,000* × $2) +	(35,000* × $3)
Work in process, ending (15,000 units)	105,000	(15,000† × $5) +	(0† × $2)	+ (10,000† × $3)
Total costs accounted for	$455,000			

*Equivalent units completed and transferred out from Solution Exhibit 17-18A, Step 2.
†Equivalent units in work in process, ending from Solution Exhibit 17-18A, Step 2.

17-20 (20 min.) **Weighted-average method, assigning costs (continuation of 17-19).**

Solution Exhibit 17-20 calculates cost per equivalent unit of work done to date in the Satellite Assembly Division of Aerospatiale, summarizes total costs to account for, and assigns costs to units completed and to units in ending work-in-process inventory.

SOLUTION EXHIBIT 17-20

Steps 3, 4, and 5: Compute Cost per Equivalent Unit, Summarize Total Costs to Account For, and Assign Total Costs to Units Completed and to Units in Ending Work in Process; Weighted-Average Method of Process Costing, Satellite Assembly Division of Aerospatiale for May 2007.

		Total Production Costs	Direct Materials	Conversion Costs
(Step 3)	Work in process, beginning (given)	$ 5,844,000	$ 4,933,600	$ 910,400
	Costs added in current period (given)	46,120,000	32,200,000	13,920,000
	Costs incurred to date		$37,133,600	$14,830,400
	Divide by equivalent units of work done to date (Solution Exhibit 17-19)		÷ 53.2	÷ 49.6
	Cost per equivalent unit of work done to date		$ 698,000	$ 299,000
(Step 4)	Total costs to account for	$51,964,000		
(Step 5)	Assignment of costs:			
	Completed and transferred out (46 units)	45,862,000	(46*× $698,000) + (46* × $299,000)	
	Work in process, ending (12 units)	6,102,000	(7.2†× $698,000) + (3.6† × $299,000)	
	Total costs accounted for	$51,964,000		

*Equivalent units completed and transferred out from Solution Exhibit 17-19, Step 2.
†Equivalent units in work in process, ending from Solution Exhibit 17-19, Step 2.

17-22 (20 min.) **FIFO method, assigning costs** (continuation of 17-21).

Solution Exhibit 17-22 calculates cost per equivalent unit of work done in May 2007 in the Satellite Assembly Division of Aerospatiale, summarizes total costs to account for, and assigns costs to units completed and to units in ending work-in-process inventory.

SOLUTION EXHIBIT 17-22

Steps 3, 4, and 5: Compute Cost per Equivalent Unit, Summarize Total Costs to Account For, and Assign Total Costs to Units Completed and to Units in Ending Work in Process; FIFO Method of Process Costing, Satellite Assembly Division of Aerospatiale for May 2007.

	Total Production Costs	Direct Materials	Conversion Costs
Work in process, beginning ($4,933,600 + $910,400)	$ 5,844,000	(costs of work done before current period)	
(Step 3) Costs added in current period (given)	46,120,000	$32,200,000	$ 13,920,000
Divide by equivalent units of work done in current period (Solution Exhibit 17-21)		÷ 46	÷ 46.4
Cost per equiv. unit of work done in current period		$ 700,000	$ 300,000
(Step 4) Total costs to account for	$51,964,000		
(Step 5) Assignment of costs:			
Completed and transferred out (46 units):			
Work in process, beginning (8 units)	$ 5,844,000		
Costs added to beginning work in process in current period	2,000,000	$(0.8^* \times \$700,000) + (4.8^* \times \$300,000)$	
Total from beginning inventory	7,844,000		
Started and completed (38 units)	38,000,000	$(38^\dagger \times \$700,000) + (38^\dagger \times \$300,000)$	
Total costs of units completed and transferred out	45,844,000		
Work in process, ending (12 units)	6,120,000	$(7.2^\# \times \$700,000) + (3.6^\# \times \$300,000)$	
Total costs accounted for	$51,964,000		

*Equivalent units used to complete beginning work in process from Solution Exhibit 17-21, Step 2.
†Equivalent units started and completed from Solution Exhibit 17-21, Step 2.
$^\#$Equivalent units in work in process, ending from Solution Exhibit 17-21, Step 2.

17-24 (25 min.) Weighted-average method, assigning costs.

1. & 2. Solution Exhibit 17-24 calculates the cost per equivalent unit of work done to date for direct materials and conversion costs, summarizes total costs to account for, and assigns these costs to units completed and transferred out and to units in ending work-in-process inventory.

SOLUTION EXHIBIT 17-24

Steps 3, 4, and 5: Compute Cost per Equivalent Unit, Summarize Total Costs to Account For, and Assign Total Costs to Units Completed and to Units in Ending Work in Process; Weighted-Average Method of Process Costing, Chatham Company for July 2007.

		Total Production Costs	Direct Materials	Conversion Costs
(Step 3)	Work in process, beginning (given)	$130,000	$ 60,000	$ 70,000
	Costs added in current period (given)	651,000	280,000	371,000
	Costs incurred to date		$340,000	$441,000
	Divide by equivalent units of work done to date (given)		÷ 50,000	÷ 42,000
	Cost per equivalent unit of work done to date		$ 6.80	$ 10.50
(Step 4)	Total costs to account for	$781,000		
(Step 5)	Assignment of costs:			
	Completed and transferred out (34,000 units)	$588,200	(34,000* × $6.80) + (34,000* × $10.50)	
	Work in process, ending (16,000 units)	192,800	(16,000† × $6.80) + (8,000† × $10.50)	
	Total costs accounted for	$781,000		

*Equivalent units completed and transferred out (given).
†Equivalent units in work in process, ending (given).

17-26 (30 min.) Standard-costing method, assigning costs.

1.　The calculations of equivalent units for direct materials and conversion costs are identical to the calculations of equivalent units under the FIFO method. Solution Exhibit 17-25A shows the equivalent unit calculations for standard costing given by the equivalent units of work done in July 2007. Solution Exhibit 17-26 uses the standard costs (direct materials, $6.60; conversion costs, $10.40) to summarize total costs to account for, and to assign these costs to units completed and transferred out and to units in ending work-in-process inventory.

2.　Solution Exhibit 17-26 shows the direct materials and conversion costs variances for

Direct materials	$16,000 U
Conversion costs	$7,000 U

SOLUTION EXHIBIT 17-26
Steps 3, 4, and 5: Compute Cost per Equivalent Unit, Summarize Total Costs to Account For, and Assign Total Costs to Units Completed and to Units in Ending Work in Process; Use of Standard Costs in Process Costing, Chatham Company for July 2007.

	Total Production Costs	Direct Materials $ 6.60	Conversion Costs $ 10.40
(Step 3) Standard cost per equivalent unit (given)			
Work in process, beginning (given)	$138,800	$(10,000 \times \$6.60) + (7,000 \times \$10.40)$	
Costs added in current period at standard costs	628,000	$(40,000 \times \$6.60) + (35,000 \times \$10.40)$	
(Step 4) Total costs to account for	$766,800		
(Step 5) Assignment of costs at standard costs:			
Completed and transferred out (34,000 units):			
Work in process, beginning (10,000 units)	$138,800		
Costs added to beg. work in process in current period	31,200	$(0^* \times \$6.60)$ + $(3,000^* \times \$10.40)$	
Total from beginning inventory	170,000		
Started and completed (24,000 units)	408,000	$(24,000^\dagger \times \$6.60)$ + $(24,000^\dagger \times \$10.40)$	
Total costs of units transferred out	578,000		
Work in process, ending (16,000 units)	188,800	$(16,000^\# \times \$6.60)$ + $(8,000^\# \times \$10.40)$	
Total costs accounted for	$766,800		
Summary of variances for current performance:			
Costs added in current period at standard costs (see Step 3 above)		$264,000	$364,000
Actual costs incurred (given)		280,000	371,000
Variance		$ 16,000 U	$ 7,000 U

*Equivalent units to complete beginning work in process from Solution Exhibit 17-25A, Step 2.
†Equivalent units started and completed from Solution Exhibit 17-25A, Step 2.
#Equivalent units in work in process, ending from Solution Exhibit 17-25A, Step 2.

17-28 (35–40 min.) **Transferred-in costs, FIFO method.**

Solution Exhibit 17-28A calculates the equivalent units of work done in the current period (for transferred-in costs, direct-materials, and conversion costs) to complete beginning work-in-process inventory, to start and complete new units, and to produce ending work in process. Solution Exhibit 17-28B calculates the cost per equivalent unit of work done in the current period for transferred-in costs, direct materials, and conversion costs, summarizes total costs to account for, and assigns these costs to units completed and transferred out and to units in ending work-in-process inventory.

SOLUTION EXHIBIT 17-28A
Steps 1 and 2: Summarize Output in Physical Units and Compute Output in Equivalent Units FIFO Method of Process Costing;
Finishing Department of Aragon Industrials for June 2007.

	(Step 1)	(Step 2)		
		Equivalent Units		
Flow of Production	Physical Units	Transferred-in Costs	Direct Materials	Conversion Costs
Work in process, beginning (given)	50	(work done before current period)		
Transferred-in during current period (given)	90			
To account for	140			
Completed and transferred out during current period:				
From beginning work in process[a]	50			
[50 × (100% – 100%); 50 × (100% – 0%); 50 × (100% – 60%)]		0	50	20
Started and completed	50[b]			
(50 × 100%; 50 × 100%; 50 × 100%)		50	50	50
Work in process, ending[c] (given)	40			
(40 × 100%; 40 × 0%; 40 × 75%)		40	0	30
Accounted for	140			
Work done in current period only		90	100	100

[a]Degree of completion in this department: Transferred-in costs, 100%; direct materials, 0%; conversion costs, 60%.

[b]100 physical units completed and transferred out minus 50 physical units completed and transferred out from beginning work-in-process inventory.

[c]Degree of completion in this department: transferred-in costs, 100%; direct materials, 0%; conversion costs, 75%.

SOLUTION EXHIBIT 17-28B

Steps 3, 4, and 5: Compute Cost per Equivalent Unit, Summarize Total Costs to Account For, and Assign Total Costs to Units Completed and to Units in Ending Work in Process;

FIFO Method of Process Costing,

Finishing Department of Aragon Industrials for June 2007.

	Total Production Costs	Transferred-in Costs	Direct Materials	Conversion Costs
		(costs of work done before current period)		
Work in process, beginning (given) ($40,000 + $0 + $20,000)	$ 60,000	$87,200	$25,000	$52,000
(Step 3) Costs added in current period (given)	164,200			
Divide by equivalent units of work done in current period (Sol. Exhibit 17-28A)		$\div$ 90	$\div$ 100	$\div$ 100
Cost per equivalent unit of work done in current period		$968.89	$ 250	$ 520
(Step 4) Total costs to account for	$224,200			
(Step 5) Assignment of costs:				
Completed and transferred out (100 units)				
Work in process, beginning (50 units)	$ 60,000			
Costs added to beginning work in process in current period	22,900	$(0^a \times \$968.89)$	$+ (50^a \times \$250)$	$+ (20^a \times \$520)$
Total from beginning inventory	82,900			
Started and completed (50 units)	86,944	$(50^b \times \$968.89)$	$+ (50^b \times \$250)$	$+ (50^b \times \$520)$
Total costs of units completed and transferred out	169,844			
Work in process, ending (40 units):	54,356	$(40^c \times \$968.89)$	$+ (0^c \times \$250)$	$+ (30^c \times \$520)$
Total costs accounted for	$224,200			

[a]Equivalent units used to complete beginning work in process from Solution Exhibit 17-28A, step 2.
[b]Equivalent units started and completed from Solution Exhibit 17-28A, step 2.
[c]Equivalent units in ending work in process from Solution Exhibit 17-28A, step 2.

17-11

17-30 (25 min.) **Weighted-average method.**

1.   Since direct materials are added at the beginning of the assembly process, the units in this department must be 100% complete with respect to direct materials. Solution Exhibit 17-30A shows equivalent units of work done to date:

Direct materials   100 equivalent units
Conversion costs   97 equivalent units

2. & 3. Solution Exhibit 17-30B calculates cost per equivalent unit of work done to date, summarizes the total Assembly Department costs for October 2007, and assigns these costs to units completed (and transferred out) and to units in ending work in process using the weighted-average method.

SOLUTION EXHIBIT 17-30A

Steps 1 and 2: Summarize Output in Physical Units and Compute Output in Equivalent Units; Weighted-Average Method of Process Costing, Assembly Department of Global Defense, Inc., for October 2007.

Flow of Production	(Step 1) Physical Units	(Step 2) Equivalent Units	
		Direct Materials	Conversion Costs
Work in process, beginning (given)	20		
Started during current period (given)	80		
To account for	100		
Completed and transferred out during current period	90	90	90
Work in process, ending* (given)	10		
10 × 100%; 10 × 70%		10	7
Accounted for	100		
Work done to date		100	97

*Degree of completion in this department: direct materials, 100%; conversion costs, 70%.

SOLUTION EXHIBIT 17-30B

Steps 3, 4, and 5: Compute Cost per Equivalent Unit, Summarize Total Costs to Account For, and Assign Total Costs to Units Completed and to Units in Ending Work in Process; Weighted-Average Method of Process Costing, Assembly Department of Global Defense, Inc., for October 2007.

		Total Production Costs	Direct Materials	Conversion Costs
(Step 3)	Work in process, beginning (given)	$ 580,000	$ 460,000	$ 120,000
	Costs added in current period (given)	2,935,000	2,000,000	935,000
	Costs incurred to date		$2,460,000	$1,055,000
	Divide by equivalent units of work done to date (Solution Exhibit 17-30A)		$\div$ 100	$\div$ 97
	Cost per equivalent unit of work done to date		$ 24,600	$10,876.29
(Step 4)	Total costs to account for	$3,515,000		
(Step 5)	Assignment of costs:			
	Completed and transferred out (90 units)	$3,192,866	$(90^* \times \$24,600) + (90^* \times \$10,876.29)$	
	Work in process, ending (10 units)	322,134	$(10^\dagger \times \$24,600) + (7^\dagger \times \$10,876.29)$	
	Total costs accounted for	$3,515,000		

[*]Equivalent units completed and transferred out from Solution Exhibit 17-30A, Step 2.
[†]Equivalent units in work in process, ending from Solution Exhibit 17-30A, Step 2.

17-32 (20 min.) **FIFO method (continuation of 17-30).**

1.   The equivalent units of work done in the current period in the Assembly Department in October 2007 for direct materials and conversion costs are shown in Solution Exhibit 17-32A.

2.   The cost per equivalent unit of work done in the current period in the Assembly Department in October 2007 for direct materials and conversion costs is calculated in Solution Exhibit 17-32B.

3.   Solution Exhibit 17-32B summarizes the total Assembly Department costs for October 2007, and assigns these costs to units completed (and transferred out) and units in ending work in process under the FIFO method.

   The cost per equivalent unit of beginning inventory and of work done in the current period differ:

	Beginning Inventory	Work Done in Current Period
Direct materials	$23,000 ($460,000 ÷ 20 equiv. units)	$25,000
Conversion costs	$10,000 ($120,000 ÷ 12 equiv. units)	$11,000

	Direct Materials	Conversion Costs
Cost per equivalent unit (weighted-average)	$24,600*	$10,876.29*
Cost per equivalent unit (FIFO)	$25,000**	$11,000**

*from Solution Exhibit 17-30B
**from Solution Exhibit 17-32B

The cost per equivalent unit differs between the two methods because each method uses different costs to calculate the numerator of the calculation. FIFO uses only the costs added during the period whereas weighted-average uses the costs from the beginning work-in-process as well as costs added during the period. Both methods also use different equivalent units in the denominator.

   The following table summarizes the costs assigned to units completed and those still in process under the weighted-average and FIFO process-costing methods for our example.

	Weighted Average (Solution Exhibit 17-30B)	FIFO (Solution Exhibit 17-32B)	Difference
Cost of units completed and transferred out	$3,192,866	$3,188,000	−$4,866
Work in process, ending	322,134	327,000	+$4,866
Total costs accounted for	$3,515,000	$3,515,000	

The FIFO ending inventory is higher than the weighted-average ending inventory by $4,866. This is because FIFO assumes that all the lower-cost prior-period units in work in process are the first to be completed and transferred out while ending work in process consists of only the higher-cost current-period units. The weighted-average method, however, smoothes out cost per equivalent unit by assuming that more of the higher-cost units are completed and transferred out, while some of the lower-cost units in beginning work in process are placed in ending work in process. So, in this case, the weighted-average method results in a higher cost of units completed and transferred out and a lower ending work-in-process inventory relative to FIFO.

SOLUTION EXHIBIT 17-32A
Steps 1 and 2: Summarize Output in Physical Units and Compute Output in Equivalent Units; FIFO Method of Process Costing,
Assembly Department of Global Defense Inc. for October 2007.

Flow of Production	(Step 1) Physical Units	(Step 2) Equivalent Units Direct Materials	Conversion Costs
Work in process, beginning (given)	20	(work done before current period)	
Started during current period (given)	80		
To account for	100		
Completed and transferred out during current period:			
From beginning work in process[§]	20		
$20 \times (100\% - 100\%); 20 \times (100\% - 60\%)$		0	8
Started and completed	70[†]		
$70 \times 100\%, 70 \times 100\%$		70	70
Work in process, ending* (given)	10		
$10 \times 100\%; 10 \times 70\%$		10	7
Accounted for	100		
Work done in current period only		80	85

[§]Degree of completion in this department: direct materials, 100%; conversion costs, 60%.

[†]90 physical units completed and transferred out minus 20 physical units completed and transferred out from beginning work-in-process inventory.

*Degree of completion in this department: direct materials, 100%; conversion costs, 70%.

SOLUTION EXHIBIT 17-32B

Steps 3, 4, and 5: Compute Cost per Equivalent Unit, Summarize Total Costs to Account For, and Assign Total Costs to Units Completed and to Units in Ending Work in Process;

FIFO Method of Process Costing, Assembly Department of Global Defense, Inc., for October 2007.

	Total Production Costs	Direct Materials	Conversion Costs
Work in process, beginning ($460,000 + $120,000)	$ 580,000	(costs of work done before current period)	
(Step 3) Costs added in current period (given)	2,935,000	$2,000,000	$935,000
Divide by equivalent units of work done in current period (Solution Exhibit 17-32A)		÷ 80	÷ 85
Cost per equivalent unit of work done in current period		$ 25,000	$ 11,000
(Step 4) Total costs to account for	$3,515,000		
(Step 5) Assignment of costs:			
Completed and transferred out (90 units):			
Work in process, beginning (20 units)	$ 580,000		
Costs added to beg. work in process in current period	88,000	$(0^* \times \$25,000) + (8^* \times \$11,000)$	
Total from beginning inventory	668,000		
Started and completed (70 units)	2,520,000	$(70^\dagger \times \$25,000) + (70^\dagger \times \$11,000)$	
Total costs of units completed & transferred out	3,188,000		
Work in process, ending (10 units)	327,000	$(10^\# \times \$25,000) + (7^\# \times \$11,000)$	
Total costs accounted for	$3,515,000		

*Equivalent units used to complete beginning work in process from Solution Exhibit 17-32A, Step 2.
†Equivelant units started and completed from Solution Exhibit 17-32A, Step 2.
#Equivalent units in work in process, ending from Solution Exhibit 17-32A, Step 2.

17-16

17-34 (30 min.) **Transferred-in costs, FIFO method (continuation of 17-33).**

1.　As explained in Problem 17-33, requirement 1, transferred-in costs are 100% complete and direct materials are 0% complete in both beginning and ending work-in-process inventory.

2.　The equivalent units of work done in October 2007 in the Testing Department for transferred-in costs, direct materials, and conversion costs are calculated in Solution Exhibit 17-34A.

3.　Solution Exhibit 17-34B calculates the cost per equivalent unit of work done in October 2007 in the Testing Department for transferred-in costs, direct materials, and conversion costs, summarizes total Testing Department costs for October 2007, and assigns these costs to units completed and transferred out and to units in ending work in process using the FIFO method.

4.　Journal entries:

a.　Work in Process—Testing Department　　3,188,000
　　　Work in Process—Assembly Department　　　　　　3,188,000
　　Cost of goods completed and transferred out
　　　during October from the Assembly Dept. to
　　　the Testing Dept.

b.　Finished Goods　　　　　　　　　　　　9,281,527
　　　Work in Process—Testing Department　　　　　　9,281,527
　　Cost of goods completed and transferred out
　　　during October from the Testing Department
　　　to Finished Goods inventory.

SOLUTION EXHIBIT 17-34A
Steps 1 and 2: Summarize Output in Physical Units and Compute Output in Equivalent Units;
FIFO Method of Process Costing,
Testing Department of Global Defense, Inc., for October 2007.

Flow of Production	(Step 1) Physical Units	(Step 2) Equivalent Units		
		Transferred-in Costs	Direct Materials	Conversion Costs
Work in process, beginning (given)	30	(work done before current period)		
Transferred-in during current period (given)	90			
To account for	120			
Completed and transferred out during current period:				
From beginning work in process[§]	30			
30 × (100% − 100%); 30 × (100% − 0%);				
30 × (100% − 70%)		0	30	9
Started and completed	75[†]			
75 × 100%; 75 × 100%; 75 × 100%		75	75	75
Work in process, ending* (given)	15			
15 × 100%; 15 × 0%; 15 × 60%		15	0	9
Accounted for	120			
Work done in current period only		90	105	93

[§] Degree of completion in this department: Transferred-in costs, 100%; direct materials, 0%; conversion costs, 70%.
[†] 105 physical units completed and transferred out minus 30 physical units completed and transferred out from beginning work-in-process inventory.
*Degree of completion in this department: transferred-in costs, 100%; direct materials, 0%; conversion costs, 60%.

SOLUTION EXHIBIT 17-34B

Steps 3, 4, and 5: Compute Cost per Equivalent Unit, Summarize Total Costs to Account For, and Assign Total Costs to Units Completed and to Units in Ending Work in Process;

FIFO Method of Process Costing,

Testing Department of Global Defense, Inc., for October 2007.

	Total Production Costs	Transferred-in Costs	Direct Materials	Conversion Costs
Work in process, beginning ($331,800 + $0 + $980,060))	$1,311,860	(Costs of work done before current period)		
(Step 3) Costs added in current period (given)	8,654,000	$3,188,000	$3,885,000	$1,581,000
Divide by equivalent units of work done in current period (Solution Exhibit 17-34A)		÷ 90	÷ 105	÷ 93
Cost per equiv. unit of work done in current period		$ 35,422.22	$ 37,000	$ 17,000
(Step 4) Total costs to account for	$9,965,860			
(Step 5) Assignment of costs:				
Completed and transferred out (105 units):				
Work in process, beginning (30 units)	$1,311,860			
Costs added to beg. work in process in current period	1,263,000	(0* × $35,422.22) + (30* × $37,000) + (9* × $17,000)		
Total from beginning inventory	2,574,860			
Started and completed (75 units)	6,706,667	(75† × $35,422.22) + (75† × $37,000) + (75† × $17,000)		
Total costs of units completed & transferred out	9,281,527			
Work in process, ending (15 units)	684,333	(15# × $35,422.22) + (0# × $37,000) + (9# × $17,000)		
Total costs accounted for	$9,965,860			

*Equivalent units used to complete beginning work in process from Solution Exhibit 17-34A, Step 2.
†Equivalent units started and completed from Solution Exhibit 17-34A, Step 2.
#Equivalent units in work in process, ending from Solution Exhibit 17-34A, Step 2.

17-19

17-36 (5–10 min.) Journal entries (continuation of 17-35).

1. Work in Process—Forming Department 70,000
  Accounts Payable   70,000
 To record direct materials purchased and
  used in production during April

2. Work in Process—Forming Department 42,500
  Various Accounts   42,500
 To record Forming Department conversion
  costs for April

3. Work in Process—Finishing Department 104,000
  Work in Process—Forming Department 104,000
 To record cost of goods completed and transferred
  out in April from the Forming Department
  to the Finishing Department

Work in Process—Forming Department

Beginning inventory, April 1	9,625	3. Transferred out to	
1. Direct materials	70,000	Work in Process—Finishing	104,000
2. Conversion costs	42,500		
Ending inventory, April 30	18,125		

17-38 (30 min.) Transferred-in costs, weighted average.

1. Solution Exhibit 17-38A computes the equivalent units of work done to date in the Spinning Department for transferred-in costs, direct materials, and conversion costs.

  Solution Exhibit 17-38B calculates the cost per equivalent unit of work done to date in the Spinning Department for transferred-in costs, direct materials, and conversion costs, summarizes total Spinning Department costs for April 2007, and assigns these costs to units completed and transferred out and to units in ending work in process using the weighted-average method.

2. Journal entries:

  a. Work in Process—Spinning Department 96,000
   Work in Process—Drawing Department 96,000
   Cost of goods completed and transferred out
    during April from the Drawing Department
    to the Spinning Department

  b. Finished Goods 166,008
   Work in Process—Spinning Department 166,008
   Cost of goods completed and transferred out
    during April from the Spinning Department
    to Finished Goods inventory

SOLUTION EXHIBIT 17-38A

Steps 1 and 2: Summarize Output in Physical Units and Compute Output in Equivalent Units; Weighted-Average Method of Process Costing, Spinning Department of Jhirmack Woolen Mills for April 2007.

| | (Step 1) | (Step 2) Equivalent Units | | |
| | Physical | Transferred- | Direct | Conversion |
Flow of Production	Units	in Costs	Materials	Costs
Work in process, beginning (given)	600			
Transferred-in during current period (given)	1,800			
To account for	2,400			
Completed and transferred out during current period:	2,000	2,000	2,000	2,000
Work in process, ending[a] (given)	400			
(400 × 100%; 400 × 0%; 400 × 60%)		400	0	240
Accounted for	2,400			
Work done to date		2,400	2,000	2,240

[a]Degree of completion in this department: transferred-in costs, 100%; direct materials, 0%; conversion costs, 60%.

SOLUTION EXHIBIT 17-38B

Steps 3, 4, and 5: Compute Cost per Equivalent Unit, Summarize Total Costs to Account For, and Assign Total Costs to Units Completed and to Units in Ending Work in Process;

Weighted-Average Method of Process Costing,

Spinning Department of Jhirmack Woolen Mills for April 2007.

		Total Production Costs	Transferred-in Costs	Direct Materials	Conversion Costs
(Step 3)	Work in process, beginning (given)	$ 31,850	$ 21,850	$ 0	$10,000
	Costs added in current period (given)	159,800	96,000	17,800	46,000
	Costs incurred to date		$117,850	$17,800	$56,000
	Divide by equivalent units of work done to date (Solution Exhibit 17-38A)		2,400	2,000	2,240
	Cost per equivalent unit of work done to date		$ 49.104	$ 8.90	$ 25
(Step 4)	Total costs to account for	$191,650			
(Step 5)	Assignment of costs:				
	Completed and transferred out (2,000 units)	$166,008	$(2,000^a \times \$49.104)$	$+ (2,000^a \times \$8.90)$	$+ (2,000^a \times \$25)$
	Work in process, ending (400 units):	25,642	$(400^b \times \$49.104)$	$+ (0^b \times \$8.90)$	$+ (240^b \times \$25)$
	Total costs accounted for	$191,650			

[a] Equivalent units completed and transferred out from Sol. Exhibit 17-38A, step 2.

[b] Equivalent units in ending work in process from Sol. Exhibit 17-38A, step 2.

17-40 (45 min.) **Transferred-in costs, weighted-average and FIFO methods.**

1.   Solution Exhibit 17-40A computes the equivalent units of work done to date in the Drying and Packaging Department for transferred-in costs, direct materials, and conversion costs. Solution Exhibit 17-40B calculates the cost per equivalent unit of work done to date in the Drying and Packaging Department for transferred-in costs, direct materials, and conversion costs, summarizes total Drying and Packaging Department costs for week 37, and assigns these costs to units completed and transferred out and to units in ending work in process using the weighted-average method.

2.   Solution Exhibit 17-40C computes the equivalent units of work done in week 37 in the Drying and Packaging Department for transferred-in costs, direct materials, and conversion costs. Solution Exhibit 17-40D calculates the cost per equivalent unit of work done in week 37 in the Drying and Packaging Department for transferred-in costs, direct materials, and conversion costs, summarizes total Drying and Packaging Department costs for week 37, and assigns these costs to units completed and transferred out and to units in ending work in process using the FIFO method.

SOLUTION EXHIBIT 17-40A

Steps 1 and 2: Summarize Output in Physical Units and Compute Output in Equivalent Units;
Weighted-Average Method of Process Costing,
Drying and Packaging Department of Frito-Lay Inc. for Week 37.

	(Step 1)	(Step 2) Equivalent Units		
Flow of Production	**Physical Units**	**Transferred-in Costs**	**Direct Materials**	**Conversion Costs**
Work in process, beginning (given)	1,250			
Transferred in during current period (given)	5,000			
To account for	6,250			
Completed and transferred out during current period	5,250	5,250	5,250	5,250
Work in process, ending* (given)	1,000			
1,000 × 100%; 1,000 × 0%; 1,000 × 40%		1,000	0	400
Accounted for	6,250			
Work done to date		6,250	5,250	5,650

*Degree of completion in this department: transferred-in costs, 100%; direct materials, 0%; conversion costs, 40%.

SOLUTION EXHIBIT 17-40B

Steps 3, 4, and 5: Compute Cost per Equivalent Unit, Summarize Total Costs to Account For, and Assign Total Costs to Units Completed and to Units in Ending Work in Process;

Weighted-Average Method of Process Costing,

Drying and Packaging Department of Frito-Lay Inc. for Week 37.

	Total Production Costs	Transferred-in Costs	Direct Materials	Conversion Costs
(Step 3) Work in process, beginning (given)	$ 38,060	$ 29,000	$ 0	$ 9,060
Costs added in current period (given)	159,600	96,000	25,200	38,400
Costs incurred to date		$125,000	$25,200	$47,460
Divide by equivalent units of work done to date (Solution Exhibit 17-40A)		÷ 6,250	÷ 5,250	÷ 5,650
Equivalent unit costs of work done to date		$ 20	$ 4.80	$ 8.40
(Step 4) Total costs to account for	$197,660			
(Step 5) Assignment of costs:				
Completed and transferred out (5,250 units)	$174,300	$(5,250* × $20) + (5,250* × $4.80) + (5,250* × $8.40)		
Work in process, ending (1,000 units)	23,360	$(1,000† × $20) + (0† × $4.80) + (400† × $8.40)		
Total costs accounted for	$197,660			

*Equivalent units completed and transferred out from Solution Exhibit 17-40A, Step 2.
†Equivalent units in work in process, ending from Solution Exhibit 17-40A, Step 2.

17-24

SOLUTION EXHIBIT 17-40C

Steps 1 and 2: Summarize Output in Physical Units and Compute Output in Equivalent Units; FIFO Method of Process Costing,
Drying and Packaging Department of Frito-Lay Inc. for Week 37.

Flow of Production	(Step 1) Physical Units	(Step 2) Equivalent Units		
		Transferred-in Costs	Direct Materials	Conversion Costs
Work in process, beginning (given)	1,250	(work done before current period)		
Transferred-in during current period (given)	5,000			
To account for	6,250			
Completed and transferred out during current period:				
From beginning work in process§	1,250			
1,250 × (100% − 100%); 1,250 × (100% − 0%); 1,250 × (100% − 80%)		0	1,250	250
Started and completed	4,000†			
4,000 × 100%; 4,000 × 100%; 4,000 × 100%		4,000	4,000	4,000
Work in process, ending* (given)	1,000			
1,000 × 100%; 1,000 × 0%; 1,000 × 40%		1,000	0	400
Accounted for	6,250			
Work done in current period only		5,000	5,250	4,650

§Degree of completion in this department: Transferred-in costs, 100%; direct materials, 0%; conversion costs, 80%.
†5,250 physical units completed and transferred out minus 1,250 physical units completed and transferred out from beginning work-in-process inventory.
*Degree of completion in this department: transferred-in costs, 100%; direct materials, 0%; conversion costs, 40%.

17-25

SOLUTION EXHIBIT 17-40D

Steps 3, 4, and 5: Compute Cost per Equivalent Unit, Summarize Total Costs to Account For, and Assign Total Costs to Units Completed and to Units in Ending Work in Process;
FIFO Method of Process Costing,
Drying and Packaging Department of Frito-Lay Inc. for Week 37.

	Total Production Costs	Transferred-in Costs	Direct Materials	Conversion Costs
Work in process, beginning ($9,060 + $0 + $28,920)	$ 37,980	(Costs of work done before current period)		
(Step 3) Costs added in current period (given)	157,600	$94,000	$25,200	$38,400
Divide by equivalent units of work done in current period (Solution Exhibit 17-40C)		÷ 5,000	÷ 5,250	÷ 4,650
Cost per equiv. unit of work done in current period		$ 18.80	$ 4.80	$ 8.258
(Step 4) Total costs to account for	$195,580			
(Step 5) Assignment of costs:				
Completed and transferred out (5,250 units):				
Work in process, beginning (1,250 units)	$ 37,980			
Costs added to beg. work in process in current period	8,065	$(0^* \times \$18.80)$	$+ (1{,}250^* \times \$4.80) +$	$(250^* \times \$8.258)$
Total from beginning inventory	46,045			
Started and completed (4,000 units)	127,432	$(4{,}000^\dagger \times \$18.80) +$	$(4{,}000^\dagger \times \$4.80) +$	$(4{,}000^\dagger \times \$8.258)$
Total costs of units completed & transferred out	173,477			
Work in process, ending (1,000 units)	22,103	$(1{,}000^\# \times \$18.80) +$	$(0^\# \times \$4.80) +$	$(400^\# \times \$8.258)$
Total costs accounted for	$195,580			

*Equivalent units used to complete beginning work in process from Solution Exhibit 17-40C, Step 2.
†Equivalent units started and completed from Solution Exhibit 17-40C, Step 2.
#Equivalent units in work in process, ending from Solution Exhibit 17-40C, Step 2.

17-42 (25-30 min.) **Operation costing, equivalent units.**

1. Materials and conversion costs of each operation, the total units produced, and the material and conversion cost per unit for the month of May are as follows:

	Extrusion	Form	Trim	Finish
1. Units produced	11,000	11,000	5,000	2,000
2. Materials costs	$132,000	$ 44,000	$15,000	$12,000
3. Materials cost per unit (2 ÷ 1)	12.00	4.00	3.00	6.00
4. Conversion costs	269,500	132,000	69,000	42,000
5. Conversion cost per unit (4 ÷ 1)	24.50	12.00	13.80	21.00

The unit cost and total costs in May for each product are as follows:

Cost Elements	Standard Model	Deluxe Model	Executive Model
Extrusion materials	$ 12.00	$ 12.00	$ 12.00
Form materials	4.00	4.00	4.00
Trim materials	–	3.00	3.00
Finish materials	–	–	6.00
Extrusion conversion	24.50	24.50	24.50
Form conversion	12.00	12.00	12.00
Trim conversion	–	13.80	13.80
Finish conversion	–	–	21.00
Total unit cost	$ 52.50	$ 69.30	$ 96.30
Multiply by units produced	× 6,000	× 3,000	× 2,000
Total product costs	$315,000	$207,900	$192,600

2.

	Unit Cost	Equivalent Units	Total Costs
Deluxe model work-in process costs at the trim operation			
Extrusion material (100% complete when transferred in)	$12.00	1,000	$12,000
Extrusion conversion (100% complete when transferred in)	24.50	1,000	24,500
Form material (100% complete when transferred in)	4.00	1,000	4,000
Form conversion (100% complete when transferred in)	12.00	1,000	12,000
Trim material (100% complete)	3.00	1,000	3,000
Trim conversion (60% complete)	13.80	600*	8,280
Work-in-process costs			$63,780

*1,000 units × 60% complete

17-44 (45 min.) **Transferred-in costs, equivalent unit costs, working backward.**

1. The equivalent units of work done in the current period for each cost category are computed in Solution Exhibit 17-44B using data on costs added in current period and cost per equivalent unit of work done in current period.

	Transferred-In Costs	Direct Materials	Conversion Costs
Costs added in current period	$58,500	$57,000	$57,200
Divided by cost per equivalent unit of work done in current period	÷ $6.50	÷ $3	÷ $5.20
Equivalent units of work done in current period	9,000	19,000	11,000

2.
$$\begin{array}{l}\text{Physical units completed} \\ \text{and transferred out}\end{array} = \begin{array}{l}\text{Physical units in beginning} \\ \text{work in process}\end{array} + \begin{array}{l}\text{Physical} \\ \text{units added}\end{array} - \begin{array}{l}\text{Physical units in ending} \\ \text{work in process}\end{array}$$

$$= 15,000 + 9,000 - 5,000 = 19,000$$

Solution Exhibit 17-44A shows the equivalent units of work done in June to complete beginning work in process and the equivalent units of work done in June to start and complete 4,000 units. Note that direct materials in beginning work in process is 0% complete because it is added only when the process is 80% complete and the beginning WIP is only 60% complete. We had calculated the total equivalent units of work done in the current period in requirement 1: transferred-in costs, 9,000; direct materials, 19,000; and conversion costs, 11,000. The missing number is the equivalent units of each cost category in ending work in process (see Solution Exhibit 17-44A).

Transferred-in costs	5,000
Direct materials	0
Conversion costs	1,000

3. Percentage of completion for each cost category in ending work in process can be calculated by dividing equivalent units in ending work in process for each cost category by physical units of work in process (5,000 units).

Transferred-in costs	5,000 ÷ 5,000 = 100%
Direct materials	0 ÷ 5,000 = 0%
Conversion costs	1,000 ÷ 5,000 = 20%

4. Solution Exhibit 17-44B summarizes the total costs to account for, and assigns these costs to units completed and transferred out and to units in ending work in process.

SOLUTION EXHIBIT 17-44A

Steps 1 and 2: Summarize Output in Physical Units and Compute Output in Equivalent Units; FIFO Method of Process Costing,
Thermo-assembly Department of Lennox Plastics for June 2007.

Flow of Production	(Step 1) Physical Units	(Step 2) Equivalent Units		
		Transferred-in Costs	Direct Materials	Conversion Costs
Work in process, beginning (given)	15,000	(work done before current period)		
Transferred-in during current period (given)	9,000			
To account for	24,000			
Completed and transferred out during current period:				
From beginning work in process§	15,000			
15,000 × (100% – 100%); 15,000 × (100% – 0%);				
15,000 × (100% – 60%)		0	15,000	6,000
Started and completed	4,000†			
4,000 × 100%; 4,000 × 100%; 4,000 × 100%		4,000	4,000	4,000
Work in process, ending* (given)	5,000			
5,000 ×100%; 5,000 ×0%; 5,000 ×20%		5,000	0	1,000
Accounted for	24,000			
Work done in current period only (from Solution Exhibit 17-44B)		9,000	19,000	11,000

§Degree of completion in this department: transferred-in costs, 100%; direct materials, 0%; conversion costs, 60%.

†19,000 physical units completed and transferred out minus 15,000 physical units completed and transferred out from beginning work-in-process inventory.

*Degree of completion in this department: transferred-in costs, 100%; direct materials, 0%; conversion costs, 20%.

SOLUTION EXHIBIT 17-44B

Steps 3, 4, and 5: Compute Cost per Equivalent Unit, Summarize Total Costs to Account For, and Assign Total Costs to Units Completed and to Units in Ending Work in Process; FIFO Method of Process Costing,

Thermo-assembly Department of Lennox Plastics for June 2007.

	Total Production Costs	Transferred -in Costs	Direct Materials	Conversion Costs
Work in process, beginning ($90,000 + $0 + $45,000)	$135,000	(Costs of work done before current period)		
(Step 3) Costs added in current period (given)	172,700	$58,500	$57,000	$57,200
Divide by equivalent units of work done in current period		÷ 9,000	÷ 19,000	÷ 11,000
Cost per equiv. unit of work done in current period		$ 6.50	$ 3	$ 5.20
(Step 4) Total costs to account for	$307,700			
(Step 5) Assignment of costs:				
Completed and transferred out (19,000 units):				
Work in process, beginning (15,000 units)	$135,000			
Costs added to beg. work in process in current period	76,200	(0* × $6.50) + (15,000* × $3) + (6,000* × $5.20)		
Total from beginning inventory	211,200			
Started and completed (4,000 units)	58,800	(4,000† × $6.50) + (4,000† × $3) + (4,000† × $5.20)		
Total costs of units completed & transferred out	270,000			
Work in process, ending (5,000 units)	37,700	(5,000# × $6.50) + (0# × $3) + (1,000# × $5.20)		
Total costs accounted for	$307,700			

*Equivalent units used to complete beginning work in process from Solution Exhibit 17-44A, Step 2.
†Equivalent units started and completed from Solution Exhibit 17-44A, Step 2.
#Equivalent units in work in process, ending from Solution Exhibit 17-44A, Step 2.

17-30

CHAPTER 18
SPOILAGE, REWORK, AND SCRAP

18-2 Spoilage—units of production that do not meet the standards required by customers for good units and that are discarded or sold at reduced prices.

Rework—units of production that do not meet the specifications required by customers but which are subsequently repaired and sold as good finished units.

Scrap—residual material that results from manufacturing a product. It has low total sales value compared to the total sales value of the product.

18-4 Abnormal spoilage is spoilage that is not inherent in a particular production process and would not arise under efficient operating conditions. Costs of abnormal spoilage are "lost costs," measures of inefficiency that should be written off directly as losses for the accounting period.

18-6 Normal spoilage typically is expressed as a percentage of good units passing the inspection point. Given actual spoiled units, we infer abnormal spoilage as follows:

Abnormal spoilage = Actual spoilage – Normal spoilage

18-8 Yes. Normal spoilage rates should be computed from the good output or from the *normal* input, not the *total* input. Normal spoilage is a given percentage of a certain output base. This base should never include abnormal spoilage, which is included in total input. Abnormal spoilage does not vary in direct proportion to units produced, and to include it would cause the normal spoilage count to fluctuate irregularly and not vary in direct proportion to the output base.

18-10 No. If abnormal spoilage is detected at a different point in the production cycle than normal spoilage, then unit costs would differ. If, however normal and abnormal spoilage are detected at the same point in the production cycle, their unit costs would be the same.

18-12 No. Unless there are special reasons for charging normal rework to jobs that contained the bad units, the costs of extra materials, labor, and so on are usually charged to manufacturing overhead and allocated to all jobs.

18-14 A company is justified in inventorying scrap when its estimated net realizable value is significant and the time between storing it and selling or reusing it is quite long.

18-16 (5–10 min.) **Normal and abnormal spoilage in units.**

1.	Total spoiled units	12,000
	Normal spoilage in units, 5% × 132,000	6,600
	Abnormal spoilage in units	5,400
2.	Abnormal spoilage, 5,400 × $10	$ 54,000
	Normal spoilage, 6,600 × $10	66,000
	Potential savings, 12,000 × $10	$120,000

Regardless of the targeted normal spoilage, abnormal spoilage is non-recurring and avoidable. The targeted normal spoilage rate is subject to change. Many companies have reduced their spoilage to almost zero, which would realize all potential savings. Of course, zero spoilage usually means higher-quality products, more customer satisfaction, more employee satisfaction, and various beneficial effects on nonmanufacturing (for example, purchasing) costs of direct materials.

18-18 (20–25 min.) **Weighted-average method, assigning costs (continuation of 18-17).**

Solution Exhibit 18-18 calculates the costs per equivalent unit for direct materials and conversion costs, summarizes total costs to account for, and assigns these costs to units completed and transferred out (including normal spoilage), to abnormal spoilage, and to units in ending work in process.

SOLUTION EXHIBIT 18-18
Compute Cost per Equivalent Unit, Summarize Total Costs to Account For, and Assign Total Costs to Units Completed, to Spoiled Units, and to Units in Ending Work in Process; Weighted-Average Method of Process Costing, Gray Manufacturing Company, November 2006.

		Total Production Costs	Direct Materials	Conversion Costs
(Step 3)	Work in process, beginning (given)	$ 2,533	$ 1,423	$ 1,110
	Costs added in current period (given)	39,930	12,180	27,750
	Costs incurred to date		13,603	28,860
	Divided by equivalent units of work done to date		÷11,150	÷ 9,750
	Cost per equivalent unit		$ 1.22	$ 2.96
(Step 4)	Total costs to account for	$42,463		
(Step 5)	Assignment of costs			
	Good units completed and transferred out (9,000 units)			
	Costs before adding normal spoilage	$37,620	$(9,000^{\#} \times \$1.22) + (9,000^{\#} \times \$2.96)$	
	Normal spoilage (100 units)	418	$(100^{\#} \times \$1.22) + (100^{\#} \times \$2.96)$	
(A)	Total cost of good units completed & transf. out	38,038		
(B)	Abnormal spoilage (50 units)	209	$(50^{\#} \times \$1.22) + (50^{\#} \times \$2.96)$	
(C)	Work in process, ending (2,000 units)	4,216	$(2,000^{\#} \times \$1.22) + (600^{\#} \times \$2.96)$	
(A)+(B)+(C)	Total costs accounted for	$42,463		

[#]Equivalent units of direct materials and conversion costs calculated in Step 2 in Solution Exhibit 18-17.

18-20 (20–25 min.) **FIFO method, assigning costs (continuation of 18-19).**

Solution Exhibit 18-20 calculates the costs per equivalent unit for direct materials and conversion costs, summarizes total costs to account for, and assigns these costs to units completed and transferred out (including normal spoilage), to abnormal spoilage, and to units in ending work in process.

SOLUTION EXHIBIT 18-20
Compute Cost per Equivalent Unit Costs, Summarize Total Costs to Account For, and Assign Total Costs to Units Completed, to Spoiled Units, and to Units in Ending Work in Process; FIFO Method of Process Costing,
Gray Manufacturing Company, November 2006.

		Total Production Costs	Direct Materials	Conversion Costs
(Step 3)	Work in process, beginning (given: $1,423 + $1,110)	$ 2,533		
	Costs added in current period (given)	39,930	$12,180	$27,750
	Divided by equivalent units of work done in current period		÷10,150	÷ 9,250
	Cost per equivalent unit		$ 1.20	$ 3
(Step 4)	Total costs to account for	$42,463		
(Step 5)	Assignment of costs:			
	Good units completed and transferred out (9,000 units)			
	Work in process, beginning (1,000 units)	$ 2,533		
	Costs added to beg. work in process in current period	1,500	(0[a] × $1.20)	+ (500[a] × $3)
	Total from beginning inventory before normal spoilage	4,033		
	Started and completed before normal spoilage (8,000 units)	33,600	(8,000[a] × $1.20)	+ (8,000[a] × $3)
	Normal spoilage (100 units)	420	(100[a] × $1.20)	+ (100[a] × $3)
(A)	Total costs of good units completed and transferred out	38,053		
(B)	Abnormal spoilage (50 units)	210	(50[a] × $1.20)	+ (50[a] × $3)
(C)	Work in process, ending (2,000 units)	4,200	(2,000[a] × $1.20)	+ (60[a] × $3)
(A)+(B)+(C)	Total costs accounted for	$42,463		

[a] Equivalent units of direct materials and conversion costs calculated in Step 2 in Solution Exhibit 18-19.

18-22 (30 min.) **FIFO method, spoilage.**

1.   Solution Exhibit 18-22A calculates equivalent units of work done in the current period for direct materials and conversion costs.

SOLUTION EXHIBIT 18-22A
Summarize Output in Physical Units and Compute Output in Equivalent Units;
FIFO Method of Process Costing with Spoilage,
Appleton Company for August 2006.

Flow of Production	(Step 1) Physical Units	(Step 2) Equivalent Units Direct Materials	Conversion Costs
Work in process, beginning (given)	2,000		
Started during current period (given)	10,000		
To account for	12,000		
Good units completed and transferred out during current period:			
From beginning work in process [a]	2,000		
[2,000 × (100% − 100%); 2,000 × (100% − 50%)]		0	1,000
Started and completed	7,000[b]		
(7,000 × 100%; 7,000 × 100%)		7,000	7,000
Normal spoilage[c]	900		
(900 × 100%; 900 × 100%)		900	900
Abnormal spoilage[d]	300		
(300 × 100%; 300 × 100%)		300	300
Work in process, ending[e] (given)	1,800		
(1,800 × 100%; 1,800 × 75%)		1,800	1,350
Accounted for	12,000		
Work done in current period only		10,000	10,550

[a] Degree of completion in this department: direct materials, 100%; conversion costs, 50%.

[b] 9,000 physical units completed and transferred out minus 2,000 physical units completed and transferred out from beginning work-in-process inventory.

[c] Normal spoilage is 10% of good units transferred out: 10% × 9,000 = 900 units. Degree of completion of normal spoilage in this department: direct materials, 100%; conversion costs, 100%.

[d] Total spoilage = Beg. units + Units started − Good units tsfd. Out - ending units = 2,000 + 10,000 − 9,000 − 1,800 = 1,200
Abnormal spoilage = Actual spoilage − Normal spoilage = 1,200 − 900 = 300 units. Degree of completion of abnormal spoilage in in this department: direct materials, 100%; conversion costs, 100%.

[e] Degree of completion in this department: direct materials, 100%; conversion costs, 75%.

2 & 3. Solution Exhibit 18-22B calculates the costs per equivalent unit for direct materials and conversion costs, summarizes total costs to account for, and assigns these costs to units completed and transferred out (including normal spoilage), to abnormal spoilage, and to units in ending work in process, using the FIFO method.

SOLUTION EXHIBIT 18-22B

Compute Cost per Equivalent Unit, Summarize Total Costs to Account For, and Assign Total Costs to Units Completed, to Spoiled Units, and to Units in Ending Work in Process; FIFO Method of Process Costing,
Appleton Company, August 2006.

		Total Production Costs	Direct Materials	Conversion Costs
(Step 3)	Work in process, beginning (given) ($17,700 + $10,900)	$ 28,600		
	Costs added in current period (given)	174,300	$ 81,300	$93,000
	Divide by equivalent units of work done in current period		÷ 10,000	÷ 10,550
	Cost per equivalent unit		$ 8.130	$ 8.8152
(Step 4)	Total costs to account for	$202,900		
(Step 5)	Assignment of costs:			
	Good units completed and transferred out (9,000 units)			
	Work in process, beginning (2,000 units)	$ 28,600		
	Costs added to beg. work in process in current period	8,815	$(0^f \times \$8.13)$	$+ (1,000^f \times \$8.8152)$
	Total from beginning inventory before normal spoilage	37,415		
	Started and completed before normal spoilage (7,000 units)	118,616	$(7,000^f \times \$8.13)$	$+ (7,000^f \times \$8.8152)$
	Normal spoilage (900 units)	15,521	$(900^f \times \$8.13)$	$+ (900^f \times \$8.8152)$
(A)	Total costs of good units completed and transferred out	171,282		
(B)	Abnormal spoilage (300 units)	5,084	$(300^f \times \$8.13)$	$+ (300^f \times \$8.8152)$
(C)	Work in process, ending (1,800 units):	26,534	$(1,800^f \times \$8.13)$	$+ (1,350^f \times \$8.8152)$
(A) + (B) + (C)	Total costs accounted for	$202,900		

^{f}Equivalent units of direct materials and conversion costs calculated in step 2 in Solution Exhibit 18-22A.

18-24 (25 min.) **Weighted-average method, spoilage.**

1.   Solution Exhibit 18-24, Panel A, calculates the equivalent units of work done to date for each cost category in September 2006.

2. & 3. Solution Exhibit 18-24, Panel B, calculates the costs per equivalent unit for each cost category, summarizes total costs to account for, and assigns these costs to units completed (including normal spoilage), to abnormal spoilage, and to units in ending work in process using the weighted-average method.

SOLUTION EXHIBIT 18-24
Weighted-Average Method of Process Costing with Spoilage;
Superchip, September 2006.

PANEL A: Steps 1 and 2—Summarize Output in Physical Units and Compute Output in Equivalent Units

	(Step 1)	(Step 2) Equivalent Units	
Flow of Production	**Physical Units**	**Direct Materials**	**Conversion Costs**
Work in process, beginning (given)	400		
Started during current period (given)	1,700		
To account for	2,100		
Good units completed and transferred out during current period:	1,400	1,400	1,400
Normal spoilage*	210		
210 × 100%; 210 × 100%		210	210
Abnormal spoilage[†]	190		
190 × 100%; 190 × 100%		190	190
Work in process, ending[‡] (given)	300		
300 × 100%; 300 × 40%		300	120
Accounted for	2,100		
Work done to date		2,100	1,920

*Normal spoilage is 15% of good units transferred out: 15% × 1,400 = 210 units. Degree of completion of normal spoilage in this department: direct materials, 100%; conversion costs, 100%.

[†]Total spoilage = 400 + 1,700 – 1,400 – 300 = 400 units; Abnormal spoilage = Total spoilage – Normal spoilage = 400 – 210 = 190 units. Degree of completion of abnormal spoilage in this department: direct materials, 100%; conversion costs, 100%.

[‡]Degree of completion in this department: direct materials, 100%; conversion costs, 40%.

18-6

SOLUTION EXHIBIT 18-24

PANEL B: Steps 3, 4, and 5—Compute Cost per Equivalent Unit, Summarize Total Costs to Account For, and Assign Total Costs to Units Completed, to Spoiled Units, and to Units in Ending Work in Process

		Total Production Costs	Direct Materials	Conversion Costs
(Step 3)	Work in process, beginning (given)	$ 74,200	$ 64,000	$ 10,200
	Costs added in current period (given)	531,600	378,000	153,600
	Costs incurred to date		$442,000	$163,800
	Divided by equivalent units of work done to date		÷ 2,100	÷ 1,920
	Cost per equivalent unit costs of work done to date		$210.476	$85.3125
(Step 4)	Total costs to account for	$605,800		
(Step 5)	Assignment of costs			
	Good units completed and transferred out (1,400 units)			
	Costs before adding normal spoilage	$414,104	$(1,400^{\#} \times \$210.476) + (1,400^{\#} \times \$85.3125)$	
	Normal spoilage (210 units)	62,116	$(210^{\#} \times \$210.476) + (210^{\#} \times \$85.3125)$	
(A)	Total cost of good units completed and transferred out	476,220		
(B)	Abnormal spoilage (190 units)	56,199	$(190^{\#} \times \$210.476) + (190^{\#} \times \$85.3125)$	
(C)	Work in process, ending (300 units)	73,381	$(300^{\#} \times \$210.476) + (120^{\#} \times \$85.3125)$	
(A)+(B)+(C)	Total costs accounted for	$605,800		

$^{\#}$ Equivalent units of direct materials and conversion costs calculated in Step 2 in Panel A.

18-26 (30 min.) Standard costing method, spoilage.

1. Solution Exhibit 18-25, Panel A, shows the computation of the equivalent units of work done in September 2006 for direct materials (1,700 units) and conversion costs (1,800 units). (This computation is the same for FIFO and standard-costing.)

2. The direct materials cost per equivalent unit of beginning work in process and of work done in September 2006 is the standard cost of $210 given in the problem.
   The conversion cost per equivalent unit of beginning work in process and of work done in September 2006 is the standard cost of $80 given in the problem.

3. Solution Exhibit 18-26 summarizes the total costs to account for, and assigns these costs to units completed (including normal spoilage), to abnormal spoilage, and to units in ending work in process using the standard costing method.

SOLUTION EXHIBIT 18-26
Standard Costing Method of Process Costing with Spoilage;
Superchip, September 2006.

Steps 3, 4, and 5—Compute Cost per Equivalent Unit, Summarize Total Costs to Account For, and Assign Total Costs to Units Completed, to Spoiled Units, and to Units in Ending Work in Process

		Total Production Costs	Direct Materials	Conversion Costs
(Step 3)	Standard costs per equivalent unit (given)	$ 290	$ 210	$ 80
	Work in process, beginning*	93,600	(400 × $210) +	(120 × $80)
	Costs added in current period at standard prices	501,000	(1,700 × $210) +	(1,800 × $80)
(Step 4)	Costs to account for	$594,600		
(Step 5)	Assignment of costs at standard costs:			
	Good units completed and transferred out (1,400 units)			
	Work in process, beginning (400 units)	$ 93,600		
	Costs added beg. work in process in current period	22,400	(0§ × $210) +	(280§ × $80)
	Total from beginning inventory before normal spoilage	116,000		
	Started and completed before normal spoilage (1,000 units)	290,000	(1,000§ × $210) +	(1,000§ × $80)
	Normal spoilage (210 units)	60,900	(210§ × $210) +	(210§ × $80)
(A)	Total costs of good units completed and transferred out	466,900		
(B)	Abnormal spoilage (190 units)	55,100	(190§ × $210) +	(190§ × $80)
(C)	Work in process, ending (300 units)	72,600	(300§ × $210) +	(120§ × $80)
(A)+(B)+(C)	Total costs accounted for	$594,600		

*Work in process, beginning has 400 equivalent units (400 physical units ×100%) of direct materials and 120 equivalent units (400 physical units × 30%) of conversion costs.
§Equivalent units of direct materials and conversion costs calculated in Step 2 in Solution Exhibit 18-25, Panel A.

18-28 (15 min.) **Reworked units, costs of rework.**

1.   The two alternative approaches to account for the materials costs of reworked units are:
   a. To charge the costs of rework to the current period as a separate expense item as abnormal rework. This approach would highlight to White Goods the costs of the supplier problem.
   b. To charge the costs of the rework to manufacturing overhead as normal rework.

2.   The $50 tumbler cost is the cost of the actual tumblers included in the washing machines. The $44 tumbler units from the new supplier were eventually never used in any washing machine and that supplier is now bankrupt. The units must now be disposed of at zero disposal value.

3.   The total costs of rework due to the defective tumbler units include the following:
   a. the labor and other conversion costs spent on substituting the new tumbler units;
   b. the costs of any extra negotiations to obtain the replacement tumbler units;
   c. any higher price the existing supplier may have charged to do a rush order for the replacement tumbler units; and
   d. ordering costs for the replacement tumbler units.

18-30 (30 min.) Weighted-average method, spoilage.

Solution Exhibit 18-30 calculates the equivalent units of work done to date for each cost category, presents computations of the costs per equivalent unit for each cost category, summarizes total costs to account for, and assigns these costs to units completed (including normal spoilage), to abnormal spoilage, and to units in ending work in process using the weighted-average method.

SOLUTION EXHIBIT 18-30
Weighted-Average Method of Process Costing with Spoilage;
Cleaning Department of the Alston Company for May.

PANEL A: Steps 1 and 2—Summarize Output in Physical Units and Compute Output in Equivalent Units

Flow of Production	(Step 1) Physical Units	(Step 2) Equivalent Units	
		Direct Materials	Conversion Costs
Work in process, beginning (given)	1,000		
Started during current period (given)	9,000		
To account for	10,000		
Good units completed and transferred out during current period:	7,400	7,400	7,400
Normal spoilage*			
740 × 100%; 740 × 100%	740	740	740
Abnormal spoilage[†]			
260 × 100%; 260 ×100%	260	260	260
Work in process, ending[‡] (given)			
1,600 × 100%; 1,600 × 25%	1,600	1,600	400
Accounted for			
Work done to date	10,000	10,000	8,800

*Normal spoilage is 10% of good units transferred out: 10% × 7,400 = 740 units. Degree of completion of normal spoilage in this department: direct materials, 100%; conversion costs, 100%.

[†]Total spoilage = 1,000 + 9,000 − 7,400 − 1,600 = 1,000 units; Abnormal spoilage = 1,000 − 740 = 260 units. Degree of completion of abnormal spoilage in this department: direct materials, 100%; conversion costs, 100%.

[‡]Degree of completion in this department: direct materials, 100%; conversion costs, 25%.

PANEL B: Steps 3, 4, and 5—Compute Cost per Equivalent Unit, Summarize Total Costs to Account For, and Assign Total Costs to Units Completed, to Spoiled Units, and to Units in Ending Work in Process

		Total Production Costs	Direct Materials	Conversion Costs
(Step 3)	Work in process, beginning (given)	$ 1,800	$ 1,000	$ 800
	Costs added in current period (given)	17,000	9,000	8,000
	Costs incurred to date		10,000	8,800
	Divided by equivalent units of work done to date		÷10,000	÷ 8,800
	Cost per equivalent unit		$ 1	$ 1
(Step 4)	Total costs to account for	$18,800		
(Step 5)	Assignment of costs			
	Good units completed and transferred out (7,400 units)			
	Costs before adding normal spoilage	$14,800	(7,400# × $1) +	(7,400# × $1)
	Normal spoilage (740 units)	1,480	(740# × $1) +	(740# × $1)
(A)	Total costs of good units completed and transferred out	16,280		
(B)	Abnormal spoilage (260 units)	520	(260# × $1) +	(260# × $1)
(C)	Work in process, ending (1,600 units)	2,000	(1,600# × $1) +	(400# × $1)
(A)+(B)+(C)	Total costs accounted for	$18,800		

#Equivalent units of direct materials and conversion costs calculated in Step 2 in Panel A above.

18-32 (35 min.) **Weighted-average method, Milling Department (continuation of 18-30).**

For the Milling Department, Solution Exhibit 18-32 calculates the equivalent units of work done to date for each cost category, presents computations of the costs per equivalent unit for each cost category, summarizes total costs to account for, and assigns these costs to units completed (including normal spoilage), to abnormal spoilage, and to units in ending work in process using the weighted-average method.

SOLUTION EXHIBIT 18-32
Weighted-Average Method of Process Costing with Spoilage;
Milling Department of the Alston Company for May.

PANEL A: Steps 1 and 2—Summarize Output in Physical Units and Compute Output in Equivalent Units

| | (Step 1) | (Step 2) Equivalent Units | | |
| | | | | |
Flow of Production	Physical Units	Transferred-in Costs	Direct Materials	Conversion Costs
Work in process, beginning (given)	3,000			
Started during current period (given)	7,400			
To account for	10,400			
Good units completed and transferred out during current period:	6,000	6,000	6,000	6,000
Normal spoilage*	300			
300 × 100%; 300 × 100%; 300 × 100%		300	300	300
Abnormal spoilage†	100			
100 × 100%; 100 ×100%, 100 × 100%		100	100	100
Work in process, ending‡ (given)	4,000			
4,000 × 100%; 4,000 × 0%; 4,000 × 25%		4,000	0	1,000
Accounted for	10,400			
Work done to date		10,400	6,400	7,400

*Normal spoilage is 5% of good units transferred out: 5% × 6,000 = 300 units. Degree of completion of normal spoilage in this department: transferred-in costs, 100%; direct materials, 100%; conversion costs, 100%.
†Total spoilage = 3,000 + 7,400 − 6,000 − 4,000 = 400 units. Abnormal spoilage = 400 − 300 = 100 units. Degree of completion of abnormal spoilage in this department: transferred-in costs, 100%; direct materials, 100%; conversion costs, 100%.
‡Degree of completion in this department: transferred-in costs, 100%; direct materials, 0%; conversion costs, 25%.

PANEL B: Steps 3, 4, and 5—Compute Cost per Equivalent Unit, Summarize Total Costs to Account For, and Assign Total Costs to Units Completed, to Spoiled Units, and to Units in Ending Work in Process

		Total Production Costs	Transferred-in costs	Direct Materials	Conversion Costs
(Step 3)	Work in process, beginning (given)	$ 8,900	$ 6,450	$ 0	$2,450
	Costs added in current period (given)	21,870	16,280*	640	4,950
	Costs incurred to date		22,730	640	7,400
	Divided by equivalent units of work done to date		÷10,400	÷ 6,400	÷7,400
	Cost per equivalent unit		$2.1856	$ 0.10	$ 1
(Step 4)	Total costs to account for	$30,770			
(Step 5)	Assignment of costs				
	Good units completed and transferred out (6,000 units)				
	Costs before adding normal spoilage	$19,713	6,000# × ($2.1856 + $0.10 + $1)		
	Normal spoilage (300 units)	986	300# × ($2.1856 + $0.10 + $1)		
(A)	Total cost of good units completed and transferred out	20,699			
(B)	Abnormal spoilage (100 units)	329	100# × ($2.1856 + $0.10 + $1)		
(C)	Work in process, ending (4,000 units)	9,742	(4,000# × $2.1856)+(0# × $0.10)+(1,000# × $1)		
(A)+(B)+(C)	Total costs accounted for	$30,770			

*Total costs of good units completed and transferred out in Step 5 Panel B of Solution Exhibit 18-30.
#Equivalent units of direct materials and conversion costs calculated in Step 2 in Panel A above.

18-34 (20–25 min.) **Job-costing spoilage and scrap.**

1. a. Materials Control   600
    Manufacturing Department Overhead Control   800
     Work-in-Process Control   1,400
    (650 + 500 + 250 = 1,400)

   b. Accounts Receivable   1,250
     Work-in-Process Control   1,250

2. a. The clause does not specify whether the 1% calculation is to be based on the input cost ($26,951 + $15,076 + $7,538) or the cost of the good output before the "1% normal spoilage" is added.

   b. *If the inputs are used to determine the 1%:*

      $26,951 + $15,076 + $7,538 = $49,565

  1% of $49,565 = $495.65 or $496, rounded. Then, the entry to leave the $496 "normal spoilage" cost on the job, remove the salvageable material, and charge manufacturing overhead would be:

    Materials Control   600
    Manufacturing Department Overhead Control   304
     Work-in-Process Control   904
    ($800 spoilage minus $496 = $304 spoilage
    cost that is taken out of the job;
    $600 salvage value plus $304 = $904; or
    $1,400 minus $496 = $904)

   If the outputs are used to determine the 1%:

     $26,951 – $650 = $26,301
      15,076 – 500 = 14,576
      7,538 – 250 =   7,288
     $49,565 $48,165

Then, $48,165 × 1% = $481.65 or $482, rounded. The journal entry would be:

    Materials Control   600
    Manufacturing Department Overhead Control   318
     Work-in-Process Control   918

18-36 (30 min.) **Job costing, scrap.**

1.   Materials Control   10,000
         Manufacturing Overhead Control   10,000
    (To record scrap common to all jobs at the time it is
    returned to the storeroom)

2.   Cash or Accounts Receivable   10,000
         Materials Control   10,000
    (To record sale of scrap from the storeroom)

3.   A summary of the manufacturing costs for HM3 and JB4 before considering the value of scrap are as follows:

	HM3	JB4	Total Costs
Direct materials	$200,000	$150,000	$350,000
Direct manufacturing labor	60,000	40,000	100,000
Manufacturing overhead			
(200% of direct manufacturing labor)	120,000	80,000	200,000
Total manufacturing costs	$380,000	$270,000	$650,000
Manufacturing cost per unit	$19	$27	
($380,000 ÷ 20,000; $270,000 ÷ 10,000)			

The value of scrap of $10,000 generated during March will reduce manufacturing overhead costs by $10,000 from $200,000 to $190,000. Manufacturing overhead will then be allocated at 190% of direct manufacturing labor costs ($190,000 ÷ $100,000 = 190%)

    The revised manufacturing cost per unit would then be:

	HM3	JB4	Total Costs
Direct materials	$200,000	$150,000	$350,000
Direct manufacturing labor	60,000	40,000	100,000
Manufacturing overhead			
(190% of direct manufacturing labor)	114,000	76,000	190,000
Total manufacturing costs	$374,000	$266,000	$640,000
Manufacturing cost per unit	$18.70	$26.60	
($374,000 ÷ 20,000; $266,000 ÷ 10,000)			

18-38 (25–35 min.) **Weighted-average method, inspection at 80% completion (chapter appendix).**

The computation and allocation of spoilage is the most difficult part of this problem. The units in the ending inventory have passed inspection. Therefore, of the 80,000 units to account for (10,000 beginning + 70,000 started), 10,000 must have been spoiled in June [80,000 – (50,000 completed + 20,000 ending inventory)]. Normal spoilage is 7,000 [0.10 × (50,000 + 20,000)]. The 3,000 remainder is abnormal spoilage (10,000 – 7,000).

Solution Exhibit 18-38, Panel A, calculates the equivalent units of work done for each cost category. We comment on several points in this calculation:

- Ending work in process includes an element of normal spoilage since all the ending WIP have passed the point of inspection—inspection occurs when production is 80% complete, while the units in ending WIP are 95% complete.
- Spoilage includes no direct materials units because spoiled units are detected and removed from the finishing activity when inspection occurs at the time production is 80% complete. Direct materials are added only later when production is 90% complete.
- Direct materials units are included for ending work in process, which is 95% complete, but not for beginning work in process, which is 25% complete. The reason is that direct materials are added when production is 90% complete. The ending work in process, therefore, contains direct materials units; the beginning work in process does not.

Solution Exhibit 18-38, Panel B, computes the costs per equivalent unit for each cost category, summarizes total costs to account for, and assigns these costs to units completed (including normal spoilage), to abnormal spoilage, and to units in ending work in process using the weighted-average method. The cost of ending work in process includes the assignment of normal spoilage costs since these units have passed the point of inspection. The costs assigned to each cost category are as follows:

Cost of good units completed and transferred out (including normal spoilage costs on good units)	$1,877,350
Abnormal spoilage	67,710
Cost of ending work in process (including normal spoilage costs on ending work in process)	734,140
Total costs assigned and accounted for	$2,679,200

SOLUTION EXHIBIT 18-38
Weighted-Average Method of Process Costing with Spoilage;
Finishing Department of the Ottawa Manufacturing Company for June.

PANEL A: Steps 1 and 2—Summarize Output in Physical Units and Compute Output in Equivalent Units

| | (Step 1) | (Step 2) Equivalent Units | | |
Flow of Production	Physical Units	Transferred-in Costs	Direct Materials	Conversion Costs
Work in process, beginning (given)	10,000			
Started during current period (given)	70,000			
To account for	80,000			
Good units completed and transferred out during current period:	50,000	50,000	50,000	50,000
Normal spoilage on good units*	5,000			
5,000 × 100%; 5,000 × 0%; 5,000 × 80%		5,000	0	4,000
Work in process, ending‡ (given)	20,000			
20,000 × 100%; 20,000 × 100%; 20,000 × 95%		20,000	20,000	19,000
Normal spoilage on ending WIP**	2,000			
2,000 × 100%; 2,000 × 0%; 2,000 × 80%		2,000	0	1,600
Abnormal spoilage†	3,000			
3,000 × 100%; 3,000 × 0%; 3,000 × 80%		3,000	0	2,400
Accounted for	80,000			
Work done to date		80,000	70,000	77,000

*Normal spoilage is 10% of good units that pass inspection: 10% × 50,000 = 5,000 units. Degree of completion of normal spoilage in this department: transferred-in costs, 100%; direct materials, 0%; conversion costs, 80%.

‡Degree of completion in this department: transferred-in costs, 100%; direct materials, 100%; conversion costs, 95%.

**Normal spoilage is 10% of the good units in ending WIP that have passed the inspection point, 10% × 20,000 = 2,000 units. Degree of completion of normal spoilage in this department: transferred-in costs, 100%; direct materials, 0%; conversion costs, 80%.

†Abnormal spoilage = Actual spoilage – Normal spoilage = 10,000 – 7,000 = 3,000 units. Degree of completion of abnormal spoilage in this department: transferred-in costs, 100%; direct materials, 0%; conversion costs, 80%.

PANEL B: Steps 3, 4, and 5—Compute Cost per Equivalent Unit, Summarize Total Costs to Account For, and Assign Total Costs to Units Completed, to Spoiled Units, and to Units in Ending Work in Process

		Total Production Costs	Transferred-in Costs	Direct Materials	Conversion Costs
(Step 3)	Work in process, beginning (given)	$ 124,900	$ 82,900	$ –	$ 42,000
	Costs added in current period (given)	2,554,300	647,500	655,200	1,251,600
	Costs incurred to date		730,400	655,200	1,293,600
	Divided by equivalent units of work done to date		÷ 80,000	÷ 70,000	÷ 77,000
	Cost per equivalent unit		$ 9.13	$ 9.36	$ 16.80
(Step 4)	Total costs to account for	$2,679,200			
(Step 5)	Assignment of costs				
	Good units completed and transferred out (50,000 units)				
	Costs before adding normal spoilage	$1,764,500	50,000# × ($9.13 + $9.36 + $16.80)		
	Normal spoilage (5,000 units)	112,850	(5,000# × $9.13) + (0# × $9.36) + (4,000# × $16.80)		
(A)	Total costs of good units completed and transferred out	1,877,350			
(B)	Abnormal spoilage (3,000 units)	67,710	(3,000# × $9.13) + (0# × $9.36) + (2,400# × $16.80)		
	Work in process, ending (20,000 units)				
	WIP ending, before normal spoilage	689,000	(20,000# × $9.13) + (20,000# × $9.36) + (19,000# × $16.80)		
	Normal spoilage on ending WIP	45,140	(2,000# × $9.13) + (0# × $9.36) + (1,600# × $16.80)		
(C)	Total costs of ending WIP	734,140			
(A)+(B)+(C)	Total costs accounted for	$2,679,200			

#Equivalent units of transferred-in costs, direct materials, and conversion costs calculated in Step 2 in Panel A.

18-40 (35 min.) **Weighted-average method, spoilage, working backward.**

1.   Equivalent units of work done to date can be calculated using Step 2 as follows:

	Direct Materials	Conversion Costs
Work in process, January 1	$ 220,000	$ 30,000
Costs added in January	1,460,000	942,000
Total costs incurred to date	$1,680,000	$972,000
Divided by cost per equivalent unit of work done to date	÷ $20	÷ $12
Equivalent units of work done to date	84,000	81,000

2.   Solution Exhibit 18-40A shows the equivalent units of work done (a) for good units completed and transferred out of inventory during January, (b) for normal spoilage, and (c) for abnormal spoilage. The sum of these equivalent units is then subtracted from the total equivalent units of work done to date (direct materials, 84,000 units, and conversion costs, 81,000 units) to determine the equivalent units in ending work in process (direct materials, 15,000, and conversion costs, 12,000). This is also shown in Solution Exhibit 18-40A.

3.   To summarize total costs to account for and to assign those costs to units completed and transferred out (including normal spoilage), to abnormal spoilage, and to ending work in process, we first need to estimate the percentage of completion of ending work in process for each cost category.   We know that there are 15,000 physical units of ending work in process. The percentage of completion of ending work in process for each cost category can then be calculated as follows:

	Direct Materials	Conversion Costs
Equivalent units of ending work in process (requirement 2)	15,000	12,000
Divided by physical units of ending work in process	÷15,000	÷15,000
Percentage of completion of ending work in process	100%	80%

Solution Exhibit 18-40B summarizes total costs to account for, and assigns these costs to units completed and transferred out (including normal spoilage), to abnormal spoilage, and to units in ending work in process.

SOLUTION EXHIBIT 18-40A
Weighted Average Method of Process Costing with Spoilage at Ferguson, Inc., for January.

Steps 1 and 2—Summarize Output in Physical Units and Compute Output in Equivalent Units

Flow of Production	(Step 1) Physical Units	(Step 2) Equivalent Units Direct Materials	Conversion Costs
Work in process, beginning (given)	10,000		
Started during current period (given)	74,000		
To account for	84,000		
Good units completed and transferred out during current period:	61,000	61,000	61,000
Normal spoilage[a]	6,100		
(6,100 × 100%; 6,100 × 100%)		6,100	6,100
Abnormal spoilage[b]	1,900		
(1,900 × 100%; 1,900 × 100%)		1,900	1,900
Work in process, ending (given)	15,000		
		15,000[c]	12,000[d]
Accounted for	84,000		
Work done to date (from Requirement 1)		84,000	81,000

[a]Normal spoilage = 10% of good units tsfd. out = 0.1 × 61,000 = 6,100 units. Degree of completion of normal spoilage direct materials, 100%; conversion costs, 100%.

[b]Abnormal spoilage = Spoiled units - Normal spoilage = 8,000 - 6,100 = 1,900 units.
 Degree of completion of abnormal spoilage: direct materials, 100%; conversion costs, 100%.

[c] Ending work in process eqvt. units of dir. matl. = 84,000 - (61,000 + 6,100 + 1,900) = 15,000 eqvt units

[d] Ending work in process eqvt. units of conv. costs = 81,000 - (61,000 + 6,100 + 1,900) = 12,000 eqvt units

SOLUTION EXHIBIT 18-40B
Weighted Average Method of Process Costing with Spoilage at Ferguson, Inc., for January.

Steps 3, 4, and 5—Compute Cost per Equivalent Unit, Summarize Total Costs to Account For, and Assign Total Costs to Units Completed, to Spoiled Units, and to Units in Ending Work in Process

		Total Production Costs	Direct Materials	Conversion Costs
(Step 3)	Work in process, beginning (given)	$ 250,000	$ 220,000	$ 30,000
	Costs added in current period (given)	2,402,000	1,460,000	942,000
	Costs incurred to date		$1,680,000	$972,000
	Divide by equivalent units of work done to date		÷ 84,000	÷ 81,000
	Cost per equivalent unit		$ 20.00	$ 12.00
(Step 4)	Total costs to account for	$2,652,000		
(Step 5)	Assignment of costs:			
	Good units completed and transferred out (61,000 units)			
	Costs before adding normal spoilage	$1,952,000	(61,000^e × $20)	+ (61,000^e × $12)
	Normal spoilage (6,100 units)	195,200	(6,100^e × $20)	+ (6,100^e × $12)
(A)	Total costs of good units completed and transferred out	2,147,200		
(B)	Abnormal spoilage (1,900 units)	60,800	(1,900^e × $20)	+ (1,900^e × $12)
(C)	Work in process, ending (15,000 units):	444,000	(15,000^e × $20)	+ (12,000^e × $12)
(A) + (B) + (C)	Total costs accounted for	$2,652,000		

^{e}Equivalent units of direct materials and conversion costs calculated in step 2 in Solution Exhibit 18-40A.

CHAPTER 19
BALANCED SCORECARD: QUALITY, TIME, AND THE THEORY OF CONSTRAINTS

19-2 Quality of design refers to how closely the characteristics of a product or service meet the needs and wants of customers. Conformance quality refers to the performance of a product or service relative to its design and product specifications.

19-4 An internal failure cost differs from an external failure cost on the basis of when the nonconforming product is detected. An internal failure is detected *before* a product is shipped to a customer, whereas an external failure is detected *after* a product is shipped to a customer.

19-6 No, companies should emphasize financial as well as nonfinancial measures of quality, such as yield and defect rates. Nonfinancial measures are not directly linked to bottom-line performance but they indicate and direct attention to the specific areas that need improvement to improve the bottom line. Tracking nonfinancial measures over time directly reveals whether these areas have, in fact, improved over time. Nonfinancial measures are easy to quantify and easy to understand.

19-8 Examples of nonfinancial measures of internal-business-process quality:
1. the percentage of defects for each product line;
2. process yield (rates of good output to total output at a particular process;
3. manufacturing lead time (the amount of time from when an order is received by production to when it becomes a finished good); and
4. number of product and process design changes

19-10 No. There is a trade-off between customer-response time and on-time performance. Simply scheduling longer customer-response time makes achieving on-time performance easier. Companies should, however, attempt to reduce the uncertainty of the arrival of orders, manage bottlenecks, reduce setup and processing time, and run smaller batches. This would have the effect of reducing both customer-response time and improving on-time performance.

19-12 No. Adding a product when capacity is constrained and the timing of customer orders is uncertain causes delays in delivering all existing products. If the revenue losses from delays in delivering existing products and the increase in carrying costs of the existing products exceed the positive contribution earned by the product that was added, then it is not worthwhile to make and sell the new product, despite its positive contribution margin. The chapter describes the negative effects (negative externalities) that one product can have on others when products share common manufacturing facilities.

19-14 The four key steps in managing bottleneck resources are:
Step 1: Recognize that the bottleneck operation determines throughput contribution of the entire system.
Step 2: Search for, and identify the bottleneck operation.
Step 3: Keep the bottleneck operation busy, and subordinate all nonbottleneck operations to the bottleneck operation.
Step 4: Increase bottleneck efficiency and capacity.

19-16 (30 min.) **Costs of quality.**

1. The ratios of each COQ category to revenues and to total quality costs for each period are as follows:

Costen, Inc.: Semi-annual Costs of Quality Report
(in thousands)

	6/30/2006			12/31/2006			6/30/2007			12/31/2007		
	Actual	% of Revenues	% of Total Quality Costs	Actual	% of Revenues	% of Total Quality Costs	Actual	% of Revenues	% of Total Quality Costs	Actual	% of Revenues	% of Total Quality Costs
	(1)	(2) = (1) ÷ $8,240	(3) = (1) ÷ $2,040	(4)	(5) = (4) ÷ $9,080	(6) = (4) ÷ $2,159	(7)	(8) = (7) ÷ $9,300	(9) = (7) ÷ $1,605	(10)	(11) = (10) ÷ $9,020	(12) = (10) ÷ $1,271
Prevention costs												
Machine maintenance	$440			$440			$390			$330		
Supplier training	20			100			50			40		
Design reviews	50			214			210			200		
Total prevention costs	510	6.2%	25.0%	754	8.3%	34.9%	650	7.0%	40.5%	570	6.3%	44.9%
Appraisal costs												
Incoming inspection	108			123			90			63		
Final testing	332			332			293			203		
Total appraisal costs	440	5.3%	21.6%	455	5.0%	21.1%	383	4.1%	23.9%	266	3.0%	20.9%
Internal failure costs												
Rework	231			202			165			112		
Scrap	124			116			71			67		
Total internal failure costs	355	4.3%	17.4%	318	3.5%	14.7%	236	2.5%	14.7%	179	2.0%	14.1%
External failure costs												
Warranty repairs	165			85			72			68		
Customer returns	570			547			264			188		
Total external failure costs	735	8.9%	36.0%	632	7.0%	29.3%	336	3.6%	20.9%	256	2.8%	20.1%
Total quality costs	$2,040	24.7%	100.0%	$2,159	23.8%	100.0%	$1,605	17.2%	100.0%	$1,271	14.1%	100.0%
Total production and revenues	$8,240			$9,080			$9,300			$9,020		

2.   From an analysis of the Cost of Quality Report, it would appear that Costen, Inc.'s program has been successful because:

- Total quality costs as a percentage of total revenues have declined from 24.7% to 14.1%.
- External failure costs, those costs signaling customer dissatisfaction, have declined from 8.9% of total revenues to 2.8% of total revenues and from 36% of all quality costs to 20.1% of all quality costs. These declines in warranty repairs and customer returns should translate into increased revenues in the future.
- Internal failure costs as a percentage of revenues have been halved from 4.3% to 2%.
- Appraisal costs have decreased from 5.3% to 3% of revenues. Preventing defects from occurring in the first place is reducing the demand for final testing.
- Quality costs have shifted to the area of prevention where problems are solved before production starts: total prevention costs (maintenance, supplier training, and design reviews) have risen from 25% to 44.9% of total quality costs. The $60,000 increase in these costs is more than offset by decreases in other quality costs.
- Because of improved designs, quality training, and additional pre-production inspections, scrap and rework costs have almost been halved while increasing sales by 9.5%.
- Production does not have to spend an inordinate amount of time with customer service since they are now making the product right the first time and warranty repairs and customer returns have decreased.

3.   To estimate the opportunity cost of not implementing the quality program and to help her make her case, Jessica Tolmy could have assumed that:

- Sales and market share would continue to decline if the quality program was not implemented and then calculated the loss in revenue and contribution margin.
- The company would have to compete on price rather than quality and calculated the impact of having to lower product prices.

Opportunity costs are not recorded in accounting systems because they represent the results of what might have happened if the company had not improved quality. Nevertheless, opportunity costs of poor quality can be significant. It is important for Costen to take these costs into account when making decisions about quality.

19-18 (25 min.) **Costs-of-quality analysis, nonfinancial quality measures.**

1. & 2.

	Frostaire	% of Revs.	Coolaire	% of Revs.
Revenues				
(20,000 units × $1,500 per unit; 40,000 units × $500/unit)	$30,000,000		$20,000,000	
Prevention costs: Design				
(7,500 hrs; 2,500 hrs × $80 per hour)	600,000	2.00%	200,000	1.00%
Appraisal: Testing and inspection				
(1 hr/unit × 20,000 units; 0.15 hr/unit × 40,000 units × $50/hour)	1,000,000	3.33%	300,000	1.50%
Internal failure: Rework				
(5% × 20,000 units × $300 per unit; 10% × 40,000 units × $120 /unit)	300,000	1.00%	480,000	2.40%
External failure: Repair				
(4% × 20,000 units × $400/unit; 8% × 40,000 units × $180/unit)	320,000	1.07%	576,000	2.88%
Lost contribution due to poor quality				
(500 × ($1,500 – $800); 4,000 × ($500 – $300))	350,000	1.17%	800,000	4.00%
Total cost of quality	$2,570,000	8.57%	$2,356,000	11.78%

- Overall, Frostaire seems to be of higher quality than Coolaire. The total cost of quality for Frostaire is 8.57% of revenues, versus 11.78% for Coolaire. This quality advantage may be related to Ambrose's ability to sell Frostaire at $1,500 per unit versus Coolaire at $500 per unit and also to the larger lost contribution due to poor quality from Coolaire than from Frostaire ($800,000 or 4% of revenues due to Coolaire; $350,000 or 1.17% of revenues due to Frostaire).
- In the Frostaire line, the focus of quality efforts is on prevention and appraisal (total of 5.33% of revenues spent on quality, versus 2.5% in the case of Coolaire); in the Coolaire line, quality resources are mostly spent on internal and external failure costs and opportunity costs (total of 9.28% of revenues versus 3.24% for Frostaire).

3.   Examples of nonfinancial quality measures that Ambrose Industries could monitor in its balanced scorecard as part of a total-quality program:

   a. number of defective units shipped to customers as a percentage of total units shipped;
   b. ratio of good output to total output at each production process; and
   c. percent of customers who would buy another Ambrose product or recommend it as their top choice to other potential buyers.

19-20 (25 min.) Quality improvement, relevant costs, and relevant revenues.

1.   Relevant costs over the next year of choosing the new lens = $55 × 20,000 copiers = $1,100,000

	Relevant Benefits over the Next Year of Choosing the New Lens
Costs of quality items	
Savings on rework costs	
$40 × 12,875 rework hours	$ 515,000
Savings in customer-support costs	
$20 × 900 customer-support-hours	18,000
Savings in transportation costs for parts	
$180 × 200 fewer loads	36,000
Savings in warranty repair costs	
$45 × 7,000 repair-hours	315,000
Opportunity costs	
Contribution margin from increased sales	900,000
Cost savings and additional contribution margin	$1,784,000

Because the expected relevant benefits of $1,784,000 exceed the expected relevant costs of the new lens of $1,100,000, Photon should introduce the new lens. Note that the opportunity cost benefits in the form of higher contribution margin from increased sales is an important component for justifying the investment in the new lens.

2. The incremental cost of the new lens of $1,100,000 is greater than the incremental savings in rework and repair costs of $884,000 ($515,000 + $18,000 + $36,000 + $315,000). Investing in the new lens is beneficial, provided it generates additional contribution margin of at least $216,000 ($1,100,000 − $884,000). Contribution margin per unit is $900,000 ÷ 150 copies = $6,000 per copier. Therefore, Photon needs additional unit sales of at least $216,000 ÷ $6,000 = 36 copiers to justify investing in the new lens on financial considerations alone.

19-22 20 min.) Waiting time, banks.

1.   If the branch expects to receive 40 customers each day and it takes 5 minutes to serve a customer, the average time that a customer will wait in line before being served is:

$$= \frac{\left(\begin{array}{c}\text{Average number} \\ \text{of customers}\end{array}\right) \times \left(\begin{array}{c}\text{Time taken to} \\ \text{serve a customer}\end{array}\right)^2}{2 \times \left[\begin{array}{c}\text{Available time} \\ \text{counter is open}\end{array} - \left[\left(\begin{array}{c}\text{Average number} \\ \text{of customers}\end{array}\right) \times \left(\begin{array}{c}\text{Time taken to} \\ \text{serve a customer}\end{array}\right)\right]\right]}$$

$$= \frac{[40 \times (5)^2]}{2 \times [300 - (40 \times 5)]} = \frac{(40 \times 25)}{2 \times (300 - 200)} = \frac{1,000}{2 \times 100} = \frac{1,000}{200} = 5 \text{ minutes}$$

2.   If the branch expects to receive 50 customers each day and the time taken to serve a customer is 5 minutes, the average time that a customer will wait in line before being served is:

$$= \frac{[50 \times (5)^2]}{2 \times [300 - (50 \times 5)]} = \frac{(50 \times 25)}{2 \times (300 - 250)} = \frac{50 \times 25}{2 \times 50} = \frac{1,250}{100} = 12.5 \text{ minutes}$$

3.   If the branch expects to serve 50 customers each day and the time taken to serve a customer is 4 minutes, the average time that a customer will wait in line before being served is:

$$= \frac{[50 \times (4)^2]}{2 \times [300 - (50 \times 4)]} = \frac{(50 \times 16)}{2 \times (300 - 200)} = \frac{50 \times 16}{2 \times 100} = \frac{800}{200} = 4 \text{ minutes}$$

19-24 (15 min.) Theory of constraints, throughput contribution, relevant costs.

1.   Finishing is a bottleneck operation. Therefore, producing 1,000 more units will generate additional throughput contribution and operating income.

Increase in throughput contribution ($72 – $32) × 1,000	$40,000
Incremental costs of the jigs and tools	30,000
Net benefit of investing in jigs and tools	$10,000

Mayfield should invest in the modern jigs and tools because the benefit of higher throughput contribution of $40,000 exceeds the cost of $30,000.

2. The Machining Department has excess capacity and is not a bottleneck operation. Increasing its capacity further will not increase throughput contribution. There is, therefore, no benefit from spending $5,000 to increase the Machining Department's capacity by 10,000 units. Mayfield should not implement the change to do setups faster.

19-26 (15 min.) Theory of constraints, throughput contribution, quality.

1. Cost of defective unit at machining operation which is not a bottleneck operation is the loss in direct materials (variable costs) of $32 per unit. Producing 2,000 units of defectives does not result in loss of throughput contribution. Despite the defective production, machining can produce and transfer 80,000 units to finishing. Therefore, cost of 2,000 defective units at the machining operation is $32 × 2,000 = $64,000.

2. A defective unit produced at the bottleneck finishing operation costs Mayfield materials costs plus the opportunity cost of lost throughput contribution. Bottleneck capacity not wasted in producing defective units could be used to generate additional sales and throughput contribution. Cost of 2,000 defective units at the finishing operation is:

Loss of direct materials $32 × 2,000	$ 64,000
Forgone throughput contribution ($72 – $32) × 2,000	80,000
Total cost of 2,000 defective units	$144,000

Alternatively, the cost of 2,000 defective units at the finishing operation can be calculated as the lost revenue of $72 × 2,000 = $144,000. This line of reasoning takes the position that direct materials costs of $32 × 2,000 = $64,000 and all fixed operating costs in the machining and finishing operations would be incurred anyway whether a defective or good unit is produced. The cost of producing a defective unit is the revenue lost of $144,000.

19-28 (30 min.) Quality improvement, relevant costs, and relevant revenues.

1. By implementing the new method, Tan would incur additional direct materials costs on all the 200,000 units started at the molding operation.

Additional direct materials costs = $4 per lamp × 200,000 lamps	$800,000
The relevant benefits of adding the new material are:	
Increased revenue from selling 30,000 more lamps	
$40 per lamp × 30,000 lamps	$1,200,000

Note that Tan Corporation continues to incur the same total variable costs of direct materials, direct manufacturing labor, setup labor and materials handling labor, and the same fixed costs of equipment, rent, and allocated overhead that it is currently incurring, even when it improves quality. Since these costs do not differ among the alternatives of adding the new material or not adding the new material, they are excluded from the analysis. The relevant benefit of adding the new material is the extra revenue that Tan would get from producing 30,000 good lamps.

An alternative approach to analyzing the problem is to focus on scrap costs and the benefits of reducing scrap.

The relevant benefits of adding the new material are:

a. Cost savings from eliminating scrap:

    Variable cost per lamp, $19[a] × 30,000 lamps $ 570,000

b. Additional contribution margin from selling
    another 30,000 lamps because 30,000 lamps
    will no longer be scrapped:

    Unit contribution margin $21[b] × 30,000 lamps   630,000

Total benefits to Tan of adding new material to improve quality $1,200,000

[a] Note that only the variable scrap costs of $19 per lamp (direct materials, $16 per lamp; direct manufacturing labor, setup labor, and materials handling labor, $3 per lamp) are relevant because improving quality will save these costs. Fixed scrap costs of equipment, rent, and other allocated overhead are irrelevant because these costs will be incurred whether Tan Corporation adds or does not add the new material.

[b] Contribution margin per unit

Selling price		$40.00
Variable costs:		
Direct materials costs per lamp	$16.00	
Molding department variable manufacturing costs		
per lamp (direct manufacturing labor, setup labor, and		
materials handling labor)	3.00	
Variable costs		(19.00)
Unit contribution margin		$21.00

On the basis of quantitative considerations alone, Tan should use the new material. Relevant benefits of $1,200,000 exceed the relevant costs of $800,000 by $400,000.

2. Other nonfinancial and qualitative factors that Tan should consider in making a decision include the effects of quality improvement on:

    a. gaining manufacturing expertise that could lead to further cost reductions in the future;

    b. enhanced reputation and increased customer goodwill which could lead to higher future revenues through greater unit sales and higher sales prices; and

    c. higher employee morale as a result of higher quality.

19-30 (30–40 min.)   **Compensation linked with profitability, on-time delivery, and external quality-performance measures.**

1.

	Jan.-June	July-Dec.
Detroit		
Add: Profitability		
2% of operating income	$33,000	$ 32,000
Add: On-time delivery		
$10,000 if >= 98%	10,000	0
Deduct: Product quality		
50% of cost of sales returns	(22,000)	(17,500)
Total: Bonus paid	$21,000	$ 14,500
Los Angeles		
Add: Profitability		
2% of operating income	$62,000	$74,000
Add: On-time delivery		
$10,000 if >= 98%	0	10,000
Deduct: Product quality		
50% of cost of sales returns	(34,500)	(25,000)
Total: Bonus paid	$27,500	$59,000

2.   *Operating income as a measure of profitability*

Operating income captures revenue and cost-related factors. However, there is no recognition of investment differences between the two plants. The Los Angeles plant's operating income is approximately double that of Detroit. This difference gives the Los Angeles plant manager the opportunity to earn a larger bonus due to investment size alone. An alternative approach would be to use return on investment (perhaps relative to the budgeted ROI).

98% on-time benchmark as a measure of on-time delivery performance

This measure reflects the ability of Pacific-Dunlop to meet a benchmark for on-time delivery. Several concerns arise with this specific measure:

  a. It is a yes-or-no cut-off. A 10% on-time performance earns no bonus, but neither does a 97.9% on-time performance. Moreover, no extra bonus is paid for performance above 98.0%. An alternative is to have the bonus be a percentage of the on-time delivery percentage.
  b. It can be manipulated by management. The Pacific-Dunlop plant manager may quote conservative delivery dates to sales people in an effort to "guarantee" that the 98% target is achieved.
  c. It reflects performance relative only to scheduled delivery date. It does not consider how quickly Pacific-Dunlop can respond to customer orders.

Problems in (b) and (c) can be overcome by measuring customer response time (how long it takes from the time a customer places an order for a product to the time the product is delivered to the customer), in addition to on-time delivery.

50% of cost of sales returns as a measure of quality

This measure incorporates one cost that arises with defective goods. However, there are several concerns with its use:

a. Not all sales returns are due to defective work by the plant manager. Some returns are due to tampering by the customer. Other returns arise from breakage during delivery and installation.

b. It does not systematically incorporate customer opinion about quality. Not all customers return defective goods.

c. It ignores important categories of the cost of defective goods. For example, dissatisfied customers may decline to make any subsequent purchases.

These last two problems with the cost of sales measure may be overcome by taking a customer satisfaction survey and incorporating a percentage of estimated lost contribution as a result of quality problems. This new measure, however, is likely to be "noisy" or very sensitive to assumptions. A combination of measures may work well as a composite measure of quality.

3.   Most companies use both financial and nonfinancial measures to evaluate performance, sometimes presented in a single report such as a balanced scorecard. Using multiple measures of performance enables top management to evaluate whether lower-level managers have improved one area at the expense of others. For example, did the on-time delivery performance of the Detroit plant manager decrease in the July–December period relative to the January–June period because the manager emphasized shipment of high-margin products to increase operating income?

If on-time delivery is dropped as a performance evaluation measure, managers will concentrate on increasing operating income and decreasing sales returns but will give less attention to on-time delivery. Consider the following situation: Suppose a manager must choose between (a) delivering a high margin order that will add to operating income while delaying a number of other orders and adversely affecting on-time performance, or (b) delaying the high margin order and sacrificing some operating income, to achieve better on-time performance. What action will the manager take? If on-time performance is excluded as a performance evaluation measure, the manager will almost certainly choose (a). Only if on-time performance is included in the manager's performance evaluation will the manager consider choosing option (b).

19-32 (60 min.) **Waiting times, relevant revenues, and relevant costs (continuation of 19-31).**

1. The direct approach is to look at incremental revenues and incremental costs.

Selling price per order of Y28, which has an average manufacturing lead time of 350 hours	$ 8,000
Variable cost per order	5,000
Additional contribution per order of Y28	3,000
Multiply by expected number of orders	× 25
Increase in expected contribution from Y28	$75,000

Expected loss in revenues and increase in costs from introducing Y28

Product (1)	Expected Loss in Revenues from Increasing Average Manufacturing Lead Times for All Products (2)	Expected Increase in Carrying Costs from Increasing Average Manufacturing Lead Times for All Products (3)	Expected Loss in Revenues Plus Expected Increases in Carrying Costs of Introducing Y28 (4) = (2) + (3)
Z39	$25,000.00[a]	$6,375.00[b]	$31,375.00
Y28	–	2,187.50[c]	2,187.50
Total	$25,000.00	$8,562.50	$33,562.50

[a] 50 orders × ($27,000 – $26,500)
[b] (410 hours – 240 hours) × $0.75 × 50 orders
[c] (350 hours – 0) × $0.25 × 25

Increase in expected contribution from Y28 of $75,000 is greater than increase in expected costs of $33,562.50 by $41,437.50. Therefore, SRG should introduce Y28.

Alternative calculations of incremental revenues and incremental costs of introducing Y28:

	Alternative 1: Introduce Y28 (1)	Alternative 2: Do Not Introduce Y28 (2)	Relevant Revenues and Relevant Costs (3) = (1) – (2)
Expected revenues	$1,525,000.00[a]	$1,350,000.00[b]	$175,000.00
Expected variable costs	875,000.00[c]	750,000.00[d]	125,000.00
Expected inv. carrying costs	17,562.50[e]	9,000.00[f]	8,562.50
Expected total costs	892,562.50	759,000.00	133,562.50
Expected revenues minus expected costs	$ 632,437.50	$ 591,000.00	$ 41,437.50

[a] (50 × $26,500) + (25 × $8,000)   [b] 50 × $27,000
[c] (50 × $15,000) + (25 × $5,000)   [d] 50 × $15,000
[e] (50 × $0.75 × 410) + (25 × $0.25 × 350)   [f] 50 × $0.75 × 240

2.

Selling price per order of Y28, which has an average manufacturing lead time of more than 320 hours	$ 6,000
Variable cost per order	5,000
Additional contribution per order of Y28	$ 1,000
Multiply by expected number of orders	× 25
Increase in expected contribution from Y28	$25,000

Expected loss in revenues and increase in costs from introducing Y28:

Product (1)	Expected Loss in Revenues from Increasing Average Manufacturing Lead Times for All Products (2)	Expected Increase in Carrying Costs from Increasing Average Manufacturing Lead Times for All Products (3)	Expected Loss in Revenues Plus Expected Increases in Carrying Costs of Introducing Y28 (4) = (2) + (3)
Z39	$25,000.00[a]	$6,375.00[b]	$31,375.00
Y28	–	2,187.50[c]	2,187.50
Total	$25,000.00	$8,562.50	$33,562.50

[a] 50 orders × ($27,000 − $26,500)
[b] (410 hours − 240 hours) × $0.75 × 50 orders
[c] (350 hours − 0) × $0.25 × 25

Increase in expected contribution from Y28 of $25,000 is less than increase in expected costs of $33,562.50 by $8,562.50. Therefore, SRG should not introduce Y28.

19-34 (20 min.) Theory of constraints, throughput contribution, relevant costs.

1.   It will cost Colorado $50 per unit to reduce manufacturing time. But manufacturing is not a bottleneck operation; installation is. Therefore, manufacturing more equipment will not increase sales and throughput contribution. Colorado Industries should not implement the new manufacturing method.

2.   Additional relevant costs of new direct materials, $2,000 × 320 units, $640,000
      Increase in throughput contribution, $25,000 × 20 units, $500,000

The additional incremental costs exceed the benefits from higher throughput contribution by $140,000, so Colorado Industries should not implement the new design.

      Alternatively, compare throughput contribution under each alternative.
      Current throughput contribution is $25,000 × 300 $7,500,000
      With the modification, throughput contribution is $23,000 × 320 $7,360,000

The current throughput contribution is greater than the throughput contribution resulting from the proposed change in direct materials. Therefore, Colorado Industries should not implement the new design.

3.   Increase in throughput contribution, $25,000 × 10 units $250,000
      Increase in relevant costs $ 50,000

The additional throughput contribution exceeds incremental costs by $200,000, so Colorado Industries should implement the new installation technique.

4.   Motivating installation workers to increase productivity is worthwhile because installation is a bottleneck operation, and any increase in productivity at the bottleneck will increase throughput contribution. On the other hand, motivating workers in the manufacturing department to increase productivity is not worthwhile. Manufacturing is not a bottleneck operation, so any increase in output will result only in extra inventory of equipment. Colorado Industries should encourage manufacturing to produce only as much equipment as the installation department needs, not to produce as much as it can. Under these circumstances, it would not be a good idea to evaluate and compensate manufacturing workers on the basis of their productivity.

19-36 (25 min.) **Quality improvement, Pareto diagram, cause-and-effect diagram.**

1.   Examples of failures in accounts receivable management include the following:
   a.   uncollectible amounts or bad debts; and
   b.   delays in receiving payments.

2.   Prevention activities that could reduce failures in accounts receivable management include the following:
   a.   credit checks on customers by salespersons based on company credit policy;
   b.   shipping the correct copier to the customer;
   c.   supporting installation of the copier and answering customer questions;
   c.   sending the correct invoice, in the correct amount, and to the correct address, promptly;
   d.   following up to see if the machine is functioning smoothly; and
   e.   offering cash discounts to encourage early payment of receivables.

3.   A Pareto diagram for the problem of delays in receiving customer payments follows:

SOLUTION EXHIBIT 19-36A
Pareto Diagram for Failures in Accounts Receivables at Murray Corporation

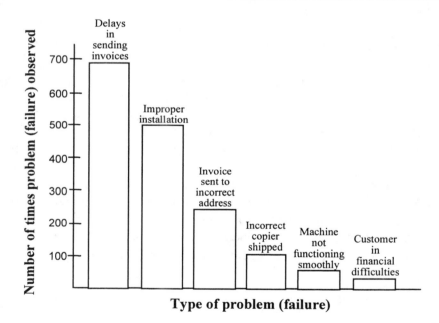

A cause-and-effect or fishbone diagram for the problem of delays in sending invoices may appear as follows:

SOLUTION EXHIBIT 19-36B
Cause-and-Effect Diagram
For Problem of Delays in Sending Invoices at Murray Corporation

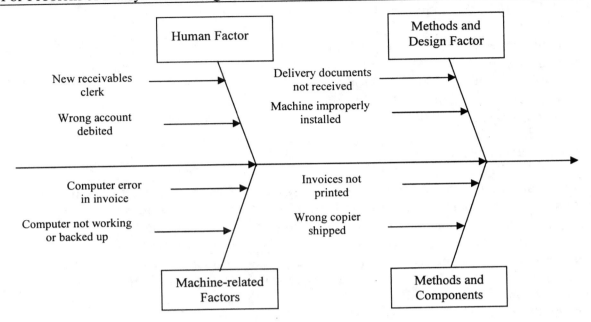

19-38 (45–50 min.) **Quality improvement, theory of constraints.**

1.   Consider the incremental revenues and incremental costs to Wellesley Corporation of purchasing additional grey cloth from outside suppliers.

Incremental revenues, $1,250 × (5,000 rolls × 0.90)		$5,625,000
Incremental costs:		
Cost of grey cloth, $900 × 5,000 rolls	$4,500,000	
Direct materials variable costs at printing		
operation, $100 × 5,000 rolls	500,000	
Incremental costs		5,000,000
Excess of incremental revenues over incremental costs		$ 625,000

Note that, because the printing department has surplus capacity equal to 5,500 (15,000 – 9,500) rolls per month, purchasing grey cloth from outside entails zero opportunity costs. Yes, the Printing Department should buy the grey cloth from the outside supplier.

2.   By producing a defective roll in the Weaving Department, Wellesley Corporation is worse off by the entire amount of revenue forgone of $1,250 per roll. Note that, since the weaving operation is a constraint, any rolls received by the Printing Department that are defective and disposed of at zero net disposal value result in lost revenue to the firm.
An alternative approach to analyzing the problem is to focus on costs of defective units and the benefits of reducing defective units.

The relevant costs of defective units in the Printing Department are:

a.	Direct materials variable costs in the Weaving Department	$ 500
b.	Direct materials variable costs in the Printing Department	100
c.	Contribution margin forgone from not selling one roll	
	$1,250 – $500 – $100	650
	Amount by which Wellesley Corporation is worse off as a	
	result of a defective unit in the Printing Department	$1,250

Note that only the variable costs of defective units of $600 per roll (direct materials in the Weaving Department, $500 per roll: direct materials in the Printing Department, $100 per roll) are relevant because improving quality will save these costs. Fixed costs of producing defective units, attributable to other operating costs, are irrelevant because these costs will be incurred whether Wellesley Corporation reduces defective units in the Printing Department or not.

Wellesley Corporation should make the proposed modifications in the Printing Department because the incremental benefits exceed the incremental costs by $125,000 per month:

Incremental benefits of reducing defective units in the Printing Department	
by 4% (from 10% to 6%)	
4% × 9,500 rolls × $1,250 per roll (computed above)	$475,000
Incremental costs of the modification	350,000
Excess of incremental benefits over incremental costs	$125,000

3.   To determine how much Wellesley Corporation is worse off by producing a defective roll in the Weaving Department, consider the payoff to Wellesley from not having a defective roll produced in the Weaving Department. The good roll produced in the Weaving Department will be sent for further processing in the Printing Department. The relevant costs and benefits of printing and selling this roll follow:

Additional direct materials variable costs incurred in the Printing Department	$ (100)
Expected revenue from selling the finished product, $1,250 × 0.9 (since 10% of the Printing Department output will be defective and will earn zero revenue)	1,125
Net expected benefit of producing a good roll in the Weaving Department	$1,025

By producing a defective roll in the Weaving Department, Wellesley Corporation is worse off by $1,025 per roll. Note that, since the weaving operation is a constraint, any rolls that are defective will result in lost revenue to the firm.

    An alternative approach to analyzing the problem is to focus on the costs and benefits of reducing defective units.

    The relevant costs of defective units in the Weaving Department are:

a.	Direct materials variable costs in the Weaving Department	$ 500
b.	Expected unit contribution margin forgone from not selling one roll, ($1,250 × 0.9) − $500 − $100	525
	Amount by which Wellesley Corporation is worse off as a result of producing a defective unit in the Weaving Department	$1,025

Note that only the variable scrap costs of $500 per roll (direct materials in the Weaving Department) are relevant because improving quality will save these costs. All fixed costs of producing defective units attributable to other operating costs are irrelevant because these costs will be incurred whether Wellesley Corporation reduces defective units in the Weaving Department or not.

    Wellesley Corporation should make the proposed improvements in the Printing Department because the incremental benefits exceed the incremental costs by $30,000 per month:

Incremental benefits of reducing defective units in the Weaving Department by 2% (from 5% to 3%)	
2% × 10,000 rolls × $1,025 per roll (computed above)	$205,000
Incremental costs of improvements	175,000
Excess of incremental benefits over incremental costs	$ 30,000

CHAPTER 20
INVENTORY MANAGEMENT, JUST-IN-TIME,
AND BACKFLUSH COSTING

20-2 Five cost categories important in managing goods for sale in a retail organization are the following:
1. purchasing costs;
2. ordering costs;
3. carrying costs;
4. stockout costs; and
5. quality costs

20-4 Costs included in the carrying costs of inventory are incremental costs for such items as insurance, rent, obsolescence, spoilage, and breakage plus the opportunity cost of capital (or required return on investment).

20-6 The steps in computing the costs of a prediction error when using the EOQ decision model are:

Step 1: Compute the monetary outcome from the best action that could be taken, given the actual amount of the cost input.

Step 2: Compute the monetary outcome from the best action based on the incorrect amount of the predicted cost input.

Step 3: Compute the difference between the monetary outcomes from Steps 1 and 2.

20-8 Just-in-time (JIT) purchasing is the purchase of materials (or goods) so that they are delivered just as needed for production (or sales). Benefits include lower inventory holdings (reduced warehouse space required and less money tied up in inventory) and less risk of inventory obsolescence and spoilage.

20.10 Disagree. Choosing the supplier who offers the lowest price will not necessarily result in the lowest total purchase cost to the buyer. This is because the price or purchase cost of the goods is only one—and perhaps, most obvious—element of cost associated with purchasing and managing inventories. Other relevant cost items are ordering costs, carrying costs, stockout costs and quality costs. A low-cost supplier may well impose conditions on the buyer—such as poor quality, or frequent stockouts, or excessively high inventories—that result in high total costs of purchase. Buyers must examine all the elements of costs relevant to inventory management, not just the purchase price.

20-12 Obstacles to companies adopting a supply-chain approach include:
- Communication obstacles—the unwillingness of some parties to share information.
- Trust obstacles—includes the concern that all parties will not meet their agreed-upon commitments.
- Information system obstacles—includes problems due to the information systems of different parties not being technically compatible.
- Limited resources—includes problems due to the people and financial resources given to support a supply chain initiative not being adequate.

20-14 Traditional normal and standard costing systems use sequential tracking, in which journal entries are recorded in the same order as actual purchases and progress in production, typically at four different trigger points in the process.

Backflush costing omits recording some of the journal entries relating to the cycle from purchase of direct materials to sale of finished goods, i.e., it has fewer trigger points at which journal entries are made. When journal entries for one or more stages in the cycle are omitted, the journal entries for a subsequent stage use normal or standard costs to work backward to "flush out" the costs in the cycle for which journal entries were not made.

20-16 (20 min.) **Economic order quantity for retailer.**

1. $D = 10{,}000, P = \$225, C = \$10$

$$EOQ = \sqrt{\frac{2\,DP}{C}} = \sqrt{\frac{2 \times 10{,}000 \times \$225}{10}}$$

$$= 670.82$$

$$\cong 671 \text{ jerseys}$$

2. Number of orders per year $= \dfrac{D}{EOQ} = \dfrac{10{,}000}{671}$

$$= 14.90$$

$$\cong \ 15 \text{ orders}$$

3. Demand each working day $= \dfrac{D}{\text{Number of working days}}$

$$= \frac{10{,}000}{365}$$

$$= 27.40 \text{ jerseys per day}$$

Purchase lead time $= 7$ days

Reorder point $= 27.40 \times 7$

$$= 191.80 \cong 192 \text{ jerseys}$$

20-18 (15 min.) **EOQ for a retailer.**

1. $D = 20{,}000,\ P = \$160,\ C = 20\% \times \$8 = \$1.60$

$$\text{EOQ} = \sqrt{\frac{2DP}{C}} = \sqrt{\frac{2 \times 20{,}000 \times \$160}{\$1.60}} = 2{,}000 \text{ yards}$$

2. Number of orders per year: $\dfrac{D}{\text{EOQ}} = \dfrac{20{,}000}{2{,}000} = 10 \text{ orders}$

3. Demand each working day $= \dfrac{D}{\text{Number of working days}}$

$= \dfrac{20{,}000}{250}$

$= 80 \text{ yards per day}$

$= 400 \text{ yards per week}$

Purchasing lead time = 2 weeks
Reorder point = 400 yards per week $\times$ 2 weeks = 800 yards

20-20 (20 min.) **Sensitivity of EOQ to changes in relevant ordering and carrying costs.**

1. A straightforward approach to the requirement is to construct the following table for EOQ at relevant carrying and ordering costs. Annual demand is 10,000 units. The formula for the EOQ model is:

$$EOQ = \sqrt{\frac{2DP}{C}}$$

where D = demand in units for a specified period of time

P = relevant ordering costs per purchase order

C = relevant carrying costs of one unit in stock for the time period used for D (one year in this problem.

Relevant Carrying Costs per Unit per Year	Relevant Ordering Costs per Purchase Order	
	$300	**$200**
$10	$\sqrt{\dfrac{2 \times 10,000 \times \$300}{\$10}} = 775$	$\sqrt{\dfrac{2 \times 10,000 \times \$200}{\$10}} = 632$
15	$\sqrt{\dfrac{2 \times 10,000 \times \$300}{\$15}} = 632$	$\sqrt{\dfrac{2 \times 10,000 \times \$200}{\$15}} = 516$
20	$\sqrt{\dfrac{2 \times 10,000 \times \$300}{\$20}} = 548$	$\sqrt{\dfrac{2 \times 10,000 \times \$200}{\$20}} = 447$

2. For a given demand level, as relevant carrying costs increase, EOQ becomes smaller. For a given demand level, as relevant order costs increase, EOQ increases.

20-22 (20 min.) **JIT production, relevant benefits, relevant costs.**

1.   Solution Exhibit 20-22 presents the annual net benefit of $315,000 to Champion Hardware Company of implementing a JIT production system.

2.   Other nonfinancial and qualitative factors that Champion should consider in deciding whether it should implement a JIT system include:
   a. The possibility of developing and implementing a detailed system for integrating the sequential operations of the manufacturing process. Direct materials must arrive when needed for each subassembly so that the production process functions smoothly.
   b. The ability to design products that use standardized parts and reduce manufacturing time.
   c. The ease of obtaining reliable vendors who can deliver quality direct materials on time with minimum lead time.
   d. Willingness of suppliers to deliver smaller and more frequent orders.
   e. The confidence of being able to deliver quality products on time. Failure to do so would result in customer dissatisfaction.
   f. The skill levels of workers to perform multiple tasks such as minor repairs, maintenance, quality testing and inspection.

SOLUTION EXHIBIT 20-22
Annual Relevant Costs of Current Production System and JIT Production System
for Champion Hardware Company

Relevant Items	Relevant Costs under Current Production System	Relevant Costs under JIT Production System
Annual tooling costs	–	$100,000
Required return on investment:		
15% per year × $1,000,000 of average inventory per year	$150,000	
15% per year × $200,000[a] of average inventory per year		30,000
Insurance, space, materials handling, and setup costs	300,000	225,000[b]
Rework costs	200,000	140,000[c]
Incremental revenues from higher selling prices	–	(160,000)[d]
Total net incremental costs	$650,000	$335,000
Annual difference in favor of JIT production	$315,000	

[a] $1,000,000 × (1 – 80%) = $200,000
[b] $300,000 × (1 – 0.25) = $225,000
[c] $200,000 × (1 – 0.30) = $140,000
[d] $4 × 40,000 units = $160,000

3.   Personal observation by production line workers and managers is more effective in JIT plants than in traditional plants. A JIT plant's production process layout is streamlined. Operations are not obscured by piles of inventory or rework. As a result, such plants are easier to evaluate by personal observation than cluttered plants where the flow of production is not logically laid out.

Besides personal observation, nonfinancial performance measures are the dominant methods of control. Nonfinancial performance measures provide most timely and easy to understand measures of plant performance. Examples of nonfinancial performance measures of time, inventory, and quality include:

- Manufacturing lead time
- Units produced per hour
- Machine setup time ÷ manufacturing time
- Number of defective units ÷ number of units completed

In addition to personal observation and nonfinancial performance measures, financial performance measures are also used. Examples of financial performance measures include:

- Cost of rework
- Ordering costs
- Stockout costs
- Inventory turnover (cost of goods sold ÷ average inventory)

The success of a JIT system depends on the speed of information flows from customers to manufacturers to suppliers. The Enterprise Resource Planning (ERP) system has a single database, and gives lower-level managers, workers, customers, and suppliers access to operating information. This benefit, accompanied by tight coordination across business functions, enables the ERP system to rapidly transmit information in response to changes in supply and demand so that manufacturing and distribution plans may be revised accordingly.

20-24 (20 min.) **Backflush costing, two trigger points, materials purchase and sale (continuation of 20-23).**

1.

(a) Purchases of direct materials	Inventory Control	2,754,000	
	Accounts Payable Control		2,754,000
(b) Incur conversion costs	Conversion Costs Control	723,600	
	Various Accounts		723,600
(c) Completion of finished goods	No entry		
(d) Sale of finished goods	Cost of Goods Sold	3,432,000	
	Inventory Control		2,692,800
	Conversion Costs Allocated		739,200
(e) Underallocated or overallocated conversion costs	Conversion Costs Allocated	739,200	
	Costs of Goods Sold		15,600
	Conversion Costs Control		723,600

2.

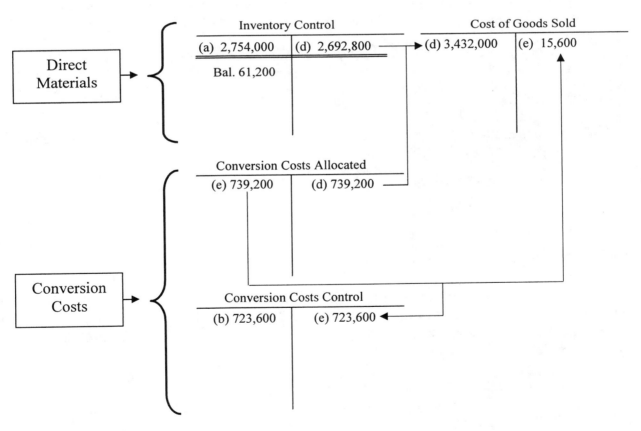

20-26 (30 min.)   **Effect of different order quantities on ordering costs and carrying costs, EOQ.**

1.

	Scenario				
	1	2	3	4	5
Demand (units) (D)	234,000	234,000	234,000	234,000	234,000
Cost per purchase order (P)	$ 81.00	$ 81.00	$ 81.00	$ 81.00	$ 81.00
Annual carrying cost per package (C)	$ 11.70	$ 11.70	$ 11.70	$ 11.70	$ 11.70
Order quantity per purchase order (units) (Q)	900	1,500	1,800	2,100	2,700
Number of purchase orders per year (D ÷ Q)	260.00	156.00	130.00	111.43	86.67
Annual ordering costs (D ÷ Q) × P	$21,060	$12,636	$10,530	$ 9,026	$ 7,020
Annual carrying costs (QC ÷ 2)	$ 5,265	$ 8,775	$10,530	$12,285	$15,795
Total relevant costs of ordering and carrying inventory	$26,325	$21,411	$21,060	$21,311	$22,815

The economic order quantity is 1,800 packages. It is the order quantity at which carrying costs equal ordering costs and total relevant ordering and carrying costs are minimized.

We can also confirm this from direct calculation. Using D = 234,000; P = $81 and C = $11.70

$$EOQ = \sqrt{\frac{2 \times 234,000 \times \$81}{\$11.70}} = 1,800 \text{ packages}$$

It is interesting to note that Koala Blue faces a situation where total relevant ordering and carrying costs do not vary very much when order quantity ranges from 1,500 packages to 2,700 packages.

2.   When the ordering cost per purchase order is reduced to $49:

$$EOQ = \sqrt{\frac{2 \times 234,000 \times \$49}{\$11.70}} = 1,400 \text{ packages}$$

The EOQ drops from 1,800 packages to 1,400 packages when Koala Blue's ordering cost per purchase order decreases from $81 to $49.

And the new relevant costs of ordering inventory $= \left(\frac{D}{Q} \times P \right) = \left(\frac{234,000}{1,400} \times \$49 \right) = \$8,190$

and the new relevant costs or carrying inventory $= \left(\frac{Q}{2} \times C \right) = \left(\frac{1,400}{2} \times \$11.70 \right) = \$8,190$

The total new costs of ordering and carrying inventory = $8,190 × 2 = $16,380

3.   As summarized below, the new Mona Lisa web-based ordering system, by lowering the EOQ to 1,400 packages, will lower the carrying and ordering costs by $4,680. Koala Blue will spend $2,000 to train its purchasing assistants on the new system. Overall, Koala Blue will still save $2,680 in the first year alone.

Total relevant costs at EOQ (from Requirement 2)	$16,380
Annual cost benefit over old system ($21,060 – $16,380)	$ 4,680
Training costs	$ 2,000
Net benefit in first year alone	$ 2,680

20-28 (20–30 min.) **EOQ, cost of prediction error.**

1. $\quad EOQ = \sqrt{\dfrac{2DP}{C}}$

$D = 2,000; \ P = \$40; \ C = \$4 + (10\% \times \$50) = \$9$

$EOQ = \sqrt{\dfrac{2 \times 2,000 \times \$40}{\$9}} = 133.333 \text{ tires} \simeq 133 \text{ tires (approximately)}$

$TRC = \dfrac{DP}{Q} + \dfrac{QC}{2} \quad$ where Q can be any quantity, including the EOQ

$\quad = \dfrac{2,000 \times \$40}{133.333} + \dfrac{133.333 \times \$9}{2} = \$600 + \$600 = \$1,200$

If students used an EOQ of 133 tires (order quantities rounded to the nearest whole number),

$TRC = \dfrac{2,000 \times \$40}{133} + \dfrac{133 \times \$9}{2} = \$601.50 + \$598.50 = \$1,200.$

Sum of annual relevant ordering and carrying costs equals $1,200.

2. $\quad$ The prediction error affects C, which is now:

$C \quad = \$4 + (10\% \times \$30) = \$7$

$D \quad = 2,000, \ P = \$40, \ C = \$7$

$EOQ = \sqrt{\dfrac{2 \times 2,000 \times \$40}{\$7}} = 151.186 \text{ tires} = 151 \text{ tires (rounded)}$

The cost of the prediction error can be calculated using a three-step procedure:

Step 1: Compute the monetary outcome from the best action that could have been taken, given the actual amount of the cost input.

$TRC \quad = \dfrac{DP}{Q} + \dfrac{QC}{2}$

$\quad = \dfrac{2,000 \times \$40}{151.186} + \dfrac{151.186 \times \$7}{2}$

$\quad = \$529.15 + \$529.15 = \$1,058.30$

Step 2: Compute the monetary outcome from the best action based on the incorrect amount of the predicted cost input.

$$\text{TRC} = \frac{DP}{Q} + \frac{QC}{2}$$

$$= \frac{2,000 \times \$40}{133.333} + \frac{133.333 \times \$7}{2}$$

$$= \$600 + \$466.67 = \$1,066.67$$

Step 3: Compute the difference between the monetary outcomes from Step 1 and Step 2:

	Monetary Outcome
Step 1	$1,058.30
Step 2	1,066.67
Difference	$ (8.37)

The cost of the prediction error is $8.37.

Note: The $20 prediction error for the purchase price of the heavy-duty tires is irrelevant in computing purchase costs under the two alternatives because the same purchase costs will be incurred whatever the order size.

Some students may prefer to round off the EOQs to 133 tires and 151 tires, respectively. The calculations under each step in this case follow:

Step 1: $\text{TRC} = \dfrac{2,000 \times \$40}{151} + \dfrac{151 \times \$7}{2} = \$529.80 + \$528.50 = \$1058.30$

Step 2: $\text{TRC} = \dfrac{2,000 \times \$40}{133} + \dfrac{133 \times \$7}{2} = \$601.50 + \$465.50 = \$1067.00$

Step 3: Difference $= \$1,058.30 - \$1,067.00 = (\$8.70)$

20-30 (25 min.) **Relevant benefits and costs of JIT purchasing, supply chain.**

Solution Exhibit 20-30 presents the cash savings of $609.90 that would result if Codleff Medical Instruments adopted the just-in-time inventory system.

SOLUTION EXHIBIT 20-30
Annual Relevant Costs of Current Purchasing Policy and JIT Purchasing Policy for Codleff Medical Instruments

| | Relevant Costs Under | |
| | Current Purchasing Policy | JIT Purchasing Policy |
Relevant Item		
Purchasing costs		
$18 per unit × 25,000 units per year	$450,000.00	
$18.02 per unit × 25,000 units per year		$450,500.00
Ordering costs		
$2 per order × 50 orders per year	100.00	
$2 per order × 500 orders per year		1,000.00
Opportunity carrying costs, required return on investment		
20% × $18 cost per unit × 250[a] units of average inventory per year	900.00	
20% × $18.02 cost per unit × 25[b] units of average inventory per year		90.10
Other carrying costs (insurance, materials handling, breakage, and so on)		
$6 per unit per year × 250[a] units of average inventory per year	1,500.00	
$6 per unit per year × 25[b] units of average inventory per year		150.00
Stockout costs		
No stockouts	0.00	
$3 per unit × 50 units per year		150.00
Total annual relevant costs	$452,500.00	$451,890.10
Annual difference in favor of JIT purchasing	$609.90	

[a] Order quantity = 25,000 ÷ 50 = 500; Average inventory = 500 ÷ 2 = 250.
[b] Order quantity = 25,000 ÷ 500 = 50; Average inventory = 50 ÷ 2 = 25.

2.   Codleff may benefit from Slocombe managing all its inventories if there is high order variability caused by randomness in when consumers purchase surgical scalpels or by trade promotions that prompt retailers to stock for the future. By coordinating their activities and sharing information about retail sales and inventory held throughout the supply chain, Slocombe can plan its manufacturing activities to ensure adequate supply of product to Codleff while keeping inventory low. For this to succeed, Codleff and Slocombe must have compatible information systems, build trust, and communicate freely.

20-32 (25 min.) **Supplier evaluation and relevant costs of quality and timely deliveries.**

Solution Exhibit 20-32 presents the $6,236 annual relevant costs difference in favor of Wayland purchasing the footballs from Bigby. On the basis of financial considerations alone, Wayland should buy the footballs from Bigby.

SOLUTION EXHIBIT 20-32
Annual Relevant Costs of Purchasing from Bigby and Kendall

Relevant Item	Relevant Costs of Purchasing from	
	Bigby	Kendall
Purchasing costs		
$40 per unit × 15,000 units per year	$600,000	
$41 per unit × 15,000 units per year		$615,000
Ordering costs		
$4 per order × 25[a] orders per year	100	
$4 per order × 25[a] orders per year		100
Inspection costs		
$0.03 per unit × 15,000 units	450	
No inspection necessary		0
Opportunity carrying costs, required return on investment		
12% × $40 × 300 units of average inventory per year	1,440	
12% × $41 × 300 units of average inventory per year		1,476
Other carrying costs (insurance, materials handling, breakage, etc.)		
$5 per unit per year × 300 units of average inventory per year	1,500	
$4.50 per unit per year × 300 units of average inventory per year		1,350
Stockout costs		
$10 per unit × 400 units per year	4,000	
$8 per unit × 100 units per year		800
Customer returns costs		
$20 per unit returned × 300 units	6,000	
$20 per unit returned × 50 units		1,000
Total annual relevant costs	$613,490	$619,726
Annual difference in favor of Bigby	$6,236	

[a]Order quantity per purchase order = 2 × average inventory held = 2 × 300 = 600 units;
   No. of orders = 15,000 units ÷ 600 units per order = 25 orders

Although Kendall is the more reliable and higher quality supplier, the financial benefits of better quality and reliability do not outweigh Kendall's higher price. Of course, Wayland should consider other financial and nonfinancial benefits of purchasing from Kendall before reaching a final decision. For example, will Kendall's higher quality and reliability
- lead to higher future sales and contribution margins? or
- improve its reputation for quality and reliability and so increase sales on other products? or
- improve employee morale?

Despite these benefits, Wayland may conclude that purchasing from Bigby is preferred, unless Kendall can lower its $41 price.

20-34 (20 min.)   **Backflush, two trigger points, materials purchase and sale (continuation of 20-33).**

1.

(a) Purchases of direct materials	Inventory Control	550,000	
	Accounts Payable Control		550,000
(b) Incur conversion costs	Conversion Costs Control	440,000	
	Various Accounts (such as Accounts Payable Control and Wages Payable Control)		440,000
(c) Completion of finished goods	No entry		
(d) Sale of finished goods	Cost of Goods Sold	900,000	
	Inventory Control		500,000
	Conversion Costs Allocated		400,000
(e) Underallocated or overallocated conversion costs	Conversion Costs Allocated	400,000	
	Cost of Goods Sold	40,000	
	Conversion Costs Control		440,000

2.

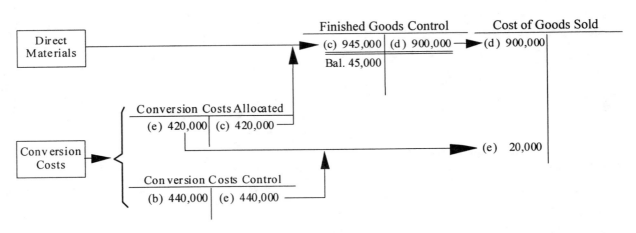

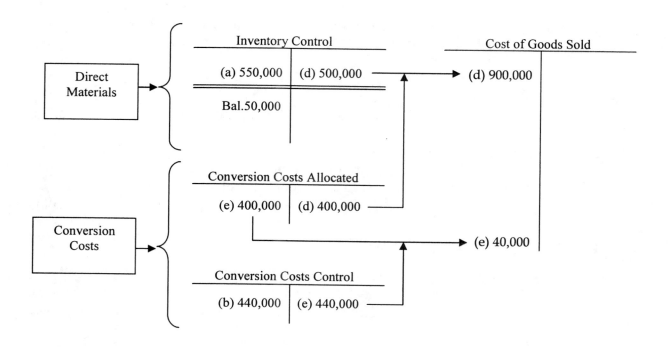

20-36 (30 min.) **Backflush costing, income manipulation, ethics.**

1.   Factors SVC should consider in deciding whether to adopt a version of backflush costing include:

    a. Effects on decision making by managers. There is a loss of information with backflushing. Supporters of backflushing maintain, however, that nonfinancial information and observation of production provide sufficient inputs to monitor production and management costs at the shop-floor level.

    b. Costs of maintaining sequential tracking vis-à-vis backflush costing.

    c. Materiality of the differences. If the production lead time is short (say, less than one day) and inventory levels are minimal (as one would anticipate with JIT), the differences between sequential tracking and backflush may be minimal.

    d. Opportunity for managers to manipulate reported numbers.

2.   Strong's concerns certainly warrant consideration. Much depends on the corporate culture at SVC. If the culture is such that quarterly or monthly reported numbers are pivotal to evaluations, and that managers "push the accounting system to facilitate meeting the numbers," Strong should raise these issues with Brown. Adopting an accounting system with an obvious opportunity for manipulation (backflush with sale as the trigger point) may well send managers the wrong message.

    Strong's concerns, however, are not by themselves sufficient to cause SVC not to adopt backflush costing. The factors mentioned in requirement 1 may well be compelling enough to support adoption of backflush costing. Brown has alternative ways to address Strong's quite legitimate concerns—see requirement 3.

3.   Ways to motivate managers not to "artificially change" reported income include:

    a. Adopting long-term measures that reduce the importance of short-run financial targets.

    b. Increasing the weight on nonaccounting-based variables—e.g., more use of stock options or customer-satisfaction measures.

    c. Penalize heavily (the "stick approach") managers who are found out to have "artificially changed" reported income. This can include withdrawal of bonuses or even termination of employment.

Chapter 20 Video Case

The video case can be discussed using only the case writeup in the chapter. Alternatively, instructors can have students view the videotape of the company that is the subject of the case. The videotape can be obtained by contacting your Prentice Hall representative. The case questions challenge students to apply the concepts learned in the chapter to a specific business situation.

REGAL MARINE: Supply Chain Management

2.   Regal Marine can benefit from a strong relationship not only with its upstream direct materials suppliers, but also from the downstream retail channel relationships. For example, retailers can provide retail sales forecasts for products that can help Regal Marine better plan production. Retailers can also provide sales information so Regal Marine knows which boats are fast-sellers and which don't seem to move off the showroom floor. Regal Marine could work with its distribution network to offer pricing and promotional deals to help boost sales and push production of higher margin products.

There are several potential challenges to strengthening the supply chain relationship with retailers. First, communication obstacles may arise if retailers are not willing to provide Regal Marine with enough information for planning and production. Second, trust issues may arise if both sides don't think the other will be able to meet commitments. Third, there may be some information systems obstacles in the form of incompatible systems if the company and its retailers try to automate the exchange of information. Lastly, both parties may face a shortage of human resources that prevent them from collecting, analyzing, and sharing information in a timely manner.

CHAPTER 21
CAPITAL BUDGETING AND COST ANALYSIS

21-2 The six stages in capital budgeting are the following:
1. An *identification stage* to determine which types of capital investments are necessary to accomplish organization objectives and strategies.
2. A *search stage* that explores alternative capital investments that will achieve organization objectives.
3. An *information-acquisition stage* to consider the expected costs and expected benefits of alternative capital investments.
4. A *selection stage* to choose projects for implementation.
5. A *financing stage* to obtain project funding.
6. An *implementation and control* stage to get projects under way and monitor their performance.

21-4 No. Only quantitative outcomes are formally analyzed in capital budgeting decisions. Many effects of capital budgeting decisions, however, are difficult to quantify in financial terms. These nonfinancial or qualitative factors (for example, the number of accidents in a manufacturing plant or employee morale) are important to consider in making capital budgeting decisions.

21-6 The payback method measures the time it will take to recoup, in the form of expected future net cash inflows, the net initial investment in a project. The payback method is simple and easy to understand. It is a handy method when screening many proposals and particularly when predicted cash flows in later years are highly uncertain. The main weaknesses of the payback method are its neglect of the time value of money and of the cash flows after the payback period.

21-8 No. The discounted cash-flow techniques implicitly consider depreciation in rate of return computations; the compound interest tables automatically allow for recovery of investment. The net initial investment of an asset is usually regarded as a lump-sum outflow at time zero. Where taxes are included in the DCF analysis, depreciation costs are included in the computation of the taxable income number that is used to compute the tax payment cash flow.

21-10 All overhead costs are not relevant in NPV analysis. Overhead costs are relevant only if the capital investment results in a change in total overhead cash flows. Overhead costs are not relevant if total overhead cash flows remain the same but the overhead allocated to the particular capital investment changes.

21-12 The categories of cash flow that should be considered are:
    1a. Initial machine investment,
     b. Initial working-capital investment,
     c. After-tax cash flow from current disposal of old machine,
    2a. Annual after-tax cash flow from operations (excluding the depreciation effect),
     b. Income tax cash savings from annual depreciation deductions,
    3a. After-tax cash flow from terminal disposal of machines, and
     b. After-tax cash flow from terminal recovery of working-capital investment.

21-14 A cellular telephone company manager responsible for retaining customers needs to consider the expected future revenues and the expected future costs of "different investments" to retain customers. One such investment could be a special price discount. An alternative investment is offering loyalty club benefits to long-time customers.

21-16   Exercises in compound interest, no income taxes.
The answers to these exercises are printed after the last problem, at the end of the chapter.

21-18 (30 min.) **Capital budgeting methods, no income taxes.**

The table for the present value of annuities (Appendix C, Table 4) shows: 10 periods at 14% = 5.216

1a.   Net present value

$$= \$28,000 \,(5.216) - \$110,000$$
$$= \$146,048 - \$110,000 \ = \$36,048$$

b.   Payback period

$$= \frac{\$110,000}{\$28,000} = 3.93 \text{ years}$$

c.   Internal rate of return:

$110,000 \quad = \quad$ Present value of annuity of $28,000 at R% for 10 years, or what factor (F) in the table of present values of an annuity (Appendix C, Table 4) will satisfy the following equation.

$$\$110,000 \ = \$28,000F$$
$$F \ = \frac{\$110,000}{\$28,000} = \ 3.929$$

On the 10-year line in the table for the present value of annuities (Appendix C, Table 4), find the column closest to 3.929; 3.929 is between a rate of return of 20% and 22%.
    Interpolation can be used to determine the exact rate:

	Present Value Factors	
20%	4.192	4.192
IRR rate	—	3.929
22%	3.923	—
Difference	0.269	0.263

Internal rate of return $= 20\% + \left[\dfrac{0.263}{0.269} \right] (2\%)$

$$= 20\% + (0.978)\,(2\%) \ = 21.96\%$$

d. Accrual accounting rate of return based on net initial investment:

Net initial investment = $110,000
Estimated useful life = 10 years
Annual straight-line depreciation = $110,000 ÷ 10 = $11,000

$$\text{Accrual accounting rate of return} = \frac{\$28,000 - \$11,000}{\$110,000}$$

$$= \frac{\$17,000}{\$110,000} = 15.46\%$$

2. Factors City Hospital should consider include:
   a. Quantitative financial aspects.
   b. Qualitative factors, such as the benefits to its customers of a better eye-testing machine and the employee-morale advantages of having up-to-date equipment.
   c. Financing factors, such as the availability of cash to purchase the new equipment.

21-20 (25 min.) **Capital budgeting with uneven cash flows, no income taxes.**

1. Present value of savings in cash operating costs:

$10,000 × 0.862	$ 8,620
8,000 × 0.743	5,944
6,000 × 0.641	3,846
5,000 × 0.552	2,760
Present value of savings in cash operating costs	21,170
Net initial investment	(23,000)
Net present value	$(1,830)

2. Payback period:

Year	Cash Savings	Cumulative Cash Savings	Initial Investment Yet to Be Recovered at End of Year
0	–	–	$23,000
1	$10,000	$10,000	13,000
2	8,000	18,000	5,000
3	6,000	24,000	–

$$\text{Payback period} = 2 \text{ years} + \frac{\$5,000}{\$6,000} = 2.83 \text{ years}$$

3. From requirement 1, the net present value is negative with a 16% required rate of return. Therefore, the internal rate of return must be less than 16%.

Year (1)	Cash Savings (2)	P.V. Factor at 14% (3)	P.V. at 14% (4) = (2) × (3)	P.V. Factor at 12% (5)	P.V. at 12% (6) = (2) × (5)	P.V. Factor at 10% (7)	P.V. at 10% (8) = (2) × (7)
1	$10,000	0.877	$ 8,770	0.893	$ 8,930	0.909	$ 9,090
2	8,000	0.769	6,152	0.797	6,376	0.826	6,608
3	6,000	0.675	4,050	0.712	4,272	0.751	4,506
4	5,000	0.592	2,960	0.636	3,180	0.683	3,415
			$21,932		$22,758		$23,619

Net present value at 14% = $21,932 − $23,000 = $(1,068)

Net present value at 12% = $22,758 − $23,000 = $(242)

Net present value at 10% = $23,619 − $23,000 = $619

$$\text{Internal rate of return} \quad = \quad 10\% + \left[\frac{619}{619 + 242} \right] (2\%)$$

$$= \quad 10\% + (0.719)(2\%) = 11.44\%$$

4. Accrual accounting rate of return based on net initial investment:

$$\text{Average annual savings in cash operating costs} \quad = \quad \frac{\$29,000}{4 \text{ years}} = \$7,250$$

$$\text{Annual straight-line depreciation} \quad = \quad \frac{\$23,000}{4 \text{ years}} = \$5,750$$

$$\text{Accrual accounting rate of return} \quad = \quad \frac{\$7,250 - \$5,750}{\$23,000}$$

$$= \quad \frac{\$1,500}{\$23,000} = 6.52\%$$

21-22 (30 min.) **Payback and NPV methods, no income taxes.**

1a.   Payback measures the time it will take to recoup, in the form of expected future cash flows, the net initial investment in a project. Payback emphasizes the early recovery of cash as a key aspect of project ranking. Some managers argue that this emphasis on early recovery of cash is appropriate if there is a high level of uncertainty about future cash flows. Projects with shorter paybacks give the organization more flexibility because funds for other projects become available sooner.

Strengths
- Easy to understand
- One way to capture uncertainty about expected cash flows in later years of a project (although sensitivity analysis is a more systematic way)

Weaknesses
- Fails to incorporate the time value of money
- Does not consider a project's cash flows after the payback period

1b.
Project A

Outflow, $3,000,000
Inflow, $1,000,000 (Year 1) + $1,000,000 (Year 2) + $1,000,000 (Year 3) + $1,000,000 (Year 4)

Payback = 3 years

Project B

Outflow, $1,500,000
Inflow, $400,000 (Year 1) + $900,000 (Year 2) + $800,000 (Year 3) etc.

$$\text{Payback} = 2 + \frac{(\$1,500,000 - \$400,000 - \$900,000)}{\$800,000} = 2.25 \text{ years}$$

Project C

Outflow, $4,000,000
Inflow, $2,000,000 (Year 1) + $2,000,000 (Year 2) + $200,000 (Year 3) + $100,000 (Year 4)
Payback = 2 years

	Payback Period
1. Project C	2 years
2. Project B	2.25 years
3. Project A	3 years

If payback period is the deciding factor, Andrews will choose Project C (payback period = 2 years; investment = $4,000,000) and Project B (payback period = 2.25 years; investment = $1,500,000), for a total capital investment of $5,500,000. Assuming that each of the projects is an all-or-nothing investment, Andrews will have $500,000 left over in the capital budget, not enough to make the $3,000,000 investment in Project A.

2.   Solution Exhibit 21-22 shows the following ranking:

	NPV
1. Project B	$ 207,800
2. Project A	$ 169,000
3. Project C	$(311,500)

3.   Using NPV rankings, Projects B and A, which require a total investment of $3,000,000 + $1,500,000 = $4,500,000, which is less than the $6,0000,000 capital budget, should be funded. This does not match the rankings based on payback period because Projects B and A have substantial cash flows after the payback period, cash flows that the payback period ignores.

Nonfinancial qualitative factors should also be considered. For example, are there differential worker safety issues across the projects? Are there differences in the extent of learning that can benefit other projects? Are there differences in the customer relationships established with different projects that can benefit Andrews Construction in future projects?

SOLUTION EXHIBIT 21-22

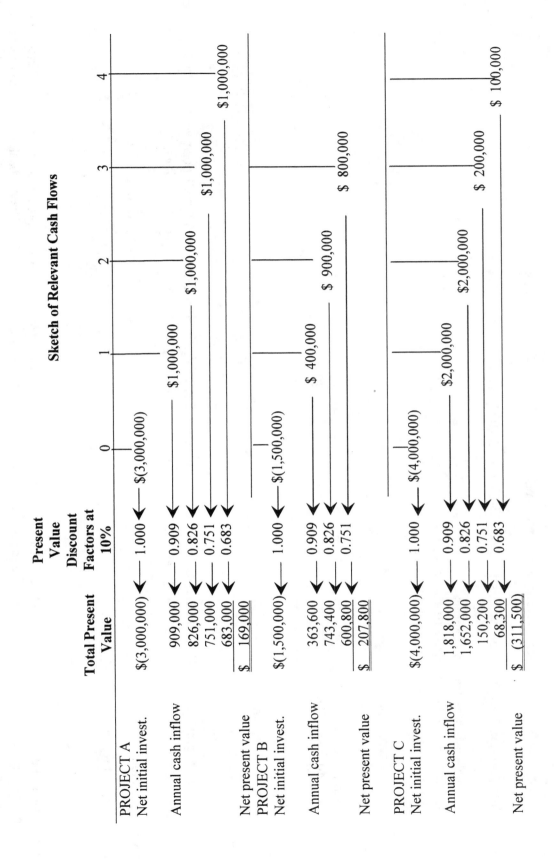

Sketch of Relevant Cash Flows

	Total Present Value	Present Value Discount Factors at 10%	0	1	2	3	4
PROJECT A							
Net initial invest.	$(3,000,000)	1.000	$(3,000,000)				
Annual cash inflow	909,000	0.909		$1,000,000			
	826,000	0.826			$1,000,000		
	751,000	0.751				$1,000,000	
	683,000	0.683					$1,000,000
Net present value	$ 169,000						
PROJECT B							
Net initial invest.	$(1,500,000)	1.000	$(1,500,000)				
Annual cash inflow	363,600	0.909		$ 400,000			
	743,400	0.826			$ 900,000		
	600,800	0.751				$ 800,000	
Net present value	$ 207,800						
PROJECT C							
Net initial invest.	$(4,000,000)	1.000	$(4,000,000)				
Annual cash inflow	1,818,000	0.909		$2,000,000			
	1,652,000	0.826			$2,000,000		
	150,200	0.751				$ 200,000	
	68,300	0.683					$ 100,000
Net present value	$ (311,500)						

21-7

21-24 (40 min.) **New equipment purchase, income taxes.**

1.   The after-tax cash inflow per year is $74,000 ($54,000 + $20,000), as shown below:

Annual cash flow from operations	$ 90,000
Deduct income tax payments (0.40 × $90,000)	36,000
Annual after-tax cash flow from operations	$ 54,000
Annual depreciation on machine	$ 50,000
[($220,000 − $20,000) ÷ 4]	
Income tax cash savings from annual depreciation deductions	20,000
(0.40 × $50,000)	

a.   Solution Exhibit 21-24A shows the NPV computation. NPV = $17,532

b. $\text{Payback} = \dfrac{\$220,000}{\$74,000} = 2.97 \text{ years}$

c.   Solution Exhibits 21-24B and 21-24C report the net present value of the project using 14% (small positive NPV) and 16% (small negative NPV). The IRR, the discount rate at which the NPV of the cash flows is zero, must lie between 14% and 16%.

By interpolation:

$\text{Internal rate of return} = 16\% - \left[\dfrac{1,908}{1,908 + 7,402} \right] \times 2\%$

$= 15.59\%$

2.   Both the net present value and internal rate of return methods use a discounted cash flow approach in which *all* expected future cash inflows and cash outflows of a project are measured as if they occurred at a single point in time. The payback method considers only cash flows up to the time when the expected future cash inflows recoup the net initial investment in a project. The payback method ignores profitability and the time value of money. However, the payback method is becoming increasingly important in the global economy. When the local environment in an international location is unstable and therefore highly risky for a potential investment, a company would likely pay close attention to the payback period for making its investment decision. In general, the more unstable the environment, the shorter the payback period desired.

SOLUTION EXHIBIT 21-24A

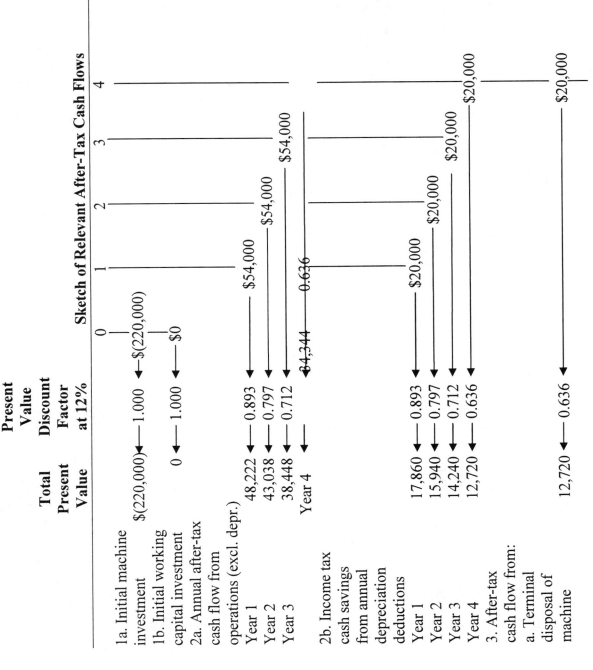

	Total Present Value	Present Value Discount Factor at 12%	Sketch of Relevant After-Tax Cash Flows

Sketch columns: 0, 1, 2, 3, 4

1a. Initial machine investment — $(220,000) — 1.000 — $(220,000) [at time 0]

1b. Initial working capital investment — 0 — 1.000 — $0 [at time 0]

2a. Annual after-tax cash flow from operations (excl. depr.)
- Year 1 — 48,222 — 0.893 — $54,000 [at time 1]
- Year 2 — 43,038 — 0.797 — $54,000 [at time 2]
- Year 3 — 38,448 — 0.712 — $54,000 [at time 3]
- Year 4 — 34,344 — 0.636 — $54,000 [at time 4]

2b. Income tax cash savings from annual depreciation deductions
- Year 1 — 17,860 — 0.893 — $20,000 [at time 1]
- Year 2 — 15,940 — 0.797 — $20,000 [at time 2]
- Year 3 — 14,240 — 0.712 — $20,000 [at time 3]
- Year 4 — 12,720 — 0.636 — $20,000 [at time 4]

3. After-tax cash flow from:
a. Terminal disposal of machine — 12,720 — 0.636 — $20,000 [at time 4]

21-9

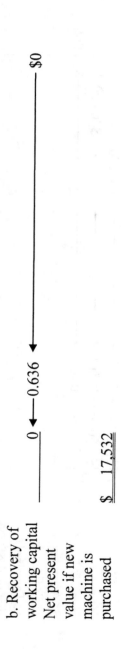

b. Recovery of
working capital   0 —0.636 → $0

Net present
value if new
machine is
purchased $ 17,532

SOLUTION EXHIBIT 21-24B

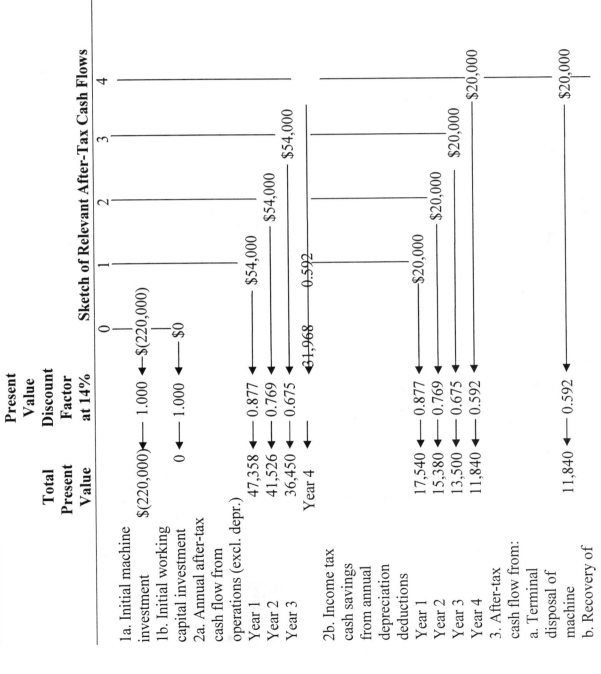

	Total Present Value	Present Value Discount Factor at 14%	**Sketch of Relevant After-Tax Cash Flows**				
			0	1	2	3	4
1a. Initial machine investment	$(220,000)	1.000	$(220,000)				
1b. Initial working capital investment	0	1.000	$0				
2a. Annual after-tax cash flow from operations (excl. depr.)							
Year 1	47,358	0.877		$54,000			
Year 2	41,526	0.769			$54,000		
Year 3	36,450	0.675				$54,000	
Year 4	31,968	0.592					$54,000
2b. Income tax cash savings from annual depreciation deductions							
Year 1	17,540	0.877		$20,000			
Year 2	15,380	0.769			$20,000		
Year 3	13,500	0.675				$20,000	
Year 4	11,840	0.592					$20,000
3. After-tax cash flow from:							
a. Terminal disposal of machine	11,840	0.592					$20,000
b. Recovery of							

21-11

SOLUTION EXHIBIT 21-24C

	Total Present Value	Present Value Discount Factor at 16%	0	1	2	3	4
1a. Initial machine investment	$(220,000)	1.000	$(220,000)				
1b. Initial working capital investment	0	1.000	$0				
2a. Annual after-tax cash flow from operations (excl. depr.)							
Year 1	46,548	0.862		$54,000			
Year 2	40,122	0.743			$54,000		
Year 3	34,614	0.641				$54,000	
Year 4	29,808	0.552					$54,000
2b. Income tax cash savings from annual depreciation deductions							
Year 1	17,240	0.862		$20,000			
Year 2	14,860	0.743			$20,000		
Year 3	12,820	0.641				$20,000	
Year 4	11,040	0.552					$20,000

Sketch of Relevant After-Tax Cash Flows

working capital | 0.592 | $0

Net present value if new machine is purchased $ 7,402

3. After-tax cash flow from:

a. Terminal disposal of machine   11,040 ←— 0.552 →$20,000

b. Recovery of working capital   0 ←— 0.552 →$0

Net present value if new machine is purchased $ (1,908)

21-26 (60 min.) **Selling a plant, income taxes.**

1. *Option 1*

Current disposal price	$9,000,000
Deduct current book value	0
Gain on disposal	9,000,000
Deduct 40% tax payments	3,600,000
Net present value	$5,400,000

Option 2

Waterford receives three sources of cash inflows:

a. Rent. Four annual payments of $2,400,000. The after-tax cash inflow is:
    $2,400,000 × (1 – 0.40) = $1,440,000 per year

b. Discount on material purchases, payable at year-end for each of the four years: $474,000
    The after-tax cash inflow is: $474,000 × (1 – 0.40) = $284,400

c. Sale of plant at year-end 2009. The after-tax cash inflow is:
    $2,000,000 × (1 – 0.40) = $1,200,000

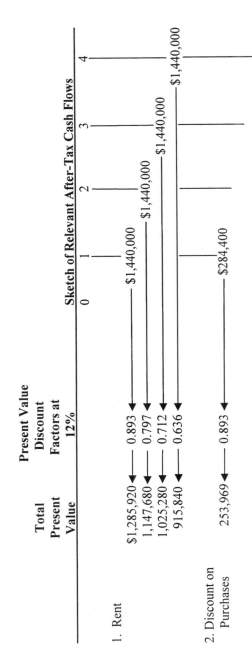

	Total Present Value	Present Value Discount Factors at 12%
1. Rent	$1,285,920	0.893
	1,147,680	0.797
	1,025,280	0.712
	915,840	0.636
2. Discount on Purchases	253,969	0.893

21-14

226,667 → 0.797 → $284,400
202,493 → 0.712 → $284,400
180,878 → 0.636 → $284,400

3. Sale of plant   763,200 → 0.636 → $1,200,000

Net present value $6,001,927

Option 3

Contribution margin per jacket:
Selling price $42.00
Variable costs   33.00
Contribution margin $ 9.00

	2006	2007	2008	2009
Contribution margin $9.00 × 200,000; 300,000; 400,000; 100,000;	$1,800,000	$2,700,000	$3,600,000	$900,000
Fixed overhead (cash) costs	200,000	200,000	200,000	200,000
Annual cash flow from operations	1,600,000	2,500,000	3,400,000	700,000
Income tax payments (40%)	640,000	1,000,000	1,360,000	280,000
After-tax cash flow from operations (excl. depcn.)	$ 960,000	$1,500,000	$2,040,000	$420,000

Depreciation: $1,500,000 ÷ 4 = $375,000 per year

Income tax cash savings from depreciation deduction: $375,000 × 0.40 = $150,000 per year

Sale of plant at end of 2009: $3,000,000 × (1 − 0.40) = $1,800,000

Solution Exhibit 21-26 presents the NPV calculations. NPV = $3,872,880

SOLUTION EXHIBIT 21-26

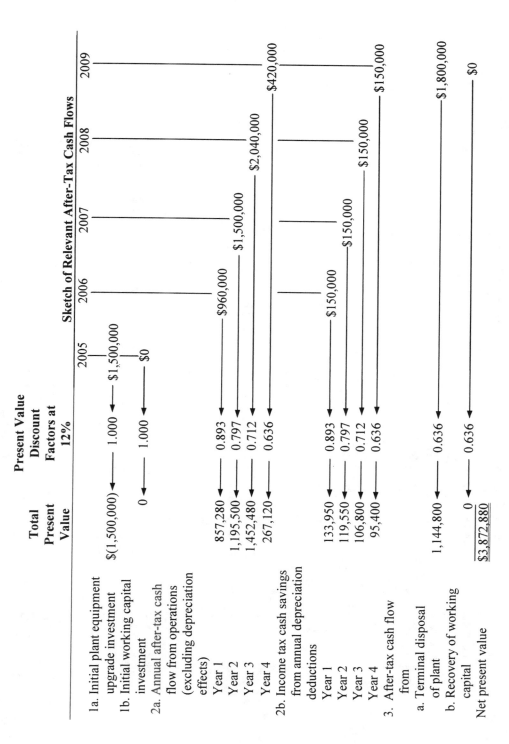

21-16

Option 2 has the highest NPV:

	NPV
Option 1	$5,400,000
Option 2	$6,001,927
Option 3	$3,872,880

2. Nonfinancial factors that Waterford should consider include the following:

- Option 1 gives Waterford immediate liquidity which it can use for other projects.
- Option 2 has the advantage of Waterford having a closer relationship with the supplier. However, it limits Waterford's flexibility if Auburn Mill's quality is not comparable to competitors.
- Option 3 has Waterford entering a new line of business. If this line of business is successful, it could be expanded to cover souvenir jackets for other major events. The risks of selling the predicted number of jackets should also be considered.

21-28 (40 min.) **Equipment replacement, income taxes (continuation of 21-27).**

1. & 2. Income tax rate = 30%

Modernize Alternative

Annual depreciation:
$28,000,000 ÷ 7 years = $4,000,000 a year.

Income tax cash savings from annual depreciation deductions:
$4,000,000 × 0.30 = $1,200,000 a year.

Terminal disposal of equipment = $5,000,000.

After-tax cash flow from terminal disposal of equipment:
$5,000,000 × 0.70 = $3,500,000.

The NPV components are:

a. Initial investment:

		NPV
Jan. 1, 2007	$(28,000,000) × 1.000	$(28,000,000)

b. Annual after-tax cash flow from operations (excluding depreciation):

Dec. 31, 2007	8,280,000 × 0.70 × 0.893	5,175,828
2008	9,180,000 × 0.70 × 0.797	5,121,522
2009	10,080,000 × 0.70 × 0.712	5,023,872
2010	10,980,000 × 0.70 × 0.636	4,888,296
2011	11,880,000 × 0.70 × 0.567	4,715,172
2012	12,780,000 × 0.70 × 0.507	4,535,622
2013	13,680,000 × 0.70 × 0.452	4,328,352

c. Income tax cash savings from annual depreciation deductions ($1,200,000 each year for 7 years):

	$1,200,000 × 4.564	5,476,800

d. After-tax cash flow from terminal sale of equipment:

	$3,500,000 × 0.452	1,582,000

Net present value of modernize alternative		$ 12,847,464

Replace alternative

Initial machine replacement = $49,000,000

Sale on Jan. 1, 2007, of equipment = $3,000,000

After-tax cash flow from sale of old equipment: $3,000,000 × 0.70 = $2,100,000

Net initial investment: $49,000,000 − $2,100,000 = $46,900,000

Annual depreciation: $49,000,000 ÷ 7 years = $7,000,000 a year

Income-tax cash savings from annual depreciation deductions: $7,000,000 × 0.30 = $2,100,000

Terminal disposal of equipment = $12,000,000

After-tax cash flow from terminal disposal of equipment: $12,000,000 × 0.70 = $8,400,000

The NPV components of the replace alternative are
a. Net initial investment
Jan. 1, 2007 $(46,900,000) × 1.000 $(46,900,000)

b. Annual after-tax cash flow from operations (excluding depreciation)
Dec. 31,   2004 $11,040,000 × 0.70 × 0.893   6,901,104
           2005   12,240,000 × 0.70 × 0.797   6,828,696
           2006   13,440,000 × 0.70 × 0.712   6,698,496
           2007   14,640,000 × 0.70 × 0.636   6,517,728
           2008   15,840,000 × 0.70 × 0.567   6,286,896
           2009   17,040,000 × 0.70 × 0.507   6,047,496
           2010   18,240,000 × 0.70 × 0.452   5,771,136

c. Income tax cash savings from annual depreciation deductions
    ($2,100,000 each year for 7 years) $2,100,000 × 4.564   9,584,400

21-19

d. After-tax cash flow from terminal sale of equipment, $8,400,000 × 0.452   3,796,800

Net present value of replace alternative $11,532,752

On the basis of NPV, Superfast should modernize rather than replace the equipment. Note that absent taxes, the replace alternative had a higher NPV than the modernize alternative.

3.   Superfast would prefer to:
   a.   have lower tax rates,
   b.   have revenue exempt from taxation,
   c.   recognize taxable revenues in later years rather than earlier years,
   d.   recognize taxable cost deductions greater than actual outlay costs, and
   e.   recognize cost deductions in earlier years rather than later years (including accelerated amounts in earlier years).

21-30 (40 min.) **NPV and customer profitability, no income taxes.**

1.

Harvey Builders	Annual Increases*	2006	2007	2008	2009
Revenues	6%	$94,500	$100,170	$106,180	$112,551
Expenses	5%	60,800	63,840	67,032	70,384
Operating Income		$33,700	$ 36,330	$ 39,148	$ 42,167

Kestle Constructors	Annual Increases*	2006	2007	2008	2009
Revenues	5%	$585,000	$614,250	$644,963	$677,211
Expenses	4%	510,000	530,400	551,616	573,681
Operating Income		$ 75,000	$ 83,850	$ 93,347	$103,530

*Given in the problem.

2.

		Harvey Builders		Kestle Constructors	
Year	PV Factor for 12%	Cash Flow from Operations	Present Value	Cash Flow from Operations	Present Value
2007	0.893	$36,330	$32,443	$ 83,850	$ 74,878
2008	0.797	39,148	31,201	93,347	74,398
2009	0.712	42,167	30,023	103,530	73,713
			$93,667		$222,989

Based on NPV at 12%, Kestle Constructors is the more valuable customer.

3.

Assuming a 10% discount on revenues for Kestle Constructors calculated in requirement 1, we have

Kestle Constructors	Annual Increases	2006	2007	2008	2009
Revenues	5%	$585,000	$552,825*	$580,466*	$609,490*
Expenses	4%	510,000	530,400	551,616	573,681
Operating Income		$ 75,000	$ 22,425	$ 28,850	$ 35,809

*Kestle Constructors' revenue from requirement 1 reduced by 10% each year.

21-22

Net present value if revenues are reduced by 10% each year relative to original estimates:

		Kestle Constructors	
		Cash Flow	
	PV Factor	from	Present
Year	for 12%	Operations	Value
2007	0.893	$22,425	$20,026
2008	0.797	28,850	22,994
2009	0.712	35,809	25,496
			$68,516

The 10% discount and reduced subsequent annual revenue reduces the NPV from $222,989 to $68,516. The NPV is still positive and so Stone Art should continue to sell to Kestle Constructors. However, this is almost a 70% drop in NPV from Kestle, and it makes Harvey the more profitable customer.

Stone Art should consider whether the price discount demanded by Kestle needs to be met in full to keep the account. The implication of meeting the full demand is that the account is minimally profitable. A serious concern is whether Harvey will also demand comparable price discounts if Kestle's demands are met. This could result in large reductions in the NPVs of all of Stone Art's customers.

Stone Art should also consider the reliability of the growth estimates used in computing the NPVs. Are the predicted differences in revenue growth rates based on reliable information? Many revenue growth estimates by salespeople turn out to be overestimates or occur over a longer time period than initially predicted.

21-23

21-32 (40 min.) Replacement of a machine, income taxes, sensitivity.

1a. Original cost of old machine: $80,000

    Depreciation taken during the first 3 years

    {[($80,000 − $10,000) ÷ 7] × 3}   30,000

    Book value   50,000

    Current disposal price: 40,000

    Loss on disposal $10,000

    Tax rate   × 0.40

    Tax savings in cash from loss on current disposal of old machine $ 4,000

1b. Difference in recurring after-tax variable cash-operating savings, with 40% tax rate:

    ($0.20 − $0.14) × (300,000) × (1− 0.40) = $10,800 (in favor of new machine)

Difference in after-tax fixed cost savings, with 40% tax rate:

    ($15,000 − $14,000) × (1 − 0.40) = $600 (in favor of new machine)

1c.

	Old Machine	New Machine
Initial machine investment	$80,000	$120,000
Terminal disposal price at end of useful life	10,000	20,000
Depreciable base	$70,000	$100,000
Annual depreciation using straight-line (7-year life)	$10,000	
Annual depreciation using straight-line (4-year life):		$ 25,000

Year (1)	Depreciation on Old Machine (2)	Depreciation on New Machine (3)	Additional Depreciation Deduction on New Machine (4) = (3) − (2)	Income Tax Cash Savings from Difference in Depreciation Deduction at 40% (4) × 40%
2006	$10,000	$25,000	$15,000	$6,000
2007	10,000	25,000	15,000	6,000
2008	10,000	25,000	15,000	6,000
2009	10,000	25,000	15,000	6,000

1d.

	Old Machine	New Machine
Original cost	$80,000	$120,000
Total depreciation	70,000	100,000
Book value of machines on Dec. 31, 2009	10,000	20,000
Terminal disposal price of machines on Dec. 31, 2009	7,000	20,000
Loss on disposal of machines	3,000	0
Add tax savings on loss (40% of $3,000; 40% of $0)	1,200	0
After-tax cash flow from terminal disposal of machines ($7,000 + $1,200; $20,000 − $0)	$ 8,200	$ 20,000

Difference in after-tax cash flow from terminal disposal of machines: $20,000 − $8,200 = $11,800.

2.   WRL Company should retain the old equipment because the net present value of the incremental cash flows from the new machine is negative. The computations, using the results of requirement 1, are presented below. In this format the present value factors appear at the bottom. All cash flows, year by year, are then converted into present values.

	After-Tax Cash Flows				
	2005[a]	2006	2007	2008	2009
Initial machine investment	$(120,000)				
Current disposal price of old machine	40,000				
Tax savings from loss on disposal of old machine	4,000				
Recurring after-tax cash-operating savings					
Variable		$10,800	$10,800	$10,800	$10,800
Fixed		600	600	600	600
Income tax cash savings from difference in depreciation deductions		6,000	6,000	6,000	6,000
Additional after-tax cash flow from terminal disposal of new machine over old machine					11,800
Net after-tax cash flows	$ (76,000)	$17,400	$17,400	$17,400	$29,200
Present value discount factors (at 16%)	1.000	0.862	0.743	0.641	0.552
Present value	$ (76,000)	$14,999	$12,928	$11,153	$16,118
Net present value	$ (20,802)				

[a]Actually January 1, 2006

3.   Let $X be the *additional* recurring after-tax cash operating savings required each year to make NPV = $0.
      The present value of an annuity of $1 per year for 4 years discounted at 16% = 2.798 (Appendix C, Table 4)
      To make NPV = 0, WRL needs to generate cash savings with NPV of $20,802.
      That is $X (2.798)   = $20,802
                      X   =   20,802 ÷ 2.798 = $7,435

WRL must generate additional annual after-tax cash operating savings of $7,435.

21-34 (40 min.) **Ethics, capital budgeting.**

1a. Referring to the specific standards of competence, confidentiality, integrity, and objectivity in "Standards of Ethical Conduct for Management Accountants" (Chapter 1), George Watson's conduct in giving Helen Dodge specific instructions on preparing the second revision of the proposal is unethical because his conduct violates the following specific standards:

Competence
Watson has the responsibility to perform his professional duties in accordance with relevant technical standards, such as using conservatism and realistic estimates in the net present value analysis. Management accountants should prepare complete and clear reports and recommendations after appropriate analyses of relevant and reliable information.

Confidentiality
Watson should refrain from using or appearing to use confidential information acquired in the course of his work for unethical advantage or personal gain (saving on commuting time and costs).

Integrity
Watson has the responsibility to advise all parties of any potential conflict of interest. Watson should communicate unfavorable as well as favorable information and professional judgments and opinions.

Objectivity
Watson has the responsibility to disclose fully all relevant information that can influence an intended user's understanding of the analysis.

1b.   Helen Dodge's revised proposal for the warehouse conversion is unethical because her actions violate the following standards:

Competence
Although the estimates used in the analysis are based on management's judgment, Dodge's action in changing reasonable estimates to assumptions that are less likely to occur is unethical. Management accountants have the responsibility to prepare complete and clear reports and recommendations after appropriate analysis of relevant and reliable information.

Integrity
Dodge has the responsibility to avoid conflicts of interest, refrain from subverting the attainment of the organization's legitimate and ethical objectives (profitability), and refrain from engaging in or supporting any activity that would discredit the profession.

Objectivity
Dodge has the responsibility to communicate information fairly and objectively and to disclose fully all relevant information that can influence an intended user's understanding.

2.   Steps that Helen Dodge should follow in attempting to resolve this situation are as follows:

- Dodge should first investigate and see if Evans Company has an established policy for resolving conflict, and she should follow this policy if it does exist.
- Since it appears that George Watson, Dodge's superior, is involved, there is no need to confront Watson or discuss this issue with him any further. Dodge should present the situation to the next higher level, the vice president of finance, for resolution.
- If the issue is not resolved to Dodge's satisfaction, she should continue to successive higher levels, including the Audit Committee and the Board of Directors.
- Dodge should clarify the concepts of the issue at hand in a confidential discussion with an objective advisor, i.e., a peer.
- If the situation is still unresolved after exhausting all levels of internal review, Dodge will have no recourse but to resign and submit an informative memorandum to an appropriate representative of the organization.
- Unless legally bound (which does not appear to be the case in this situation), it is inappropriate to have communication about this situation with authorities and individuals not employed or engaged by the organization.

21-36 (30 min.) **Relevant costs, outsourcing, capital budgeting, no income taxes.**

1. Relevant operating cash outflows and operating cash savings each year if Part No. 789 is outsourced:

	2006	2007 to 2010
Operating cash outflows for purchasing Part No. 789	$(50,000)	$(50,000)
Relevant operating cash savings from outsourcing Part No. 789:		
Direct materials	22,000	22,000
Direct manufacturing labor	11,000	11,000
Variable manufacturing overhead	7,000	7,000
Product and process engineering	–	4,000
Rent	1,000	1,000
Total relevant operating cash savings	41,000	45,000
Net relevant operating cash outflows if Part No.789 purchased from Gabriella	$ (9,000)	$ (5,000)

NPV of cash inflows and outflows if Part No. 789 purchased from outside (in thousands):

End of Year	Total Present Value	Present Value of $1 Discounted at 12%	Sketch of Relevant Cash Flows					
			2003	2004	2005	2006	2007	2008
1. Disposal price of machine	$15.000 ← 1.000 ← $15							
2. Recurring operating cash flows	(8.037) ← 0.893 ←			$(9)				
	(3.985) ← 0.797 ←				$(5)			
	(3.560) ← 0.712 ←					$(5)		
	(3.180) ← 0.636 ←						$(5)	
	(2.835) ← 0.567 ←							$(5)
Net present value	$(6.597)							

The decision to purchase Part No. 789 from Gabriella has a negative NPV of $6,597. Strubel should continue to make Part No. 789 in-house based on quantitative, financial considerations.

Note the following:

  a. Equipment depreciation is a noncash cost and, in a scenario without taxes, irrelevant for the NPV analysis.

  b. Product and process engineering is irrelevant for 2006, since $4,000 in costs will be incurred in 2004 whether Part No. 789 is outsourced or manufactured in-house. But product and process engineering is relevant from 2007 to 2010. These cash costs will be saved if Strubel decides to outsource Part No. 789.

  c. The allocated rent costs of $2,000 are irrelevant for NPV analysis, but the $1,000 rent saved for outside storage if Strubel outsources Part No. 789 is a relevant cash savings, under the "outsourcing" alternative.

  d. Allocation of general plant overhead costs of $5,000 is irrelevant since these costs will not change in total whether Part No. 789 is outsourced or manufactured in-house.

2. Sensitivity analysis with respect to the quantity of Part No. 789 required seems desirable.

   - If demand for Part No. 789 decreases, Gabriella is willing to supply a lower quantity at the same price of $50 per part. If Strubel continued to manufacture part No. 789, the costs it would incur may not decrease quite as fast with lower quantities of production because of fixed costs. Furthermore, the net cash outflows of outsourcing calculated in requirement 1 will be smaller if lower quantities of Part No. 789 are demanded. For example, if only 900 units per year are required, the net relevant cash outflows if Part No. 789 is purchased from Gabriella will be less by $5,000 in years 2005 through 2008. Note that cash inflow from selling the machine is still $15,000. This would make outsourcing Part No. 789 more attractive.
   - If, on the other hand, Strubel's demand for Part No. 789 increases, Strubel will continue to prefer manufacturing the part in-house.

3. Other nonfinancial and qualitative factors that Lin should consider before making a decision are

   a. Whether Gabriella will deliver Part No. 789 according to the agreed-upon delivery schedule.
   b. Whether Gabriella will produce Part No. 789 according to the desired quality standards.
   c. Whether Gabriella will be in a position to accommodate modifications in Part No. 789 if Strubel's requirements change.
   d. Whether Gabriella will continue in business for the next five years and continue to make Part No. 789 based on Strubel's demands.

4. Compute the effects of relevant items on operating income under the alternatives of outsourcing versus making Part No. 789 in-house.

	Increase (Decrease) in Strubel's Operating Income in 2006 (in thousands)
Relevant accounting costs if Part No. 789 is made in-house	
Direct materials	$22,000
Direct manufacturing labor	11,000
Variable manufacturing overhead	7,000
Depreciation on machine	10,000
Relevant costs for operating income calculations if Part No. 789 is manufactured in-house	$50,000
Relevant accounting cost of outsourcing part No. 789	
Purchase costs of Part No. 789	$50,000
Savings in rent	(1,000)
Loss on sale of machine[a]	35,000
Relevant costs to consider for operating income computations if Part No. 789 is outsourced	$84,000
[a] Proceeds from sale of machine	$15,000
Deduct book value of machine ($60,000 − $10,000)	50,000
Loss on sale of machine	$35,000

Lin will maximize reported operating income in 2006 by manufacturing Part No. 789 in-house (relevant accounting costs of $50,000 by manufacturing in-house versus $84,000 by outsourcing). In this case, there is no conflict between the conclusion Lin will reach based on NPV and operating income analysis. Note, however, that if the sale of the machine was postponed for another year, Lin will prefer to outsource Part No. 789 (relevant outsourcing costs of $49,000 versus relevant manufacturing costs of $50,000).

Note the following:

a. Machine depreciation is relevant for operating income computations. This cost will only be incurred if Strubel continues to manufacture Part No. 789.

b. Product and process engineering costs, allocated rent and allocated general plant overhead costs are irrelevant because these costs will continue to be incurred in total whether Part No. 789 is outsourced or manufactured in-house. The savings in rent of $1,000 will only occur if Part No. 789 is outsourced. These savings are relevant and are, therefore, included in the calculation of operating income under the "outsource Part No. 789" alternative.

CHAPTER 22
MANAGEMENT CONTROL SYSTEMS, TRANSFER PRICING, AND MULTINATIONAL CONSIDERATIONS

22-2 To be effective, management control systems should be (a) closely aligned to an organization's strategies and goals, (b) designed to fit the organization's structure and the decision-making responsibility of individual managers, and (c) able to motivate managers and employees to put in effort to attain selected goals desired by top management.

22-4 The chapter cites five benefits of decentralization:
1. Creates greater responsiveness to local needs
2. Leads to gains from faster decision making
3. Increases motivation of subunit managers
4. Assets management development and learning
5. Sharpens the focus of subunit managers

The chapter cites four costs of decentralization:
1. Leads to suboptimal decision making
2. Focuses managers' attention on the subunit rather than the company as a whole
3. Increases costs of gathering information
4. Results in duplication of activities

22-6 No. A transfer price is the price one subunit of an organization charges for a product or service supplied to another subunit of the same organization. The two segments can be cost centers, profit centers, or investment centers. For example, the allocation of service department costs to production departments that are set up as either cost centers or investment centers is an example of transfer pricing.

22-8 Transfer prices should have the following properties. They should
1. promote goal congruence,
2. be useful for evaluating subunit performance,
3. motivate management effort, and
4. preserve a high level of subunit autonomy in decision making.

22-10 Transferring products or services at market prices generally leads to optimal decisions when (a) the market for the intermediate product market is perfectly competitive, (b) interdependencies of subunits are minimal, and (c) there are no additional costs or benefits to the company as a whole from buying or selling in the external market instead of transacting internally.

22-12 Reasons why a dual-pricing approach to transfer pricing is not widely used in practice include:
1. In this approach, the manager of the supplying division uses a cost-based method to record revenues and does not have sufficient incentives to control costs.
2. This approach does not provide clear signals to division managers about the level of decentralization top management wants.
3. This approach tends to insulate managers from the frictions of the marketplace because costs, not market prices, affect the revenues of the supplying division.

4. It leads to problems in computing the taxable income of subunits located in different tax jurisdictions.

22-14 Yes. The general transfer-pricing guideline specifies that the minimum transfer price equals the *incremental cost per unit* incurred up to the point of transfer *plus* the *opportunity cost per unit* to the supplying division. When the supplying division has idle capacity, its opportunity cost per unit is zero; when the supplying division has no idle capacity, its opportunity cost per unit is positive. Hence, the minimum transfer price will vary depending on whether the supplying division has idle capacity or not.

22-16 (15min.) **Management control systems, balanced scorecard.**
Durham produces and sells furniture of unique design and outstanding quality. Clearly, it is pursuing a product-differentiation strategy, and its balanced-scorecard-based management control system should reflect that strategy and measure and communicate the degree to which the organization meets its strategic goals. Some possible financial and non-financial measures are:

> Financial measures (for financial perspective): Profit margins, stock price, net income, return on investment, cash flow from operations, design costs as a percentage of sales.

> Non-financial measures: market share in the high-end furniture segment, customer repeat purchases, number of mentions of Durham furniture in design and architecture magazines (customer perspective), recognized quality certifications, number of innovative designs, (internal business process perspective), ability to attract and keep the best designers, employee satisfaction, employee pride in Durham's identity (learning-and-growth perspective).

22-18 (15 min.) **Decentralization, goal congruence, responsibility centers.**

1. The environmental-management group appears to be decentralized because its managers have considerable freedom to make decisions. They can choose which projects to work on and which projects to reject. Top management will adjust the size of the environmental-management group to match the demand for the group's services by operating divisions.

2. The environmental-management group is a cost center. The group is required to charge the operating divisions for environmental services at cost and not at market prices that would help earn the group a profit.

3. The benefits of structuring the environmental-management group in this way are:
   a. The operating managers have incentives to carefully weigh and conduct cost-benefit analyses before requesting the environmental group's services.
   b. The operating managers have an incentive to follow the work and the progress made by the environmental team.
   c. The environmental group has incentives to fulfill the contract, to do a good job in terms of cost, time, and quality, and to satisfy the operating division to continue to get business.

The problems in structuring the environmental-management group in this way are:

a. The contract requires extensive internal negotiations in terms of cost, time, and technical specifications.

b. The environmental group needs to continuously "sell" its services to the operating division, and this could potentially result in loss of morale.

c. Experimental projects that have long-term potential may not be undertaken because operating division managers may be reluctant to undertake projects that are costly and uncertain, whose benefits will be realized only well after they have left the division.

To the extent that the focus of the environmental-management group is on short-run projects demanded by the operating divisions, the current structure leads to goal congruence and motivation. Goal congruence is achieved because both operating divisions and the environmental-management group are motivated to work toward the organizational goals of reducing pollution and improving the environment. The operating divisions will be motivated to use the services of the environmental-management group to achieve the environmental goals set for them by top management. The environmental-management group will be motivated to deliver high-quality services in a cost-effective way to continue to create a demand for their services. The one issue that top management needs to guard against is that experimental projects with long-term potential that are costly and uncertain may not be undertaken under the current structure. Top management may want to set up a committee to study and propose such long-run projects for consideration and funding by corporate management.

22-20 (30 min.) **Transfer-pricing methods, goal congruence.**

1. *Alternative 1:* Sell as raw lumber for $200 per 100 board feet:

Revenue	$200
Variable costs	100
Contribution margin	$100 per 100 board feet

Alternative 2: Sell as finished lumber for $275 per 100 board feet:

Revenue		$275
Variable costs:		
Raw lumber	$100	
Finished lumber	125	225
Contribution margin		$ 50 per 100 board feet

British Columbia Lumber will maximize its total contribution margin by selling lumber in its raw form.

An alternative approach is to examine the incremental revenues and incremental costs in the Finished Lumber Division:

Incremental revenues, $275 – $200	$ 75
Incremental costs	125
Incremental loss	$ (50) per 100 board feet

2. Transfer price at 110% of variable costs:
    = $100 + ($100 × 0.10)
    = $110 per 100 board feet

	Sell as Raw Lumber	Sell as Finished Lumber
Raw Lumber Division		
Division revenues	$200	$110
Division variable costs	100	100
Division operating income	$100	$ 10
Finished Lumber Division		
Division revenues	$ 0	$275
Transferred-in costs	—	110
Division variable costs	—	125
Division operating income	$ 0	$ 40

The Raw Lumber Division will maximize reported division operating income by selling raw lumber, which is the action preferred by the company as a whole. The Finished Lumber Division will maximize division operating income by selling finished lumber, which is contrary to the action preferred by the company as a whole.

3. Transfer price at market price = $200 per 100 board feet.

	Sell as Raw Lumber	Sell as Finished Lumber
Raw Lumber Division		
Division revenues	$200	$200
Division variable costs	100	100
Division operating income	$100	$100
Finished Lumber Division		
Division revenues	$ 0	$275
Transferred-in costs	—	200
Division variable costs	—	125
Division operating income	$ 0	$ (50)

Since the Raw Lumber Division will be indifferent between selling the lumber in raw or finished form, it would be willing to maximize division operating income by selling raw lumber, which is the action preferred by the company as a whole. The Finished Lumber Division will maximize division operating income by not further processing raw lumber and this is preferred by the company as a whole. Thus, transfer at market price will result in division actions that are also in the best interest of the company as a whole.

22-22 (30 min.) Transfer pricing, general guideline, goal congruence.

1. Using the general guideline presented in the chapter, the minimum price at which the Airbag Division would sell airbags to the Tivo Division is $90, the incremental costs. The Airbag Division has idle capacity (it is currently working at 80% of capacity). Therefore, its opportunity cost is zero—the Airbag Division does not forgo any external sales and as a result, does not forgo any contribution margin from internal transfers. Transferring airbags at incremental cost achieves goal congruence.

2. Transferring products internally at incremental cost has the following properties:

   a. Achieves goal congruence—Yes, as described in requirement 1 above.
   b. Useful for evaluating division performance—No, because this transfer price does not cover or exceed full costs. By transferring at incremental costs and not covering fixed costs, the Airbag Division will show a loss. This loss, the result of the incremental cost-based transfer price, is not a good measure of the economic performance of the subunit.
   c. Motivating management effort—Yes, if based on budgeted costs (actual costs can then be compared to budgeted costs). If, however, transfers are based on actual costs, Airbag Division management has little incentive to control costs.
   d. Preserves division autonomy—No. Because it is rule-based, the Airbag Division has no say in the setting of the transfer price.

3.   If the two divisions were to negotiate a transfer price, the range of possible transfer prices will be between $90 and $125 per unit. The Airbag Division has excess capacity that it can use to supply airbags to the Tivo Division. The Airbag Division will be willing to supply the airbags only if the transfer price equals or exceeds $90, its incremental costs of manufacturing the airbags. The Tivo Division will be willing to buy airbags from the Airbag Division only if the price does not exceed $125 per airbag, the price at which the Tivo division can buy airbags in the market from external suppliers. Within the price range or $90 and $125, each division will be willing to transact with the other and maximize overall income of Quest Motors. The exact transfer price between $90 and $125 will depend on the bargaining strengths of the two divisions. The negotiated transfer price has the following properties.

     a. Achieves goal congruence—Yes, as described above.
     b. Useful for evaluating division performance—Yes, because the transfer price is the result of direct negotiations between the two divisions. Of course, the transfer prices will be affected by the bargaining strengths of the two divisions.
     c. Motivating management effort—Yes, because once negotiated, the transfer price is independent of actual costs of the Airbag Division. Airbag Division management has every incentive to manage efficiently to improve profits.
     d. Preserves subunit autonomy—Yes, because the transfer price is based on direct negotiations between the two divisions and is not specified by headquarters on the basis of some rule (such as Airbag Division's incremental costs).

4.   Neither method is perfect, but negotiated transfer pricing (requirement 3) has more favorable properties than the cost-based transfer pricing (requirement 2). Both transfer-pricing methods achieve goal congruence, but negotiated transfer pricing facilitates the evaluation of division performance, motivates management effort, and preserves division autonomy, whereas the transfer price based on incremental costs does not achieve these objectives.

22-24 (30 min.) **Multinational transfer pricing, goal congruence (continuation of 22-23).**

1.   After-tax operating income if Mornay Company sells all 1,000 units of Product 4A36 in the United States:

Revenues, $600 × 1,000 units	$600,000
Full manufacturing costs, $500 × 1,000 units	500,000
Operating income	100,000
Income taxes at 40%	40,000
After-tax operating income	$ 60,000

From Exercise 22-23, requirement 1, Mornay Company's after-tax operating income if it transfers 1,000 units of Product 4A36 to Austria at full manufacturing cost and sells the units in Austria is $112,000. Therefore, Mornay should sell the 1,000 units in Austria.

2.   Transferring Product 4A36 at the full manufacturing cost of the U.S. Division minimizes import duties and taxes (Exercise 22-23, requirement 2), but creates zero operating income for the U.S Division. Acting autonomously, the U.S. Division manager would maximize division operating income by selling Product 4A36 in the U.S. market, which results in $60,000 in after-tax division operating income as calculated in requirement 1, rather than by transferring Product 4A36 to the Austrian division at full manufacturing cost. Thus, the transfer price calculated in requirement 2 of Exercise 22-23 will not result in actions that are optimal for Mornay Company as a whole.

3.   The minimum transfer price at which the U.S. division manager acting autonomously will agree to transfer Product 4A36 to the Austrian division is $600 per unit. Any transfer price less than $600 will leave the U.S. Division's performance worse than selling directly in the U.S. market. Because the U.S. Division can sell as many units that it makes of Product 4A36 in the U.S. market, there is an opportunity cost of transferring the product internally equal to $250 (selling price $600 − variable manufacturing costs, $350).

$$\begin{matrix} \text{Minimum transfer} \\ \text{price per unit} \end{matrix} = \begin{matrix} \text{Incremental cost per} \\ \text{unit up to the point of} \\ \text{transfer} \end{matrix} + \begin{matrix} \text{Opportunity cost per} \\ \text{unit to the selling} \\ \text{(U. S.) division} \end{matrix}$$

$$= \quad \$350 + \$250 = \$600$$

This transfer price will result in Mornay Company as a whole paying more import duties and taxes than the answer to Exercise 22-23, requirement 2, as calculated below:

U.S. Division

Revenues, $600 × 1,000 units	$600,000
Full manufacturing costs	500,000
Division operating income	100,000
Division income taxes at 40%	40,000
Division after-tax operating income	$ 60,000

Austrian Division

Revenues, $750 × 1,000 units	$750,000
Transferred in costs, $600 × 1,000 units	600,000
Import duties at 10% of transferred-in price, $60 × 1,000 units	60,000
Division operating income	90,000
Division income taxes at 44%	39,600
Division after-tax operating income	$ 50,400

Total import duties and income taxes at transfer prices of $500 and $600 per unit for 1,000 units of Product 4A36 follow:

		Transfer Price of $500 per Unit (Exercise 22-23, Requirement 2)	Transfer Price of $600 per Unit
(a)	U.S. income taxes	$ 0	$ 40,000
(b)	Austrian import duties	50,000	60,000
(c)	Austrian income taxes	88,000	39,600
		$138,000	$139,600

The minimum transfer price that the U.S. division manager acting autonomously would agree to results in Mornay Company paying $1,600 in additional import duties and income taxes.

A student who has done the calculations shown in Exercise 22-23, requirement 2, can calculate the additional taxes from a $600 transfer price more directly, as follows:

Every $1 increase in the transfer price per unit over $500 results in additional import duty and taxes of $0.016 per unit

So, a $100 increase ($600 – $500) per unit will result in additional import duty and taxes of $0.016 × 100 = $1.60

For 1,000 units transferred, this equals $1.60 × 1,000 = $1,600

22-26 (5 min.) **Transfer-pricing problem (continuation of 22-25).**

The company as a whole would benefit in this situation if Division C purchased from external suppliers. The $15,000 disadvantage to the company as a whole as a result of purchasing from external suppliers would be more than offset by the $30,000 contribution margin of Division A's sale of 1,000 units to other customers:

Purchase costs paid to external suppliers, 1,000 units × $135		$135,000
Deduct variable cost savings, 1,000 units × $120		120,000
Net cost to the company as a result of purchasing from external suppliers		$ 15,000
Division A's sales to other customers, 1,000 units × $155		$155,000
Deduct:		
Variable manufacturing costs, $120 × 1,000 units	$120,000	
Variable marketing costs, $5 × 1,000 units	5,000	
Total variable costs		125,000
Contribution margin from selling units to other customers		$ 30,000

22-28 (20–30 min.) **Pertinent transfer price.**

This problem explores the "general transfer-pricing guideline" discussed in the chapter.

1.   No, transfers should not be made to Division B if there is no unused capacity in Division A. An incremental (outlay) cost approach shows a positive contribution for the company as a whole:

Selling price of final product		$300
Incremental cost per unit in Division A	$120	
Incremental cost per unit in Division B	150	270
Contribution margin per unit		$ 30

However, if there is no excess capacity in Division A, any transfer will result in diverting products from the market for the intermediate product. Sales in this market result in a greater contribution for the company as a whole. Division B should not assemble the bicycle since the incremental revenue Europa can earn, $100 per unit ($300 from selling the final product – $200 from selling the intermediate product) is less than the incremental cost of $150 to assemble the bicycle in Division B. Alternatively, Europa's contribution margin from selling the intermediate product exceeds Europa's contribution margin from selling the final product:

Selling price of intermediate product	$200
Incremental (outlay) cost per unit in Division A	120
Contribution margin per unit	$ 80

Using the general guideline described in the chapter,

$$\begin{array}{rl} \text{Minimum} \\ \text{transfer price} \end{array} = \left(\begin{array}{c} \text{Additional } \textit{incremental } \text{cost} \\ \textit{per unit} \text{ incurred up} \\ \text{to the point of transfer} \end{array} \right) + \left(\begin{array}{c} \textit{Opportunity } \text{cost} \\ \textit{per unit} \text{ to the} \\ \text{supplying division} \end{array} \right)$$

$$= \$120 + (\$200 - \$120)$$
$$= \$200, \text{ which is the market price}$$

The market price is the transfer price that leads to the correct decision; that is, do not transfer to Division B unless there are extenuating circumstances for continuing to market the final product. Therefore, Division B must either drop the product or reduce the incremental costs of assembly from $150 per bicycle to less than $100 (selling price, $300 – transfer price, $200).

2.   If (a) A has excess capacity, (b) there is intermediate external demand for only 800 units at $200, and (c) the $200 price is to be maintained, then the opportunity costs per unit to the supplying division are $0. The general guideline indicates a minimum transfer price of: $120 + $0 = $120, which is the incremental or outlay costs for the first 200 units. B would buy 200 units from A at a transfer price of $120 because B can earn a contribution of $30 per unit [$300 – ($120 + $150)]. In fact, B would be willing to buy units from A at any price up to $150 per unit because any transfers at a price of up to $150 will still yield B a positive contribution margin.

Note, however, that if B wants more than 200 units, the minimum transfer price will be $200 as computed in requirement 1 because A will incur an opportunity cost in the form of lost contribution of $80 (market price, $200 – outlay costs of $120) for every unit above 200 units that are transferred to B.

The following schedule summarizes the transfer prices for units transferred from A to B:

Units	Transfer Price
0–200	$120–$150
200–1,000	$200

For an exploration of this situation when imperfect markets exist, see the next problem.

3.   Division B would show zero contribution, but the company as a whole would generate a contribution of $30 per unit on the 200 units transferred. Any price between $120 and $150 would induce the transfer that would be desirable for the company as a whole. A motivational problem may arise regarding how to split the $30 contribution between Division A and B. Unless the price is below $150, B would have little incentive to buy.

Note: The transfer price that may appear optimal in an economic analysis may, in fact, be totally unacceptable from the viewpoints of (1) preserving autonomy of the managers, and (2) evaluating the performance of the divisions as economic units. For instance, consider the simplest case discussed previously, where there is idle capacity and the $200 intermediate price is to be maintained. To direct that A should sell to B at A's variable cost of $120 may be desirable from the viewpoint of B and the company as a whole. However, the autonomy (independence) of the manager of A is eroded. Division A will earn nothing, although it could argue that it is contributing to the earning of income on the final product.

If the manager of A wants a portion of the total company contribution of $30 per unit, the question is: How is an appropriate amount determined? This is a difficult question in practice. The price can be negotiated upward to somewhere between $120 and $150 so that some "equitable" split is achieved. A dual transfer-pricing scheme has also been suggested, whereby the supplier gets credit for the full intermediate market price and the buyer is charged with only variable or incremental costs. In any event, when there is heavy interdependence between divisions, such as in this case, some system of subsidies may be needed to deal with the three problems of goal congruence, management effort, and subunit autonomy. Of course, where heavy subsidies are needed, a question can be raised as to whether the existing degree of decentralization is optimal.

22-30 (30–35 min.) **Effect of alternative transfer-pricing methods on division operating income.**

1.

Pounds of cranberries harvested	500,000
Gallons of juice processed (500 gals per 1,000 lbs.)	250,000
Revenues (250,000 gals. × $2.10 per gal.)	$525,000
Costs	
Harvesting Division	
Variable costs (500,000 lbs. × $0.10 per lb.) $ 50,000	
Fixed costs (500,000 lbs. × $0.25 per lb.) 125,000	
Total Harvesting Division costs	175,000
Processing Division	
Variable costs (250,000 gals. × $0.20 per gal.) $ 50,000	
Fixed costs (250,000 gals. × $0.40 per gal.) 100,000	
Total Processing Division costs	150,000
Total costs	325,000
Operating income	$200,000

2.

	200% of Full Costs	Market Price
Transfer price per pound (($0.10 + $0.25) × 2; $0.60)	$0.70	$0.60
1. Harvesting Division		
Revenues (500,000 lbs. × $0.70; $0.60)	$350,000	$300,000
Costs		
Division variable costs (500,000 lbs. × $0.10 per lb.)	50,000	50,000
Division fixed costs (500,000 lbs. × $0.25 per lb.)	125,000	125,000
Total division costs	175,000	175,000
Division operating income	$175,000	$125,000
Harvesting Division manager's bonus (5% of operating income)	$8,750	$6,250
2. Processing Division		
Revenues (250,000 gals. × $2.10 per gal.)	$525,000	$525,000
Costs		
Transferred-in costs	350,000	300,000
Division variable costs (250,000 gals. × $0.20 per gal.)	50,000	50,000
Division fixed costs (250,000 gals. × $0.40 per gal.)	100,000	100,000
Total division costs	500,000	450,000
Division operating income	$ 25,000	$ 75,000
Processing Division manager's bonus (5% of operating income)	$1,250	$3,750

3.   Bonus paid to division managers at 5% of division operating income is computed above and summarized below:

	Internal Transfers at 200% of Full Costs	Internal Transfers at Market Prices
Harvesting Division manager's bonus (5% × $175,000; 5% × $125,000)	$8,750	$6,250
Processing Division manager's bonus (5% × $25,000; 5% × $75,000)	$1,250	$3,750

The Harvesting Division manager will prefer to transfer at 200% of full costs because this method gives a higher bonus. The Processing Division manager will prefer transfer at market price for its higher resulting bonus.

Crango may resolve or reduce transfer pricing conflicts by:

- Basing division managers' bonuses on overall Crango profits in addition to division operating income. This will motivate each manager to consider what is best for Crango overall and not be concerned with the transfer price alone.
- Letting the two divisions negotiate the transfer price between themselves. However, this may result in constant re-negotiation between the two managers each accounting period.
- Using dual transfer prices However, a cost-based transfer price will not motivate cost control by the Harvesting Division manager. It will also insulate that division from the discipline of market prices.

22-32 (40 min.) **Multinational transfer pricing, global tax minimization.**

This is a two-country two-division transfer-pricing problem with two alternative transfer-pricing methods.

Summary data in U.S. dollars are:

South Africa Mining Division

Variable costs:	560 ZAR ÷ 7 = $80 per lb. of raw diamonds
Fixed costs:	1,540 ZAR ÷ 7 = $220 per lb. of raw diamonds
Market price:	3,150 ZAR ÷ 7 = $450 per lb. of raw diamonds

U.S. Processing Division

Variable costs = $150 per lb. of polished industrial diamonds
Fixed costs = $700 per lb. of polished industrial diamonds
Market price = $5,000 per lb. of polished industrial diamonds

1. The transfer prices are:
    a. *200% of full costs*
        Mining Division to Processing Division
        = 2.0 × ($80 + $220) = $600 per lb. of raw diamonds
    b. *Market price*
        Mining Division to Processing Division
        = $450 per lb. of raw diamonds

	200% of Full Cost	Market Price
South Africa Mining Division		
Division revenues, $600, $450 × 2,000	$1,200,000	$ 900,000
Costs		
Division variable costs, $80 × 2,000	160,000	160,000
Division fixed costs, $220 × 2,000	440,000	440,000
Total division costs	600,000	600,000
Division operating income	$ 600,000	$ 300,000
U.S. Processing Division		
Division revenues, $5,000 × 1,000	$5,000,000	$5,000,000
Costs		
Transferred-in costs, $600, $450 × 2,000	1,200,000	900,000
Division variable cost, $150 × 1,000	150,000	150,000
Division fixed costs, $700 × 1,000	700,000	700,000
Total division costs	2,050,000	1,750,000
Division operating income	$2,950,000	$3,250,000

2.

	200% of Full Cost	Market Price
South Africa Mining Division		
Division operating income	$600,000	$300,000
Income tax at 18%	108,000	54,000
Division after-tax operating income	$492,000	$246,000
U.S. Processing Division		
Division operating income	$2,950,000	$3,250,000
Income tax at 30%	885,000	975,000
Division after-tax operating income	$2,065,000	$2,275,000

3.

	200% of Full Cost	Market Price
South Africa Mining Division:		
After-tax operating income	$ 492,000	$ 246,000
U.S. Processing Division:		
After-tax operating income	2,065,000	2,275,000
Industrial Diamonds:		
After-tax operating income	$2,557,000	$2,521,000

The South Africa Mining Division manager will prefer the higher transfer price of 200% of full cost and the U.S. Processing Division manager will prefer the lower transfer price equal to market price. Industrial Diamonds will maximize companywide net income by using the 200% of full cost transfer-pricing method. This method sources more of the total income in South Africa, the country with the lower income tax rate.

4.   The Surveys of Company Practice Box in the chapter lists the factors executives state to be important in decisions on transfer pricing:
   a. Performance evaluation
   b. Management motivation
   c. Pricing and product emphasis
   d. External market recognition

Factors specifically related to multinational transfer pricing include:
   a. Overall income of the company
   b. Income or dividend repatriation restrictions
   c. Competitive position of subsidiaries in their respective markets

22-34 (30 min.) **Transfer pricing, goal congruence.**

1.   See column (1) of Solution Exhibit 22-34. The net cost of the in-house option is $230,000.

2.   See columns (2a) and (2b) of Solution Exhibit 22-34. As the calculations show, if Johnson Corporation offers a price of $38 per tape player, Orsilo Corporation should purchase the tape players from Johnson; this will result in an incremental net cost of $210,000 (column 2a). If Johnson Corporation offers a price of $45 per tape player, Orsilo Corporation should manufacture the tape players in-house; this will result in an incremental net cost of $230,000 (column 2b).

SOLUTION EXHIBIT 22-34

	Transfer 10,000 tape players to Assembly. Sell 2,000 in outside market at $35 each (1)	Buy 10,000 tape players from Johnson at $38. Sell 12,000 tape players in outside market at $35 each (2a)	Buy 10,000 tape players from Johnson at $40. Sell 12,000 tape players in outside market at $35 each (2x)	Buy 10,000 tape players from Johnson at $45. Sell 12,000 tape players in outside market at $35 each (2b)
Incremental cost of Cassette Division supplying 10,000 tape players to Assembly Division $25 × 10,000; 0; 0; 0	$(250,000)	$ 0	$ 0	$ 0
Incremental costs of buying 10,000 tape players from Johnson $0; $38 × 10,000; $40 × 10,000; $45 × 10,000	0	(380,000)	(400,000)	(450,000)
Revenue from selling tape players in outside market $35 × 2,000; 12,000; 12,000; 12,000	70,000	420,000	420,000	420,000
Incremental costs of manufacturing tape players for sale in outside market $25 × 2,000; 12,000; 12,000; 12,000	(50,000)	(300,000)	(300,000)	(300,000)
Revenue from supplying head mechanism to Johnson $20 × 0; 10,000; 10,000; 10,000	0	200,000	200,000	200,000
Incremental costs of supplying head mechanism to Johnson $15 × 0; 10,000; 10,000; 10,000	0	(150,000)	(150,000)	(150,000)
Net costs	$(230,000)	$(210,000)	$(230,000)	$(280,000)

Comparing columns (1) and (2a), at a price of $38 per tape player from Johnson, the net cost of $210,000 is less than the net cost of $230,000 to Orsilo Corporation if it made the tape players in-house. So, Orsilo Corporation should outsource to Johnson.

Comparing columns (1) and (2b), at a price of $45 per tape player from Johnson, the net cost of $280,000 is greater than the net cost of $230,000 to Orsilo Corporation if it made the tape players in-house. Therefore, Orsilo Corporation should reject Johnson's offer.

Now consider column (2x) of Solution Exhibit 22-34. It shows that at a price of $40 per tape player from Johnson, the net cost is exactly $230,000, the same as the net cost to Orsilo Corporation of manufacturing in-house (column 1). Thus, for prices between $38 and $40, Orsilo will prefer to purchase from Johnson. For prices greater than $40 (and up to $45), Orsilo will prefer to manufacture in-house.

3. The Cassette Division can manufacture at most 12,000 tape players and it is currently operating at capacity. The incremental costs of manufacturing a tape player are $25 per unit. The opportunity cost of manufacturing tape players for the Assembly Division is (1) the contribution margin of $10 (selling price, $35 minus incremental costs $25) that the Cassette Division would forgo by not selling tape players in the outside market plus (2) the contribution margin of $5 (selling price, $20 minus incremental costs, $15) that the Cassette Division would forgo by not being able to sell the head mechanism to external suppliers of tape players such as Johnson (recall that the Cassette division can produce as many head mechanisms as demanded by external suppliers, but their demand will fall if the Cassette Division supplies the Assembly Division with tape players). Thus, the total opportunity cost to the Cassette Division of supplying tape players to Assembly is $10 + $5 = $15 per unit.

Using the general guideline,

$$\begin{array}{ccc} \text{Minimum transfer} \\ \text{price per tape player} \end{array} = \begin{array}{c} \text{Incremental cost per} \\ \text{tape player up to the} \\ \text{point of transfer} \end{array} + \begin{array}{c} \text{Opportunity cost per} \\ \text{tape player to the} \\ \text{selling division} \end{array}$$

$$= \$25 + \$15 = \$40$$

Thus, the minimum transfer price that the Cassette Division will accept for each tape player is $40. Note that at a price of $40, Orsilo is indifferent between manufacturing tape players in-house or purchasing them from an external supplier.

4a. The transfer price is set to $40 + $1 = $41 and Johnson is offering the tape players for $40.50 each. Now, for an outside price per tape player below $41, the Assembly Division would prefer to purchase from outside; above it, the Assembly Division would prefer to purchase from the Cassette Division. So, the Assembly division will buy from Johnson at $40.50 each and the Cassette Division will be forced to sell its output on the outside market.

4b. But for Orsilo, as seen from requirements 1 and 2, an outside price of $40.50, which is greater than the $40 cut-off price, makes inhouse manufacture the optimal choice. So, a mandated transfer price of $41 causes the division managers to make choices that are sub-optimal for Orsilo.

4c. When selling prices are uncertain, the transfer price should be set at the minimum acceptable transfer price. It is only if the price charged by the external supplier falls below $40 that Orsilo Corporation as a whole is better off purchasing from the outside market. Setting the transfer price at $40 per unit achieves goal congruence. The Cassette division will be willing to sell to the Assembly Division, and the Assembly Division will be willing to buy in-house and this would be optimal for Orsilo, too.

22-36 (20 min.) **Ethics, transfer pricing.**

1.   The contribution margin for 10,000 units of R47 if variable costs are $14 and $16 per unit, respectively, are as follows:

	Variable Costs of $14 per Unit	Variable Costs of $16 per Unit
Transfer price at 200% of variable costs	$ 28	$ 32
Variable cost per unit	14	16
Contribution margin per unit	$ 14	$ 16
Contribution margin for 10,000 units		
$14 × 10,000; $16 × 10,000	$140,000	$160,000

2.   In assessing the situation, the specific "Standards of Ethical Conduct for Management Accountants," described in Chapter 1 that the management accountant should consider are listed below.

Competence
Clear reports using relevant and reliable information should be prepared. Reports prepared on the basis of incorrectly identifying variable costs would violate the management accountant's responsibility to competence. It is unethical for Lasker to suggest that Tanner should change the variable cost numbers that were prepared for costing product R47 and, hence, the transfer price for R47. The methodology to calculate variable costs has been in place for some time at Durham Industries. The company could certainly re-evaluate this methodology but Tanner cannot do so on his own.

Integrity
The management accountant has a responsibility to avoid actual or apparent conflicts of interest and advise all appropriate parties of any potential conflict. Increasing the variable costs allocated to R47 will increase the transfer price and as a result, the revenues of the Belmont Division. If they changed the method of determining variable costs, Lasker and Tanner would appear to favor the Belmont Division (that manufactures R47) over the Alston Division (that uses R47). This action could be viewed as violating the responsibility for integrity. The Standards of Ethical Conduct require the management accountant to communicate favorable as well as unfavorable information. In this regard, both Lasker's and Tanner's behavior (if Tanner agrees to increase variable costs) could be viewed as unethical.

Objectivity
The "Standards of Ethical Conduct for Management Accountants" require that information should be fairly and objectively communicated and that all relevant information should be disclosed. From a management accountant's standpoint, increasing the variable costs of a product to earn higher revenue for a division, in violation of company policy, clearly violates both these precepts. For the various reasons cited above, the behavior of Lasker and Tanner (if he goes along with Lasker's wishes) is unethical.

Tanner should indicate to Lasker that the variable costs of R47 are indeed appropriate, given that the methods for computing variable costs and fixed costs have been in place for some time. If Lasker still insists on making the changes and increasing the variable costs of making R47, Tanner should raise the matter with Lasker's superior. If, after taking all these steps, there is continued pressure to increase the variable cost component, Tanner should consider resigning from the company and not engage in unethical behavior.

Some students may raise the issue of whether variable cost transfer pricing is appropriate in this context. The problem does not provide enough details for a complete discussion of this issue. Management may well conclude that the transfer price should not be set as a multiple of variable costs. But that is a management decision. The management accountant should not unilaterally use methods of calculating variable costs that are in direct violation of accepted past practice.

CHAPTER 23
PERFORMANCE MEASUREMENT, COMPENSATION, AND
MULTINATIONAL CONSIDERATIONS

23-2   The six steps in designing an accounting-based performance measure are:
1.   Choose performance measures that align with top management's financial goals
2.   Choose the time horizon of each performance measure in Step 1
3.   Choose a definition of the components in each performance measure in Step 1
4.   Choose a measurement alternative for each performance measure in Step 1
5.   Choose a target level of performance
6.   Choose the timing of feedback

23-4   Yes. Residual income (RI) is not identical to return on investment (ROI). ROI is a percentage with investment as the denominator of the computation. RI is an absolute monetary amount which includes an imputed interest charge based on investment.

23-6   Definitions of investment used in practice when computing ROI are:
1.   Total assets available
2.   Total assets employed
3.   Total assets employed minus current liabilities
4.   Stockholders' equity

23-8   Special problems arise when evaluating the performance of divisions in multinational companies because
    a.   The economic, legal, political, social, and cultural environments differ significantly across countries.
    b.   Governments in some countries may impose controls and limit selling prices of products.
    c.   Availability of materials and skilled labor, as well as costs of materials, labor, and infrastructure may differ significantly across countries.
    d.   Divisions operating in different countries keep score of their performance in different currencies.

23-10   Moral hazard describes situations in which an employee prefers to exert less effort (or to report distorted information) compared with the effort (or accurate information) desired by the owner because the employee's effort (or validity of the reported information) cannot be accurately monitored and enforced.

23-12   Benchmarking or relative performance evaluation is the process of evaluating a manager's performance against the performance of other similar operations. The ideal benchmark is another operation that is affected by the same noncontrollable factors that affect the manager's performance. Benchmarking cancels the effects of the common noncontrollable factors and provides better information about the manager's performance.

23-14 Disclosures required by the Securities and Exchange Commission are:
   a. A summary compensation table showing the salary, bonus, stock options, other stock awards, and other compensation earned by the five top officers in the previous three years
   b. The principles underlying the executive compensation plans, and the performance criteria, such as profitability, sales growth, and market share used in determining compensation
   c. How well a company's stock performed relative to the stocks of other companies in the same industry

23-16 (30 min.) **ROI, comparisons of three companies.**

1.   The separate components highlight several features of return on investment not revealed by a single calculation:
   a. The importance of investment turnover as a key to income is stressed.
   b. The importance of revenues is explicitly recognized.
   c. The important components are expressed as ratios or percentages instead of dollar figures. This form of expression often enhances comparability of different divisions, businesses, and time periods.
   d. The breakdown stresses the possibility of trading off investment turnover for income as a percentage of revenues so as to increase the average ROI at a given level of output.

2.   (Filled-in blanks are in bold face.)

	Companies in Same Industry		
	A	B	C
Revenue	$1,000,000	$ 500,000	**$10,000,000**
Income	$ 100,000	$ 50,000	$ **50,000**
Investment	$ 500,000	**$5,000,000**	$ 5,000,000
Income as a % of revenue	**10%**	10%	0.5%
Investment turnover	**2.0**	0.1	2.0
Return on investment	**20%**	1%	**1%**

Income and investment alone shed little light on comparative performances because of disparities in size between Company A and the other two companies. Thus, it is impossible to say whether B's low return on investment in comparison with A's is attributable to its larger investment or to its lower income. Furthermore, the fact that Companies B and C have identical income and investment may suggest that the same conditions underlie the low ROI, but this conclusion is erroneous. B has higher margins but a lower investment turnover. C has very small margins (1/20th of B) but turns over investment 20 times faster.

   I.M.A. Report No. 35 (page 35) states:

   "Introducing revenues to measure level of operations helps to disclose specific areas for more intensive investigation. Company B does as well as Company A in terms of income margin, for both companies earn 10% on revenues. But Company B has a much lower turnover of investment than does Company A. Whereas a dollar of investment in Company A supports two dollars in revenues each period, a dollar investment in Company B supports only ten cents in revenues each period. This suggests that the analyst should look carefully at Company B's investment. Is the company keeping an inventory larger than necessary for its revenue level?

Are receivables being collected promptly? Or did Company A acquire its fixed assets at a price level that was much lower than that at which Company B purchased its plant?"

"On the other hand, C's investment turnover is as high as A's, but C's income as a percentage of revenue is much lower. Why? Are its operations inefficient, are its material costs too high, or does its location entail high transportation costs?"

"Analysis of ROI raises questions such as the foregoing. When answers are obtained, basic reasons for differences between rates of return may be discovered. For example, in Company B's case, it is apparent that the emphasis will have to be on increasing turnover by reducing investment or increasing revenues. Clearly, B cannot appreciably increase its ROI simply by increasing its income as a percent of revenue. In contrast, Company C's management should concentrate on increasing the percent of income on revenue."

23-18 (10–15 min.) **ROI and RI.**

1. Operating income = (Contribution margin per unit × 150,000 units) – Fixed costs
= ($360 – $250) × 150,000 – $15,000,000 = $1,500,000

$$\text{ROI} = \frac{\text{Operating income}}{\text{Investment}} = \frac{\$1,500,000}{\$24,000,000} = 6.25\%$$

2. Operating income = ROI × Investment

[No. of pairs sold (Selling price – Var. cost per unit)] – Fixed costs = ROI × Investment

Let $X = minimum selling price per unit to achieve a 25% ROI

150,000 ($X – $250) – $15,000,000 = 25% ($24,000,000)
$150,000X = $6,000,000 + $15,000,000 + $37,500,000 = $58,500,000
X = $390

3. Let $X = minimum selling price per unit to achieve a 20% rate of return

150,000 ($X – $250) – $15,000,000 = 20% ($24,000,000)
$150,000X = $4,800,000 + $15,000,000 + $37,500,000 = $57,300,000
X = $382

23-20 (25 min.) **Financial and nonfinancial performance measures, goal congruence**.

1.   Operating income is a good summary measure of short-term financial performance. By itself, however, it does not indicate whether operating income in the short run was earned by taking actions that would lead to long-run competitive advantage. For example, Summit's divisions might be able to increase short-run operating income by producing more product while ignoring quality or rework. Harrington, however, would like to see division managers increase operating income without sacrificing quality. The new performance measures take a balanced scorecard approach by evaluating and rewarding managers on the basis of direct measures (such as rework costs, on-time delivery performance, and sales returns). This motivates managers to take actions that Harrington believes will increase operating income now and in the future. The nonoperating income measures serve as surrogate measures of future profitability.

2.   The semiannual installments and total bonus for the Charter Division are calculated as follows:

Charter Division Bonus Calculation
For Year Ended December 31, 2006

January 1, 2006 to June 30, 2006

Profitability	$(0.02 \times \$462,000)$	$ 9,240
Rework	$(0.02 \times \$462,000) - \$11,500$	(2,260)
On-time delivery	No bonus—under 96%	0
Sales returns	$[(0.015 \times \$4,200,000) - \$84,000] \times 50\%$	(10,500)
Semiannual installment		$ (3,520)
Semiannual bonus awarded		$ 0

July 1, 2006 to December 31, 2006

Profitability	$(0.02 \times \$440,000)$	$ 8,800
Rework	$(0.02 \times \$440,000) - \$11,000$	(2,200)
On-time delivery	96% to 98%	2,000
Sales returns	$[(0.015 \times \$4,400,000) - \$70,000] \times 50\%$	(2,000)
Semiannual installment		$ 6,600
Semiannual bonus awarded		$ 6,600
Total bonus awarded for the year		$ 6,600

The semiannual installments and total bonus for the Mesa Division are calculated as follows:

Mesa Division Bonus Calculation
For Year Ended December 31, 2006

January 1, 2006 to June 30, 2006

Profitability	(0.02 × $342,000)	$ 6,840
Rework	(0.02 × $342,000) – $6,000	0
On-time delivery	Over 98%	5,000
Sales returns	[(0.015 × $2,850,000) – $44,750] × 50%	(1,000)
Semiannual bonus installment		$10,840
Semiannual bonus awarded		$10,840

July 1, 2006 to December 31, 2006

Profitability	(0.02 × $406,000)	$ 8,120
Rework	(0.02 × $406,000) – $8,000	0
On-time delivery	No bonus—under 96%	0
Sales returns	[(0.015 × $2,900,000) – $42,500] which is greater than zero, yielding a bonus	3,000
Semiannual bonus installment		$11,120
Semiannual bonus awarded		$11,120
Total bonus awarded for the year		$21,960

3.   The manager of the Charter Division is likely to be frustrated by the new plan, as the division bonus has fallen by more than $20,000 compared to the bonus of the previous year. However, the new performance measures have begun to have the desired effect—both on-time deliveries and sales returns improved in the second half of the year, while rework costs were relatively even. If the division continues to improve at the same rate, the Charter bonus could approximate or exceed what it was under the old plan.

The manager of the Mesa Division should be as satisfied with the new plan as with the old plan, as the bonus is almost equivalent. On-time deliveries declined considerably in the second half of the year and rework costs increased. However, sales returns decreased slightly. Unless the manager institutes better controls, the bonus situation may not be as favorable in the future. This could motivate the manager to improve in the future but currently, at least, the manager has been able to maintain his bonus with showing improvement in only one area targeted by Harrington.

Ben Harrington's revised bonus plan for the Charter Division fostered the following improvements in the second half of the year despite an increase in sales:

- An increase of 1.9% in on-time deliveries.
- A $500 reduction in rework costs.
- A $14,000 reduction in sales returns.

However, operating income as a percent of sales has decreased (11% to 10%).

The Mesa Division's bonus has remained at the status quo as a result of the following effects:

- An increase of 2.0 % in operating income as a percent of sales (12% to 14%).
- A decrease of 3.6% in on-time deliveries.
- A $2,000 increase in rework costs.
- A $2,250 decrease in sales returns.

This would suggest that revisions to the bonus plan are needed. Possible changes include:

- increasing the weights put on on-time deliveries, rework costs, and sales returns in the performance measures while decreasing the weight put on operating income;
- a reward structure for rework costs that are below 2% of operating income that would encourage managers to drive costs lower;
- reviewing the whole year in total. The bonus plan should carry forward the negative amounts for one six-month period into the next six-month period incorporating the entire year when calculating a bonus; and
- developing benchmarks, and then giving rewards for improvements over prior periods and encouraging continuous improvement.

23-22 (25 min.) **ROI, RI, EVA®.**

1. The required division ROIs using total assets as a measure of investment is shown in the row labeled (1) in Solution Exhibit 23-22.

SOLUTION EXHIBIT 23-22

		Truck Rental Division	Transportation Division
	Total assets	$11,000,000	$9,500,000
	Current liabilities	$2,200,000	$2,800,000
	Operating income	$825,000	$855,000
	Required rate of return	12%	12%
	Total assets – current liabilities	$8,800,000	$6,700,000
(1)	ROI (based on total assets) ($825,000 ÷ $11,000,000; $855,000 ÷ $9,500,000)	7.5%	9.0%
(2)	RI (based on total assets – current liabilities) ($825,000 – (12% × $8,800,000); $855,000 – (12% × $6,700,000))	($231,000)	$51,000
(3)	RI (based on total assets) ($825,000 – (12% × $11,000,000); $855,000 – (12% × $9,500,000))	($495,000)	($285,000)

2. The required division RIs using total assets minus current liabilities as a measure of investment is shown in the row labeled (2) in the table above.

3. The row labeled (3) in the table above shows division RIs using assets as a measure of investment. Even with this new measure that is insensitive to the level of short-term debt, the truck rental division has a relatively worse RI than the transportation division. Both RIs are negative, indicating that the divisions are not earning the 12% required rate of return on their assets.

4. After-tax cost of debt financing = $(1 - 0.4) \times 10\% = 6\%$
After-tax cost of equity financing = 15%

$$\text{Weighted average cost of capital} = \frac{\$9,000,000 \times 6\% + 6,000,000 \times 15\%}{\$9,000,000 + 6,000,000} = 9.6\%$$

	Truck Rental Division	Transportation Division
Operating income after tax 0.6 × operating income before tax (0.6 × $825,000; 0.6 × $855,000)	$ 495,000	$ 513,000
Required return for EVA 9.6% × Investment (9.6% × $8,800,000; 9.6% × $6,700,000)	844,800	643,200
EVA (Optg. inc. after tax – reqd. return)	$(349,800)	$(130,200)

5. Both the residual income and the EVA calculations indicate that the Transportation Division is performing nominally better than the Truck Rental Division. The Transportation Division has a higher residual income. The negative EVA for both divisions indicates that, on an after-tax basis, the divisions are destroying value—the after-tax economic returns from them are less than the required returns.

23-24 (20 min.) **Multinational performance measurement, ROI, RI.**

1a.　U.S. Division's ROI in 2006 $= \dfrac{\text{Operating income}}{\text{Total assets}} = \dfrac{\text{Operating income}}{\$8,000,000} = 15\%$

Hence, operating income $= 15\% \times \$8,000,000 = \$1,200,000$.

1b.　Swedish Division's ROI in 2006 (based on kronas) $= \dfrac{8,100,000 \text{ kronas}}{52,500,000 \text{ kronas}} = 15.43\%$

2.　Convert total assets into dollars using the December 31, 2005 exchange rate, the rate prevailing when the assets were acquired (7 kronas = $1):

$$\dfrac{52,500,000 \text{ kronas}}{7 \text{ kronas per dollar}} = \$7,500,000$$

Convert operating income into dollars at the average exchange rate prevailing during 2006 when operating income was earned (7.5 kronas = $1):

$$\dfrac{8,100,000 \text{ kronas}}{7.5 \text{ kronas per dollar}} = \$1,080,000$$

Comparable ROI for Swedish Division $= \dfrac{\$1,080,000}{\$7,500,000} = 14.4\%$

The Swedish Division's ROI based on kronas is helped by the inflation that occurs in Sweden in 2006 (that caused the Swedish krona to weaken against the dollar from 7 kronas = $1 on 12-31-2005 to 8 kronas = $1 on 12-31-2006). Inflation boosts the division's operating income. Since the assets are acquired at the start of the year 2006, the asset values are not increased by the inflation that occurs during the year. The net effect of inflation on ROI calculated in kronas is to use an inflated value for the numerator relative to the denominator. Adjusting for inflationary and currency differences negates the effects of any differences in inflation rates between the two countries on the calculation of ROI. After these adjustments, the U.S. Division earned a higher ROI than the Swedish Division.

3.　U.S. Division's RI in 2006 $= \$1,200,000 - (12\% \times \$8,000,000)$
　　　　　　　　　　　　　　$= \$1,200,000 - \$960,000 = \$240,000$

Swedish Division's RI in 2006 (in U.S. dollars) is calculated as:

$\$1,080,000 - (12\% \times \$7,500,000) = \$1,080,000 - \$900,000 = \$180,000$.

The U.S. Division's RI also exceeds the Swedish Division's RI in 2006 by $60,000 ($240,000 − $180,000).

23-26 (20–30 min.) **Risk sharing, incentives, benchmarking, multiple tasks.**

1.   An evaluation of the three proposals to compensate Marks, the general manager of the Dexter Division follows:

(i)   Paying Marks a flat salary will not subject Marks to any risk, but it will provide no incentives for Marks to undertake extra physical and mental effort.

(ii)   Rewarding Marks only on the basis of Dexter Division's ROI would motivate Marks to put in extra effort to increase ROI because Marks's rewards would increase with increases in ROI. But compensating Marks solely on the basis of ROI subjects Marks to excessive risk because the division's ROI depends not only on Marks's effort but also on other random factors over which Marks has no control. For example, Marks may put in a great deal of effort, but, despite this effort, the division's ROI may be low because of adverse factors (such as high interest rates or a recession) which Marks cannot control.

To compensate Marks for taking on uncontrollable risk, AMCO must pay him additional amounts within the structure of the ROI-based arrangement. Thus, compensating Marks only on the basis of performance-based incentives will cost AMCO more money, on average, than paying Marks a flat salary. The key question is whether the benefits of motivating additional effort justify the higher costs of performance-based rewards.

Furthermore, the objective of maximizing ROI may induce Marks to reject projects that, from the viewpoint of the organization as a whole, should be accepted. This would occur for projects that would reduce Marks's overall ROI but which would earn a return greater than the required rate of return for that project.

(iii)   The motivation for having some salary and some performance-based bonus in compensation arrangements is to balance the benefits of incentives against the extra costs of imposing uncontrollable risk on the manager.

2.   Marks's complaint does not appear to be valid. The senior management of AMCO is proposing to benchmark Marks's performance using a relative performance evaluation (RPE) system. RPE controls for common uncontrollable factors that similarly affect the performance of managers operating in the same environments (for example, the same industry). If business conditions for car battery manufacturers are good, all businesses manufacturing car batteries will probably perform well. A superior indicator of Marks's performance is how well Marks performed relative to his peers. The goal is to filter out the common noise to get a better understanding of Marks's performance. Marks's complaint will be valid only if there are significant differences in investments, assets, and the business environment in which AMCO and Tiara operate. Given the information in the problem, this does not appear to be the case.

Of course, using RPE does not eliminate the problem with the ROI measure itself. To keep ROI high, Marks will still prefer to reject projects whose ROI is greater than the required rate of return but lower than the current ROI.

3.   Superior performance measures change significantly with the manager's performance and not very much with changes in factors that are beyond the manager's control. If Marks has no authority for making capital investment decisions, then ROI is not a good measure of Marks's performance—it varies with the actions taken by others rather than the actions taken by Marks. AMCO may wish to evaluate Marks on the basis of operating income rather than ROI.

ROI, however, may be a good measure to evaluate Dexter's economic viability. Senior management at AMCO could use ROI to evaluate if the Dexter Division's income provides a reasonable return on investment, regardless of who has authority for making capital investment decisions. That is, ROI may be an inappropriate measure of Marks's performance but a reasonable measure of the economic viability of the Dexter Division. If, for whatever reasons—bad capital investments, weak economic conditions, etc.—the Division shows poor economic performance as computed by ROI, AMCO management may decide to shut down the division even though they may simultaneously conclude that Marks performed well.

4.   There are two main concerns with Marks's plans. First, creating very strong sales incentives imposes excessive risk on the sales force because a salesperson's performance is affected not only by his or her own effort, but also by random factors (such as a recession in the industry) that are beyond the salesperson's control. If salespersons are risk averse, the firm will have to compensate them for bearing this extra uncontrollable risk. Second, compensating salespersons only on the basis of sales creates strong incentives to sell, but may result in lower levels of customer service and sales support (this was the story at Sears auto repair shops where a change in the contractual terms of mechanics to "produce" more repairs caused unobservable quality to be negatively affected). Where employees perform multiple tasks, it may be important to "blunt" incentives on those aspects of the job that can be measured well (for example, sales) to try and achieve a better balance of the two tasks (for example, sales and customer service and support). In addition, the division should try to better monitor customer service and customer satisfaction through surveys, or through quantifying the amount of repeat business.

23-28 (40–50 min.)   **ROI performance measures based on historical cost and current cost.**

1.   ROI using historical cost measures:

Calistoga $\dfrac{\$130,000}{\$340,000}$ = 38.24%

Alpine Springs $\dfrac{\$220,000}{\$1,150,000}$ = 19.13%

Rocky Mountains $\dfrac{\$380,000}{\$1,620,000}$ = 23.46%

The Calistoga Division appears to be considerably more efficient than the Alpine Springs and Rocky Mountain Divisions.

2.   The gross book values (i.e., the original costs of the plants) under historical cost are calculated as the useful life of each plant (12 years) × the annual depreciation:

Calistoga	12 × $70,000	=	$ 840,000
Alpine Springs	12 × $100,000	=	$1,200,000
Rocky Mountains	12 × $120,000	=	$1,440,000

Step 1: Restate long-term assets from gross book value at historical cost to gross book value at current cost as of the end of 2007.

Gross book value of long-term assets   × $\dfrac{\text{Construction cost index in 2007}}{\text{Construction cost index in year of construction}}$
at historical cost

Calistoga	$ 840,000 × (170 ÷ 100)	=	$1,428,000
Alpine Springs	$1,200,000 × (170 ÷ 136)	=	$1,500,000
Rocky Mountain	$1,440,000 × (170 ÷ 160)	=	$1,530,000

Step 2: Derive net book value of long-term assets at current cost as of the end of 2007. (Estimated useful life of each plant is 12 years.)

Gross book value of long-term assets   × $\dfrac{\text{Estimated remaining useful life}}{\text{Estimated total useful life}}$
at current cost at the end of 2007

Calistoga	$1,428,000 × (2 ÷ 12)	=	$ 238,000
Alpine Springs	$1,500,000 × (9 ÷ 12)	=	$1,125,000
Rocky Mountains	$1,530,000 × (11 ÷ 12)	=	$1,402,500

Step 3: Compute current cost of total assets at the end of 2007. (Assume current assets of each plant are expressed in 2007 dollars.)

Current assets at the end   +   Net book value of long-term assets at
of 2007 (given)   current cost at the end of 2007 (Step 2)

Calistoga	$200,000 + $238,000	=	$ 438,000
Alpine Springs	$250,000 + $1,125,000	=	$1,375,000
Rocky Mountains	$300,000 + $1,402,500	=	$1,702,500

Step 4: Compute current-cost depreciation expense in 2007 dollars.

Gross book value of long-term assets at current cost at the end of 2007 (from Step 1) ÷ 12

Calistoga	$1,428,000 ÷ 12 = $119,000
Alpine Springs	$1,500,000 ÷ 12 = $125,000
Rocky Mountains	$1,530,000 ÷ 12 = $127,500

Step 5: Compute 2007 operating income using 2007 current-cost depreciation expense.

$$\text{Historical-cost operating income} - \left(\begin{array}{c} \text{Current-cost} \\ \text{depreciation expense in} \\ \text{2007 dollars (Step 4)} \end{array} - \begin{array}{c} \text{Historical-cost} \\ \text{depreciation expense} \end{array} \right)$$

Calistoga	$130,000 – ($119,000 – $70,000)	= $ 81,000
Alpine Springs	$220,000 – ($125,000 – $100,000)	= $195,000
Rocky Mountains	$380,000 – ($127,500 – $120,000)	= $372,500

Step 6: Compute ROI using current-cost estimates for long-term assets and depreciation expense.

$$\frac{\text{Operating income for 2007 using current cost depreciation expense in 2007 dollars (Step 5)}}{\text{Current cost of total assets at the end of 2007 (Step 3)}}$$

Calistoga	$ 81,000 ÷ $ 438,000	= 18.49%
Alpine Springs	$195,000 ÷ $1,375,000	= 14.18%
Rocky Mountains	$372,500 ÷ $1,702,500	= 21.88%

	ROI: Historical Cost	ROI: Current Cost
Calistoga	38.24%	18.49%
Alpine Springs	19.13	14.18
Rocky Mountains	23.46	21.88

Use of current cost results in the Rocky Mountains Division appearing to be the most efficient. The Calistoga ROI is reduced substantially when the ten-year-old plant is restated for the 70% increase in construction costs over the 1997 to 2007 period.

3.   Use of current costs increases the comparability of ROI measures across divisions' operating plants built at different construction cost price levels. Use of current cost also will increase the willingness of managers, evaluated on the basis of ROI, to move between divisions with assets purchased many years ago and divisions with assets purchased in recent years.

23-30 (25 min.) **ROI, RI, ROS, management incentives**.

1.   If Mason Industries uses ROI to measure the Jump-Start Division's (JSD's) performance, Grieco may be reluctant to invest in the new plant because, as shown below, ROI for the plant of 19.2% is lower than JSD's current ROI of 24%.

Operating income for new plant	$480,000
New investment	$2,500,000
Return on investment for new plant	19.2%

Investing in the new plant would lower JSD's ROI and as a result, limit Grieco's bonus.

2.   The residual income computation for the new plant is as follows:

Residual income = Income − (Required rate of return × Investment)

Investment	$2,500,000
Operating income	$ 480,000
Required return	
(Investment, $2,500,000 × 15%)	375,000
Residual income	$ 105,000

Investing in the new plant would add $105,000 to JSD's residual income. Consequently, if Mason Industries could be persuaded to use residual income to measure performance, Grieco would be more willing to invest in the new plant.

3.   Return on Sales (ROS) $= \dfrac{\text{Operating income}}{\text{Sales}} = \dfrac{480,000}{2,400,000} = 20\%$

If Mason Industries uses ROS to determine Grieco's bonus, Grieco will be more willing to invest in the new plant because ROS for the new plant of 20% exceeds the current ROS of 19%.

The advantages of using ROS are (a) that it is simpler to calculate and (b) that it avoids the negative short-run effects of ROI measures that may induce Grieco to not make the investment in the new plant. Grieco may favor ROS because she believes that eventually increases in ROS will increase ROI and RI.

The main disadvantage of using ROS is that it ignores the amount of investment needed to earn a return. For example, ROS may be high but not high enough to justify the level of investment needed to earn the required return on an investment.

23-32 (30–40 min.) **ROI, RI, DuPont method, investment decisions, balanced scorecard.**

1.

2006	$\dfrac{\text{Revenue}}{\text{Total Assets}}$	$\times$	$\dfrac{\text{Operating Income}}{\text{Revenues}}$	$=$	ROI $=$ $\dfrac{\text{Operating Income}}{\text{Total Assets}}$
Newspapers	0.939 ($9,660 ÷ $10,290)		0.239 ($2,310 ÷ $9,660)		0.224 ($2,310 ÷ $10,290)
Television	2.133 ($13,440 ÷ $6,300)		0.025 ($ 336 ÷ $13,440)		0.053 ($ 336 ÷ $ 6,300)

The Newspapers Division has a relatively high ROI because of its high income margin relative to Television. The Television Division has a low ROI despite a high investment turnover because of its very low income margin.

2.   Although the proposed investment is small, relative to the total assets invested, it earns less than the 2006 return on investment (0.224) (All dollar numbers in millions):

$$2006 \text{ ROI (before proposal)} \quad = \quad \frac{\$2,310}{\$10,290} \quad = \quad 0.224$$

$$\text{Investment proposal ROI} \quad = \quad \frac{\$60}{\$400} \quad = \quad 0.150$$

$$2006 \text{ ROI (with proposal)} \quad = \quad \frac{\$2,310 + \$60}{\$10,290 + \$400} = \frac{\$2,370}{\$10,690} = 0.222$$

Given the existing bonus plan, any proposal that reduces the ROI is unattractive.

3a.   Residual income for 2006 (before proposal, in millions):

	Operating Income		Imputed Interest Charge		Division Residual Income
Newspapers	$2,310	–	$1,235 (0.12 × $10,290)=		$1,075
Television	336	–	756 (0.12 × $6,300) =		(420)

3b.   Residual income for proposal (in millions):

Operating Income		Imputed Interest Charge		Residual Income
$60	–	$48 (0.12 × $400)	=	$12

Investing in the fast-speed printing press will increase the Newspapers Division's residual income. As a result, if Kearney is evaluated using a residual income measure, Kearney would be much more willing to adopt the printing press proposal.

4.   As discussed in requirement 3b, Bronson could consider using RI. The use of RI motivates managers to accept any project that makes a positive contribution to net income after the cost of the invested capital is taken into account. Making such investments will have a positive effect on Media Group's customers.

Bronson may also want to consider nonfinancial measures such as newspaper subscription levels, television audience size, repeat purchase patterns, and market share. These measures will require managers to invest in areas that have favorable long-run effects on Media Group's customers.

23-34 (25 min.)   **Ethics, manager's performance evaluation** (A. Spero, adapted).

1a.   Variable manufacturing cost per unit = $2
Fixed manufacturing cost per unit = $9,000,000 ÷ 500,000 = $18
Total manufacturing cost per unit = $2 + $18 = $20

Revenues, $20 × 500,000	$10,000,000
Variable manufacturing costs, $2 × 500,000	1,000,000
Fixed manufacturing costs, $18 × 500,000	9,000,000
Fixed marketing costs	400,000
Total costs	10,400,000
Operating loss	$ (400,000)

Ending inventory: $0

1b.   Variable manufacturing cost per unit = $2
Fixed manufacturing cost per unit = $9,000,000 ÷ 600,000 = $15
Total manufacturing cost per unit = $2 + $15 = $17

Revenues, $20 × 500,000	$10,000,000
Variable manufacturing costs, $2 × 500,000	1,000,000
Fixed manufacturing costs, $15 × 500,000	7,500,000
Fixed marketing costs	400,000
Total costs	8,900,000
Operating income	$ 1,100,000

Ending inventory = $17 per unit × 100,000 units = $1,700,000

2.   It would not be ethical for Jones to produce more units just to show better operating results. Professional managers are expected to take better operating actions that are in the best interests of their shareholders. Jones's action would benefit him at the cost of shareholders. Jones's actions would be equivalent to "cooking the books," even though he may achieve this by producing more inventory than was needed, rather than through fictitious accounting. Some students might argue that Jones's behavior is not unethical—he simply took advantage of the faulty contract the board of directors had given him when he was hired.

3.   Asking distributors to take more products than they need is also equivalent to "cooking the books." In effect, distributors are being coerced into taking more product. This is a particular problem if distributors will take less product in the following year or alternatively return the excess inventory next year. Some students might argue that Jones's behavior is not unethical—it is up to the distributors to decide whether to take more inventory or not. So long as Jones is not forcing the product on the distributors, it is not unethical for Jones to push sales this year even if the excess product will sit in the distributors' inventory.

23-36 (30 min.) ROI, RI, division manager's compensation, balanced scorecard.

1. $ROS = \dfrac{\text{Operating Income}}{\text{Sales}} = \dfrac{1,800,000}{15,000,000} = 12\%$

        $ROI = \dfrac{\text{Operating Income}}{\text{Total Assets}} = \dfrac{1,800,000}{10,000,000} = 18\%$

2a. $ROI = 20\% = \dfrac{\text{Operating income}}{\text{Total Assets}} = \dfrac{X}{10,000,000}$

Hence, operating income = 20% × 10,000,000 = $2,000,000
Operating income = Revenue − Costs
Therefore, Costs = $15,000,000 − $2,000,000 = $13,000,000
Currently,
Costs = Revenues − Operating income = $15,000,000 − $1,800,000 = $13,200,000

Costs need to be reduced by $200,000 ($13,200,000 − $13,000,000).

2b. $ROI = 20\% = \dfrac{\text{Operating income}}{\text{Total assets}} = \dfrac{\$1,800,000}{X}$

Hence X = $1,800,000 ÷ 20% = $9,000,000
PD would need to decrease total assets in 2007 by $1,000,000 ($10,000,000 − $9,000,000).

3.   RI = Income − (Required rate of return × Investment)
         = $1,800,000 − (0.15 × $10,000,000)
         = $300,000

4.   PD wants RI to increase by 50% × $300,000 = $150,000
    That is, PD wants RI in 2007 to be $300,000 + $150,000 = $450,000
    If PD cuts costs by $45,000 its operating income will increase to
        $1,800,000 + $45,000 = $1,845,000
             RI_{2007} = $450,000 = $1,845,000 − (0.15 × Assets)
        $1,395,000 = 0.15 × Assets
          Assets = $1,395,000 ÷ 0.15 = $9,300,000
    PD would need to decrease total assets by $700,000 ($10,000,000 − $9,300,000).

5.   Barrington could focus more on revenues and ROS. Then, it will focus less on cutting costs and reducing assets and put more emphasis on customers, actual revenues, and how they translate into operating income.

Barrington may also want to consider nonfinancial measures such as customer satisfaction and market share, quality, yield, and on-time performance as well as monitor employee satisfaction and the development of employee skills. Maintaining high performance along these measures will have a favorable long-run effect on PD's customers.